D1637421

THE SHATTERING OF
TEXAS UNIONISM

The Shattering of Texas Unionism

Politics in the Lone Star State During the Civil War Era

Dale Baum

Louisiana State University Press

Baton Rouge

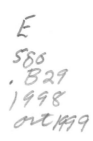

Copyright © 1998 by Louisiana State University Press
All rights reserved
Manufactured in the United States of America
First printing
07 06 05 04 03 02 01 00 99 98   5 4 3 2 1

Designer: Glynnis Weston
Typefaces: display, Willow; text, Bembo
Typesetter: Wilsted & Taylor Publishing Services
Printer and binder: Edwards Brothers, Inc.

Portions of Chapter 1 were first published, in somewhat different form, by the author and Robin E. Baker as "The Texas Voter and the Crisis of the Union, 1859–1861," *Journal of Southern History*, LIII (August, 1987), 395–420.

Portions of Chapter 2 first appeared, in somewhat different form, as "Pinpointing Apparent Fraud in the 1861 Texas Secession Referendum" and are reprinted from the *Journal of Interdisciplinary History*, XXII (1991), 201–21, with the permission of the editors of the *Journal of Interdisciplinary History* and the MIT Press, Cambridge, Massachusetts. Copyright © 1991 by the Massachusetts Institute of Technology and the editors of the *Journal of Interdisciplinary History*.

Portions of Chapter 5 were first published, in somewhat different form, as "Chicanery and Intimidation in the 1869 Texas Gubernatorial Race," *Southwestern Historical Quarterly*, XCVII (July, 1993), 37–54.

Library of Congress Cataloging-in-Publication Data
Baum, Dale, 1943–
    The shattering of Texas unionism : politics in the Lone Star state
during the Civil War era / Dale Baum.
        p.   cm.
    Includes bibliographical references and index.
    ISBN 0-8071-2245-9 (cloth : alk. paper)
    1. Texas—Politics and government—1861–1865.   I. Title.
E580.B29   1998
976.4'05—dc21   98-10534
                                                                          CIP

*For the small group of Texas unionists
who, after the Civil War,
linked their political fortunes with the hopes
of freedom's first generation of African Americans
and tried to build an interracial democracy on the ashes of slavery.*

CONTENTS

ILLUSTRATIONS

MAPS

PHOTOGRAPHS
(following page 132)

TABLES

ACKNOWLEDGMENTS

I welcome this opportunity to acknowledge the assistance of many people and institutions during the years this book was in preparation. What this book owes to my teachers, J. Joseph Huthmacher, Peyton McCrary, and Carroll Quigley, anyone familiar with their writings and ideas will know. I wish to express my thanks to my former and present colleagues, notably Walter L. Buenger, Robert A. Calvert, Walter D. Kamphoefner, and Eric H. Walther, who shared my interest in Texas history. I will always be grateful for their empathetic camaraderie. This book also owes a great deal to my former students, including Robin E. Baker, Donald Scott Barton, and Ihor Bemko, who shared my interest in analyzing popular voting behavior. I especially want to thank Joseph G. Dawson, who read parts of earlier drafts of this book and helped clarify both its ideas and style. I am, of course, responsible for the errors and inadequacies that remain.

Many persons at Texas A&M University deserve my gratitude for the help they gave me. At the Evans Library the Inter-Library Loan division efficiently filled my many requests for newspapers and documents on microfilm, and the staffs of the Microtext and Special Collections divisions brought me a wealth of material that would otherwise have escaped my attention. Avi Harpaz, Roger Sorrells, Ching-Yun Wang, and many others at the computer "help desks" on campus were indispensable in giving me technical assistance with my quantitative work.

The resources of the American History Center at the University of Texas provided much of the research material on which this book is based. Mike Musick and the staff of the Military Reference Branch of the National Archives extended me every courtesy and assistance during my visit to this overwhelming repository. Michael Green and his staff at the Archives Division of the Texas State Library guided me to the manuscript election returns and contested election files on which the quantitative analyses of this study are grounded and many of its conclusions are based.

I am also under obligation to the staff at Louisiana State University Press for all of their assistance, and I thank Executive Editor John Easterly in particular for his encouragement and professional guidance. In addition, I am grateful for the meticulous copy editing of Eivind Boe that greatly improved the final version of my manuscript. I should mention many more individuals here, but the list would stretch too long. I am indebted to all of them.

On a final and more personal note, I would like to express my appreciation to my wife, Ann Todd Baum. Without her love, patience, and companionship this book would never have come into existence.

Abbreviations Used in Notes

AHC	Austin History Center, Austin Public Library
BRFAL	Bureau of Refugees, Freedmen, and Abandoned Lands
BTHC	Eugene C. Barker Texas History Collections, Center for American History, the University of Texas at Austin
COCADT	Correspondence of the Office of Civil Affairs of the District of Texas, the Fifth Military District, and the Department of Texas, 1867–1870
HFMD	Headquarters, Fifth Military District
NA	National Archives, Washington, D.C.
RG	Record Group
TSL	Archives Division, Texas State Library, Austin

THE SHATTERING OF
TEXAS UNIONISM

Introduction

Unionist sentiment in Texas, as elsewhere in the American South throughout the Civil War era, lacked a common ideology or shared agenda. Although prewar unionism was a prime source of anti-secessionists, wartime dissenters, and postwar Republicans, the term *unionist,* as a comprehensive term for those southerners opposing the Democratic party, can be a misleading characterization. Moreover, the precise point at which a Texan ceased to be a unionist varied initially according to his assessment of the value of the American Union, and later according to the ability of the United States government or the Republican party to promote his interests. Because the motivations of unionists were remarkably diverse, the inherent weaknesses of unionism perhaps guaranteed its failure in party building. Of far more interest are the attempts, for whatever reasons, by various leaders and groups throughout the turbulent years of secession, war, emancipation, and Reconstruction to create a viable political alternative to the dominant Democratic party.

Historians of the American South have found anti-secessionists, wartime dissenters, and Republicans or "scalawags" difficult to pin down and describe. Many were persistent Whigs who were emotionally incapable of supporting the Democratic party. Others were nonslaveholding or upcountry farmers and lower-class whites who lived in the poorest regions of the South and often harbored resentment toward the planter elites. A few were prewar political leaders, prominent men from old wealthy plantation areas, or urban merchants promoting a modernized New South. Others have been uncharitably described as just "nobodies." Counterparts for each of these groups can be found in Texas. The Lone Star State was not unlike other states of the Confederacy, but Texas was also distinctive in that it was the only Southern state with an international boundary, an extensive western frontier, and a sizable population of Mexicans and Germans. Although Texas dissenters must be included in what Carl Degler has aptly labeled the "other South," they dissented, so to speak, with a characteristic Texas twang.[1]

---

1. Carl N. Degler, *The Other South: Southern Dissenters in the Nineteenth Century* (New York, 1974), 99–263 (quotation on p. 195). There is considerable literature on the nature of political dissent in the antebellum, wartime, and postwar South. For a synthesis of the scholarship devoted to the scalawags, see

This book defines more precisely the distinctive nature of political dissent in Texas during the late antebellum, wartime, and immediate postwar period. It represents the first attempt to compare the leadership of the legendary Sam Houston and other prewar unionist politicians who followed in his footsteps, such as Elisha M. Pease, Andrew J. Hamilton, and Edmund J. Davis, with the electoral basis of the state's politics before, during, and after the war. Although historians have noted many reasons for Houston's spectacular comeback victory in the 1859 gubernatorial election, few have analyzed the composition of his coalition, especially in terms of previous voting alignments in the late 1850s. None has detailed accurately the degree to which Houston voters embodied a unifying sentiment, or how and why the coalition rapidly unraveled after John Brown's raid and the resulting breakup of the national Democratic party. Scholars have documented how Texas politicians during the war years faced new problems and rehashed older ones within the confines of their collective memories. Nevertheless, questions persist concerning the extent to which late antebellum voting alignments, especially the "no-vote" cast in the state's secession referendum, influenced or shaped the outcome of major wartime elections. Although the story of the gradual melting away, in the immediate postwar years, of the old prewar opposition to the Southern Rights Democrats has been told elsewhere, obstacles remain in the task of uncovering the extent to which anti-secessionist sentiment remained intact during Presidential and Congressional Reconstruction.[2]

A broad theme and recurrent pattern unify the saga of Texas unionism. Innate frailties within Houston's 1859 anti-Democratic coalition led to its double collapse. Texas unionism shattered first during the secessionist movement and then splintered again after the war when confronted with black freedom. During the secession crisis the forces of reaction from the

---

Eric Foner, *Reconstruction: America's Unfinished Revolution, 1863–1867* (New York, 1988), 297–303. See also: Thomas B. Alexander, "Persistent Whiggery in the Confederate South, 1860–1877," *Journal of Southern History,* XXVII (1961), 305–29; William L. Barney, *The Secessionist Impulse: Alabama and Mississippi in 1860* (Princeton, 1974); Steven A. Channing, *Crisis of Fear: Secession in South Carolina* (New York, 1974); David H. Donald, "The Scalawag in Mississippi Reconstruction," *Journal of Southern History,* X (1944), 447–60; Otto H. Olsen, "Reconsidering the Scalawags," *Civil War History,* XII (1966), 304–20; and Allen W. Trelease, "Who Were the Scalawags?" *Journal of Southern History,* XXIX (1963), 445–68. For Texas, see James Marten, *Texas Divided: Loyalty and Dissent in the Lone Star State, 1856–1874* (Lexington, 1990).

2. For a discussion of the voluminous literature on Texas politics during the Civil War period, see Randolph B. Campbell, "Statehood, Civil War, and Reconstruction, 1846–76," in Walter L. Buenger and Robert A. Calvert, eds., *Texas Through Time: Evolving Interpretations* (College Station, 1991), 165–96.

political right tested the mettle of men who, in rejection of the Democratic party, had voted for Houston. After the war the subsequent pressures of radicalism from the political left during Congressional Reconstruction challenged the resilience of white Texans who otherwise might have joined the Republican party. Both the formation of the Confederacy and the abolition of slavery aimed to bring about extraordinary and unprecedented change during this period. The former sought to isolate Texas from the contagion of abolition by taking the state out of the American Union. Paradoxically, the failure of secession and Southern independence unleashed the very transformation that Texas disunionists had tried to prevent. A second revolution began with the emancipation of the slaves and culminated with efforts during Congressional Reconstruction to give them full civic and political rights. The time of Republican party, or scalawag, control of the Texas government became the most controversial era in the state's history, and represented, at most, an unfinished remodeling of Texas society.[3]

Many Texas secessionists considered their attempt to obtain independence to be a revolution in the image of 1776. Their commitment to secession and probable war in 1861 was not, however, a revolution in the usual sense of the word. Their purpose was in the broadest sense to preserve, not alter or change, existing institutions. Foremost among these institutions was slavery, which constituted the cornerstone of their cherished "Southern way of life." In effect, the Texas secessionists launched "a counterrevolution of independence" to avoid the possibility of any harm being done by the Republican party to the value of their slave property. On the other hand, emancipation and subsequent policies of Congressional Reconstruction inaugurated genuine and unmistakable revolutionary change. In the two years following the end of the Civil War, Texans found their way of life severely disrupted by the emancipation of the slaves. Then, in March of 1867, they found their world completely turned upside down by the First Reconstruction Act adopted by the United States Congress. In seeking to win and protect new freedoms for former slaves, northern Republicans initiated extraordinary undertakings aimed at radically transforming social and political structures throughout the South.[4]

What the reader will find in the following pages is mainly an inquiry into

3. *Ibid.*, 196.

4. James M. McPherson, *Ordeal by Fire: The Civil War and Reconstruction* (New York, 1982), 129–32; and Randolph B. Campbell, *A Southern Community in Crisis: Harrison County, Texas, 1850–1880* (Austin, 1983), 192–97.

the voting behavior of Texans in a series of elections, including Houston's dramatic defeat of a pro-slavery Democratic incumbent governor in 1859, the calamitous decision of Texans to leave the Union in a statewide popular referendum held in 1861, and the remarkable election of Edmund J. Davis, a radical Republican scalawag, to the governorship in 1869 with the support of tens of thousands of newly enfranchised African Americans. The use of regression equations to estimate voter transition probabilities from one election to the next meticulously tracks the course of subsets of voters in subsequent elections. The probable impact, for example, of opponents of secession in 1861 can be discerned in wartime or postwar elections. The quantitative methodology employed thus permits far more nuanced conclusions than the impressionistic generalizations that have too long encrusted Texas political history. This methodology also provides a more comprehensive picture of the rapport between the posturing of politicians and the attitudes of various social, economic, and religious groups within the Texas electorate.

The Texas voting returns and comparable demographic information analyzed here—in conjunction with more traditional evidence—also expose the social dynamics of political dissension, including its appeal among men who owned no slaves, were born in Mexico or Germany, or lived on the western frontier. The results thus help to identify those Texans who rejected the Democratic party and secession on the eve of the Civil War, were antagonistic to the Confederacy during the war, and became Republicans during Reconstruction. The statistical techniques generate estimates of probable rates of voter participation, which, in turn, are useful in reaching conclusions about the mobilization of new voters and the apathy of others. In addition, the estimates provide an objective foundation for determining the magnitude of voter fraud and manipulation—a very important issue, given the state's violent political history. A thorough investigation of the 1869 governor's race, one of the most controversial and consequential elections ever held in Texas, provides a solid foundation for debate about whether radical Republicans stole the election. It also reveals the extent to which voting irregularities, especially intimidation of black voters by Democrats and former Confederates, also influenced the election's outcome.

In short, this book explains why Sam Houston's triumphant anti-Democratic coalition arose and why it fragmented during the secession crisis only to reemerge, though weaker than ever, during Reconstruction. It evaluates the social and economic basis of voting in the secession referendum, and appraises the extent to which intimidation of anti-secessionists shaped the state's decision to leave the American Union. By examining the subsequent voting behavior of Confederate Texans, this study shows precisely how antebellum alignments and issues carried over into the war years. By investigating the impact on the state's electoral politics of President Andrew Johnson's policies and the ensuing broad program of revolutionary changes under Congressional Reconstruction, it exposes the degree to which the "Union Republican" ballots cast in the 1866 gubernatorial election represented a subset of the 1861 vote cast against secession and clarifies the limits to which radical Republicans, in turn, attracted prewar anti-secessionists and supporters of the hapless 1866 Union Republican ticket. The findings of this book serve to illuminate the most turbulent political period in the history of Texas and interpret both the weight of continuity and the force of change that swept over it before, during, and immediately after the American Civil War.

1
LATE ANTEBELLUM TEXAS: THE POLITICAL RESURRECTION OF SAM HOUSTON

It is apparent that at this moment General Houston has a stronger hold upon the confidence and affection of the masses, not only in Texas, but throughout the whole of the United States, than any man who has been concerned with public affairs since the days of General Andrew Jackson.
—*Southern Intelligencer* (Austin), August 10, 1859

The great issues between the North and South are not yet permanently settled; and upon them the heart of Texas pulsates true and firm.
—Galveston *Weekly News,* August 4, 1859

In 1857 the southern slave states appeared to be in firm command of the national political system. The increasing power of southern leaders in national party counsels accompanied Democratic party ascendancy in Texas and in other states below the Mason-Dixon Line. Extreme "southern rights" exponents had played key roles in the nomination of James Buchanan and were among his most influential advisers after he became president. Southerners and pro-slavery northerners also controlled the Supreme Court, which in the Dred Scott decision embraced the extreme pro-slavery interpretation of the constitutional debate over slavery in the western territories. When President Buchanan's efforts to secure the admission of Kansas to the Union on the basis of the fraudulent Lecompton constitution alienated Stephen A. Douglas, the leader of the "popular sovereignty" element in the Democratic party, Buchanan stripped the influential Illinois senator of his control over federal patronage. Buchanan's action was possible because, although the Republican party had a slight edge in the House of Representatives, the Senate remained under control of the pro-slavery Democrats.[1]

1. Roy F. Nichols, *The Disruption of American Democracy* (New York, 1948), 18–19, 26–27, 29–31,

Despite their great political power, southern planters frequently expressed their concern over the ability of the American Union to protect their investment in slaves and worried over how best to neutralize abolitionist and Republican party attacks on their "peculiar institution." Southern leaders, particularly within the Democratic party, saw the geographical expansion of slavery as essential to the health of their regional economy. Their demands for a federal slave code for the territories and their interest in acquiring Cuba, in expanding into Mexico, and in filibustering expeditions in Central America were expressions of their concern for what would later be called Lebensraum. Arguing that the acquisition of new lands would be of little use without the enlargement of the slave labor force, pro-slavery extremists went as far as demanding the reopening of the African slave trade. They confidently predicted that Texas would become the "Empire State of the South" once a revitalized slave trade increased the state's black population tenfold, to two million. More successful was the demand for the reenslavement of free blacks.[2]

Accompanying these efforts to expand the plantation economy was a growing fear of innovative political change. The antebellum South was a region that lived on the unwilling labor of millions of the descendants of black Africans. It found the apology for slavery in the supposed character of the people it enslaved. Most white southerners regarded Africans and their offspring as inferior beings who without the discipline of slavery would become dangerous and uncontrollable wards of the state. Consequently, slaveholders frequently exhibited the anxiety that often typifies a society under siege. This fear, in turn, created a degree of defensiveness, stifled the free exchange of ideas, and provoked staunch justifications for the status quo. As the Galveston *Weekly News* stated it, "Those who are not for us, must be against us." Ironically, when southern politicians tried to explain the restiveness of the slave population as the work of abolitionist agitators from the North, they gave credence to one of their worst fears, namely, the concern that northern anti-slavery radicals were a veritable revolutionary vanguard that would someday come south to incite slave insurrections.[3]

170, 174, 228–29; McPherson, *Ordeal by Fire*, 94–96, 98–105; Kenneth M. Stampp, *America in 1857: A Nation on the Brink* (New York, 1990), 46–109, 329–31.

2. Eugene Genovese, "The Origins of Slavery Expansionism," in *The Political Economy of Slavery: Studies in the Economy and Society of the Slave South* (New York, 1965), 243–74; Ronald T. Takaki, *A Proslavery Crusade: The Agitation to Reopen the African Slave Trade* (New York, 1971); William L. Barney, *The Secessionist Impulse*, 3–49; *Texas State Gazette* (Austin), July 17, 1858.

3. Stampp, *America in 1857*, 117; Galveston *Weekly News*, March 3, 1857, quoted in Randolph B. Campbell, *An Empire for Slavery: The Peculiar Institution in Texas, 1821–1865* (Baton Rouge, 1989), 256.

A gubernatorial election in the summer of 1859 momentarily check-mated the tendency for Texas to adhere to the extreme pro-slavery Democratic party stance that was popular in the lower South during the late antebellum period. Democratic governor Hardin R. Runnels, who had often asserted that Texas might be forced to secede from the Union, lost his reelection bid to Sam Houston, the old hero of the Texas Revolution. Only two years earlier Runnels had dealt Houston, who was then still in the United States Senate, his first setback ever at the polls. Houston's defeat in 1857 had been anticipated, for his pro-northern voting record on slavery issues in Congress and endorsement of the American, or Know-Nothing, party had alienated most of his constituents who increasingly looked upon themselves as Democrats and southerners.[4]

Houston had voted for the organization of Oregon under the slavery prohibition contained in the Northwest Ordinance of 1787, had favored every item in the Compromise of 1850, and had signed, by his own ad-mission, his "political death warrant in Texas" by voting against Douglas' Kansas-Nebraska bill. Houston never recanted his Oregon vote, his support for the Compromise of 1850, or his vote against the repeal of the Missouri Compromise. In addition, he had declared in 1856 that patriotic duty would have required him to submit to a Republican party administration if John C. Frémont had won the presidency. Nor did he retract his denunciation the following year of the Supreme Court's pro-southern Dred Scott deci-sion. In seeking northern backing for a possible presidential campaign, he had discounted the potential injury to his position at home. As his oppo-nents constantly reminded voters during the 1859 campaign, "*Whenever* the opportunity presented itself," Houston had "in most instances voted with the North, against the South" and had expressed "no contrition for such unnatural conduct."[5]

Traditional accounts of Houston's dramatic comeback victory have been based primarily on the impressions of contemporaries of the period who

4. Stampp, *America in 1857*, 315–16; Llerena B. Friend, *Sam Houston: The Great Designer* (Austin, 1954, paperback edition, 1979), 162–269; Marion K. Wisehart, *Sam Houston: American Giant* (Washington, D.C., 1962), 523–76; Randolph B. Campbell, *Sam Houston and the American Southwest* (New York, 1993), 114–44; Marquis James, *The Raven: A Biography of Sam Houston* (1929; rpr. Austin, 1988), 372–412; Gregg Cantrell, "Sam Houston and the Know-Nothings: A Reappraisal," *Southwestern Historical Quarterly*, XCVI (1993), 327–43.

5. Sam Houston, quoted in Jeff Hamilton, *"My Master": The Inside Story of Sam Houston* (Dallas, 1940), 36; Galveston *News*, quoted in the Dallas *Herald*, June 22, 1859; William Henry Giesenschlag, Jr., "The Texas Gubernatorial Elections of 1857 and 1859" (M.A. thesis, Texas A&M University, 1970), 16–17, 21–28, 41–42; and Campbell, *Sam Houston*, 120–21, 128–29, 135.

recorded their observations in newspapers and letters.[6] Reasons for the reversal of the 1857 outcome are many, including actions taken by Senator Houston to propitiate his constituents, unstoppable Indian problems on the frontier that plagued Governor Runnels' administration, and intramural battles within the Texas Democratic party between southern rights zealots and their more moderate opponents. In the space of two years a radical change in public sentiment occurred. Although historians will never know as much as they would like about the motivations of voters at the time of the 1859 election, speculation regarding why Texans voted as they did must be grounded in an examination of actual voting returns.

Conventional wisdom holds that "thousands of Texans had to change their decision of 1857" to produce Houston's 1859 victory. Because Houston won in 1859 by roughly the margin by which he had lost in 1857, the notion that his victory was contingent upon his winning over many who had voted against him two years earlier is, at first glance, a compelling one. (In 1857 Runnels defeated Houston by 32,552 to 23,628 votes; in 1859 Runnels lost to Houston by 36,527 to 27,691 votes.) Yet not one 1857 Runnels supporter needed to have switched in 1859 to the Opposition, or "Union Democratic," camp in order to elect Houston. Texans who between 1857 and 1859 exited and entered the active or participating electorate could have caused Runnels' defeat. For example, Houston could have benefited from a large influx of new voters or 1857 nonvoters to the polling places, while Runnels could have failed to mobilize vast numbers of men who had previously voted for him.[7]

Because voter turnout fluctuated extensively in statewide elections in late antebellum Texas, any analysis of Houston's political resurrection must take into account changes in voter participation, especially between 1857 and 1859. Voting returns reported in the 1859 election from El Paso, Medina, Bowie, and Tyler Counties demonstrate the necessity of calculating voting totals based on potentially eligible voters rather than ballots cast (see table 1). In these four counties a negative relationship exists between the per-

6. In addition to the list of secondary source materials on late antebellum Texas politics contained in Walter L. Buenger, *Secession and the Union in Texas* (Austin, 1984), 229–46, see: Giesenschlag, "The Texas Gubernatorial Elections"; Robert Kingsley Peters, "Texas: Annexation to Secession" (Ph.D. dissertation, University of Texas at Austin, 1977); Joe T. Timmons, "Texas on the Road to Secession" (2 vols.; Ph.D. dissertation, University of Chicago, 1973).

7. Billy D. Ledbetter, "Politics and Society: The Popular Response to Political Rhetoric in Texas, 1857–1860," *East Texas Historical Journal,* XIII (Fall, 1975), 14; Buenger, *Secession and the Union,* 36–37. For the source of all voting returns cited here and elsewhere, see Appendix.

TABLE 1

SUPPORT FOR CANDIDATES IN THE 1859 GOVERNOR'S RACE:
PERCENTAGE OF BALLOTS CAST VERSUS
PERCENTAGE OF TOTAL ELECTORATE

Calculating the Democratic Share of the 1859 Gubernatorial Vote

County	Percentage of Ballots Cast for Hardin R. Runnels	Percentage of Total Electorate Voting for Hardin R. Runnels
El Paso	88	35
Medina	78	45
Bowie	72	50
Tyler	60	53

Calculating the Opposition Share of the 1859 Gubernatorial Vote

County	Percentage of Ballots Cast for Sam Houston	Percentage of Total Electorate Voting for Sam Houston
Kerr	81	25
Orange	73	28
Jackson	70	37
Shelby	62	57

Source: The source of the 1859 gubernatorial returns is the *Texas Senate Journal: Eighth Legislature,* Austin, 1860, pp. 44–47. "Total electorate" in 1859 in the above counties is an estimate of the number of adult white males, a surrogate measure for legally qualified voters, and was calculated by assuming that the rate of growth in the adult white male population between 1859 and 1860 equaled the rate of growth between 1860 and 1861. The estimation procedure used to calculate the size of the 1860 potential voting population follows the method employed by Joe T. Timmons in his "The Referendum in Texas on the Ordinance of Secession, February 23, 1861: The Vote," *East Texas Historical Journal,* XI (Fall, 1973), 18–19, table 2. The estimated number of adult white males for El Paso County for 1860 has been corrected here to equal 1,372. Because the figures in the 1858 state census on "qualified electors" are incomplete (and are missing for Tyler County) and underrepresent the potential electorate statewide (and underrepresent the voting populations in El Paso, Jackson, Medina, and Orange Counties), they were not used in the extrapolation procedures here. See "Census of the State of Texas for 1858," in *The Texas Almanac for 1859* (Galveston, 1858), 208–11.

centages of ballots cast for Governor Runnels and the rates at which all potentially eligible voters turned out and voted for him. Likewise, the knowledge of percentages of ballots cast for Houston in Kerr, Orange, Jackson, and Shelby Counties in 1859 is a false predictor of the levels at which potential voters in these counties turned out and voted for Houston. Calculating voting shares based on ballots cast can thus be a misleading indicator of the relative strength of a candidate or political party in regions where sizable variations in voter turnout occurred. More important, ignoring changes in turnout from one election to the next can convey the incorrect, although widely held, assumption that masses of Texas voters throughout the 1850s "quite frequently changed their factional or party allegiance."[8]

8. Giesenschlag, "The Texas Gubernatorial Elections," 260. On the strength of party loyalties in Texas between 1848 and 1852, see Randolph Campbell, "The Whig Party of Texas in the Elections of 1848 and 1852," *Southwestern Historical Quarterly,* LXXIII (1969), 17–34. On the necessity of calculating

Fluctuations in turnout from one election to the next can be accounted for by using a statistical technique known as ecological regression. The coefficients generated by ecological regression equations provide approximations of the shifts in voting and nonvoting between two elections. Because this technique is based on assumptions that in reality are seldom entirely satisfied, the results must be viewed as merely estimates or probabilities of how individuals voted. The method assumes that the behavior of a particular group of voters is consistent over the county units reporting votes (that is, a group votes the same way in, for instance, a heavily Democratic or a heavily anti-Democratic county), or at least the variation is random and not systematic throughout the counties. Although these assumptions are not easy to test or always accurate, the closer they are satisfied guarantees a smaller margin of error in the estimates of actual voting behavior.[9]

The results of the regression analysis reveal that except for the 1860 presidential contest, differential rates of turnout were more important in shaping outcomes of elections in antebellum Texas than voters switching allegiances between the Democrats and their opponents (see table 2). Throughout the 1850s, the extent to which Texans changed their partisan loyalties from one election to the next never exceeded one-sixth of the total electorate. According to the estimates of voter transition probabilities between the 1857 and 1859 gubernatorial elections, less than 3 percent, or roughly 1,000 votes, of Houston's 1859 total came from former Runnels men. (The estimate of less than 3 percent is derived from the information in table 2 in the following manner: $1\% \div [24\% + 1\% + 12\%] = 2.7\%$.) Another, although similar, analysis, which is based on a much lower number of geographical units in order to account for the creation of new counties throughout the 1850s, estimates that about 3,500 votes in Houston's total came from former Runnels men.[10] This higher estimate still militates against the commonly held notion that the endorsement of Houston in 1859 by many prominent Democratic leaders, including some who had worked to

voting percentages on the basis of all potentially eligible voters, see J. Morgan Kousser, "Ecological Regression and the Analysis of Past Politics," *Journal of Interdisciplinary History*, IV (Autumn, 1973), 250.

9. For a discussion of the technique of ecological regression, see: E. Terrence Jones, "Ecological Inference and Electoral Analysis," *Journal of Interdisciplinary History*, II (Winter, 1972), 249–62; Kousser, "Ecological Regression," 237–62; Laura Irwin Langbein and Allan J. Lichtman, *Ecological Inference*, Sage University Paper series on Quantitative Applications in the Social Sciences, series no. 17-010 (Beverly Hills, 1978).

10. Robin E. Baker and Dale Baum, "The Texas Voter and the Crisis of the Union, 1859–1861," *Journal of Southern History*, LIII (1987), 397. For explanations for the differences between the analysis employed by Baker and Baum and the results presented here, see the note to table 2.

revitalize their party during the Know–Nothing challenge in the mid–1850s, provoked a massive defection of rank–and–file Democrats into Houston's column. Because Houston defeated Runnels by nearly 9,000 votes, Democratic defections alone could not have provided Houston with his margin of victory.[11]

Further examination of the quantitative evidence presented here suggests that Houston won his rematch with Runnels because of a combination of two occurrences. First, Runnels failed to mobilize about one-third of his 1857 supporters to the polls to vote for him again in 1859. These former Runnels men preferred, for whatever reasons, to sit out the 1859 balloting. According to the estimated relationships between voting patterns in 1857 and 1859, about 10,664 former Runnels voters (11 percent of 96,948 potentially eligible voters in 1859) abstained from voting in 1859. (By way of contrast, an insignificant number of former Houston voters subsequently did not vote.) If Runnels had managed to mobilize his former supporters to the polls in 1859 at the same rate as Houston, Runnels would have retained the Texas governorship by about 1,800 votes.

Secondly, Runnels failed to match Houston's success in attracting new voters and previous nonvoters. Almost one-third of Houston's total, or about 11,634 votes, consisted of men who either had sat out the balloting in the first Houston-Runnels contest or had not been part of the state's voting population in 1857. Because the state's population expanded almost threefold between 1850 and 1860, new voters alone in any given year represented a powerful force in the state's electoral politics. They must be taken into account in an analysis of the relationships between voting patterns in pairs of successive elections.

Between 1857 and 1859 the potential Texas voting population, in terms of adult white males, increased by an estimated 12,892 men. Using counties as the units of analysis implicitly assumes there existed some continuity over time of the voting population within them, but constant mobility and population turnover caused by in-and-out migration were salient characteristics of Texas society in the late antebellum period. If the men who cast ballots in consecutive elections were, for the most part, not the same individuals, then the assumptions underlying this analysis are admittedly called into

---

11. On the abandonment of the Texas Democratic party by many of its moderate leaders in 1859, see Walter L. Buenger, "Texas and the Riddle of Secession," *Southwestern Historical Quarterly*, LXXXVII (1983), 166. For estimated rates at which Texans turned out and voted in statewide elections in late antebellum Texas, see Appendix.

TABLE 2

TRANSITION PROBABILITIES OF VOTING BEHAVIOR IN SELECTED ELECTIONS

(in percentages of adult white males)

Election Pair	Actual Number of Cases	Repeat Dem. (%)	Repeat Opp. (%)	Repeat Not Voting (%)	(Total Stability) (%)	Dem. to Opp. (%)	Opp. to Dem. (%)	New Dem. (%)	New Opp. (%)	Dem. Dropout (%)	Opp. Dropout (%)	(Total Instability) (%)
Successive Gubernatorial Elections and the Secession Referendum, 1855–1861												
1855–1857	59	18	14	27	(59)	6	8	13	8	6	0	(41)
1857–1859	109	22	24	23	(69)	1	0	7	12	11	0	(31)
1859–1861	119	21	7	28	(56)	0	16	6	7	4	11	(44)
Successive Presidential Elections and the Secession Referendum, 1852–1861												
1852–1856	58	19	7	38	(64)	0	0	22	14	0	0	(36)
1856–1860	60	18	7	27	(52)	2	8	21	6	11	0	(48)
1860–1861	123	38	11	33	(82)	0	0	5	3	7	3	(18)
Successive Presidential, Gubernatorial, and Judicial Elections and the Secession Referendum, 1852–1861												
1852–1855	58	21	8	39	(68)	0	0	14	18	0	0	(32)
1855–1856	59	17	12	26	(55)	4	11	13	5	2	0	(45)
1856–1857	59	33	18	33	(84)	5	1	6	5	0	0	(17)
1857–1858[a]	107	22	20	30	(62)	3	3	3	5	11	3	(28)
1858[a]–1859	116	16	26	25	(67)	2	0	13	10	9	0	(34)
1859–1860	119	20	9	31	(60)	3	19	6	2	4	5	(39)
1860–1861	123	38	11	33	(82)	0	0	5	3	7	3	(18)

[a] The 1858 judicial election for Texas Supreme Court justices in which Constantine W. Buckley, the only Democratic party nominee who faced opposition, was defeated by James H. Bell.

Source: For the sources for the county election returns, which were the units of analysis in generating the above estimates, see the Appendix. The column labeled "Opposition" represents the Whig party in 1852, the American, or Know-Nothing, party in 1855 and 1856, the "Independent" vote in 1857 and 1858, the "Union Democratic" vote in 1857 and 1858, the anti-Breckinridge "Fusion" vote in 1860, and the vote cast against secession in 1861. Opposition votes also include, rather arbitrarily in some instances, all votes not cast for "regular" Democratic candidates. Thus the category includes "Independent Whig" and "Southern Rights" ballots in 1852 and ballots cast for minor candidates in 1855. The 1861 anti-secessionist vote, however, does not include improperly marked pro-secessionist ballots (*e.g.,* "For an Independent Texas") that were cast independently of the standard secession ballot.

Note: The figures above represent the percentage of adult white males, a substitute measure for the number of legally qualified voters. The 1845 Texas State Constitution defined "qualified electors" as all free adult male citizens except convicted felons, untaxed Indians, Africans and their descendants, and members of the United States military. Except for city elections there were no property or tax-paying restrictions on voting. State law established only one additional restriction: a residency requirement of one year in Texas and six months in the county or city. In the absence of more detailed census information, the potential voting population as calculated here is unavoidably inflated by the number of adult white men who were newcomers, aliens, soldiers, and felons. See Hans Peter Nielson Gammel, comp., *Laws of Texas,* (10 vols.; Austin, 1898), II, 62. In calculating the above voter transition probabilities between pairs of elections between 1852 and 1861, logically but not statistically impossible estimates falling outside the 0–100 percent range were arbitrarily set at their respective minimum or maximum limits and the values of the remaining estimates were then adjusted according to the restraints of the marginal values of the contingency tables. To adjust for the varying populations of counties, the variables used in the regression equations were "weighted" by the number of adult white males. For the procedures used, see Laura Irwin Langbein and Allan J. Lichtman, *Ecological Inference,* Sage University Paper series on Quantitative Applications in the Social Sciences, Series No. 07-010 (Beverly Hills, 1984), 15–21. County boundary changes between 1850 and 1860 immensely complicated the analysis of voting returns achieved here. Of the 123 counties in existence in 1860, only 52 of them had stable boundaries between 1850 and 1860. The organization, especially between 1852 and 1856, of new counties from territory formerly included in neighboring areas has been compensated for by aggregating the new counties back into the original county or counties from which they were formed. The strategy used here to create geographical comparability is taken from Paul R. Scott, "The Democrats and Their Opposition: A Statistical Analysis of Texas Elections, 1852–1861" (typescript in Texas A&M University Archives). In several respects the procedures used in the analysis of voting returns presented above differ from those employed by Baker and Baum in their "The Texas Voter," table 1, pp. 398–99. First, the mistakes made by Timmons in his "The Referendum in Texas," table 2, pp. 18–19, in calculating the number of adult white males living in 1860 in Cherokee, El Paso, Fayette, Hopkins, Maverick, and Wood Counties have been corrected here. (These errors underestimated the potential voting population in 1860 by about 1,000 potential voters.) Second, estimates of the potential electorate in each county for noncensus years were derived by straight-line extrapolations, rather than by use of a growth-rate formula that assumed a curvilinear pattern of increase (or decline) in the number of adult white males between 1850 and 1860. Third, in order to maximize the number of cases or counties used in the regression analysis, estimates of the number of all possible voters in each county after 1856 were derived by assuming that the growth rate of the adult white male population between each year from 1857 to 1860 equaled the growth rate between 1860 and 1861. Information on the number of "qualified electors" in the 1858 census was used in the extrapolation procedures only where the reported number of legal voters exceeded the estimation of the number of adult white males. Finally, estimates of voting between 1857 and 1859 and between 1859 and 1861 are the adjusted estimates that reflect parameters generated by construction of multidimensional contingency tables. For example, the 1857, 1858, and 1859 voting returns were analyzed by multiple ecological regressions, taking the percentages of choices of potentially eligible voters in the 1859 governor's race for Runnels, Houston, and not voting as the dependent variables. The independent variables, analyzed separately for each choice, were (1) the proportions of the electorate voting in 1857 for Runnels, Houston, and in 1858 for Buckley and Bell, and (2) all first-order interactions among these four variables. To avoid multicollinearity, the 1857 and 1858 nonvoting percentages were not used. For instance, to estimate the proportion of Runnels and Buckley voters who subsequently favored Runnels in his rematch election with Houston, the intercept of the equation for the 1859 Runnels percentage was added to the slopes for "proportion voting for Runnels in 1857," "proportion voting for Buckley in 1858," and the appropriate interaction. This sum estimated the proportion for Runnels in 1859 for a hypothetical county consisting solely of 1857 Runnels and 1858 Buckley supporters: in other words, the proportion of such voters favoring Runnels in 1859. All variables were "weighted" by the estimate of the 1859 adult white male population. For the weighting procedure, see *SPSS-X User's Guide* (3rd ed.; Chicago, 1988), 186–87. Similarly, the estimates of voting between 1859 and 1861 are also adjusted estimates that reflect parameters generated by construction of a multidimensional contingency table based on voting in 1859, 1860, and 1861. These changes produced some different estimates of voting behavior and eliminated illogical estimates of voting between 1860 and 1861.

question. On one hand, transients could have been too mobile, disorganized, and powerless to make a mark on the counties through which they passed. On the other, antebellum party allegiances, being independent of place, were relied on by politicians of every stripe to help integrate masses of strangers into the county electorates at every election. With these admonitions in mind, the evidence suggests that voting for Houston in 1859 were about 4,847 adult men who in 1857 had either not yet reached the age of twenty-one years or not yet arrived in the state (see table 2). Houston also received the votes of approximately 6,786 men who had been present in 1857 but in this year had not voted for governor.[12]

Deeply ingrained in accounts by historians of Houston's 1859 victory is the notion that the outcome of the 1858 judicial elections foreshadowed Runnels' defeat.[13] A resignation from the Texas Supreme Court had triggered a special election of a new associate justice. Traditionally, groups of prominent attorneys operating independently of party politics drafted and nominated likely candidates for the high court. However, for the vacated seat on the supreme bench the Texas Democratic party in an unprecedented action endorsed Constantine W. Buckley, a member of the state legislature from Fort Bend County (southwest of Houston). Buckley was a disciple of John C. Calhoun, but he was also a notorious heavy drinker and a suspected perjurer. An immediate backlash to his nomination occurred.[14]

Fearing that Buckley's election would endanger the independence of the judiciary by allowing politics to corrupt the law, two of the state's most well known lawyers organized an anti-Buckley movement: George W. Paschal, a longtime Democrat who had served as chief justice of the Arkansas Supreme Court, and William P. Ballinger, a former Whig who had served as United States district attorney for the Texas District. They put up James H.

---

12. For the calculation of the growth rate of the potentially eligible Texas electorate between 1857 and 1860, see Appendix. The relationship between wholesale migration and patterns of political participation is explored by Kenneth J. Winkle in his *The Politics of Community: Migration and Politics in Antebellum Ohio* (New York, 1988). An uncomplicated interpolation method of estimating the electorate in every county for the years where census data are unavailable will admittedly misrepresent population growth as unwavering. This presents another problem, because in actuality growth rates varied in different years. See Barnes F. Lathrop, *Migration Into East Texas, 1835–1860: A Study from the United States Census* (Austin, 1949), 24, 33. Lists of potential or registered voters in the 1850s are rare; see "List of the Registered Voters of Galveston, 1853–1873" (Regional Historical Resource Depository, Texas State Library, Austin).

13. Buenger, *Secession and the Union,* 35–36; Peters, "Texas: Annexation to Secession," 262.

14. William P. Ballinger to Guy M. Bryan, May 27, 1858, in Guy M. Bryan Papers (Bryan-Ballinger Correspondence, 1857–1887), BTHC; *Southern Intelligencer* (Austin), January 13 and 20, 1858; Giesenschlag, "The Texas Gubernatorial Elections," 118–21.

Bell, a state district judge from Brazoria County (west of Galveston), to run against Buckley. Bell, a Harvard-educated native Texan who disliked pro-slavery extremists, was also a candidate for the state supreme court. He had, however, refused to allow his name to be placed before the convention because of his opposition to judicial nominations. When he entered the race as the candidate defending an independent judiciary, the *Texas State Gazette*, a semi-official organ of the Texas Democracy, condemned him and his followers as deserters having the "shameless audacity" of northern abolitionists: "Like Judas Iscariot, they [the Bell supporters] should go off and hang themselves."[15]

On election day Bell defeated Buckley by the razor-thin margin of 421 votes out of 50,229 cast. It remains questionable, however, whether "a new political coalition began to take form" because of Bell's victory.[16] The evidence offered here suggests that the votes of disaffected Democrats undeniably gave Bell his slim victory over Buckley. However, Houston's subsequent election to the governorship did not depend on the Opposition party's retention within its ranks of a single 1858 Democratic bolter (see table 2). According to the estimates of voting behavior presented here, most 1858 Democratic defectors came back to their party's fold and voted again in 1859 for Runnels. Thus, the shuffling of voters across party lines in 1858 was, for the most part, temporary and not permanent.[17]

In one respect, however, Bell's victory over Buckley had presaged the 1859 gubernatorial outcome. The abstention rates among 1857 Runnels men were high in both 1858 and 1859. Initial Runnels men who subsequently sat out the balloting in the 1858 judicial contest and in the 1859 rematch election, constituted over one tenth of the potentially eligible electors in both 1858 and 1859 (see table 2). Within the Democratic leadership the division over judicial nominations tended to coincide with the split between pro-slavery zealots and their opponents. The unionist sentiments of Bell, Paschal, and Ballinger thus had more than a little to do with their

15. *Texas State Gazette* (Austin), May 15 and 29, 1858, quoted in Giesenschlag, "The Texas Gubernatorial Elections," 123–124; Peters, "Texas: Annexation to Secession," 262; Oran Lonnie Sinclair, "Crossroads of Conviction: A Study of the Texas Political Mind, 1856–1861" (Ph.D. dissertation, Rice University, 1975), 93–114; Buenger, *Secession and the Union,* 35–36; and John Moretta, "William Pitt Ballinger and the Travail of Texas Secession," *Houston Review,* XI (1989), 3–26.

16. Buenger, *Secession and the Union,* 35.

17. For mistaken insinuations of fraud in the Bell-Buckley contest, see Peters, "Texas: Annexation to Secession," 263. In Cass County, Bell received 308 votes rather than zero votes as alleged by Peters; in Angelina County, Buckley polled 59 votes, not zero votes as claimed by Peters. See *Executive Record Book* [Gov. Hardin R. Runnels], 181–84, RG 301, TSL.

opposition to Buckley and the Democratic "organization." The Democratic party's unnecessary championship of extreme pro-slavery views caused the alienation of many who otherwise would have been in its ranks in 1858 as much as the fear that without nonpartisan judicial elections a political clique would instruct justices on how to rule or would nominate them by the "dictation of hungry spoilsmen."[18]

To what extent did issues touching on slavery shape the result of the 1857 and 1859 elections? Part of the answer is found in the behavior of nonslaveholders, especially those living outside the East Texas and the Galveston-Houston areas. Their votes, according to the analysis presented here, determined the outcomes in both elections (see tables 3 and 4). More than 70 percent of Texas families owned no slaves by the end of the 1850s. Although a large percentage of men who exercised political power at the state, county, and local levels of government were members of the slave-holding class, Texas had no taxpaying or property restrictions on voting. Any free adult male citizen—but not free Negroes, untaxed Indians, con-victed felons, or members of the United States armed forces—could vote or hold political office. Therefore, the votes cast by nonslaveholders were crit-ical in deciding the outcomes of late antebellum elections.[19]

Had the votes of nonslaveholders been disallowed and only slaveholder ballots counted in the Houston-Runnels elections, Houston would have won in 1857 and lost in 1859—exactly the opposite of what occurred (see table 4). In other words, Houston lost in 1857 because he had been unable to win the votes of nonslaveholders, and he would have lost again in 1859 had he failed to carry their votes. The finding here that Texans who owned no slaves decided the outcome of both elections is consistent with the re-alignments of voting behavior that occurred between 1857 and 1859 in areas with few slaves—namely, the Rio Grande valley, the western frontier, and North Texas. One important key to understanding the outcome of the 1859 election thus lies in explaining these regional realignments that bene-fited Houston.

Obvious socioeconomic explanations of Texas voting patterns in the 1850s have proven elusive. Although in many communities election out-comes often hinged on the ability of politicians to capitalize on intrastate

18. Dallas *Herald,* August 14, 1858, p. 3; *Texas State Gazette* (Austin), December 21, 1857.

19. Randolph B. Campbell and Richard G. Lowe, *Wealth and Power in Antebellum Texas* (College Station, 1977), 99, 122; Hans Peter Nielson Gammel, comp., *Laws of Texas* (10 vols.; Austin, 1898), II, 62.

rivalries and popular resentment toward powerful interest groups, political conflict in antebellum Texas invariably occurred within a defense of southern interests. Outside of this pro-slavery consensus a free exchange of beliefs was likely to be suppressed. Genuine differences of opinion over how to promote slave labor and cotton agriculture, however, allowed plenty of room for political discussion and conflict. While few questioned the necessity and advantages of slavery, many disliked the extreme measures put forth to preserve it. Even the most emotional issue in antebellum Southern politics, namely, how best to protect slavery within the American Union, divided the planter elites as well as the nonslaveholding yeomanry. Consequently, voters rarely divided along economic and class lines. Nevertheless, the presence of large Opposition majorities in many nonslaveholding areas of the state in 1859 have led some historians to conclude that Houston, by successfully campaigning on "the theme that the Democratic party represented only the planting interests of the state," became the "most successful manipulator against the plantation leadership that controlled the [Texas] government in the antebellum period."[20]

According to the estimates of voting behavior presented here, Texans who owned no slaves voted in 1859 for Houston over Runnels at a rate of three to two. However, if Houston's candidacy in 1859 had been uniquely successful in mobilizing the peripheral and hinterland areas against the political and economic dominance of the slaveholding areas, one would expect his vote to be more closely associated than in 1857 with the distribution of real and personal property. One could also hypothesize that a geographical polarization of the vote would make knowledge of the regional location of a county a better predictor of the voting results in 1859 than in 1857. The quantitative evidence offers little, if any, support for these suppositions. In 1857 virtually no relationship ($r = -.00$) existed between Houston's voting strength and per capita wealth; in 1859 the comparable correlation ($r = -.03$) was essentially unchanged.[21] Nor did the amount of variation in Houston's vote explained by mere knowledge of the region in which

20. Carl H. Moneyhon, *Republicanism in Reconstruction Texas* (Austin, 1980), 16; Charles W. Ramsdell, "The Frontier and Secession," in *Studies in Southern History and Politics* (New York, 1914), 61–79; Campbell, *A Southern Community in Crisis,* 147–79; Roger A. Griffin, "Intrastate Sectionalism in the Texas Governor's Race of 1853," *Southwestern Historical Quarterly,* LXXVI (1972), 142–60; Campbell and Lowe, *Wealth and Power,* 107–23.

21. Per capita wealth, calculated for each county by dividing the total value of real and personal property by the number of free inhabitants, correlated very slightly with the vote for Runnels in both 1857 and 1859: $r = +.14$ and $+.20$ and actual $N = 98$ and 117, respectively.

TABLE 3

INCREASE AND DECREASE IN THE GUBERNATORIAL VOTE
FROM 1857 TO 1859, BY REGION

(in percentages of 1857 and 1859 regional electorates)

Comparison of Votes Cast for Runnels in 1857 and 1859, By Region

Region	Percentage of 1857 Electorate Favoring Runnels	(Difference Between Regions[a])	Percentage of 1859 Electorate Favoring Runnels	(Difference Between Regions[a])	Percentage Increase or Decrease
Rio Grande Valley	56	(+20)	29	(0)	−27
East Texas	42	(+7)	33	(+6)	−9
Elsewhere	35	(−3)	28	(0)	−9
Galveston–Houston Hub	33	(−4)	29	(0)	−4
North Texas	32	(−6)	26	(−3)	−6
Western Frontier	21	(−17)	10	(−19)	−11
All Texas	39		29		−10

Comparison of Votes Cast for Houston in 1857 and 1859, By Region

Region	Percentage of 1857 Electorate Favoring Houston	(Difference Between Regions[a])	Percentage of 1859 Electorate Favoring Houston	(Difference Between Regions[a])	Percentage Increase or Decrease
East Texas	33	(+8)	43	(+7)	+10
Elsewhere	29	(+3)	38	(0)	+9
Galveston–Houston Hub	25	(−2)	33	(−5)	+8
North Texas	23	(−4)	39	(+1)	+16
Western Frontier	21	(−6)	46	(+9)	+25
Rio Grande Valley	6	(−22)	12	(−28)	+6
All Texas	28		38		+10

[a] Differences between regions were obtained by employing "dummy," or nominal, variables that coded the absence or presence of the geographical characteristics (or locations) of the counties. For example, the finding above that the Rio Grande valley region had an impact of 20 percentage points on the vote for Runnels in 1857 was derived by first scoring the counties in the Rio Grande valley region as "1" and all other counties as "0." Regressing the percentage Runnels upon the dummy variable then yielded the following values: $y = 0.36 + 0.20(x)$, where y equals the Runnels percentage and x equals the dummy variable for the Rio Grande valley region. Here the intercept (36%) is the average 1857 Runnels vote in counties outside the Rio Grande valley area (when x equals "0"), whereas the intercept added to the slope (36% + 20%, or 56%) equals the average Runnels vote in 1857 in the valley region.

Source: The source for the 1857 gubernatorial returns is *Texas House Journal: Seventh Biennial Session* (Austin, 1857), 15–17. For the source for the 1859 gubernatorial returns, see table 1 above. The "unofficial" 1859 gubernatorial vote cast in Henderson County in East Texas is included here in the computations. See Secretary of State, MSS Election Returns for 1859, RG 307, TSL.

Note: The Rio Grande valley region includes the counties along the Mexican border from El Paso to Cameron, plus San Patricio and Nueces; "North Texas" comprises the counties along the Red River from Cooke to Red River, plus Denton, Collin, Hunt, Tarrant, and Dallas; "Galveston-Houston Hub" encircles the fourteen counties either linked in 1860 by railroad lines to Houston or located between the Brazos and Trinity Rivers south of Robertson and Leon

TABLE 3

(continued)

Counties; "East Texas" includes all counties east of the Trinity River, including Chambers and Polk (but not Walker and Liberty, which are located within the Galveston-Houston commercial hub) and excluding the counties contained in North Texas; "Western Frontier" represents counties on the band of settlements where fears of possible Indian depredations still existed in 1860, including (from north to south) Montague, Young, Jack, Wise, Palo Pinto, Parker, Erath, Comanche, Coleman, Brown, Hamilton, McCulloch, San Saba, Mason, Llano, Gillespie, Kerr, Bandera, and Uvalde; and "Elsewhere" encompasses all remaining counties, centered primarily in the central hill country, the north-central, and the south-central areas of the state.

a county was located dramatically increase between 1857 and 1859 (see table 3).[22]

Houston's 649-vote margin over Runnels in the Galveston-Houston commercial hub provides another reservation to the claim that he so effectively orchestrated nonslaveholder disapproval of the political power of the slaveholding elites in 1859 that "the cleavage between the west and the cotton planters showed deeper at this election than ever before."[23] Fertile river bottomlands had made the area surrounding Galveston a dynamic center of slave agriculture and economic wealth. Although the region in 1860 was the home of only 15 percent of the state's adult white males, it contained one-fourth of the state's slave population. The region's per capita wealth, based on the total value of real estate and personal property divided by the free population, equaled $2,214.23. (Elsewhere per capita wealth was equal to $926.40.) Throughout the 1850s politicians representing the area had secured state financial aid to build hundreds of miles of railroad track emanating from Galveston and nearby Houston, which were the two most rapidly growing cities in the state. The region had fought attempts to lend state money for the construction of a competing transcontinental railroad through northeastern Texas—a route that Houston had supported in Congress.[24]

Houston's popularity in 1859 in slaveholding regions, including the Galveston-Houston area, was built upon the core of support he had always enjoyed among slaveholders in the old Know-Nothing strongholds, espe-

22. In regressing the vote for Houston in 1857 and 1859 upon the "dummy" or nominal variables that coded the regional locations of the counties in table 3 above, the category for "Elsewhere" was left out of the equations to avoid multicollinearity. For percentage Houston in 1857 and 1859, $R^2 = .27$ and .30; for percentage Runnels in the same years, $R^2 = .32$ and .23. Actual N for 1857 and 1859 = 109 and 119, respectively.

23. Ramsdell, "The Frontier and Secession," 74; Galveston *Weekly News,* August 9, 1859.

24. U.S. Census Bureau, *Eighth Census, 1860: Population,* 340–51. In 1859 Houston carried twelve of the nineteen Texas counties having 10,000 acres or more of land in cotton production in 1860. See U.S. Census Bureau, *Eighth Census, 1860: Agriculture,* 2–176; *Texas Senate Journal: Eighth Legislature,* 44–47.

TABLE 4

ESTIMATED RELATIONSHIPS BETWEEN SLAVEOWNERSHIP AND VOTING IN THE 1857 GUBERNATORIAL, 1858 JUDICIAL, AND 1859 GUBERNATORIAL RACES

(by percent)

The 1857 Gubernatorial Election (Actual $N = 109$)

	Percent for Runnels	Percent for Houston	Percent Not Voting
All Slaveholders	30	66	4
Slaveholders by Number of Slaves Owned			
Large (over 20)	58	42	0
Medium (4 to 20)	29	69	2
Small (1 to 3)	21	69	10
Nonslaveholders	41	17	42
All Voters[a]	39	28	33

The 1858 Judicial Election (Actual $N = 116$)

	Percent for Buckley	Percent for Bell	Percent Not Voting
All Slaveholders	32	62	6
Slaveholders by Number of Slaves Owned			
Large (over 20)	31	69	0
Medium (4 to 20)	35	65	0
Small (1 to 3)	29	56	16
Nonslaveholders	26	18	56
All Voters[a]	28	28	44

The 1859 Gubernatorial Election (Actual $N = 119$)

	Percent for Runnels	Percent for Houston	Percent Not Voting
All Slaveholders	46	42	12
Slaveholders by Number of Slaves Owned			
Large (over 20)	86	5	10
Medium (4 to 20)	53	38	9
Small (1 to 3)	30	55	14
Nonslaveholders	24	36	41
All Voters[a]	29	38	34

[a] Actual, not estimated, statewide percentages of adult white males.

Source: For the sources of the 1857 and 1859 gubernatorial returns, see tables 1 and 3 above. The source for the 1858 judicial election returns is Executive Record Book [Gov. Hardin R. Runnels], 181–84, RG 301, TSL. The information on slaveholders is from U.S. Census Bureau, *Eighth Census, 1860: Agriculture,* Unnumbered Table, 240–42.

Note: There were 21,878 slaveholders in Texas in 1860. "Small" slaveholders were arbitrarily defined as slaveholders having 1 to 3 slaves in 1860; "Medium" as owning 4 to 20 slaves; and "Large" as holding over 20 slaves. Given these definitions and assuming that slaveholders were primarily adult white men, Texas small slaveholders represented approximately 9.3 percent of the state's adult white male population in 1860, and medium and large slaveholders constituted

TABLE 4

(continued)

9.9 percent and 2.1 percent, respectively. The lack of data on the size of slaveholder holdings for the years immediately prior to 1860 made it necessary to assume that these proportions remained constant in every county over the period from 1857 to 1859. The regression equations used to generate the above estimates were run *backwards,* predicting slaveholder status from the voting decisions of the electorate. For example, in the first table above, the percentage of large slaveholders voting for Runnels in 1857 was derived by running a multiple regression with the percent large slaveholder as dependent and the 1857 Runnels and Sam Houston percentages as independent variables. In a hypothetical Texas county that voted 100 percent for Runnels in 1857, the predicted large-slaveholder percentage was constant (or intercept) plus the regression coefficient for "percentage Runnels." This sum equaled the estimated proportion of Runnels voters who were large slaveholders. Likewise, constant plus the coefficient for "percentage Houston" gave the estimated proportion of Houston voters who were large slaveholders. The constant was the estimated proportion of those not voting in the 1857 gubernatorial election who were large slaveholders. These estimated proportions were, in turn, multiplied by the respective statewide percentages for Runnels, Houston, and nonvoters. The resulting percentages of the entire electorate were then divided by the percentage of the electorate consisting of large slaveholders. These quotients yielded, in turn, the percentages of large slaveholders voting for Runnels, Houston, and not voting. This roundabout procedure is both necessary and valid for the following reasons: First, the artifact of backward regression provides a method for circumventing multicollinearity problems caused by high intercorrelations among the slaveholding variables. Second, causality is not posited here; slaveholder status does not cause the vote in 1859, any more than the latter causes the former.

cially in the long-established towns in the interior river valley counties of eastern Texas. Here "small" and "medium" slaveholders, or (as arbitrarily defined here as) those who owned from 1 to 3 slaves and from 4 to 20 slaves, respectively, were among his most loyal supporters (see table 4). Although two years later Houston failed to carry the votes of the Texas slaveholders who turned out and voted in his rematch election with Runnels, Houston managed, nevertheless, to win the votes of the state's small slaveholders, and his support among medium slaveholders remained strong. Only at the hands of wealthy, or "large," planters, who owned more than twenty slaves, had he fared poorly. Although large slaveholders voted more than 15 to 1 in favor of Runnels in 1859, Houston had remained competitive with Runnels among all slaveholders because the overwhelming majority of them were not so wealthy. Approximately 90 percent of the state's slaveholders owned fewer than twenty-one slaves. Houston's strong showing among slaveholders in both 1857 and 1859 merely attested to the enduring personal popularity of "Old Sam," as many affectionately called him, in the eastern half of the state.[25]

Until the events at Harpers Ferry and the resulting breakup of the national Democratic party caused most Texas slaveowners to reconsider the value of being part of the American Union, their electoral decisions hinged largely on traditional party loyalties and reasons internal to Texas. If in 1857 their recollections of Houston's votes in the nation's capital on slavery ex-

25. Marcus de LaFayette Herring to Oran M. Roberts, July 15, 1857, quoted in Friend, *Sam Houston,* 251.

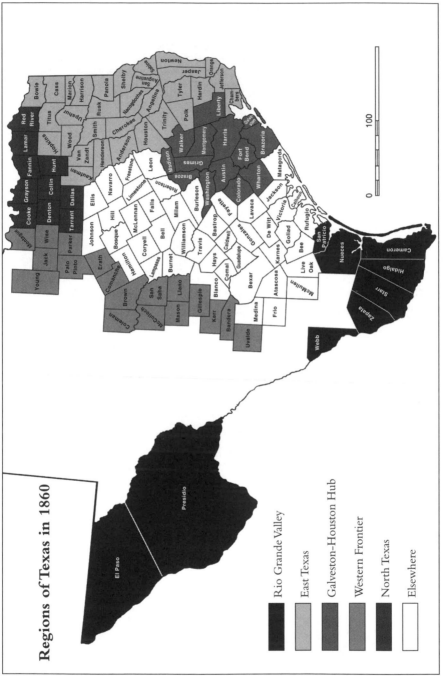

Regions of Texas in 1860

- Rio Grande Valley
- East Texas
- Galveston–Houston Hub
- Western Frontier
- North Texas
- Elsewhere

The maps designed for this book are adapted from the map of Texas, 1870, created by T. D. Rabenhorst and C. V. Earle, and included in the Histori-cal U.S. County Outline Map Collection, 1840–1980, University of Maryland, Baltimore County, Department of Geography, 1984.

pansionism had not injured his traditional strength among small and medium slaveholders, then the "traitor-to-the-South" rebuke hurled at him by the Democrats could hardly have accounted in that year's election for his lackluster showing at the hands of Texas nonslaveholders. More important, in 1857 accusations of nativism directed at Houston kept Mexican Texans and normally unionist German Texans squarely in Runnels' column. In addition, Houston's legendary goodwill toward the Indians and his belief that the white man was most often responsible for persistent Indian problems had the same consequences for settlers on the western frontier. Considering these circumstances, a Democratic defeat would have been extraordinary, but the prevailing view that an Opposition victory would have given aid and comfort to Northern Republicans had precluded it altogether.[26]

Houston's only chance of winning the 1857 gubernatorial election would have been to exploit purely state and local questions that had the potential of splintering the state Democratic party. His avoidance of state issues played into the hands of Runnels, who deliberately ran, for the sake of harmony in Democratic ranks, on a platform that dodged all local questions. Houston unwisely spent most of his time defending his record in the United States Senate or vilifying the Democratic campaigners who followed him around on his strenuous speaking tours. He also failed to appreciate the new power of the Democratic party organization, which assembled numerous speakers on behalf of Runnels, who hardly campaigned at all. Democratic spokesmen and newspaper editors hammered away at Houston's Know-Nothing connections, his endorsement in 1856 of the unpopular Millard Fillmore, and his willingness to acquiesce in the possibility of a Black Republican administration. They denounced Houston's voting record in Congress, claiming that his purpose had been to betray his constituency and the entire South in order to position himself for a run for the presidency with northern antislavery support.[27]

Houston, who was essentially a candidate without a party in 1857, allowed the Democrats to frame the principal issue as "Houston versus anti-Houston." This kept the focus of the campaign riveted on the extent to

26. For Houston's views concerning management of the Plains Indians, see his speech on January 31, 1857, in the United States Senate in Amelia W. Williams and Eugene C. Barker, eds., *The Writings of Sam Houston, 1813–1863* (8 vols.; Austin, 1941), VI, 410–18.

27. Galveston *News*, July 21, 1857; *Texas State Gazette* (Austin), August 15, 1857; Dallas *Herald*, October 4, 1856; Ernest William Winkler, ed., *Platforms of the Political Parties in Texas*, Bulletin of the University of Texas, no. 53 (Austin, 1916), 71–72; Friend, *Sam Houston*, 248–54; Cantrell, "Sam Houston and the Know Nothings," 340–42.

Vote Cast in the 1859 Gubernatorial Election

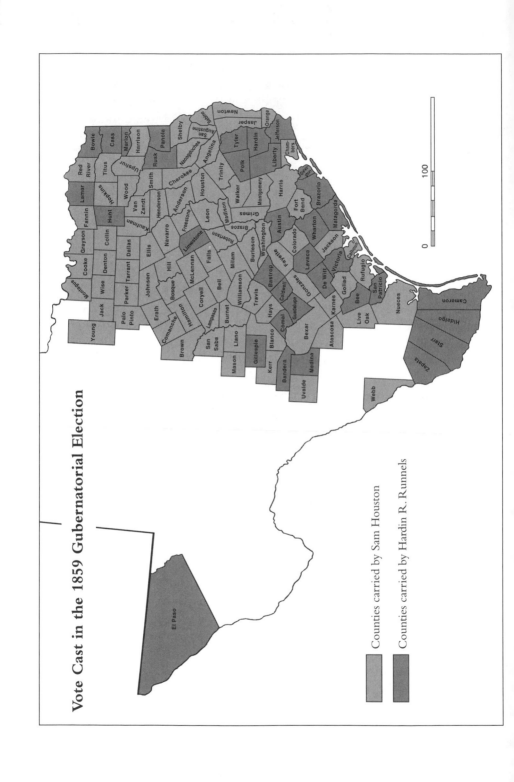

Counties carried by Sam Houston

Counties carried by Hardin R. Runnels

0   100

which Houston had become an unreliable defender of southern interests and a friend of the national foes of the Democratic party—the party which had controlled Texas politics since statehood. By 1859, however, the situation was vastly different. Runnels had to run on his record of failure to bring peace to the frontier and had to defend the introduction into state politics of unwarranted issues, such as the nominating of candidates for supreme judgeships, the reopening of the African slave trade, and the raising of the possibility of southern states's secession from the Union. The advancement of these matters by Runnels and the extreme pro-slavery Democrats coincided with their penchant to censure anyone in their party's ranks who disagreed with them. Houston's support of the Buchanan administration prevented Runnels' friends from claiming, as they had in 1857, that a defeat of the Texas Democratic party would only give solace to northern abolitionists and anti-slavery Republicans.[28]

An inspection of the regions where the largest decreases in the Democratic gubernatorial vote occurred between 1857 and 1859 reveals the geographical locations of many disaffected Democrats (see table 3). In addition, evidence suggesting where Houston attracted new or previous nonvoters can be gathered by identifying areas where his popularity markedly increased between the two elections. The two regions of the state where Runnels' vote declined the most were the Rio Grande valley and the western frontier. Houston's greatest electoral gains occurred on the western frontier and in North Texas. Although the 1859 gubernatorial vote was free of allegations of vote fraud, circumstances in two specific counties require explanations.

The vote in Young County (Fort Belknap) on the extreme northwestern frontier was inflated with pro-Houston ballots when Indian agent Robert S. Neighbors opened an unauthorized polling place for a few men associated with the Brazos and Clear Fork Indian Reservations. Because the county judge subsequently authorized the vote totals submitted by Neighbors, the Young County returns probably did not violate the voters' intentions. The larger vote cast than there were possible voters in Lampases County (northwest of Austin) suggests, at first glance, that voting irregularities occurred in this central Texas county. Here, however, during the summer months hundreds of people, seeking relief from a variety of infirmities, came to the county's white sulfur and chalybeate springs. With local hotels fully occupied, many camped out near the springs, creating a veritable town of camp-

28. Galveston *Weekly News,* August 18, 1857; Friend, *Sam Houston,* 248.

ers that "solidly covered" twenty acres of ground. State law allowed Texas citizens who were away from home on election day to vote for national and state offices wherever in the state they happened to be.[29]

For the purposes of analysis, the regions of Texas defined here are mutually exclusive areas (see table 3). However, if the definition of a frontier region is expanded to include localities where threats from marauding Indians or Mexican bandits were definite possibilities in the late 1850s, then much of the Rio Grande valley and North Texas would qualify as a "frontier." By this definition the Texas frontier stretched along the Red River, which separated Texas from Indian Territory (Oklahoma), then southward irregularly from Young County (Fort Belknap) to Uvalde County (Fort Inge), then to the Gulf of Mexico below Corpus Christi, where it almost hugged the shoreline until Brownsville (Fort Brown), then up and along the Rio Grande to Eagle Pass (Fort Duncan), and finally westward to El Paso County (Fort Bliss). Although many Anglo frontiersmen desired to "run all the Mexicans into the Rio Grande and all the Indians into the Red River," this attitude alone did not directly translate in 1859 into votes for Houston.[30]

Many living along the line of white settlement in West Texas blamed Governor Runnels for mismanaging the problem of frontier defense. Newspapers in the late 1850s commonly reported depredations caused by nomadic Indians, such as the Comanches, Kiowas, Kickapoos, and Lipan Apaches, but Indians on government reservations were also often blamed for raiding frontier settlements when they strayed off reservation land to hunt. During the 1859 campaign, Houston had accused Governor Runnels of shamefully neglecting to protect settlers on the frontier and recklessly advocating disunionist proposals, such as acquiring Cuba and reopening the African slave trade. Frontiersmen living far from the center of plantation country and relying on the federal government to fend off roving plains Indians were opposed to agitating unnecessarily the slavery issue. Likewise, many in North Texas questioned the wisdom of fire-eating rhetoric because they depended on government agencies in nearby Indian Territory to buy their surplus wheat and corn.[31]

29. Carrie J. Crouch, *Young County; History and Biography* (1937; rpr. Austin, 1956), 109–10; Walter Prescott Webb, H. Bailey Carroll, and Eldon Stephen Branda, eds., *The Handbook of Texas* (3 vols.; Austin, 1952, 1976), II, 17–18; F. M. Cross, *A Short Sketch-History from Personal Reminiscences of Early Days in Central Texas* (Brownwood, Tex., 1912), 30; *The Texas Almanac for 1859* (Galveston, 1858), 175–78; Gammel, *Laws of Texas,* II, 1, 280.

30. D. W. Meinig, *Imperial Texas: An Interpretive Essay in Cultural Geography* (Austin, 1969), 45–46; Walter Prescott Webb, *The Texas Rangers: A Century of Frontier Defense* (Boston, 1935), 127.

31. Buenger, *Secession and the Union,* 36–38.

In addition, the unpopular "pre-emption law" threatened to cost Runnels and the Democrats many votes in the low-slaveholding areas of settlement in West Texas. Opposition to laws allowing genuine settlers, not land speculators, to claim vacant land on the public domain on reasonable terms came traditionally from slaveholding areas in East Texas. Slaveholders perceived preemption laws as attracting only nonslaveholders. In 1858 the Democratic-dominated legislature had passed a law giving settlers the right to preempt 160 acres of land on the surveyed portion of the public domain for every three slaves owned by them within the state. Because the 1858 law restoring preemption rights had added this additional land for slaveholders as a price for its passage, the law was unpopular in the western counties. The legislature subsequently repealed the law in early 1860.[32]

In 1859, it will be recalled, Houston ran dramatically better on the western frontier and in North Texas. In their first contest, Houston and Runnels had divided the votes of western frontiersmen who had settled in a band of counties running from Fort Belknap, in the extreme northwest, to Fort Inge, located west of San Antonio. In the North Texas belt of counties along the Red River (from Cooke to Red River and including also Denton, Collin, Hunt, Tarrant, and Dallas Counties), Runnels had outpolled Houston in 1857 by a three-to-one margin. In 1859 Runnels' voting strength on the western frontier and in North Texas declined by 19 and 3 percentage points, respectively, whereas Houston's vote increased by an amazing 25 percentage points in the western frontier region and by 16 percentage points in North Texas.

These results suggest that Houston, by dissociating himself from Know-Nothingism and embracing the Buchanan administration, attracted the votes of many newcomers and previously apathetic men who believed in the party of Andrew Jackson but doubted the commitment of Runnels and the Democratic firebrands to solving local problems peculiar to their regions. Chiding Runnels for caring less about the lawless conditions on the frontier than about a "free-soil" constitution for Kansas, one disgusted frontiersman wrote that if northern abolitionists had hidden themselves in the Wichita Mountains (Oklahoma Territory) to lure away from the state "half a dozen squads of negroes," Runnels would have shown more concern, but in the absence of any abolitionist threat "an interest of equal importance is neglected." Nor had Houston damaged his appeal among settlers on the

32. Ramsdell, "The Frontier and Secession," 66–67; Peters, "Texas: Annexation to Secession," 172.

frontier and in North Texas by his restatement of support for a southern route for a transcontinental railroad and for the encouragement of a system of public education that would be "as free as possible."[33]

Also, it will be recalled, in 1857 Runnels had run exceptionally well and Houston had fared abysmally in the Rio Grande valley—a region which encompassed all the counties along the "Great River" dividing Texas from Mexico, plus San Patricio and Nueces (Corpus Christi) Counties in South Texas. In this region in 1859 Houston made his smallest gains and Runnels witnessed his largest declines. It is of special interest that the rate of nonvoting in the Rio Grande valley spiraled up by twenty-two percentage points between 1857 and 1859 to a remarkably high 60 percent—a figure over twice as high as the statewide rate of 29 percent. (In 1857 the rate of nonvoting in the region had roughly equaled the statewide rate.) The explanation of the 1859 voting outcome in the Rio Grande valley lies in the distinctiveness of this area, in which large concentrations of Mexican Texans, or Tejanos, were separated from smaller numbers of Anglos by class and cultural differences.

Most Tejanos had been born Mexican citizens and acquired United States citizenship under the Treaty of Guadalupe Hidalgo, which had ended the Mexican War. Most had a strong sense of locality and little identification with the United States government—a government that had failed to enforce the rights guaranteed to them under the 1848 treaty. Often unfairly divested of their lands and subjected to tremendous prejudice, Tejanos had little love for Anglos and were unsympathetic to slavery. Many who retained their Mexicanness were largely poor and illiterate people found in barrios and rancherias. Even in areas where they predominated, their votes were often manipulated by unprincipled cliques of powerful Anglo and European merchants. Disputes within the merchant community over land titles frequently lay behind the divisions between the "Colorados," or "Reds" (usually Democrats), and "Azules," or "Blues" (often anti-Democrats). Local elections were often so hotly contested "that school children even wore red and blue shoestrings to represent their families' political feelings." However, the lopsided support for Runnels and the Democratic party in 1857 among Tejanos had stemmed mainly from their genuine hostility to all former Know-Nothings.[34]

33. "R" to the editors of the *Intelligencer*, n.d., quoted in the *Southern Intelligencer* (Austin), February 23, 1859; Sam Houston's Speech at Nacogdoches, July 9, 1859, in Williams and Barker, eds., *The Writings of Sam Houston*, VII, 358–59, 363–65.

34. Frederick Law Olmsted, *A Journey Through Texas; Or, a Saddle-Trip on the Southwestern Frontier:*

The American, or Know-Nothing, party reached its zenith in Texas in the mid-1850s. In 1855 the party's gubernatorial candidate with the support of Houston fell short of victory by about 7,000 votes. Believing that the American party could best throttle both fire-eating rhetoric in the South and unrestrained free-soilism in the North, Houston in 1856 had made speeches for Fillmore. After Fillmore carried only Maryland nationwide and only eight counties in the Lone Star State, the American party rapidly declined in strength. By 1857 the fusion of its remnants with the anti-Runnels Democrats marked the end of its separate existence in Texas. Although the "black lantern" order had initially attracted Houston more by its strong nationalistic and reformist agenda than by its nativistic and anti-Catholic doctrines, the Know-Nothings had, nevertheless, made considerable political capital out of the claim that the state's two largest minority groups among the free population, the Mexicans and Germans, were not reliable on the slavery issue. Therefore, in 1857 when Houston ran as a "Jacksonian Democrat" or "independent anti-caucus" candidate with disorganized remnants of American party support, his past associations with the nativists still tainted him in the eyes of Tejano voters. Consequently, in the Rio Grande valley region, Runnels had polled more than nine votes for every vote received by Houston.[35]

Paradoxically, Runnels' vote dropped off most dramatically in 1859 in the Rio Grande valley—the same region where in 1857 he had fared better than anywhere else in the state (see table 4). In 1857 Runnels had captured 56 percent of the potentially eligible voters in the region, but in 1859 he attracted only 29 percent of them. Reasons for Runnels' decline are many. Houston's supporters had reminded Tejanos that among Governor Runnels' most powerful allies in 1859 were men who had led in 1854 the movement to exclude transient Mexicans from Travis County. Anti-Runnels advocates also linked attempts to reopen the African slave trade with plans to reestablish a system of peonage to regulate the labor of Mexican Texans. More important, in the wake of renewed Indian raids on the outlying regions of

With a Statistical Appendix (1857; rpr. New York, 1978), 163, 245, 427, 456; Arnoldo De León, The Tejano Community, 1836–1900 (Albuquerque, 1982), xiii–xv; Stephen Powers to Elisha M. Pease, August 8, 1857, in the Pease-Graham-Niles Collection, AHC; James Robert Crews, "Reconstruction in Brownsville, Texas" (M.A. thesis, Texas Tech University, 1969), 39; Buenger, Secession and the Union, 86–92.

35. The Texas Sentinel, July 18, 1857, quoted in Litha Crews, "The Know Nothing Party in Texas" (M.A. thesis, University of Texas, 1925), 170; Sinclair, "Crossroads of Conviction," 26–49; Buenger, Secession and the Union, 26–31; Friend, Sam Houston, 292–97; Giesenschlag, "The Texas Gubernatorial Elections," 68; Stampp, America in 1857, 185.

Laredo and Eagle Pass during his administration, Runnels' immoderate pro-slavery utterances had clashed with the local desire to expand federal gov-ernment operations at Forts McIntosh and Duncan. Moreover, Houston had improved his stature among Tejanos by lashing out at John C. Watrous, the federal judge for the First Texas Judicial District who had for years used his official position to benefit himself and his business partners. Houston's denunciation was translated into Spanish and widely circulated in the areas of South Texas where a land company associated with Watrous had been bringing suits to take advantage of hard-to-prove land titles. In 1859 Tejanos were thus caught between their traditional allegiance to the Democrats, on one hand, and their appreciation for Houston's censure of Judge Watrous, on the other. Alienated by Runnels' disunionist dogmas in defense of slav-ery, but still unable to bring themselves to vote for the Opposition ticket, many Rio Grande valley residents resolved their dilemma in 1859 by staying away from the polls.[36]

Throughout Texas in 1859 Houston's winning coalition was less excep-tional than has commonly been assumed. In both 1857 and 1859 Houston ran extremely well in his traditional area of support in East Texas—a region defined here as including all counties east of the Trinity River except those in the Galveston-Houston commercial hub and in North Texas (see table 4). Although his most dramatic gains occurred in North Texas and on the sparsely settled western frontier, Houston improved upon his 1857 totals in every region, including East Texas and the Galveston-Houston area. By way of contrast, Runnels lost support throughout every region, but suffered his largest declines in the Rio Grande valley and on the western frontier. In 1857 Houston's candidacy had been closely competitive with Runnels' only on the western frontier, but in 1859 Houston failed to carry only the Rio Grande valley region.

Nevertheless, conventional wisdom still holds that Houston assembled in 1859 a "curious" or "strange" coalition of renegade anti-secessionist Dem-ocrats, on one hand, and former members of the moribund Whig and Know-Nothing parties, on the other.[37] The evidence presented here, how-

36. James Marten, *Texas Divided,* 69; Gilberto Miguel Hinojosa, *A Borderlands Town in Transition: Laredo, 1755–1870* (College Station, 1983), 69; Friend, *Sam Houston,* 264–66; Giesenschlag, "The Texas Gubernatorial Elections," 257–58; Robert E. Lane, *Political Life: Why and How People Get Involved in Politics* (Glencoe, Ill., 1959), 197–203; Seymour Martin Lipset, *Political Man: The Social Basis of Politics* (Garden City, N.Y., 1963), 211–26.

37. James Alex Baggett, "The Constitutional Union Party in Texas," *Southwestern Historical Quar-terly,* LXXXII (1979), 236; Earl Wesley Fornell, *The Galveston Era: The Texas Crescent on the Eve of Secession* (Austin, 1961), 146 n. 16.

ever, suggests that antiquated partisan divisions and Democratic bolters played no peculiar role in shaping Houston's victory. As estimated above, 1857 Democrats, including possible German Texans who switched from Runnels to Houston, made up less than 10 percent of Houston's 1859 total. In addition, according to the estimates of the relationships between voting in the 1857 and 1859 elections and prior voting in the 1856 presidential election, Houston in his rematch with Runnels fared worse at the hands of former Fillmore voters compared with his appeal among them in 1857 (see table 5). The pro-Runnels press repeatedly claimed that many former prominent Know-Nothings, along with others described as "Bolters, Faggots, Frazzles, Stubs and Tail-ends of all parties," had joined the Union Democrats and endorsed Houston. However, neither the behavior of political elites nor the unflattering portrait of Houston men by the pro-slavery firebrands was a reliable guide to the actions of the masses of Texas voters.[38]

According to the evidence presented here, Houston's voting strength in 1859 declined in the old Fillmore strongholds, increased among 1856 Buchanan voters, and dramatically expanded among previous nonvoters and new voters (see table 5). In 1857 Houston, in a losing cause, had captured all but a small percentage of the 1856 Know-Nothings, but in winning in 1859 he attracted only about three-fourths of them. In addition, between 1857 and 1859 Houston made substantial inroads into the ranks of former Buchanan supporters. In 1857 he had captured only about 13 percent of the 1856 Democrats, but in 1859, when he dissociated himself with the defunct American party and accepted the Union Democratic label, he attracted over one-third of them. In net results, quondam Know-Nothings, former Buchanan supporters, and men who either had sat out the balloting in the 1856 presidential race or had not yet become part of the state's voting population, constituted in 1859 roughly equal proportions of Houston's total vote. By way of contrast, these same Know-Nothings, Democrats, and men who either had abstained or had not yet become eligible to vote in 1856 had made up about 64 percent, 18 percent, and 18 percent, respectively, of Houston's 1857 total vote.

Nominated along with Houston at the Union Democratic convention in 1859 were Edward Clark for lieutenant governor and Frank M. White for land commissioner. The delegates also chose Andrew J. Hamilton, who would later serve as the state's military and provisional governor under the

38. *Standard* (Clarksville), June 4, 1859, p. 2. For a rare exception to the conventional wisdom about the nature of Houston's 1859 coalition, see Peters, "Texas: Annexation to Secession," 319–20.

TABLE 5

ESTIMATED RELATIONSHIPS BETWEEN VOTING IN THE
1856 PRESIDENTIAL ELECTION AND VOTING IN THE
1857 AND 1859 GUBERNATORIAL ELECTIONS

(in percentages of 1857 and 1859 electorates)

The 1857 Gubernatorial Election and 1856 Presidential Election (Actual $N = 59$)

	Percentage Having Voted for Buchanan	Percentage Having Voted for Fillmore	Percentage Having Not Voted for President	Percentage Having Been Ineligible to Vote	Totals
Runnels Voters	33	1	6	0	39
Houston Voters	5	18	1	4	28
Voters Not Voting for Governor	0	0	28	5	33
Totals	38	19	35	8	100

The 1859 Gubernatorial Election and 1856 Presidential Election (Actual $N = 59$)

	Percentage Having Voted for Buchanan	Percentage Having Voted for Fillmore	Percentage Having Not Voted for President	Percentage Having Been Ineligible to Vote	Totals
Runnels Voters	20	4	5	0	29
Houston Voters	12	13	0	13	38
Voters Not Voting for Governor	1	0	26	7	34
Totals	33	17	31	20	100

Source: The source of the 1856 presidential returns is Walter Dean Burnham, *Presidential Ballots, 1836–1892* (Baltimore, 1955), 764–813. For the source for the 1857 and 1859 gubernatorial returns, see tables 1 and 3 above. For the strategy used to aggregate counties in order to achieve areal comparability, see table 2 above.

Note: The cell entries in the above contingency table represent the percentages of 1857 and 1859 adult white males and not the conventional percentage of ballots cast. Thus, if the percentage of 1857 adult white males voting for Runnels (39 percent) is added to the percentage for Houston (28 percent), the sum equals the turnout for the 1857 election. (*Cf.* table 2 above.) All calculations here and elsewhere were carried to three decimal places, but in order to avoid the impression that the estimates are precise, all figures in the tables have been rounded off to the nearest whole percentage. Rounding procedures occasionally produce totals greater or less than 100 percent. In order to take into account increases in the size of the voting population from one election to another, the votes for each party or candidate in the first election were divided by the adult white male population at the time of the second election. Ideally, if more information were available, another category could be created for men who were present at the time of the 1856 election but who were not able to vote in 1857 or 1859 because of death or migration. For a detailed discussion of the multiple regression technique used to generate the above tables, see Langbein and Lichtman, *Ecological Inference,* 50–62. The equations used to generate estimates were weighted by the number of adult white males in order to ensure that sparsely populated counties would not be overrepresented in the analysis. In the table above, the actual number of cases (or counties) equals 59. Logically but not statistically impossible estimates which fell outside the 0 to 100 percent range were arbitrarily set at their respective minimum or maximum limits and the values of the remaining estimates were then adjusted according to the restraints of the marginal values of the contingency table.

Abraham Lincoln and Andrew Johnson administrations, to run on their ticket for Congress. Hamilton's opponent in the Second Congressional District—commonly referred to as the "western district"—was Thomas N. Waul, a Democrat of long standing and a pro-slavery zealot who would be later remembered for his reassuring pledge to "drink all the blood" that would be spilled as a consequence of secession. Although Hamilton in defeating Waul ran slightly behind Houston, a remarkably high level of straight-ticket voting characterized the 1859 election in the Western District (see table 6). In the First Congressional District, however, the balloting was less disciplined and more complex.[39]

Events in the First Congressional District—the "eastern district"—illustrated the extent to which ultra-pro-slavery Democrats were out of touch with the masses of Texas voters. Incumbent Democratic congressman John H. Reagan, who later served as postmaster general in the Confederacy and whose renomination and reelection for Congress in 1859 was a certainty, had written to his constituents an open letter claiming that only "very crazy" men would destroy the Union "for the ignoble . . . privilege of being permitted to kidnap . . . a parcel of the savages of Africa." Without mentioning names, Reagan left no doubt that he aimed his accusations at his inveterate enemy, Governor Runnels, and at other "croakers of evil" such as Lieutenant Governor Francis R. Lubbock and Central Committee chairman John Marshall. Nevertheless, out of party loyalty, Reagan endorsed, but never actively campaigned for, the Runnels-Lubbock ticket. The opposition to Reagan did not arise from Houston's followers. The Union Democrats had officially praised Reagan for his "love of the Union." Rather, in a hopeless attempt to deny Reagan reelection, a splinter group of secessionist Democrats endorsed William B. Ochiltree, one of the founders of the Lone Star Republic and a former Whig and Know-Nothing leader who had recently moved toward an extreme southern-rights position. Ochiltree should not be confused with his son, Thomas Peck Ochiltree, who as a precocious young man of nineteen years of age in 1859 was elected secretary of the Texas Democratic convention.[40]

39. Thomas N. Waul quoted in *Flake's Daily Bulletin* (Galveston), January 16, 1866; Giesenschlag, "The Texas Gubernatorial Elections," 221–23.

40. John H. Reagan to the Voters of the First Congressional District, April 12, 1859, quoted in the *Texas Republican* (Marshall), April 22, 1859; Resolution of the "Union Democratic" Convention quoted in the *Southern Intelligencer* (Austin) May 25, 1859; Ben H. Procter, *Not Without Honor: The Life of John H. Reagan* (Austin, 1962), 109–13; Ledbetter, "Politics and Society," 15; Claude H. Hall, "The Fabulous Tom Ochiltree: Promoter, Politician, and Raconteur," *Southwestern Historical Quarterly*, LXXI (1968), 349–50.

TABLE 6

ESTIMATED RELATIONSHIPS BETWEEN VOTING IN THE 1859 GOVERNOR'S RACE AND VOTING IN CONGRESSIONAL ELECTIONS, BY DISTRICT

(in percentages of 1859 electorate)

The First Congressional District (Actual $N = 43$)

	Percentage Voting for Runnels	Percentage Voting for Houston	Percentage Not Voting for Governor	Totals
Reagan Voters	27	31	2	60
Ochiltree Voters	1	8	0	9
Voters Not Voting for Congressman	4	5	22	31
Totals	32	43	24	100

The Second Congressional District (Actual $N = 74$)

	Percentage Voting for Runnels	Percentage Voting for Houston	Percentage Not Voting for Governor	Totals
Waul Voters	26	3	0	29
Hamilton Voters	1	32	0	33
Voters Not Voting for Congressman	0	0	38	38
Totals	27	35	38	100

Source: For the source of the 1859 gubernatorial returns, see table 1 above. The 1859 congressional returns are from *Executive Record Book* (Gov. Hardin R. Runnels), 355, 369, RG 301 TSL.

Although many, including Reagan, probably believed that Runnels had encouraged Ochiltree's candidacy, the overwhelming majority of the Eastern District voters who cast their ballots in the hopeless cause of electing Ochiltree were paradoxically also found in Houston's column (see table 6). In this instance, former party allegiances rather than ideological considerations had caused most of the Ochiltree voters to favor Houston over Runnels. Putting aside other possible reasons why Ochiltree voters had shunned Runnels, the results in the First District clearly showed that Runnels, not Reagan, was the "weak" candidate on the Democratic ticket. The foolish attack on Reagan by the southern-rights extremists alienated them from a potential ally whom they desperately needed to defeat the Houston-Clark ticket. But for the unusual position of Reagan in reluctantly upholding the slave-trade wing of his party, Houston and the Opposition ticket would have probably been elected by even a greater margin.[41]

Dominated in 1859 by so-called Calhoun Democrats, or ultra-southern-rights men, the Democratic state convention had given serious attention to, but had not passed, a resolution demanding the reopening of the African slave trade. When asked to explain his position on the unrealistic attempts to reopen the illegal trade, Runnels lamely responded that his party had taken no particular position on the issue. Why, asked the pro-Houston press, was Runnels precluded from speaking his own mind on this issue while candidates on the Union Democratic ticket were not? To many Texans it appeared that pro-slavery zealots had riddled the Democratic ticket with dangerous secessionist doctrines which party spokesmen now ironically tried to camouflage by a type of Know-Nothing secrecy and deception. This perception became so injurious that even Runnels' supporters eventually pleaded with him to explain his views in order to salvage his reelection bid.[42]

Runnels thus found himself in much the same defensive position as Houston had two years earlier. In 1857 Texas voters rebuked Houston for his opposition to the Kansas-Nebraska Act and his toleration for the enemies of the national Democracy. In 1859 the election result hinged, in part, upon Runnels' failure to bring peace to the western frontier. However, to an even greater extent the outcome had turned upon the Texas Democratic party's needless injection of sectional issues regarding slavery into state politics at a time when federal policies had been, in the candid words of one anti-Houston newspaper, "all that Southern men could desire."[43]

Criticism of the Texas Democratic party in the late antebellum period centered on the premise that the party promoted concerns of no practical importance, but instead agitated sectional issues that alienated people in the North from the South, and, consequently, unnecessarily endangered the survival of the Union. It was the North, not the South, that was on the defensive after the Supreme Court's decision in the Dred Scott case and the Buchanan administration's pro-slavery course in accepting the Lecomp-

41. Oran M. Roberts, "The Political, Legislative, and Judicial History of Texas for Its Fifty Years of Statehood, 1845–1895," in Dudley G. Wooten, ed., *A Comprehensive History of Texas, 1685–1897* (2 vols.; Dallas, 1898), II, 55; Giesenschlag, "The Texas Gubernatorial Elections," 227–29; Peters, "Texas: Annexation to Secession," 331; *Southern Intelligencer* (Austin), August 10, 1859.

42. Ledbetter, "Politics and Society," 13–14; *Standard* (Clarksville), July 2, 1859; Dallas *Herald*, August 10, 1859; Timmons, "Texas on the Road to Secession," I, 306.

43. The Crockett *Argus*, quoted in the Galveston *Weekly News*, August 23, 1859.

ton constitution for Kansas and attempting to annex Cuba. In the summer of 1859 most Texans doubted the wisdom of discussing extreme measures, even disunion, in order to evade hypothetical troubles conjured up in the imaginations of extreme pro-slavery Democrats. However, after John Brown's raid in October on the federal arsenal at Harpers Ferry, most Texas voters abandoned their suspicions of a pro-slavery extremism that arrogantly condemned men who had genuinely questioned whether slavery would be safer out of, rather than within, the Union.

Although Brown's raid had been a sorrowful failure, it was not a theoretical evil. Brown had launched a movement to foment a massive slave rebellion and create a free-soil republic on the ruins of the plantation South. His actions appeared to fulfill the paranoid prophecies of pro-slavery Democratic party zealots who had warned for years that northern abolitionists might someday come to the South to incite slave uprisings. Moreover, when many northerners elevated Brown to martyrdom and rang church bells on the day Virginia officials hanged him, it appeared to most Texans that the North was sanctioning the use of violence to overthrow slavery. Southern sentiment turned against the national government and prompted most Texans to reconsider whether the American nation could be trusted to protect the interests of the South.

In the months which followed the Harpers Ferry raid, Texas Democratic party leaders determined among themselves to attend their party's 1860 national convention with a set of nonnegotiable demands. They insisted that the party reject the notion of "squatter sovereignty," which was closely associated with Senator Douglas, and incorporate in its platform their own goal of federal protection for the right of slaveholders to take their property into the western territories. Even more critical was their veto of Douglas as the party's presidential nominee. Control of the White House by a sympathetic commander in chief seemed even more important after John Brown: could the South trust Douglas to dispatch federal troops to the rescue the next time the emergency arose? The question provided the litmus test of a presidential candidate's acceptability. Many Texas delegates saw the Illinois Democrat as no better than a Black Republican. When it became clear at the convention that he had the necessary votes to win the nomination, the Texans, including former Governor Runnels, walked out. The probability that a split in their party would assure the election for the hated Republicans was apparently a risk that the Texas delegates were willing to take. For those in their ranks who were already inclined toward secession, the election of a

Republican—which many Texans regarded as indisputable grounds for secession—was perhaps less a calculated risk than a means to an end.[44]

In the midst of the irreparable breach in national Democratic party ranks,
elements of the Opposition party in Texas tried to obtain the nomination of
Houston as the presidential candidate of the newly formed Constitutional
Union party. Houston's supporters and the Constitutional Unionists shared
the belief that the breakup on the national level of the otherwise Democratic
party majority would lead to a Republican victory and, in turn, to the
probable dissolution of the Union. They thus hoped to provide a basis on
which the patriotic men of all parties in every section of the country could
unite. They also hoped that the nominee of the Constitutional Union party
would have a chance to attract enough votes to devolve the national election into the House of Representatives. The party was dominated by former
Whigs and Know-Nothings, to whom voting Democratic was anathema.
Thus, unfortunately for Houston, the party was predictably unreceptive to
a self-styled "Democrat of the Old School" who continued to emphasize
his devotion to Jacksonian principles. The Constitutional Unionists chose
former Whig John Bell of Tennessee as their candidate for president.[45]

Meanwhile, the Democrats were failing to reconcile their differences.
Northern and southern wings of the party nominated separate candidates.
The Southern Democrats, including the Texas delegates and a smattering of
westerners and northerners, nominated John C. Breckinridge of Kentucky
for president; the remainder of the national party nominated Douglas. At
the same time the Republican party held its convention and nominated
Abraham Lincoln of Illinois. Thus, by the middle of June, four candidates—
Lincoln, Douglas, Bell, and Breckinridge—were in the race for the American presidency.[46]

For a short period after that, Houston's supporters contemplated running
him as an independent candidate, but with dwindling support for him outside his home state, the Texas Opposition gradually, although reluctantly,
turned to the lackluster Bell. As a former Whig with lingering ties to the
Know-Nothings, Bell held little appeal for many disaffected Democrats who

44. Francis Richard Lubbock, *Six Decades in Texas or Memoirs of Francis Richard Lubbock, Governor of Texas in War-Time, 1861–63; A Personal Experience in Business, War, and Politics*, ed. C. W. Raines (Austin, 1900), 259–80; Buenger, *Secession and the Union*, 48–51; Nichols, *The Disruption of American Democracy*, 245, 254, 279, 288–307.

45. Sam Houston's Speech at Nacogdoches, July 9, 1859, in Williams and Barker, eds., *The Writings of Sam Houston*, VII, 344.

46. Lubbock, *Six Decades in Texas*, 280–94; Buenger, *Secession and the Union*, 50.

had voted for Houston in 1859—voters who would be crucial to prospects of an Opposition victory in the 1860 November presidential balloting. Nonetheless, Bell at least shared Houston's national vision, which promised to triumph over the narrow sectional appeals of Breckinridge and Lincoln. To expand upon the limited charisma of Bell, the leadership of the Texas Opposition fielded what it termed a "Union Electoral Ticket." It was a delicately balanced combination of Bell and Douglas supporters pledged to vote for whichever candidate had the best chance of defeating Lincoln. The Texas "fusionist" ticket, which was the only one of its kind achieved in the South, caused a few initial problems because it involved modifying the Constitutional Union party ticket supporting Bell and thus alienated some anti-Breckinridge voters who could not accept Douglas. If the fusionists had won, the Texas presidential electors would have been pledged to vote in the Electoral College for either Bell, Douglas, or if necessary even Breckinridge to defeat Lincoln. Houston actively campaigned for the Union, or fusion, ticket which seemed, at least momentarily, to have reinvigorated the Texas Opposition.[47]

Unfortunately for the fusionists, during the summer of 1860 a series of major fires in Dallas and North Texas spread rumors that slave arsonists and abolitionist emissaries were at work. In the resulting panic, vigilance committees terrorized traveling strangers and hanged as many as forty to fifty slaves. Soon the contagion, known as the "Texas Troubles" in the southern press, spread eastward into Louisiana and other states of the Lower South. It gradually took on serious political connotations. For the most part, the pro-Breckinridge press breathed life into the rumors of abolitionist incendiarism, whereas the Bell and Douglas forces discounted the reports. Although the hysteria died down by the time of the November election, the Breckinridge camp had capitalized on fears that Texans could expect to find on their doorsteps "the torch of the incendiary" if a hostile party gained control of the federal administration.[48]

The Breckinridge forces swept to victory in Texas by a lopsided majority of three to one. Nevertheless, their hopes for a national victory were futile, because, as most political observers recognized during the closing weeks of the 1860 campaign, Lincoln's strength in the northern states was more than

---

47. *Harrison Flag* (Marshall) September 22, October 13 and 20, 1860; Buenger, *Secession and the Union,* 52–53.

48. *Texas State Gazette* (Austin), September 8, 1860; Donald E. Reynolds, *Editors Make War: Southern Newspapers in the Secession Crisis* (Nashville, 1966), 97–117.

sufficient to win. Voter turnout in Texas was virtually the same as it had been in the 1856 presidential election, but was less than in the two preceding gubernatorial elections featuring the races between Houston and Runnels—a testimony perhaps to the realization that Lincoln's election was all but inevitable. Nonetheless, even when the Texas Southern Rights Democrats sensed their certain defeat at the hands of the Republicans, their zeal did not lessen. After they tacitly conceded Lincoln's election, their goal was to plan and coordinate the impending secessionist movement.

The outcome in Texas of the 1860 presidential election permanently destroyed the coalition that had elected Houston to the governorship: nearly three-fifths of his 1859 supporters subsequently voted for Breckinridge (see table 2). The result obliterated any illusion that Houston's victory in the 1859 gubernatorial election embodied a unionist sentiment that could be tapped under dramatically changed circumstances to prevent the secession of Texas from the Union. This is not to say that Texas unionism was completely dead in the wake of Lincoln's election. To the contrary, there remained a small minority of Texans, including Governor Houston himself, who were unconditionally committed to the United States and who hoped to exploit lingering doubts about the wisdom and legitimacy of secession.

In hindsight, however, Governor Runnels' defeat for reelection in the 1859 governor's race was an aberration. A temporary voter disapproval of his administration, along with opposition to the extreme pro-slavery wing of his party, precipitated his ouster from office. Only on the surface of Texas politics had Houston's dramatic comeback victory won for him a true measure of vindication. Unluckily for Houston, the slavery issue moved Lone Star State politics from beneath. His 1859 victory merely testified to the unpopularity of fire-eating rhetoric at a time when the South had not yet suffered from the double trauma of, first, experiencing on its own soil a genuine northern abolitionist attempt to foment slave rebellion and, second, losing its dominion, which had been assured for years prior to 1860 by the influence of its slaveholders in the national Democratic party, over the American political system.

2
THE SOCIAL DYNAMICS OF THE BALLOTING FOR AND AGAINST SECESSION

We prefer the enslavement of the African race, because we believe it is right—that it is sanctioned by revelation, and by the immemorial custom of mankind, and was never questioned until lately—very lately—when British interests and religious bigotry made the discovery, that it was exceedingly sinful.
—Oran M. Roberts, quoted in the *Texas State Gazette* (Austin),
December 8, 1860

"What the hell's it all about, anyway?"
"The nigger," someone answered.
"The nigger! H——l. I ain't got no nigger. Give me a nigger, some of you, and I'll fight for it as long as any of you. I ain't going to fight for somebody else's nigger."
—Speechmaking on the steps of the Capitol in Austin in the spring of 1861, quoted in Noah Smithwick, *The Evolution of a State*

The February 23, 1861, popular referendum on secession was in many respects the most crucial election in Texas history, for it witnessed a unique instance in which citizens voted—in what might loosely be termed a free election—for the alternative of political rebellion. Texans endorsed disunion by a three-to-one majority, triggering the edict that formally merged their state with the newly formed Confederate States of America and moved the American nation closer to civil war. (The actual vote favoring secession was 46,188 to 15,149.) Although the secessionist movement had accelerated three months earlier in November, with news of Abraham Lincoln's election to the presidency, Governor Sam Houston, who remained unwavering in his resolve to adhere to the Union, had exercised all the possible delaying tactics at his disposal to prevent what he termed the "whipsters and demagogues" from bringing upon Texas "civil strife and bloodshed." The suspense generated by Houston's obstructionist efforts ended in mid-March, when he refused to take a required oath of loyalty to the new southern nation and rejected suggestions that he try to hold the governorship by force.[1]

During the secession crisis, Houston had hoped that the people would either repudiate at the ballot box the work of the Texas Secession Convention or "unfurl again the banner of the Lone Star [Republic]." The chances for either scenario were virtually nil. The 1860 presidential balloting had already ripped apart the fragile Opposition, or "Union Democratic," coalition that had elected Houston to the governorship (see table 7). The John C. Breckinridge–Joseph Lane Southern Rights Democratic ticket had easily defeated the Houston-endorsed John Bell–Stephen A. Douglas "fusion" ticket by a margin of 48,155 to 15,618 votes. Breckinridge had been the only candidate during the campaign who, according to his adherents, had spoken unequivocally for the protection of slavery and could be counted upon in the future to safeguard Texas from abolitionist incendiaries.[2]

In a losing cause, the Bell-Douglas fusionists had captured only about 27 percent of the 1859 Opposition, or Houston, supporters (or almost 10,000 votes), attained over one-tenth of the 1859 Democrats (or approximately 3,000 votes), and attracted roughly 2,000 votes cast by men who either had abstained from voting in the 1859 governor's race or had not yet become part of the voting population in 1859 (see table 7).

The remarkable similarity between the statewide voting totals in the 1860 November presidential election and the subsequent February secession referendum has seduced many historians into incorrectly concluding that the latter result was shaped by the mere reappearance of the coalitions in the presidential balloting.[3] Although a negligible number of Breckinridge men subsequently opposed secession and an insignificant number of fusionists favored it, large variations in voter turnout occurred in many localities between November and February (see tables 2 and 8). An examination of

---

1. Campbell, *Sam Houston,* 150–57 (quotation on p. 150); Friend, *Sam Houston,* 329–49 (quotation on p. 339); Buenger, *Secession and the Union,* 123–25, 141, 143, 147–49.

2. Sam Houston, quoted in Campbell, *Sam Houston,* 152; Reynolds, *Editors Make War,* 97–117.

3. The misconception that voter sentiment in the 1861 secession referendum balloting was almost the same as in the 1860 presidential election is traceable to Frank W. Johnson, *A History of Texas and Texans* (5 vols.; Chicago, 1916), I, 538. For a more accurate assessment, see Baggett, "The Constitutional Union Party," 252–53; Joe T. Timmons, "The Referendum in Texas on the Ordinance of Secession, February 23, 1861: The Vote," *East Texas Historical Journal,* XI (Fall 1973), 24 n. 8.

TABLE 7

ESTIMATED RELATIONSHIPS BETWEEN VOTING IN THE
SECESSION REFERENDUM AND PRIOR VOTING

Voter Group	Percentage of 1860 Electorate[a]	Percentage Voting For Secession	Percentage Voting Against Secession	Percentage Not Voting
Runnels (1859) and Breckinridge	20	100[b]	0[b]	0[b]
Runnels (1859) and Fusion	3	0[b]	0[b]	100[b]
Runnels (1859) and Not Voting in 1860	4	[0–25]	0[b]	[75–100]
Houston (1859) and Breckinridge	19	[74–84]	0[b]	[16–26]
Houston (1859) and Fusion	9	0[b]	100[b]	0[b]
Houston (1859) and Not Voting in 1860	5	0[b]	0[b]	100[b]
Not Voting (1859) and Breckinridge	6	67	0	33
Not Voting (1859) and Fusion	2	0[b]	100[b]	0[b]
Not Voting (1859) and Not Voting in 1860	31	6	16	77
All Voters	100	43	14	43

[a] The percentages of the 1860 electorate are the estimated percentages for the respective segments of the electorate presented in table 2 above for election pair 1859 and 1860.

[b] Logically but not statistically impossible estimates falling outside of the 0–100 percent range were arbitrarily set at their respective minimum or maximum limits.

Source: For the source of the 1859 gubernatorial returns, see table 1 above. The 1860 presidential election returns are the official returns that are reproduced in Burnham, *Presidential Ballots*, 764–813. Included here are returns omitted from Burnham's compilation for Atascosa, Bee, and Milam Counties. See MSS Election Returns for 1860, RG 307, TSL. The 1861 secession-referendum returns are taken from Timmons, "The Referendum in Texas," 15–16, table 1. In following Timmons' characterization of the "scattered" returns, the totals against secession in Goliad, Grimes, Hays, Nacogdoches, and San Patricio Counties have been calculated as 41, 10, 116, 105, and 7, respectively, and the secessionist vote in Wood County has been computed as 452. Because the five improperly designated votes cast at the Wallisville precinct in Chambers County were marked "Union," they have been added here to the county's total cast against secession, but the few unidentified scattered votes reported by Nueces County have necessarily been ignored. The "unofficial" or "informal" reports of votes polled in Presidio and Coleman Counties were left out of the analysis because no balloting for governor and president occurred in these counties in 1859 and 1860. The 1861 Brown County vote has been corrected here to tally 29 to 0 for secession. See Baum, "Pinpointing Apparent Fraud," 208–209.

Note: The voting returns were analyzed by multiple ecological regressions, taking the percentages of choices of potentially eligible voters in the secession referendum (*i.e.,* "for secession," "against secession," and not voting) as the dependent variables. The independent variables, analyzed separately for each choice, were (1) the proportions of the 1861 electorate that had voted in 1859 for Hardin R. Runnels, Sam Houston, and in 1860 for John C. Breckinridge, and the John Bell–Stephen A. Douglas "fusion," or combination, ticket; and (2) all first-order interactions among these four variables. To avoid multicollinearity, the 1859 and 1860 nonvoting percentages were not used. To estimate, for instance, the proportion of Runnels-Breckinridge voters who subsequently favored secession, the intercept of the equation for the secessionists was added to the slopes for "proportion voting for Runnels in 1859," "proportion voting for Breckinridge in 1860," and the appropriate interaction. This sum estimated the proportion secessionist in 1861 for a hypothetical county composed solely of Runnels and Breckinridge voters: in other words, the proportion of such voters favoring secession. All variables were weighted by the adult white male population. For the weighting procedure, see *SPSS-X User's Guide*, 186–87. For the equation predicting "Voted for Secession": $R^2 = .57$; standard error $= .07$; and actual $N = 119$. For the equation predicting "Voted against Secession": $R^2 = .39$; standard error $= .08$; and actual $N = 119$. For the equation predicting "Did Not Vote on Secession": $R^2 = .54$; standard error $= .07$; and actual $N = 119$.

county voting returns grouped into regions reveals the disappearance in eastern Texas, including the Galveston-Houston area, of fragments of the Bell-Douglas opposition (see table 8). In other words, a few fusionists in East Texas apparently sat out the secession-referendum balloting. Most were former Whigs, Know-Nothings, or Houston supporters who boycotted the referendum balloting because they considered it unauthorized or believed their chances of preventing secession were hopeless. Some, however, were genuinely crossed-pressured by their lofty principles regarding the value of the American Union and their economic stake in the institution of slavery.[4]

The analysis of county voting returns also exposes an anti-secessionist influx of previous nonvoters to the polls in North Texas and on the central western frontier (see table 8). Texans who had not voted three months earlier in the presidential election constituted over one-fifth of the anti-secessionist vote (see table 2). In other words, a few formerly apathetic men, mainly nonslaveholders in northern and western Texas, entered the political arena to vote against secession (see tables 7, 8, and 9). Many were European immigrants who had avoided the polling places in both 1859 and 1860 presumably because of their aversion to the pro-slavery sectionalism of Governor Runnels and Breckinridge, on one hand, and the former nativistic or Know-Nothing associations of Houston and Bell, on the other. These slight shifts between November and February square with the standard interpretation that planter-dominated areas of eastern Texas orchestrated secession, while nonslaveholding areas in northern and western Texas not only held back, but also witnessed a few previous nonvoters drawn to the polling places to stand against the tide of disunion.[5]

To uncover further the demographic patterns of support for and against secession, the divisions of the electorate in the referendum were regressed upon twenty-five background variables that measured both social and economic characteristics of the state's counties (see tables 10 and 11). The procedure used, stepwise regression analysis, reveals the relative effect of each background or explanatory variable on the percentages of the electorate voting for secession, against secession, and abstaining, for whatever reason, in the referendum balloting. The analysis thus disentangles statistically the effects of all the background variables in order to learn what importance might be assigned to each in an explanation of voting behavior. All data in the regression equations were treated as descriptions of the social and eco-

4. Baggett, "The Constitutional Union Party," 253–54.
5. Buenger, Secession and the Union, 159–77.

TABLE 8

INCREASE AND DECREASE IN BRECKINRIDGE-SECESSIONIST AND OPPOSITION VOTING STRENGTH BETWEEN NOVEMBER 1860 AND FEBRUARY 1861, BY REGION

(in percentages of 1860 and 1861 regional electorates)

Comparison of Votes Cast for Breckinridge with For Secession

Region	Percentage of 1860 Electorate Favoring Breckinridge	(Difference Between Regions[a])	Percentage of 1861 Electorate Favoring Secession	(Difference Between Regions[a])	Percentage Increase or Decrease
East Texas	52	(+7)	47	(+6)	−5
Western Frontier	48	(+1)	33	(−10)	−15
Galveston-Houston Hub	46	(−1)	52	(+11)	+6
Elsewhere	46	(−1)	44	(+2)	−2
North Texas	45	(−2)	29	(−16)	−16
Rio Grande Valley	33	(−15)	34	(−9)	+1
All Texas	47		43		−4

Comparison of Votes Cast for Fusion with Against Secession

Region	Percentage of 1860 Electorate Favoring Fusion	(Difference Between Regions[a])	Percentage of 1861 Electorate Against Secession	(Difference Between Regions[a])	Percentage Increase or Decrease
North Texas	20	(+6)	31	(+19)	+11
Elsewhere	16	(+1)	17	(+5)	+1
East Texas	15	(0)	7	(−11)	−8
Galveston-Houston Hub	14	(−1)	7	(−9)	−7
Western Frontier	13	(−3)	22	(+8)	+9
Rio Grande Valley	4	(−12)	7	(−7)	+3
All Texas	15		15		0

[a] The difference between regions was obtained by employing a dummy variable that coded the absence or presence of the geographical characteristic (or location) of the counties. For a discussion of the procedure used and listings of counties included in each region, see table 3 above.

Source: For the sources for the 1860 presidential and 1861 secession referendum returns, see table 7 above.

nomic environment or milieu affecting individual voting decisions. Therefore, the behavior of geographical voting units, in this case counties, and not the behavior of individual voters, was under study.

In order to assess the influence of ethnocultural factors, church seating accommodations held by all major denominations were used as a measure of religious preferences, and the percentage of adult white males who were foreign-born provided a rough index of ethnicity. Agricultural variables

TABLE 9

ESTIMATED RELATIONSHIPS BETWEEN SLAVEOWNERSHIP AND VOTING
IN THE 1860 PRESIDENTIAL ELECTION AND 1861 SECESSION REFERENDUM

(by percent)

The 1860 Presidential Election (Actual N = 116)			
	Percent for Breckinridge	*Percent for Fusion*	*Percent Not Voting*
All Slaveholders	61	27	8
Slaveholders by Number of Slaves Owned			
Large (over 20)	81	14	5
Medium (4 to 20)	64	28	7
Small (1 to 3)	58	30	11
Nonslaveholders	43	12	45
All Voters[a]	47	15	38

The 1861 Secession Referendum (Actual N = 123)			
	Percent for Secession	*Percent against Secession*	*Percent Not Voting*
All Slaveholders	81	5	14
Slaveholders by Number of Slaves Owned			
Large (over 20)	100[b]	0[b]	0[b]
Medium (4 to 20)	90	3	7
Small (1 to 3)	70	11	19
Nonslaveholders	32	16	52
All Voters[a]	43	14	43

[a] Actual, not estimated, statewide percentages of adult white males.

[b] Logically but not statistically impossible estimates falling outside of the 0–100 percent range were arbitrarily set at their respective minimum or maximum limits.

Source: For the sources of the 1860 presidential and 1861 secession referendum returns, see table 7 above. For the source of the slaveholding data, see table 4 above.

Note: "Small" slaveholders were arbitrarily defined as slaveholders having 1 to 3 slaves in 1860; "medium" as owning 4 to 20 slaves; and "large" as holding over 20 slaves. Given these definitions and assuming that slaveholders were primarily adult white men, Texas small slaveholders represented approximately 9.3 percent of the state's adult white male population in 1860, and medium and large slaveholders constituted 9.9 percent and 2.1 percent, respectively. For a discussion of the procedures used to generate the above estimates, see table 4 above.

included indices of cattle, sheep, hog, wheat, tobacco, and cotton production. Because of regional differences in the use of draft animals, a ratio of horses to mules was also computed. The proportion of the adult male population that owned slaves and the per capita valuation (measured by real and personal property) among the free population served as measures of slaveholding influence and economic wealth. The rate of growth in the slave population and the frequency at which slaves were taxed were also calculated. In order to provide an intracounty measure of distribution in the

TABLE 10

DESCRIPTIONS, MEANS, AND STANDARD DEVIATIONS OF VARIABLES SELECTED FOR STEPWISE REGRESSION ANALYSIS

Variable Name	Amplified Description	Mean	Standard Deviation
For Secession	Percent of electorate voting for secession in 1861	42.8	.157
Against Secession	Percent of electorate voting against secession in 1861	14.0	.149
Not Voting	Percent of electorate not voting in the 1861 secession referendum	43.1	.148
Baptist	Church seating accommodations, Baptist, divided by free population, 1860	.205	.215
Disciples of Christ	Church seating accommodations, Disciples of Christ, divided by free population, 1860	.041	.083
Episcopalian	Church seating accommodations, Episcopalian, divided by free population, 1860	.025	.064
Lutheran	Church seating accommodations, Lutheran, divided by free population, 1860	.010	.028
Presbyterian	Church seating accommodations, United and Cumberland Presbyterian, divided by free population, 1860	.103	.138
Catholic	Church seating accommodations, Roman Catholic, divided by free population, 1860	.031	.073
Methodist	Church seating accommodations, Methodist, divided by free population, 1860	.276	.279
All Other Churches	Church seating accommodations, all other churches, divided by free population, 1860	.029	.056
Sex Ratio	The number of white males divided by the number of white females in 1860, and multiplied by 100.0	118.3	6.1
Cattle	An index of cattle production calculated by taking the county with the highest ratio of cattle to white population in 1860, assigning it a value of 1.00, and expressing the white per capita production of cattle in each of the remaining counties as a percentage of the maximum	.075	.090
Sheep	An index of sheep production based on the number of sheep in 1860, and computed as above for cattle	.059	.059
Hog	An index of hog production based on the number of hogs in 1860, and computed as above for cattle	.177	.099
Wheat	An index of wheat production based on the number of bushels of wheat produced in 1860, and computed as above for cattle	.020	.031
Cotton	An index of cotton production based on the number of bales of cotton produced in 1860, and computed as above for cattle	.067	.100
Tobacco	An index of tobacco production based on the number of pounds of tobacco produced in 1860, and computed as above for cattle	.025	.109

Variable	Description		
Gini Index	Gini Index of inequality of farmland distribution based on the number of farms in 1860 within the following size brackets: 3 to under 10 acres, 10 to under 20 acres, 20 to under 50 acres, 50 to under 100 acres, 100 to under 500 acres, 500 to under 1,000 acres, and 1,000 acres and over	.533	.058
Slave Growth Rate	A rate of slave growth calculated by dividing the increase in the number of slaves taxed by the state between 1860 and 1861 by the number of slaves taxed in 1860	.086	.182
Horse:Mule	A horse-mule ratio calculated by dividing the number of horses by the number of mules in 1860	6.64	5.92
Slaves Taxed	Percent of slaves taxed by the state in 1860	85.6	.130
Slaveholders	The number of slaveholders divided by the number of adult white males in 1860	.225	.101
Twenties	Percent of adult white males older than 19 but less than 30 years of age in 1860	40.9	.035
Foreign-born	Number of foreign-born white males divided by the total number of white males in 1860	.101	.157
Valuation	Per capita valuation among the free population of real and personal property, 1860	$1,189.05	—
Unimproved:Improved	Ratio of unimproved to improved acres of farmland in 1860	11.50	20.68
Livestock	Value of farm livestock per farm in 1860	$1,656.26	1,330.09

Source: For the source for the 1861 secession referendum returns, see table 7 above. For the sources for church: seating accommodations and the value of real estate and personal property, see *Eighth Census, 1860: Statistics,* 471–73, and "Miscellaneous Statistics," table 3. Agricultural data, including the number of farms within different size brackets and the number of slaveholders, are from the *Eighth Census, 1860: Agriculture,* 2–176, 216–17, 240–42. Taxation of personal property entailed an enumeration of slaves in county tax rolls. See the Records of the Comptroller of Public Accounts, Ad Valorem Tax Division, County Real and Personal Property Tax Rolls for 1860 and 1861, TSL. The source for all other variables is *Eighth Census, 1860: Population,* 472–77, 487–89.

Note: Some potential explanatory variables had to be deleted from consideration because of "multicollinearity" problems. Whenever two independent variables correlated at .75 or above, one of them was discarded. For a discussion of the problem of multicollinearity, see Donald E. Farrar and Robert R. Glauber, "Multicollinearity in Regression Analysis: The Problem Revisited," *Review of Economics and Statistics,* XLIX (February, 1967), 92–107. The construction of the indices for livestock and crop production follows procedures used by Thomas B. Alexander, Peggy Duckworth Elmore, Frank M. Lowrey, and Mary Jane Pickens Skinner, "The Basis of Alabama's Ante-bellum Two-Party System: A Case Study in Party Alignment and Voter Response in the Traditional Two-Party System of the United States by Quantitative Analysis Methods," *Alabama Review,* XIX (October, 1966), 243–76. The Gini Index of concentration of land holdings is calculated from the formula presented in Charles M. Dollar and Richard J. Jensen, *Historian's Guide to Statistics: Quantitative Analysis and Historical Research* (New York, 1971), 122–25. In computing the index for each county using the number of farms within a certain size bracket, it is necessary to assume arbitrarily that the middle value for any given farm size category constituted the average; for example, the mean landholding in the 10-to-under-20-acre bracket is assumed to be 15 acres. *Cf.,* with Randolph B. Campbell, "Planters and Plain Folk: Harrison County, Texas, as a Test Case, 1850–1860," *Journal of Southern History,* XL (1974), 369–98, who constructed Gini indices for a single county from detailed information drawn from the manuscript schedules of the 1850 and 1860 federal censuses. A check on the accuracy of the indices calculated here is not possible just by comparing the result for Harrison County with Campbell's figure. His index of concentration of improved acreage among Harrison County's farm operators in 1860 is .562, whereas the index for Harrison County calculated by the method outlined here is .472. In the regression analyses that follow, however, systematic underrepresentation of the actual extent of inequality in land holdings in each county would make no difference either in the correlation or in regression coefficients. A check on the accuracy of the county indices computed here would entail comparing them with comparable indices constructed in the same manner employed by Campbell for Harrison County—a task requiring an enormous investment in time and energy.

TABLE 11

INFLUENCE OF SELECTED EXPLANATORY VARIABLES ON VOTING PATTERNS IN THE 1861 SECESSION REFERENDUM

Determinants of Secessionist Voting Strength

Dependent Variable: For Secession [R^2 = .61; std. err. = .10; and actual N = 90]

Explanatory Variables	Simple r	Regression Coefficients	Adjusted Standard Errors of Regression Coefficients	Beta Coefficients	Change in R^2
Slaveholders	.65	.37	.31	.24	.42
Hog	.63	.48	.22	.30	.07
Sex Ratio	.23	.01	.00	.21	.02
Methodist	.41	.09	.07	.16	.02
Sheep	.06	.59	.32	.22	.02
Gini Index	−.01	.24	.29	.09	.00
Disciples of Christ	.03	−.12	.19	−.06	.00
Presbyterian	.26	.11	.14	.10	.00
Baptist	.39	.11	.09	.15	.00
Foreign-born	−.37	−.25	.26	−.25	.00
Catholic	−.21	.39	.30	.18	.00
Cattle	.17	−.23	.25	−.13	.00
Slaves Taxed	.20	−.24	.23	−.20	.00
Unimproved:Improved	−.19	−.00	.00	−.37	.01
Slave Growth Rate	−.04	.12	.13	.14	.00
Livestock	−.04	.00	.00	.17	.00
Episcopalian	.01	−.12	.28	−.05	.00
All Other Churches	.21	.12	.28	.04	.00
Horse:Mule	−.27	.00	.00	.04	.00
Twenties	−.02	−.22	.56	−.05	.00
Tobacco	−.01	−.05	.19	−.03	.00
Wheat	−.19	−.10	.70	−.02	.00
Cotton	.45	.04	.18	.03	.00
Valuation	.49	−.00	.00	−.02	.00
Lutheran	−.17	−.07	.79	−.01	.00

Determinants of Anti-Secessionist Voting Strength

Dependent Variable: Against Secession [R^2 = .50; std. err. = .11; and actual N = 90]

Explanatory Variables	Simple r	Regression Coefficients	Adjusted Standard Errors of Regression Coefficients	Beta Coefficients	Change in R^2
Wheat	.48	1.48	.63	.30	.23
Methodist	−.38	−.13	.06	−.23	.09
Sex Ratio	−.22	−.01	.00	−.24	.03
Lutheran	.10	.48	.71	.04	.03
Gini Index	−.19	−.67	.30	−.26	.01
Baptist	−.33	−.15	.08	−.22	.01
Disciples of Christ	.07	.31	.17	.17	.02

TABLE 11

(continued)

Explanatory Variables	Simple r	Regression Coefficients	Adjusted Standard Errors of Regression Coefficients	Beta Coefficients	Change in R²
Presbyterian	−.21	−.16	.12	−.15	.01
Valuation	−.24	.00	.00	.20	.01
Cotton	−.29	−.16	.17	−.11	.01
Hog	−.30	−.32	.20	−.22	.01
Cattle	−.05	.30	.23	.18	.01
Unimproved:Improved	−.09	.00	.00	.03	.01
Catholic	−.05	−.22	.27	−.11	.00
Episcopalian	−.15	−.18	.25	−.08	.00
Foreign-born	.00	.15	.23	.15	.00
Slaveholders	−.32	.24	.28	.16	.00
Horse:Mule	.27	.00	.00	.11	.00
Sheep	.07	−.22	.29	−.09	.00
All Other Churches	−.02	.07	.26	.03	.00
Livestock	−.02	−.00	.00	−.05	.00
Slave Growth Rate	−.12	−.04	.12	−.05	.00
Twenties	.07	−.17	.51	−.04	.00
Tobacco	−.13	−.08	.17	−.05	.00
Slaves Taxed	.05	.02	.21	.02	.00

Determinants of Nonvoting in the Secession Referendum

Dependent Variable: Not Voting [$R^2 − .45$; std. err. = .11; and actual $N = 90$]

Explanatory Variables	Simple r	Regression Coefficients	Adjusted Standard Errors of Regression Coefficients	Beta Coefficients	Change in R²
Valuation	−.28	−.00	.00	−.18	.08
Wheat	−.28	−1.38	.77	−.28	.07
Slaveholders	−.37	−.61	.34	−.42	.03
Lutheran	.07	−.40	.87	−.08	.02
Horse:Mule	.02	−.00	.00	−.15	.02
All Other Churches	−.20	−.19	.31	−.07	.01
Tobacco	.14	.12	.21	.09	.01
Sheep	−.13	−.37	.35	−.15	.01
Episcopalian	.14	.31	.31	.13	.01
Gini Index	.20	.43	.32	.17	.01
Cattle	−.14	−.07	.28	−.04	.01
Unimproved:Improved	.29	.00	.00	.37	.00
Slaves Taxed	−.26	.22	.26	.19	.01
Disciples of Christ	−.10	−.19	.21	−.10	.00
Methodist	−.05	.03	.07	.06	.00
Slave Growth Rate	.17	−.07	.14	−.09	.00
Catholic	.27	−.16	.33	−.08	.00
Twenties	−.05	.39	.62	.09	.00

(continued)

TABLE 11

(continued)

Explanatory Variables	Simple r	Regression Coefficients	Adjusted Standard Errors of Regression Coefficients	Beta Coefficients	Change in R²
Foreign-born	.39	.11	.29	.11	.00
Livestock	.07	−.00	.00	−.12	.00
Hog	−.36	−.15	.25	−.10	.00
Cotton	−.18	.12	.20	.08	.00
Baptist	−.08	.04	.10	.06	.00
Presbyterian	−.07	.05	.15	.05	.00
Sex Ratio	−.03	.00	.00	.02	.00

Note: In order to ensure that smaller counties are not overrepresented in the analysis, the equations are weighted by the estimate of the number of adult white males in 1861. Standard errors of the regression coefficients, however, are computed according to the original, unweighted number of counties and are thus essentially the standard deviations of actual voting percentages from voting percentages predicted by the regression lines. R^2 estimates the proportion of variation in voting percentages explained by the independent variables. The procedure used is the SPSS stepwise regression program (see SPSS-X User's Guide, 850–52). Unreported in the above table is the finding that the increase in R^2 obtained by the addition of the 1860 Breckinridge percentage in the equation for the secessionist vote is 14 percent (or $R^2 = .75$). In like manner, the additional variance explained in the anti-secessionist vote by combining the 1860 fusionist percentage with the twenty-five explanatory variables is 16 percent (or $R^2 = .66$).

ownership of farmland, a Gini Index of inequality was computed for each county. The ratio of unimproved to improved acres of farmland and the value of livestock per farm were also calculated. Finally, the percentage of adult white males who were in their twenties served as an indicator of the relative youthfulness of a county's population, and the number of white males divided by the number of white females generated a sex-ratio variable.

Regarding the socioeconomic environment that underpinned the Texas secessionist movement, the results of the regression analysis confirm the conventional wisdom. As anticipated, the best single predictor of secessionist voting strength was the percentage of slaveholders in the electorate (see table 11). Consistent with the association of slaveholding with secessionist support were other variables that were also highly correlated with the level of voter turnout for secession. Disunionism tended to be strongest in wealthy plantation areas characterized by high levels of hog and cotton production, low ratios of horses to mules, large native-born percentages among their white population, and considerable concentrations of Methodists, Baptists, and Presbyterians.

On the other hand, the most influential variable in explaining the variation in the anti-secessionist vote was the level of wheat production (see table 11). Anti-secessionist sentiment was strong in the wheat-growing counties in North Texas, especially in the counties stretching southward from the

Red River valley to the Blackland prairies. This region contained, besides a smattering of Yankees, many upper South and border-state immigrants, especially natives of Tennessee and Kentucky. Wheat was not only the principal cash crop but also part of the agricultural heritage of many of the region's transplanted yeomen farmers, who often depended upon the United States government to buy their surplus foodstuffs for distribution in Indian Territory (later Oklahoma). This area of the state was also exposed to the greatest military danger in case of civil war.[6]

Opposition to secession, based on correlations of other variables with the level of voter turnout against secession, was also strong in counties with concentrations of Lutherans and Disciples of Christ. The majority of Lutherans were German-born Texans and their children, who in 1860 accounted for almost 8 percent of the state's free population. They were clustered in two bands of counties, stretching from Galveston and Matagorda on the coast to Medina and Gillespie near San Antonio in the interior. The inaccurate portrayal of some German-born settlers as abolitionists, especially those German immigrants living in West Texas, stemmed from exaggerated attention given to a small group of university-educated "liberals" who had fled to Texas in the aftermath of the abortive 1848 democratic uprisings in central Europe. Nevertheless, Germans throughout Texas showed very little sympathy for slavery. The overwhelming majority of Saxon and Hessian peasants (or "Dutchmen," as they were commonly called) who made up the bulk of the Texas German population would have unquestionably preferred that issues of secession and possible civil war had never arisen. Their lack of enthusiasm for extreme pro-slavery arguments was widely known. During the secession crisis German immigrants were often "watched" for evidence of "treason" and frequently denounced as "less patriotic" than "the African Negro." Among the German Texans who participated in the referendum balloting, most voted against secession.[7]

6. Descriptions of North Texas are found in Meinig, *Imperial Texas*, 48–50; Terry G. Jordan, "Imprint of the Upper and Lower South on Mid-Nineteenth Century Texas," *Annals of the Association of American Geographers*, LVII (December, 1967), 667–90; Buenger, *Secession and the Union*, 64–71.

7. Buenger, *Secession and the Union*, 81; Terry G. Jordan, *German Seed in Texas Soil: Immigrant Farmers in Nineteenth-Century Texas* (Austin, 1966), 182; Fornell, *The Galveston Era*, 288–89; Terry G. Jordan, "Germans and Blacks in Texas," in *States of Progress: Germans and Blacks in America over 300 Years; Lectures from the Tricentennial of the Germantown Protest Against American Slavery*, ed. Randall M. Miller (Philadelphia, 1989), 92. For a bibliography on the European immigrant experience in nineteenth-century Texas, see W. Phil Hewitt, *Land and Community: European Migration to Rural Texas in the 19th Century* (Boston, 1981), 63–69. The small group of Norwegian Lutherans also tended to oppose slavery. See Zoie Odom Newsome, "Antislavery Sentiment in Texas, 1821–1861" (M.A. thesis, Texas Technological College, 1968), 68–70.

The association of German Texans with anti-secessionist convictions comes as no surprise, but the same cannot be said for the Disciples of Christ, who, incidentally, were often called "Campbellites" after their cofounder, Alexander Campbell. The strong connection between anti-secessionist voting strength and the presence of the Disciples of Christ is the most remarkable finding of the regression analysis. Even after controlling for all of the other explanatory variables, the variable measuring the percentage of the free population belonging to the Disciples of Christ, or "Christian," church still had a positive impact on the level of turnout against secession (see table 11).

In contrast to their evangelical Protestant brethren, who resided in large numbers throughout East Texas, the Disciples of Christ were scattered in about forty congregations found mostly in North Texas. Although the Disciples had a strong anti-slavery tradition stemming from the Stonite wing of their denomination, they allegedly owned more slaves per capita throughout the South in the late antebellum period than members of any other religious group. In spite of the extent of slaveholding within their ranks, the Disciples apparently often managed to annoy their Methodist and Baptist neighbors. The Disciples, who stressed New Testament notions of God's love and mercy, had a reputation for treating their slaves leniently. They also engaged in proselytizing among community members who were already churchgoers. Although most Texas churches were structurally dependent on church organizations outside the state, the Disciples were the only evangelical Protestant denomination that was not dominated by their coreligionists elsewhere. Whereas Baptist churches were closely aided by the Georgia Baptist Convention, and Methodists and Presbyterians had previously been in the charge of their Mississippi counterparts, only the Disciples of Christ, with their emphasis on biblical literalism and fear of ecclesiastic control, remained independent of strong denominational ties stretching into other southern states.[8]

By calling for peace, unity, and fellowship between northern and south-

---

8. Sandra L. Myres, ed., *Force Without Fanfare: The Autobiography of K. M. Van Zandt* (Fort Worth, 1968), 65–66; Campbell, *A Southern Community in Crisis,* 104, 133, 194; Carter E. Boren, *Religion on the Texas Frontier* (San Antonio, 1968), 45–46; John W. Storey, "Battling Evil: The Growth of Religion in Texas," in *Texas: A Sesquicentennial Celebration,* ed. Donald W. Whisenhunt (Austin, 1985), 374–78; David T. Bailey, *Shadow on the Church: Southwestern Evangelical Religion and the Issue of Slavery, 1783–1860* (Ithaca, 1985), 171–77. Stephen Daniel Eckstein, Jr., in his *History of the Churches of Christ in Texas, 1824–1950* (Austin, 1963), claims that the Texas Disciples were pro-Southern during the Civil War era—an assertion that ignores considerable evidence to the contrary that he himself provides on pages 71–78.

ern Christians, the Disciples firmly believed that slavery was a political and not a religious problem. In this regard, they found themselves oddly out of step with their pietistic southern Protestant brethren, namely the Methodists, Baptists, and Presbyterians. The slaveholding ethic was mostly a natural product of a beleaguered southern evangelical Protestantism. In response to northern criticism of their "peculiar institution," southern pietists developed a biblical defense of slavery and argued that salvation and self-development of blacks were more practicable under the tutelage of Christian slaveholders than under heathen and uncivilized conditions in Africa.[9]

The Disciples of Christ, by deemphasizing questions of slavery and disunion and calling for the cooperation and understanding among the brethren of Christ, surprisingly found themselves in the company of the Lutherans, Episcopalians, and Roman Catholics. In terms of serving non-Hispanic parishioners and European immigrants, Roman Catholics and Lutherans were relative newcomers to Texas. The Lutheran Church in the late antebellum period became a cohesive cultural and religious entity providing for needs of northern European (mostly German) immigrants. On the eve of the Civil War the Vatican dispatched missionaries to Texas with orders to assist settlements of Roman Catholic immigrants (mostly German and Czech) from Bavaria, Bohemia, and Moravia. The Episcopal Church, which was notably one of urban areas, did not have a resident bishop until 1859 and by 1860 possessed only nineteen church buildings in the state.[10]

In the midst of the secession crisis, the Episcopal bishop of the Diocese of Texas pleaded for moderation in the "perilous" times that loomed ahead and noted that the true Christian mission must be "a peaceful and highly exalted one." As outsiders, the German Lutherans wrestled with their instinctive belief that only by obeying the Constitution and the laws of their adopted land would they prove that they were full-fledged American citizens. The Roman Catholic Church was practically silent on the issue of slavery. German, Alsatian, Polish, Czech, and other war-weary European immigrants in its fold feared becoming enmeshed again in the unpredictability of civil strife. In addition, Roman Catholics of Mexican heritage had

9. Donald G. Mathews, *Religion in the Old South* (Chicago, 1977), chaps. 4 and 6; Anne C. Loveland, *Southern Evangelicals and the Social Order, 1800–1860* (Baton Rouge, 1980), 202; "The Christianization of Negroes," *Texas Baptist,* March 7, 1961.

10. Joseph Blount Cheshire, *The Church in the Confederate States: A History of the Protestant Episcopal Church in Texas* (New York, 1912), 5–38; Du Bose Murphy, *A Short History of the Protestant Episcopal Church in Texas* (Dallas, 1935); Carlos E. Castañeda, *Our Catholic Heritage in Texas, 1519–1936* (7 vols.; Austin, 1936–1958), VII, 216–18.

little sympathy for Protestant Anglos, had a strong sense of locality, and had little, if any, financial or emotional stake in the debate over slavery.[11]

Estimates of the relationship between religious affiliation and voting in the referendum election suggest that the Disciples of Christ and the Lutherans voted either against secession or sat out the balloting altogether (see table 12). The strong commitment of the German Lutherans to the Union, with the conspicuous exception of their behavior in Comal County, endured after Lincoln's election fragmented opinion among their leading spokesmen. Although abstention in the referendum balloting was extraordinarily high among Roman Catholic voters, those who went to the polls, according to the estimates of voting, cast secessionist ballots—a finding that reflects manipulation of many Hispanic Roman Catholic votes in extreme South Texas. Whatever was the case, the evidence shows that, because of Roman Catholic voter apathy, support for secession was much higher among the electorate-at-large than among Roman Catholics. A stay-at-home tendency also characterized Episcopalians, who, like the Roman Catholics, turned out to support secession at a lower rate than the state average.[12]

Explaining why about one-quarter of the Texans who went to the polling places in February of 1861 voted against secession is made easier by first identifying groups of men, such as wheatgrowers in North Texas and Lutherans in Central Texas, who were most likely to be in the ranks of the anti-secessionists. However, the more difficult task is to clarify why three out of four Texans *favored* secession. Among nonslaveholders, who constituted over three-quarters of the state's voters, a two-to-one majority for secession represented a resounding endorsement of the disunionist goals of the slaveholding class. (It will be recalled that three out of every five nonslaveholders who voted in 1859 had favored Houston over Runnels.) Although in 1860 the Democrats articulated views that were singularly sympathetic to the interests of the state's slaveholders, their party's political ideology obviously had a much wider appeal as well. From the point of view of the Southern Rights Democrats, the Republican party, or "the

11. Alexander Gregg, quoted in the Dallas *Herald,* January 23, 1861; Boren, *Religion on the Texas Frontier,* 32; *Daily Ranchero* (Corpus Christi), January 5, 1861; "Letter from a German Citizen" in the Galveston *Weekly News,* February 19, 1861; Thomas T. McAvoy, "The Formation of the Catholic Minority in the United States, 1820–1860," in John M. Mulder and John F. Wilson, eds., *Religion in American History: Interpretive Essays* (Englewood Cliffs, N.J., 1978), 254–69.

12. Jordan, *German Seed in Texas Soil,* 182–83; Walter L. Buenger, "Secession and the Texas German Community: Editor Lindheimer vs. Editor Flake," *Southwestern Historical Quarterly,* LXXXII (1979) 379–402.

TABLE 12

ESTIMATED RELATIONSHIPS BETWEEN RELIGIOUS AFFILIATION AND VOTING IN THE 1860 PRESIDENTIAL ELECTION AND 1861 SECESSION REFERENDUM

The 1860 Presidential Election   (Actual $N = 95$)

	Percentage for Breckinridge	Percentage for Fusion	Percentage Not Voting
Roman Catholics	[0–1]	0[a]	[99–100]
Lutherans	4	50	46
Episcopalians	10	15	75
Disciples of Christ	30	25	45
Nonchurchgoers	46	17	38
Methodists	51	8	41
Baptists	58	21	21
Presbyterians	59	25	16
Members of All Other Churches	65	27	8
All Voters[a]	47	15	38

The 1861 Secession Referendum Election   (Actual $N = 95$)

	Percentage for Secession	Percentage against Secession	Percentage Not Voting
Lutherans	0[a]	[81–100]	[0–19]
Disciples of Christ	0[a]	[66–71]	[29–34]
Nonchurchgoers	34	23	42
Roman Catholics	[2–35]	0[a]	[65–98]
Episcopalians	35	11	53
Presbyterians	48	12	40
Baptists	51	6	43
Methodists	52	7	41
Members of All Other Churches	[92–100]	0[a]	[0–8]
All Voters[a]	43	14	43

[a] Negative estimates have been arbitrarily set at 0 percent and the parameters of the corresponding estimates have been placed in brackets.

Source: For the source for the church seating accommodations, see table 10 above. For the source of the 1860 presidential and 1861 secession referendum returns, see table 7 above.

Note: Church seating accommodations divided by the free population in 1860 is, admittedly, an extremely crude measure of the percentage of adult white males who were formally affiliated with a specific church. Roman Catholics, moreover, are underrepresented by just counting "seats." Accommodations belonging to the Roman Catholic Church constituted only 5.7 percent of the total number of seating accommodations in 1860. Roman Catholic churches probably held three or four masses per Sunday in the same church building, thus serving more parishioners than the mere number of seats would indicate; whereas there was relatively less duplication among Protestant denominations in plantation areas, where slaves were frequently admitted to church services or even membership. However, systematic under- or overcounting of a denomination's share of church seats would make no difference in the above estimates from what they would be if, for example, the particular denomination's seats were doubled or tripled and all other church seatings were left unchanged. Nevertheless, the above estimates could have been easily biased by leaving out other possible determinants of the vote, such as citizenship status and extent of slaveownership.

revolutionary party of the North" as it was frequently called, threatened Texas with an imminent assault upon established laws and procedures. They saw in the creation of a new southern nation an opportunity to seal off their state from what they saw as the contagion of abolition—an evil that would render property in slaves worthless and cause the slaves themselves "to descend to the vilest barbarism." Democratic party spokesmen were thus able to portray secession to nonslaveholders as the best way to ensure social stability and maintain economic prosperity. This, in brief, was the genius of the Democratic strategy, and explains why the wealthy East Texas planters who launched the secession juggernaut were able to mobilize popular support for rebellion and probable war.[13]

Another, and a far more difficult, question is to what extent did intimidation of Texas unionists and deliberate miscounting of votes affect the outcome of the February balloting. The allegations, made at the time by unionists and often repeated subsequently, that Texas secessionists coerced and silenced many voters or miscounted the votes to their advantage, were often sweeping and intensely emotional charges supported with little, if any, solid evidence. Typical of the generalized, but largely unsubstantiated, accusations were the charges made by unionist refugees that "many" of the reported secessionist majorities were "false" and that threats and intimidation caused "thousands" of anti-secessionists to vote for secession or not vote at all. Unionists claimed that paramilitary and secret groups, such as the Knights of the Golden Circle, had illegally intimidated the majority of Texans who otherwise would have voted against secession. Congressman Andrew J. Hamilton, a staunch supporter of Governor Houston, caustically remarked that unionists had stayed away from the polls because they preferred "reading about martyrs to being martyrs."[14]

Most current historical accounts, while acknowledging that intimidation and miscounting played some part—albeit far short of a determining one—in shaping the outcome of the secession referendum, have interpreted the complaints of the Texas unionists as consequences of the secessionist cur-

---

13. Oran M. Roberts, quoted in the *State Gazette* (Austin), December 8, 1860.

14. James P. Newcomb, *Sketch of Secession Times in Texas and Journal of Travel from Texas Through Mexico to California, Including a History of the "Box Colony"* (San Francisco, 1863), 8; Gilbert D. Kingsbury [F. F. Fenn], "Lectures, Reports, and Writings 1855–1867," II, 20, in Gilbert D. Kingsbury Papers, BTHC; George S. Denison, "Some Letters of George Stanton Denison, 1854–1866: Observations of a Yankee on Conditions in Louisiana and Texas," ed. James A. Padgett, *Louisiana Historical Quarterly,* XXIII (1940), 1172–73; Andrew Jackson Hamilton, "Origin and Objects of the Slaveholders' Conspiracy Against Democratic Principles, As Well As Against the National Union" (New York, 1862), 6.

tailment of political debate during the winter of 1860–1861. Only in scattered localities where "being a unionist remained socially and politically legitimate" and "established leaders could not be muffled" did opposition to secession make its voice heard. Evidence showing precisely where and how secessionists fraudulently smothered unionist sentiment remains not only impressionistic, but also uncorroborated.[15]

Specific and detailed allegations of trickery, ballot-box stuffing, miscounting, and falsification of returns are rare. Claims by prominent unionists that the election procedures had not been fair centered on the flimsy accusation that, because the date when returns were to be received by the secretary of state was apparently the same date when the ordinances of secession were to take effect, many unionists, mistakenly believing that their anti-secessionist ballots would be cast in vain, stayed away from the polls. This charge skirted the new unfolding events that unionists could acknowledge with only impotent resentment: namely, that the Texas Secession Convention had, for all practical purposes, already taken Texas out of the Union by first effectively seizing control of the state away from Governor Houston and then forcibly securing the surrender of all federal property and the evacuation of the command of the United States government's top military man in the state. Although unionists tried to discredit the legitimacy of a secessionist movement that condoned force and illegal methods, opposition to secession was arguably fenced in at the outset.[16]

To probe more systematically the issue of election fraud in the secession referendum, procedures for pinpointing counties where possible voting irregularities might have occurred must take into account the expected or "normal" voting patterns for the voting units for which election returns are available. The same equations that generate voter transition probabilities between pairs of elections can also be used to "predict" or estimate the levels of turnout for political parties, candidates, or outcomes in each voting unit under study. The secession referendum followed in the wake of two statewide elections which were comparably free of allegations of fraud: the

15. Buenger, *Secession and the Union,* 157, 161, 173–74, 176; Buenger, "Texas and the Riddle of Secession," 174. Charles William Ramsdell's undocumented statement that "charges of unfair tactics and of fraud came up from all parts of the state against the secessionists," was uncritically accepted in much of the older historical literature (*Reconstruction in Texas* [1910; rpr. Austin, 1970], 19).

16. John T. Sprague, *The Treachery in Texas, the Secession of Texas, and the Arrest of the United States Officers and Soldiers Serving in Texas* (New York, 1862); James Oldam Wallace, "San Antonio During the Civil War" (M.A. thesis, St. Mary's University, 1940), 36; Buenger, "Texas and the Riddle of Secession," 174; Buenger, *Secession and the Union,* 153–54.

1860 presidential race in which Breckinridge had easily defeated the Bell–Douglas fusion ticket, and the August, 1859, gubernatorial race that incumbent governor Runnels lost in dramatic fashion to Sam Houston. When the secessionist percentage of the possible vote is regressed upon the Breckinridge, Bell-Douglas-fusion, Houston, and Runnels percentages, the resulting equation produces a predicted secessionist percentage that is a weighted linear composite of the previous divisions of the electorate.[17]

In other words, the predicted secessionist percentages express whatever sources of variance in the secessionist vote are due to the divisions of the electorate in the 1859 gubernatorial and 1860 presidential elections. Therefore, if they are subtracted from the actual secessionist percentages, the remainders, or residual values, should express sources of variance *other* than those due to the prior voting patterns in the gubernatorial and presidential elections. Voting-units with the largest residual values are called "outliers," which are, in effect, the data points that fall the greatest distances from the regression line. What constitutes an outlier can vary from one study to the next, but here it is defined arbitrarily as a value falling two standard errors from the regression line (see table 13).[18]

When an outlier county in table 13 has a *positive* residual listed under "For Secession" (or "Against Secession") it means that, given the proportions of its constituency that supported Houston and Runnels in 1859, and Breckinridge and Bell-Douglas fusion in 1860, and given the statewide relationships between the support for Houston, Runnels, Breckinridge, and fusion on the one hand, and the secessionist (or anti-secessionist) vote on the other, the county favored disunion (or staying in the union) at a rate much higher than it would have had it behaved in the same way as all other counties. Counties where the secessionists (or anti-secessionists) polled an unexplainably low number of votes have *negative* residuals. Because the set

17. For an introduction to multiple linear regression, see Fred N. Kerlinger, *Foundations of Behavioral Research* (3rd ed.; New York, 1986), 531–36. For a description of the equation used here to predict the vote in the 1861 secession referendum, see table 7 above.

18. The standard error of the estimate is essentially the standard deviation of the actual voting percentages from the values predicted by the regression line. For the value of analyzing the residuals of ecological regressions used in voting behavior studies, see Ivor Crewe and Clive Payne, "Another Game with Nature: An Ecological Regression Model of the British Two-Party Vote Ratio in 1970," *British Journal of Political Science,* VI (January, 1976), 43–81. On the use of regression analysis as a method for the study of election fraud, see Lawrence N. Powell, "Correcting for Fraud: A Quantitative Reassessment of the Mississippi Ratification Election of 1868," *Journal of Southern History,* LV (1989), 633–58; Dale Baum, "Pinpointing Apparent Fraud in the 1861 Texas Secession Referendum," *Journal of Interdisciplinary History,* XXII (Autumn, 1991), 221.

TABLE 13

OUTLIER COUNTIES IN THE 1861 SECESSION REFERENDUM

(in percentages of 1861 county electorates)

Abnormally High Turnout "For" and "Against" Secession

County	Residual Values Above Expected Turnout "For" Secession (%)	County	Residual Values Above Expected Turnout "Against" Secession (%)
Young	37	Blanco	46
Grimes	27	Gillespie	38
Brazoria	21	Uvalde	34
San Saba	21	Medina	33
Fort Bend	20	Montague	30
Zapata	19	Williamson	26
Coryell	16	Mason	26
Harrison	16	Grayson	25
Navarro	15	Collin	22
Bandera	15	Lamar	21
		Atascosa	20
		Travis	18
		Caldwell	15

Abnormally Low Turnout "For" and "Against" Secession

County	Residual Values Below Expected Turnout "For" Secession (%)	County	Residual Values Below Expected Turnout "Against" Secession (%)
Uvalde	−35	Starr	−24
Jack	−28	Harrison	−22
Titus	−25	Lampasas	−21
Montague	−23	Karnes	−20
Tyler	−20	Goliad	−19
Van Zandt	−20	Bandera	−16
Hunt	−19	Wise	−16
Cass	−16		

Source: For the sources of the 1859 gubernatorial, 1860 presidential, and 1861 secession referendum returns used in this table, see tables 1 and 7 above.

Note: The residual values or scores above are the differences between the actual percentages of the county electorates voting for and against secession, on one hand, and the corresponding estimated or predicted levels of secessionist and anti-secessionist turnout, on the other. The predicted levels for this table are based on voting in the 1859 gubernatorial and 1860 presidential elections. Outliers are arbitrarily defined here as having residual values falling at least two standard errors above or below the respective regression lines generated by the equations predicting the secession referendum results in table 7 above. For the description of the equations used, amount of variation explained, standard errors, and actual number of cases, see table 7 above.

of residual values for all Texas counties contains all of the available information on the ways in which the divisions of the vote in the gubernatorial and presidential elections fail to predict the result in the secession referendum, there may be many explanations other than vote fraud to account for the behavior of outlier counties. If no other explanation applies, the county must be examined more thoroughly because it remains under suspicion of being a locality where voting irregularities occurred.

Because the sole purpose of using regression equations in this manner is to predict a particular voting outcome, it is permissible to include as many legitimate predictors in the regression equation as possible plus every legitimate interaction among them, including, if necessary, second-, third-, and higher-order interactions. Even multicollinearity—which exists when two or more independent variables are highly correlated or when one is a linear combination of several others—poses no problem, for in the case of "predicting" voting outcomes (rather than "explaining" them by determining which factors best account for the variation in the vote) the relative magnitudes of the coefficients are ignored. The difficulty lies in deciding what constitutes a "legitimate" variable. Adding nonpolitical variables into the equations could conceal the impact of fraud. For example, if slave-related variables or cotton production indices were correlated with the incidence of fraud, their inclusion in the equations would yield more accurate predictions of actual voting outcomes, but counties where unionists were intimidated or "counted out" would not exhibit unusually low levels of anti-secessionist voting. Instead, voting patterns would appear normal or predictable, when in truth they should show no-vote totals below predicted levels of unionist support.

The net loss or gain accruing to the secessionist or anti-secessionist cause as a result of the idiosyncratic voting behavior in any county can be calculated by subtraction of the comparable residual values. For example, in Harrison County, located in the center of cotton plantation agriculture in the extreme northeastern part of the state, the vote for secession was sixteen full percentage points, or about 249 votes, above the share of the possible vote that the secessionists would have polled had the Harrison County electorate behaved in the same way as all of the Texas county electorates between 1859 and 1861. However, the net gain of the secessionist crusade over the unionist cause in the county was thirty-eight percentage points (+16 minus −22), or 591 votes, because the turnout "against secession" was twenty-two percentage points below its predicted level. Unusually large net gains in favor of secession could have been, but did not necessarily have to have been, fabricated by ballot-box stuffing or miscounting of the returns by secessionists in control of the local election machinery (see table 14).

Although in the literature on Texas secession there is no hint of any election fraud perpetrated by unionists, the circumstances around the vote in Uvalde County, the most "unpredictable" county identified by the statistical analysis presented here, demand further examination (see table 14). If unionist officials in any county had fraudulently transposed the voting results, the pattern of aberrant support against secession would resemble that of Uvalde County in that the amount of inflated unionist strength would exactly match the extent of discounted secessionist ballots.

Throughout Texas the number of Breckinridge voters who subsequently cast ballots against secession was insignificant. However, if all Uvalde County voters who participated in the 1860 election returned to the polls three months later to vote in the secession referendum, then over half of them would have had to "switch" from the Southern Rights Democracy to the unionist camp to achieve the overwhelming anti-secessionist vote registered in their county. Uvalde County cast 81 votes for Breckinridge and 16 votes for the fusion ticket, but in the secession referendum the county voted negatively 76 to 16. If 56 of the estimated 73 county voters who sat out the November presidential balloting had subsequently joined the 20 fusionists in opposing secession and if 65 former Breckinridge men had not voted, for whatever reason, in the secession referendum, then it would have been theoretically possible, but highly unlikely, that not one voter in the county would have had to "switch" from Breckinridge to against secession to have produced the 1861 result. Because three of the county's four precincts mysteriously failed to report returns, this scenario of large conversions of Breckinridge men into unionists is even more improbable.[19]

The influx of a smattering of foreign settlers and doubts during the secession crisis over the ability of a southern Confederacy to defend frontier areas against Indian depredations explain only a minor part of the strong unionist showing in Uvalde County. In this southwestern county whose first elected

---

19. Black's handwritten note on the certification of returns states: "no returns from three precinct[s?] received yet" (Secretary of State, MSS Election Returns for 1861, RG 307, TSL). For estimates of insignificant anti-secessionist support among former Breckinridge voters, see Peyton McCrary, Clark Miller, and Dale Baum, "Class and Party in the Secession Crisis: Voting Behavior in the Deep South, 1856–1861," *Journal of Interdisciplinary History*, VIII (Winter, 1978), 446–47; Robin E. Baker and Dale Baum, "The Texas Voter and the Crisis of the Union," 400. *Cf.* Timmons, "Texas on the Road to Secession," II, 715–16, who ignores the impact of differentials in voter participation rates between the 1860 presidential balloting and subsequent voting in the secession referendum.

TABLE 14

LARGEST NET GAINS FOR AND AGAINST SECESSION
IN TERMS OF VOTER SUPPORT ABOVE OR BELOW PREDICTED LEVELS

(in percentages of 1861 county electorates)

Residual Net Gains Greater Than 18 Percentage Points "For" Secession

County	Net Gain "For" Secession (%)	Estimated Size of 1861 Electorate
Grimes *(Navasota)*	42	1,317
Harrison *(Marshall)*	38	1,555
Goliad	33	662
Starr	33	751
Lampases	32	213
Austin *(Bellville)*	31	1,731
Brazoria	29	646
Navarro *(Corsicana)*	27	1,049
Hays	27	335
San Saba	27	197
Zapata	25	196
Coryell	25	541
Young	24	196
Rusk *(Henderson)*	24	2,261
Karnes	23	374
Fort Bend	22	647
Gonzales *(Gonzales)*	21	1,298
Jasper	21	528
Falls	19	476
Guadalupe	19	893
Smith *(Tyler)*	19	1,973
Upshur *(Gilmer)*	19	1,628

Residual Net Gains Greater Than 18 Percentage Points "Against" Secession

County	Net Gain "Against" Secession (%)	Estimated Size of 1861 Electorate
Uvalde	69	174
Montague	53	190
Gillespie	53	683
Blanco	51	309
Medina	39	473
Grayson *(Sherman)*	38	1,696
Jack	38	241
Mason	38	214
Van Zandt	34	764
Collin *(McKinney)*	33	1,953
Lamar *(Paris)*	32	1,756
Williamson	31	849
Atascosa	30	394
Hunt *(Greenville)*	30	1,348

TABLE 14

(continued)

County	Net Gain "Against" Secession (%)	Estimated Size of 1861 Electorate
Fannin *(Bonham)*	29	1,783
Titus *(Mount Pleasant)*	28	1,660
Bastrop *(Bastrop)*	26	1,086
Tyler	23	727
Kaufman	23	806
Travis *(Austin)*	21	1,325
Brazos	19	475

Source: For the sources of the 1859 gubernatorial, 1860 presidential, and 1861 secession referendum returns, see tables 1 and 7 above. For the procedure used to estimate potentially eligible voters in 1861, see table 7 above.

Note: The above percentages represent the net gain (in terms of shares of estimated 1861 potentially eligible voters) for and against secession due to idiosyncratic county voting behavior above or below the statewide trends estimated in table 7 above. The statewide trends are based on prior voting in the 1859 gubernatorial and 1860 presidential elections. For example, the finding that disunionism benefited in Grimes County from a 42 percentage point advantage was calculated by subtracting the 15 percentage points the anti-secessionist cause received *below* the predicted level from the 27 percentage points the secessionist cause received *above* the predicted level (or 27 percent minus −15 percent = 42 percent). In other words, the secessionist cause in Grimes County benefited from a 553-vote (42 percent of 1,317) margin over and above the margin of support disunionism would have had in the county had the county merely behaved in the same way as all of the counties in Texas between 1859 and 1861.

officials in 1856 were all experienced Indian fighters with connections to Fort Inge, the referendum outcome was shaped by the excessive influence of Reading W. Black, a New Jersey–born Quaker, former Whig, and ardent anti-secessionist. Black's successful speculation in land and prosperity as an Indian trader had made him Uvalde County's most prominent citizen. In his capacity as chief justice (county judge), he certified the lopsided unionist majority in the referendum balloting. After the outbreak of war Black crossed the border into Mexico to elude, in his words, "rebels & cut-throats." Upon returning home after the war, he served as one of the few anti-Democratic "Unionists" in the state legislature. After he welcomed the prospect of congressional control of Reconstruction and tried to organize a local Republican party "Loyal League," angry ex-Confederates successfully arranged his assassination. The subsequent failure to extradite Black's murderer from a Mexican jail had implications that reached the halls of the U.S. Congress and was one of the many reasons why Winfield S. Hancock was deposed in March, 1868, of a Southern command.[20]

20. Webb, Carroll, and Branda, eds., *The Handbook of Texas,* I, 167–68; Reading Wood Black, *The Life and Diary of Reading W. Black; A History of Early Uvalde,* comp. Ike Moore (Austin, 1934), 27–30, and 28 n. 69; El Progreso Club, *A Proud Heritage: A History of Uvalde County, Texas* (Uvalde, Tex., 1975), 12–13, 193–96; San Antonio *Express,* October 5, 1867; Thomas Tyree Smith, "Fort Inge: Sharps,

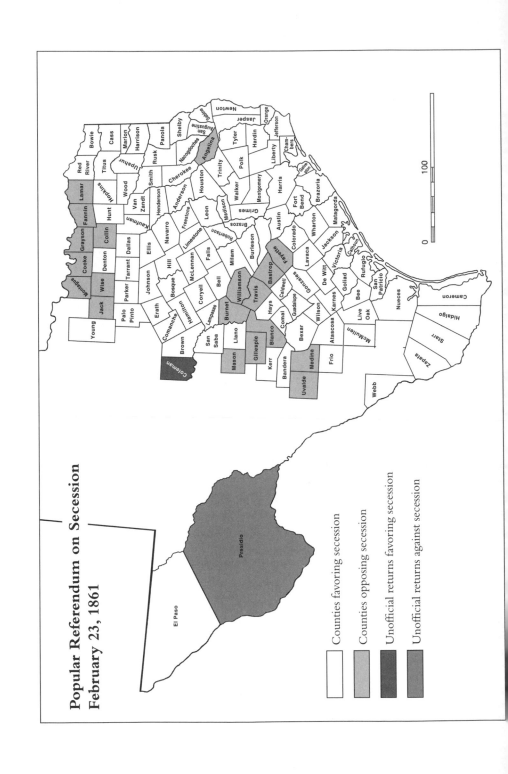

Popular Referendum on Secession
February 23, 1861

Counties favoring secession
Counties opposing secession
Unofficial returns favoring secession
Unofficial returns against secession

If Black had transposed the voting totals, which the quantitative evidence suggests was precisely the case, it would seem reasonable to assume that someone would have noticed this obvious fraud when the results of the balloting were made public. Moreover, mention of the suspicion of vote fraud would have presumably surfaced subsequently during the war years or at the time of the investigation of Black's murder. Until now, no hint of possible chicanery on Black's part has been suggested or uncovered in any secondary or primary historical source.[21] There remains, however, a plausible alternative explanation for the unpredictably large anti-secessionist vote in Uvalde County.

Company C of the 2nd U.S. Cavalry was at Fort Inge on the day of the referendum balloting, even though General David E. Twiggs's orders to abandon the post had been received five days earlier. Company commander James Oakes and his highest-ranking lieutenant, Abraham K. Arnold, were both Pennsylvania-born unionists who subsequently fought for the North. No southern secessionist officers served at the post. Of the post's full complement of seventy-seven men, a large percentage was European-born. Black, who was on excellent terms with the fort's personnel, might have allowed the soldiers to vote at the voting precinct established at the settlement next to the fort. The remaining three precincts, at Waresville (present-day Utopia), at Patterson Settlement (present-day Sabinal), and at the town of Uvalde, could have failed to have reported returns possibly because Black deliberately avoided arranging for the polls in these localities to be open.[22]

Unionists also carried Montague County, the second-most-unpredictable county flagged for possible voting irregularities in the secession referendum. Like Uvalde County, Montague County was located on the sparsely populated frontier, although much farther north. It shared its surprisingly strong unionist sentiment with neighboring Jack County. Both counties

---

Spurs, and Sabers on the Texas Frontier, 1849–1869" (MS in possession of Thomas Tyree Smith, College Station, Tex.), 178–83.

21. Living in the Fort Inge and Fort Clark area during the secession crisis was Belgian astronomer and journalist Jean-Charles Houzeau, who later, as the editor of the radical Republican New Orleans *Tribune,* became "one of the most remarkable men to take part in the saga of Reconstruction" (Foner, *Reconstruction,* 63). Houzeau's eyewitness accounts of the repression of unionist sentiment in Texas fail to mention Black or Uvalde County politics. See Jean-Charles Houzeau, *La terreur blanche au Texas et mon évasion* (Brussels, 1862).

22. U.S. Bureau of the Census, *Population Schedules of the Eighth Census of the United States, 1860, State of Texas,* Reel #1307, RG 29 (Washington, D.C., NA, Microfilm edition), 657–68; Smith, "Fort Inge," 127, 129–30, 142; Colonel Harold B. Simpson, *Cry Comanche: The 2nd U.S. Cavalry in Texas, 1855–1861* (Hillsboro, Tex., 1979), 160–65, 172, 174.

contained many settlers with upper-South and border-state origins. They also embraced many settlers from Illinois, Indiana, and Ohio, causing contemporaries to call the region "Yankee Country." The resounding no-vote by homesteaders in these two counties by well over a two-to-one majority reflected their fear of exposure to Indian raids if federal troops abandoned Fort Belknap in nearby Young County and Fort Cobb across the Red River in Indian Territory. The vote in Jack County (where election managers conspicuously wrote on the official tally sheet "Against Secession—for the Union Forever!") might have been polled by an unauthorized *viva voce* procedure or an improper "reading out loud" of voters' ballots. A list of the names of men voting for and against secession appears without comment in a local memoir.[23]

Glaring exceptions to the phenomenon of "frontier unionism" are Young and San Saba Counties, which are also flagged by the statistical analysis by virtue of their abnormally large margin for secession (see table 14). Young County had grown up around Fort Belknap, one of the larger military posts in northwestern Texas and a stop on the Butterfield Overland Mail route where horses were changed for mules on the way west. In the secession referendum the total vote cast in Young County was virtually the same as the number of possible "qualified electors," and this extraordinary turnout heavily favored the disunionist cause. (Young County favored secession by a vote of 166 to 31, but had only 196 "qualified electors" in 1861.) Unionists later surmised that either the ballot box was stuffed or "the prairie-dogs were original secessionists and were counted." Though the vote was probably "padded," the county's voting behavior strikingly illustrates that the army was capable of provoking negative as well as positive reactions among settlers on the western Texas frontier.[24]

In 1859 deadly and vituperative conflicts arose within and around Young County between local cattlemen, on one side, and the soldiers, Indians, and their agent Robert S. Neighbors, who was the highest federal Indian official

---

23. Ida Lasater Huckabay, *Ninety-Four Years in Jack County, 1854–1948* (Waco, 1949), 53–60, 76–77; Glenn O. Wilson, "Montague County: 'The Texas County of Trails,' " in Jeff S. Henderson, ed., *100 Years in Montague County, Texas* (Saint Jo, Tex., 1958); Floyd F. Ewing, Jr., "Unionist Sentiment on the Northwest Texas Frontier," *West Texas Historical Association Year Book*, XXXIII (October, 1957), 70. Lists of voters revealing how each of them voted are rare and have been uncovered for the secession referendum for only two other frontier counties. See folders for Brown and Coleman Counties in Secretary of State, MSS Election Returns for 1861, RG 307, TSL.

24. Ewing, "Unionist Sentiment on the Northwest Texas Frontier," 58–70; Carrie J. Crouch, *Young County*, 29; Webb, Carroll, and Branda, eds., *Handbook of Texas*, II, 948–49; "How Texas Was Surrendered: A Military Sketch," *New Jersey Magazine*, May 1, 1867, p. 42.

in Texas, on the other. Problems stemmed from the management of the Brazos and Clear Fork Indian Reservations. Many white settlers resented appropriations of land and food to the reserve Indians, who were often blamed, when they strayed off reservation lands to hunt, for pillaging frontier settlements. Complaining whites, however, made little, if any, effort to distinguish between the peaceful reserve Indians and the nonreserve Indians who carried out most of the raids against whites and reserve Indians alike. For Fort Belknap officials, the job of supplying and supervising some 2,000 Indians dependent upon the army for protection from lawless Texans and terrifying "wild" Comanches was an expensive and unrewarding task. Convinced that the settlers were the real troublemakers, Neighbors, at the time of the removal of the reservation Indians north of the Red River into Indian Territory, inflated the Young County 1859 gubernatorial vote with a few questionable Houston ballots cast at an unauthorized polling place. Shortly afterward, Neighbors was assassinated at the village of Fort Belknap. Following his murder many difficulties arose in maintaining local and county government. By the time of the secession-referendum balloting, the army had already abandoned the area.[25]

Although it is doubtful that virtually every possible voter in Young County appeared at the polls on the day of the referendum, historians have not found any evidence to suggest that voters' intentions were violated. The county's election managers, including its pro-secessionist chief justice, presumably justified the "full poll" as accurately reflecting the local sentiment that the army had for too long defended Indians rather than frontiersmen. A prominent Texas Indian fighter recalled his conversion to disunionism after realizing, at the height of his efforts to have the Indians expelled from the area, that the U.S. Congress "thought more of an Indian, a foreigner and a free negro than it did of American citizens."[26]

25. George Klos, "'Our People Could Not Distinguish One Tribe from Another': The 1859 Expulsion of the Reserve Indians from Texas," *Southwestern Historical Quarterly*, XCVII (1994), 599–619 (quotation on p. 610); James K. Greer, ed., *A Texas Ranger and Frontiersman: The Days of Buck Barry in Texas* (Dallas, 1932), 111–17; Buenger, *Secession and the Union*, 106, 111–12; Webb, Carroll, and Branda, eds., *Handbook of Texas*, I, 209–10, II, 267–68; Barbara Neal Ledbetter, *Civil War Days in Young County, Texas* (Newcastle, Tex., 1965), 1; Crouch, *Young County*, 19–25, 109–13; Kenneth F. Neighbours, "Indian Exodus Out of Texas in 1859," *West Texas Historical Association Year Book*, XXXVI (October, 1960), 85–86; Kenneth Franklin Neighbours, *Robert Simpson Neighbors and the Texas Frontier, 1836–1859* (Waco, 1975), 273.

26. MSS Election Returns for 1861; Ledbetter, *Civil War Days in Young County*, 19; James Buckner Barry, quoted in B. P. Gallaway, ed., *The Dark Corner of the Confederacy: Accounts of Civil War Texas as Told by Contemporaries* (Dubuque, Iowa, 1968), 17.

Following Montague County, the next most unpredictable county, Gillespie County (Fredericksburg), shares its unusually large margin against secession with five other counties (Blanco, Medina, Mason, Williamson, Bastrop, and Travis) in the same central Texas Hill Country region (see table 14). Because Gillespie County was the only Texas county to report majorities for the Bell-Douglas fusion ticket and against secession, historians have regarded it as "the model of consistency" between the two elections. This assessment, however, ignores the large differential in voter turnout in the county between the presidential balloting and the February referendum. Centered near Gillespie County on the fringes of the cotton-growing South were ten of the nineteen Texas counties that voted against secession. Sensitive to the rhetoric of influential unionists in the state capital of Austin, the counties shared some additional characteristics, such as the unimportance of slavery in their local economies, concentrations of Anglo frontiersmen with origins outside the Deep South, and large numbers of European, principally German, immigrants. The area produced many uncompromising unionists who subsequently fled the state, took to the "bush" to avoid conscript officers, and suffered greatly under Confederate rule. Geographical proximity, shared social characteristics, and statements by contemporaries of the period dictate unqualified acceptance of the unionist majorities registered in each of these counties, especially in Blanco.[27]

Local elections in Blanco County in 1860 had been hotly contested, and apparently the defeated candidates stepped up the crusade to make the western part of the county a separate "union county"—a movement that led in 1862 to the creation of Kendall County. After the Civil War Kendall County citizens gathered up the remains of thirty-six German unionist refugees who had been massacred while trying to escape from Texas via Mexico to the North. Over their common grave was later erected a monument with the inscription *Treue der Union*. During Reconstruction in Blanco County, grand juries handed down seventy-three indictments from homicides of unionists who had resisted Confederate army arrest. The Nueces

27. Timmons, "The Referendum in Texas," 15; Frank H. Smyrl, "Unionism in Texas, 1856–1861," *Southwestern Historical Quarterly*, LXVIII (1964), 172–95; Claude Elliot, "Union Sentiment in Texas, 1861–1865," *Southwestern Historical Quarterly*, L (1947), 449–77; John W. Speer, *A History of Blanco County*, ed. Henry C. Armbruster (Austin, 1965), 23; John Stribling Moursund, *Blanco County History* (Burnet, Tex., 1979), 196; Mary Starr Barkley, *A History of Central Texas* (Austin, 1970), 219–20; William L. Mann, "Early History of Williamson County," in *Williamson County Centennial, 1848–1948* (Georgetown, Tex., 1948), 5–16; Clara Stearns Scarbrough, *Land of Good Water—Takachue Pouetsu: A Williamson County, Texas, History* (Georgetown, Tex., 1973), 110–11, 141, 168–69, 184–85.

Treue der Union monument is today one of the few monuments to the Union outside of National Cemeteries in former Confederate states.[28]

Conspicuously, although predictably, absent from the ranks of the central Texas counties that voted against secession is Comal County (New Braunfels). Located southeast of Blanco and the most thoroughly German Texan of any county in the state in 1860, Comal registered a large pro-secession majority. Its heavy yes-vote was attributable to a local German-language newspaper that supported Breckinridge and disunion for pragmatic reasons. The editor of the *Neu-Braunfelser Zeitung,* Ferdinand Lindheimer, believed that disunion was inevitable. Consequently, he told his readers that they would be wiser to be on the winning, rather than on the losing, side. Although Lindheimer's defense of disunion propelled a handful of infuriated New Braunfelsers to toss his newspaper's type into the Comal River, the local German settlers, as a reward for heeding his advice, were subsequently sheltered from Confederate atrocities and persecutions committed during the war on German unionists elsewhere in the region.[29]

According to the analysis presented here, the result in Comal County was anticipated, for the breakdown of the county's vote in the 1859 gubernatorial and 1860 presidential elections comes close to predicting the outcome in the secession referendum (see table 11). This is not true, however, for neighboring Hays and Guadalupe Counties, where a sizable German population existed only in the latter and slaves constituted over one-fourth of the population of both counties. In Hays and Guadalupe Counties the regression equations underpredicted secessionist strength by 13 and 4 percentage points, respectively, and overpredicted unionist support by 14 and 15 percentage points, respectively, resulting in a net gain for secession of 27 percentage points, or about 90 votes in Hays County, and a disunionist net gain in Guadalupe County of 19 percentage points, or about 170 votes. Lacking any allegations of election irregularities, the result in heavily Anglo-American Hays County must be accepted at face value. The abnormally low

28. Speer, *History of Blanco County,* 19, 29, 40–41; Robert W. Shook, "The Battle of the Nueces, August 10, 1862," *Southwestern Historical Quarterly,* LXVI (1962), 31–42; Gilbert J. Jordan, *Yesterday in the Texas Hill Country* (College Station, 1979), 14–15; [Comfort Chamber of Commerce], "Discover Yesterday in the Comfort of Today" (Comfort, Tex., 1986).

29. Minetta Altgelt Goyne, *Lone Star and Double Eagle: Civil War Letters of a German-Texas Family* (Fort Worth, 1982), 16; Buenger, "Secession and the Texas German Community," 379–402; Jordan, *German Seed in Texas Soil,* 180–85; Ada Marie Hall, "The Texas Germans in State and National Politics, 1850–1865" (M.A. thesis, University of Texas at Austin, 1938), 107; and Walter D. Kamphoefner, "Texas Germans and Civil War Issues: The Evidence from Immigrant Letters," *Journal of the German-Texan Heritage Society,* XIII (Spring, 1991), 16.

unionist turnout in Guadalupe County suggests, but does not prove, that many German Texans abstained from voting.

Following Blanco County, the next-most-unpredictable county is Grimes County (see table 14). By virtue of its large voter turnout—which heavily contributed to the disunionist cause—and its geographical location, Grimes belongs with three other counties (Austin, Brazoria, and Fort Bend) that also exhibited a disproportionate turnout for secession. All were located on the rich alluvial lands lying in the lower part of the Brazos River valley and were well within the orbit of the Galveston-Houston commercial hub. Here, only a few men stood against the inevitable tide of disunion: the combined vote in favor of secession in these four counties was 2,745 to 223. Nowhere within this region—where white inhabitants were often a self-conscious minority among much larger slave populations—did unionists complain that the outpouring of enthusiasm for secession was anything other than completely genuine. Here, a combination of exhilaration and resolve captivated voters. The confidence of the local planters, who following the news of Lincoln's election had coordinated the decision to call a secession convention, saturated Brazoria County. At the polling places zealous men distributed fancy, boldly printed, colored cardboard ballots marked "For Secession."[30]

A similar conviction of purpose characterized voters in the cotton plantation region in the northeastern part of the state, especially in Harrison County (Marshall). More slaves lived here on the eve of the Civil War than in any other Texas county. Although Houston had carried Harrison County in 1859 and the Bell-Douglas fusion ticket had made a respectable showing in 1860, the lopsided secessionist margin was attributable as much to the disappearance of the opposition as to the enthusiasm for secession (see table 14). Harrison County is the next-least-predictable county after Grimes, and shares its pattern of statistical abnormality with nearby Smith (Tyler), Upshur (Gilmer), and Rusk (Henderson) Counties (see table 14). Rusk County, the most populous county in the state, had witnessed its county seat destroyed by fire in the summer of 1860. Shortly after, a mob lynched a northern unionist and a female slave in retaliation.[31]

If excitement and resolve on the day of the secession referendum gripped

30. Webb, Carroll, and Branda, eds., *The Handbook of Texas*, I, 86–87, 208–209, 620, 738; Clarence R. Wharton, *Wharton's History of Fort Bend County* (San Antonio, 1939), 153; James A. Creighton, *A Narrative History of Brazoria County* (Waco, 1975), 230.

31. Campbell, *A Southern Community in Crisis*, 3–4, 170–76, 189–91; Dorman H. Winfrey, *A History of Rusk County, Texas* (Waco, 1961), 40–41.

voters in the plantation country of the lower Brazos River and the extreme northeastern parts of the state, there were other areas, especially in North Texas, where dismay and apprehension prevailed. Following Harrison County in its degree of unpredictability was Grayson County (Sherman). Located along the Red River where the Butterfield Mail route to the east exited into Indian Territory, Grayson and seven other northern counties (Van Zandt, Collin, Lamar, Hunt, Fannin, Titus, and Kaufman) produced remarkably high unionist gains above the statewide trend. Although contemporaries commented on the unusual interest in the referendum in these counties, there were no allegations by secessionists that the respective no-votes were inflated by election-day skulduggery. Grayson, Collin, Fannin, and Lamar Counties were part of a band of eight anti-secessionist counties, including Cooke, Montague, Wise, and Jack, in extreme northern Texas, where before the announcement of the secession referendum a futile attempt had been made to form a separate state and apply for admission to the Union.[32]

Reasons for the strong unionist showing in the Red River valley counties are plentiful. The region contained, in addition to a few Yankees, transplanted yeoman farmers from the upper South who depended upon government agencies in nearby Indian Territory to buy their surplus wheat and corn. Many of the region's residents believed that in the event of civil war their homes would be exposed to military danger, whether from raiding Indians or invading Union troops. Here, a few Methodists had refused to affiliate with the southern branch of the Methodist Episcopal Church, and many Disciples of Christ had placed the fellowship of all Christians ahead of the rights of slaveholders. In the old Whig strongholds of North Texas, to a greater extent than in the Hill Country, a "last resort" conditional unionism had prevailed during the secession crisis. However, the reason for the greater intensity of support for the unionist cause in Grayson, Collin, and Lamar Counties was directly attributable to their outspoken and venerable unionist leadership.[33]

During the secession crisis ninety-four-year-old Collin McKinney, one of the first state leaders of the Disciples of Christ, a signer of the Texas Declaration of Independence, and the man for whom the county and

32. Elliot, "Union Sentiment in Texas," 453.

33. Meinig, *Imperial Texas,* 48–50; Jordan, "Imprint of the Upper and Lower South," 667–90; Buenger, *Secession and the Union,* 64–71; Campbell, *An Empire for Slavery,* 220; Baker and Baum, "The Texas Voter and the Crisis of the Union," 410–11, 416–17.

county seat were named, lectured his neighbors on the evils of secession. The pages of the McKinney *Messenger* and the Sherman *Patriot* echoed his arguments against disunion. E. Junius Foster, the editor of the latter paper, courageously, although foolhardily, continued to publish his opinions until silenced by assassins in front of his print shop in the fall of 1862. Anti-Confederates in these counties during the war joined secret unionist societies, resulting in the deaths of many of them after vigilante "treason" trials determined their guilt. More fortunate was Christopher C. Binkley, Sherman's most prosperous citizen in the late antebellum period. He survived his unconditional unionist stand to become a power in the Republican party for many years after the war. More influential than McKinney and Binkley was former Whig and Know-Nothing James W. Throckmorton, a Collin County unionist delegate to the Texas Secession Convention who, after the war, was elected governor. Lamar County had sent to the convention a solid delegation of unionists, including George W. Wright, the county's most prominent "pioneer settler," who energetically canvassed the county against secession.[34]

Of the remaining counties flagged for abnormally large net gains for secession, the voting returns reported from adjoining Starr and Zapata Counties in extreme South Texas require an explanation that differs from any offered for statewide trends. Voter turnout, especially along all of the counties on the rough frontier border with Mexico, was historically very low—only small percentages of Mexican Texans, or Tejanos, voted, and when allowed to exercise their franchise, they commonly received their ballots from wealthy patrons. Overall, prejudice against the poorer classes of Tejanos was pervasive. Anglos accorded the vast majority of Tejanos less than equal rights and even regarded them at times as merely, in the words of one traveler from the North, "vermin, to be exterminated."[35]

---

34. Grayson County Frontier Village, *The History of Grayson County, Texas* (n.p., 1979), I, 155–56; Graham Landrum and Allan Smith, *Grayson County: An Illustrated History of Grayson County, Texas* (Fort Worth, 1967), 63–65; Mattie Davis Lucas and Mita Holsapple Hall, *A History of Grayson County, Texas* (Sherman, Tex., 1936), 115; Richard B. McCaslin, "Wheat Growers in the Cotton Confederacy: The Suppression of Dissent in Collin County, Texas, During the Civil War," *Southwestern Historical Quarterly*, XCVI (1993), 532; J. Lee Stambaugh and Lillian J. Stambaugh, *A History of Collin County, Texas* (Austin, 1958), 64, 90–91; A. W. Neville, *The History of Lamar County* (Paris, Tex., 1937), 65, 239; Ralph A. Wooster, *The Secession Conventions of the South* (Princeton, 1962), 131 n. 23, 132, table 29.

35. David Montejano, *Anglos and Mexicans in the Making of Texas, 1836–1986* (Austin, 1987), 37–41; Arnoldo De León, *They Called Them Greasers: Anglo Attitudes Toward Mexicans in Texas, 1821–1900* (Austin, 1983), 14–86; Olmsted, *A Journey Through Texas,* 245; Marilyn McAdams Sibley, *Travelers in Texas, 1761–1860* (Austin, 1967), 129.

In other predominantly Tejano border counties there was also little opposition to secession, and, as in Starr and Zapata, cliques of powerful Anglo
and European merchants and their Hispanic landowner allies traditionally
monopolized land, sources of credit, and political offices. Late antebellum
politics in Webb County (Laredo) fell under the sphere of two groups of
competing elites, one of them led by the Benavides family. Santos Benavides, a native-born Texan and an ardent supporter, although a nonslaveholder, of the secessionist cause, was the patriarch of one of the most wealthy
families in the lower Rio Grande valley. The inevitability of Texas secession
provided him and his family with a way to advance their political influence.
Not one vote was cast against secession in Webb County. Most of the small
percentages of Tejanos who voted in other border counties in South Texas
were also manipulated economically or politically into doing so by powerful
patrons. However, the flagrant falsification of the Zapata returns—the
county voted 212–0 to take Texas out of the Union—is a fascinating story
if only because of the subsequent rebellion there that broke out in April of
1861.[36]

Ysidro Vela, a large stock farmer and the county's chief justice, and
Henry Redmond, an English immigrant who had built up a trading empire
from his ranch at the county seat of Carrizo (later renamed Zapata), orchestrated the disunionist sentiment in Zapata County. (Carrizo, often confused
with Carrizo Springs in Dimmit County, was settled at least as early as 1767
and is known today as the lost town of "old Zapata," which is submerged
beneath the Falcon Reservoir.) When Vela certified as "true and correct"
the report of referendum returns showing approximately a dozen more
secessionist votes cast than there were legally qualified voters in the county,
it marked only another incident in a series of arrogant acts that had earned
Vela and Redmond the resentment of many of the county's poor, largely
landless, Spanish-speaking citizens.[37]

Before the election Judge Vela had threatened to fine certain individuals
fifty dollars each unless they voted in favor of secession. After the election
serious trouble began when the county sheriff, who lacked proper arrest
warrants, tried to apprehend some of the men whom Vela had intimidated.

---

36. Montejano, *Anglos and Mexicans*, 36; Jerry D. Thompson, *Mexican Texans in the Union Army*,
Southwestern Studies No. 78 (El Paso, 1986), 1–10.
37. MSS Election Returns for 1861; Georgia Lee Tatum, *Disloyalty in the Confederacy* (1934; rpr.
New York, 1970), 45; Lauraine Miller, "The Lost Town of Zapata," *Texas Magazine*, August 15, 1993,
pp. 6–14; Dave Harmon, "Zapata's Falcon Lake Awash with Memories, Future Promise," Dallas *Morning News*, December 5, 1993, pp. 64A–65A.

On the day before the surrender of Fort Sumter, forty to eighty armed Tejanos seized control of the southern part of Zapata County, declared their loyalty to the United States government, and marched on Carrizo allegedly to prevent local county officials from taking the oath of allegiance to the Confederacy. Although admiration of the American Union might have genuinely motivated some of them, few had been followers of the debates over slavery between the North and South in the 1850s. Most proclaimed their anti-Confederate sentiments in order to get revenge for past grievances or pay back old political and economic debts. By May this unionist-inspired resistance led to the sacking of the courthouse and customhouse in Carrizo. Whether the rebellion in Zapata County should be placed in the larger context of the Juan Cortina insurgency is problematic. More important, this Tejano defiance of the Confederacy continued throughout the Civil War, and for many in Zapata County it culminated in December of 1862 with the lynching of Judge Vela at his ranch in the sight of his hysterical wife and children.[38]

Because the degree of fraud in the referendum election presumably varied from one county to the next, predictions of the levels of secessionist and anti-secessionist support can be used to corroborate more traditional evidence of voter intimidation, ballot-box stuffing, miscounting, and other irregularities (see table 15). For example, witnesses to the balloting in Bexar County (San Antonio) maintained that the pro-secession and pro-slavery Knights of the Golden Circle policed the polling places and that any man who "dared to vote" against secession "*was marked,* in the common parlance of the day." The vote in Bexar County was 827 to 709 for secession, although the vote in the county seat of San Antonio went against secession. The city's unionists also accused secessionists of trying to sway voters by distributing anti-secessionist tickets with the words "the negro must be equal to the white man in this government" printed on them. Nevertheless, the quantitative evidence presented here offers no support for the conclusion that secessionist harassment or browbeating prevented many Bexar County unionists from casting their votes against secession. The equations underpredicted the unionist vote and overpredicted the secessionist vote. If the county had merely reflected the statewide voting trends between 1859

---

38. Gilberto Miguel Hinojosa, *A Borderlands Town in Transition: Laredo, 1755–1870* (College Station, 1983), 83–84; Gardner W. Pierce to John Z. Leyendecker, June 1, 1861, in John Z. Leyendecker Papers, BTHC; Thompson, *Mexican Texans in the Union Army,* 2–10; Robert J. Rosenbaum, *Mexicano Resistance in the Southwest: "The Sacred Right of Self-Preservation"* (Austin, 1981), 42–45; Jerry Thompson, *Vaqueros in Blue and Gray* (Austin, 1976), 18–23.

TABLE 15

NET GAINS FOR OR AGAINST SECESSION IN COUNTIES WHERE UNIONISTS CLAIMED VOTING IRREGULARITIES OCCURRED

(in percentages of 1861 county electorates)

Intimidation of Unionist Voters

County	Net Gain "For" Secession (%)	Net Gain "Against" Secession (%)	Estimated Size of 1861 Electorate
Anderson *(Palestine)*	3		1,581
Bexar *(San Antonio)*		16	3,516
Cameron *(Brownsville)*	16		1,969
Cass *(Linden)*		9	1,141
Colorado *(Columbus)*	13		1,265
Hamilton		6	112

Ballot-Box Stuffing, Miscounting, and Incomplete Polling of Votes

County	Net Gain "For" Secession (%)	Net Gain "Against" Secession (%)	Estimated Size of 1861 Electorate
Chambers		6	233
El Paso *(San Elizario)*		6	1,431
Nueces	4		784
Young	24		196

Trickery and Deceit by Secessionists

County	Net Gain "For" Secession (%)	Net Gain "Against" Secession (%)	Estimated Size of 1861 Electorate
Kaufman		23	806

Source: For the sources of the 1859 gubernatorial, 1860 presidential, and 1861 secession referendum returns, see tables 1 and 7 above.

Note: On the calculation of the residual net gains, see table 14 above. Not a shred of evidence can be found to support the notion that secessionists in any county violated the requirement of a paper ballot by insisting on a *viva voce* vote to intimidate voters; *cf.* Timmons, "The Referendum in Texas," 12–28, who confuses the election procedures followed in the February referendum with the manner in which many delegates for the Texas Secession Convention were selected in a quasi-legal election held on January 8, 1861. For the manner in which the Texas Secession Convention prescribed and Governor Sam Houston ordered the holding of the secession referendum, see "Proclamation by the Governor of the State of Texas," [signed by] Sam Houston, February 9, 1861, Texas Broadsides Collection, BTHC; and Ernest William Winkler, ed., *Journal of the Secession Convention of Texas, 1861* (Austin, 1912), 58–59, and note 10 on p. 59.

and 1861, then about 563 more votes would have inflated the secessionist margin of victory.[39]

Bexar is not the only county where Texas unionists used the rhetoric of

39. Sprague, *The Treachery in Texas*, 140; *Alamo Express* (San Antonio), February 23, 1861.

fraud to characterize localities that, according to the quantitative evidence, do not appear to have "unexpected" or idiosyncratic voting patterns. A unionist refugee who fled to California before the outbreak of war hinted that the secessionist vote in El Paso County was inflated by Mexicans who waded across the Rio Grande to vote. (The county voted 871 to 2 for secession.) The statistical evidence does not support his frequently quoted insinuation. More detailed accounts of the balloting in this outermost western county on the Chihuahua–to–Santa Fe trail suggest that a pro-southern clique of Anglos manipulated the large secessionist majority, but that their actions were consistent with their previous control and management of the county's voters and elections.[40]

Contentions that the referendum did not constitute a "full poll" are rare, although some precinct managers failed to hold an election or did not report returns. The chief justice of Nueces County (Corpus Christi) related that he had not received returns from three precincts. No traditional evidence suggests that the county's unionist voters protested that their ballots went uncounted, and the quantitative evidence reveals no unusually large secessionist margin in Nueces County (see table 15). In Chambers County (east of Houston) a daughter's account of her mother's recollections contends that, in the balloting in the Double Bayou precinct, local election officials incorrectly reported the unionist vote. However, the analysis presented here offers no additional support for the contention, which could have been accurate, that a misreporting of the voting returns placed the unionist cause at a disadvantage in Chambers County.[41]

The staunchly unionist McKinney *Messenger* accused secessionists of trickery and deceit in Kaufman County (east of Dallas). Ballots prepared there for the election were allegedly printed with the words "For Submission" (rather than "Against Secession") in order to confuse unionists who did not know the precise legal wording to be used. The analysis presented here, however, leaves little room for the assumption that this deception cost the unionists votes. Although Kaufman County voted for secession, the unionist cause received an unexpected 185-vote advantage in the county above the statewide trend.[42]

40. Noah Smithwick, *The Evolution of a State,* or *Recollections of Old Texas Days,* comp. Nanna Smithwick Donaldson, Barker Texas History Center Series, No. 5 (Austin, 1983), 256; C. L. Sonnichsen, *Pass of the North: Four Centuries on the Rio Grande* (2 vols.; El Paso, 1968, 1980), I, 151–52.

41. MSS Election Returns for 1861; Agnes Paschal McNeir, "Did Texas Secede?" *Quarterly of the Texas State Historical Association,* V (July, 1901–April, 1902), 168–69.

42. *McKinney Messenger,* March 1, 1861.

A week before the election in Hamilton County (west of Waco) a mass meeting of secessionists declared the county's chief justice, James A. Mc-Barron, guilty of being an abolitionist and ordered him to leave the county within five days, "or else abide the verdict of an indignant community." McBarron, whose only transgression was his staunch unionism, read between the lines of the mob's edict and apparently left the county before the referendum balloting. His illegal ouster from office, however, generated no unusually large secessionist margin in Hamilton County.[43]

A better case for corroborating election-day intimidation of unionists can be made for southernmost Cameron County (Brownsville). Here, the secessionists carried the election by a vote of 600 to 37. On the day of the referendum balloting, armed men at the polling places gave each suspected unionist voter a "friendly warning" either to leave the state or never to vote again, and "by way of emphasizing their assurance, slapped their hands on their revolvers." Had the county's voting population mirrored the statewide voting trends, the secessionist margin would have been reduced by about 315 votes. This finding suggests that aggressive advocates of disunion cowed the opposition in Cameron County. Many potential unionists presumably accepted ballots marked "for secession" from the armed men policing the polls.[44]

In plantation country in southeastern Texas, at least thirty German immigrants at Frelsburg in Colorado County apparently avoided the polls because they hoped to "escape the responsibility of the consequences" of voting against secession or believed their votes would be of no consequence. The unusually large secessionist margin in Colorado County suggests that the Frelsburg Germans might not have been alone in their fears of reprisals or in their skepticism about the purpose of even bothering to turn out and vote. On the other hand, local unionists had speculated before the election that the anti-secessionist vote in the county would be only "about 300"—a prediction that proved remarkably accurate and that might have taken into account the likelihood of the Frelsburg Germans staying away from the polls.[45]

From Cass County, bordering on Arkansas and Louisiana, a local unionist leader reported that the secessionists were successful only because unionists,

---

43. *Texas State Gazette* (Austin), March 9, 1861; Marten, *Texas Divided*, 59.
44. Kingsbury [F. F. Fenn], "Lectures, Reports, and Writings," 20, in Kingsbury Papers.
45. Hall, "The Texas Germans," 57; Kidder N. Walker to Elisha M. Pease, February 10, 1861, in Pease-Graham-Niles Collection, AHC.

denounced as Black Republicans and "insulted at every corner," refused to vote. While this allegation might have been true, the quantitative findings show that the secessionists in the county were apparently more prone to sit out the balloting than the unionists (see tables 13 and 15). The secessionist total was substantially below normal in Cass County and in neighboring Titus County. This relative lack of enthusiasm for secession in extreme northeastern Texas could have been attributable to worries about the security of the border with Arkansas, where secessionists in early 1861 were ostensibly still in the minority.[46]

Although many unionists in plantation counties with large secessionist majorities could have abstained from voting less out of fear for their personal safety than from the realization that they formed a minority with virtually no hope to win, the calculus of self-preservation dictated circumspection and unquestionably affected their behavior. As a Robertson County unionist who failed to vote put it, "The numbers in favor of the act" were so considerable that differing with them was likely "to involve those who were opposed to secession in unpleasant and frequently dangerous altercations." Unfortunately, historians will never know as much as they would like about the motivations of Texas voters at the time of the referendum. Consequently, much of the impressionistic evidence regarding intimidation of unionist voters will remain difficult to evaluate.[47]

On the upper Trinity River in Anderson County, often described as "the raw head and bloody bones" of the rebellion in Texas, the decisive moment for the county's handful of anti-secessionist voters came after the February balloting, when they faced far more profound and potentially dangerous decisions, such as whether to remain in the state after the result of the referendum election was announced, give lip service to the Confederate cause, or reluctantly join the Confederate army. The finding here that the net gain for secession was only three percentage points in overwhelmingly secessionist Anderson County neither proves nor disproves the statement of one local resident who later claimed that he had not voted against secession because "it would have been as much as my life was worth to vote against it" (see table 15). Had he advocated abolitionism or "Negro equality" along with his unionist sentiments, he might have been shot on the streets of the county seat sooner than a mad dog. However, for the many disorganized

46. J. C. McAlpine to Sam Houston, February 27, 1861, Governors' Papers: Sam Houston, RG 301, TSL; Wooster, *The Secession Conventions,* 157.

47. Josephus Cavitt to Andrew Johnson, September 7, 1865, quoted in Marten, *Texas Divided,* 44.

and quiescent conditional unionists who remained faithful to the American Union only while northern force of arms did not coerce the lower southern states into submission, an unadorned no-vote in the referendum was not necessarily a pronouncement of disloyalty to the newly formed Confederacy or a rejection of the principle of white supremacy.[48]

In hindsight, the decision for disunion opened a tragic chapter in Texas history. Because few who voted for secession foresaw that their state was on the threshold of tremendous loss of life and extreme privation, some historians have wondered if irrationality and miscalculation eclipsed reason and reality at the time of the February balloting.[49] Although secession reflected a rational appraisal of the perils posed by the coming to power of a national administration hostile to the South's way of life, an unwillingness to look ahead to the consequences of the decision to break up the American Union unquestionably characterized the Texas secessionists. Most of them simply discounted the probable repercussions of their action. They genuinely believed that they had no basis to fear the results of any likely ensuing conflict with the North. The Texas unionists were obviously more pessimistic.

No matter whether one in the early months of 1861 prophesied either the terrible end of the Confederacy or its triumphant success, very few correctly predicted that the popular decision to secede would quickly provoke the very changes that the most zealous secessionists had sought to prevent. One exception was Sam Houston. Typical of his prophetic wisdom, which was unmatched at this crucial moment among leaders and politicians throughout the South, Houston informed John H. Reagan: "Our people are going to war to perpetuate slavery, and the first gun fired in the war will be the knell of slavery."[50]

48. W. V. Tunstall to Joseph J. Reynolds, March 26, 1868, in Governors' Papers: Elisha M. Pease, RG 301, TSL; J. D. Rankin to Charles E. Morse, November 18, 1869, Reel #18, COCADT, *Records of the U.S. Army Continental Commands, 1821–1920,* RG 393 (Washington, D.C., NA, Microfilm edition); Buenger, *Secession and the Union,* 157, 161, 173; Buenger, "Texas and the Riddle of Secession," 174.

49. Buenger, *Secession and the Union,* 9, 161, 159–77.

50. John H. Reagan, "A Conversation with Governor Houston," *Quarterly of the Texas State Historical Association,* III (1900), 280.

3
CIVIL WAR ELECTIONS AND ANTEBELLUM VOTING ALIGNMENTS

It is high time for the people of Texas to determine whether they will invite the fate of Louisiana and Mississippi, and allow a few men more distinguished for shallow brains and loud talk, than other capacity, and who have little stomach for the suffering they prepare for others, to drag them down to inevitable ruin.
—broadside entitled *Common Sense* and signed by "one who was at Vicksburg," Dallas County, Texas, September, 1863

Your homes have already been promised to the scum of Europe, the negroe, and—the worse than either—vindictive, miserable, puritanical Yankees. . . . Reconstruction *means, simply, subjugation.*
—speech of Private Z. J. Harman of Texas to fellow Confederate soldiers in the Army of Northern Virginia, January 15, 1865

The first historians of Civil War Texas politics were the men who were involved in the secessionist movement and the resulting struggle for southern independence. Prominent ex-Confederates at the turn of the century put forth misleading, although enduring, notions about the character of state politics during the war. According to their interpretation, from 1861 to 1865 Texans were united by the necessity of protecting their homes from possible northern invasion. In the crucible of this war-induced solidarity, the old antebellum allegiances, issues, and rivalries vanished. Preoccupation with military matters eclipsed attentions normally given to local concerns. After anti-secessionist leaders had either joined the southern cause or withdrawn from public life, like-minded Confederates dominated the political scene. Consequently, there was "little controversy of a political character in Texas" during the war years. Without political parties and nominating conventions, the outcome of wartime elections hinged on the strengths of the personalities of the self-announced candidates. Victorious candidates were invariably men who had been more persuasive in their promises to wage war energetically against the North.[1]

This idea of a Confederate Texas united politically against northern adversaries was shaped more by nostalgic fantasies than by wartime realities. Putting aside the quelling of unionist sentiment by vigilante groups, which led to the murders of many alleged northern sympathizers, Texas Civil War history is, for the most part, a morose story of intragovernmental rivalries coupled with wide-ranging disaffection that prevented effective implementation of statewide wartime policies. During the war years many apolitical men put profits or personal ends ahead of the common or public good, while their town and county governments often refused to cast aside local prerogatives for the greater welfare of the state, not to mention the Richmond government. In the winter of 1863, Texas lawmakers reached the nadir of wartime leadership by proposing initiatives that would have catapulted their state on a collision course with Confederate authorities. By 1864 Governor Pendleton Murrah's aversion for "centralizing" war measures generated by Jefferson Davis' "dictatorial power" propelled him into obstructive resistance to the Confederate government. Only the eventual defeat on the battlefield and the subsequent policies of Congressional Reconstruction accomplished what flag-waving orations and a prolonged bloodletting could not: the fiction of a united Confederacy to which all Anglo Texans had proclaimed their allegiance.[2]

Nothing approaching the moral strength of the northern anti-slavery crusade sustained the southern cause. In the euphoria of the secessionist

1. Roberts, "The Political, Legislative, and Judicial History of Texas," 142 and *passim;* Lubbock, *Six Decades in Texas,* 314–527 and *passim.* Historical accounts of Texas wartime politics that assume that political activity ceased in the absence of traditional two-party division include Robert P. Felgar, "Texas in the War for Southern Independence, 1861–1865" (Ph.D. dissertation, University of Texas, 1935); James T. De Shields, *They Sat in High Places: The Presidents and Governors of Texas* (San Antonio, 1940); Stephen B. Oates, "Texas Under the Secessionists," *Southwestern Historical Quarterly,* LXVII (1963), 167–212; Billy D. Ledbetter, "Confederate Texas: A Political Study, 1861–1865" (M.S. thesis, North Texas State University, 1969); Ernest Wallace, *Texas in Turmoil: The Saga of Texas, 1849–1875* (Austin, 1965); Seymour V. Connor, *Texas: A History* (Arlington Heights, Ill., 1971), 202–204; Webb, Carroll, and Branda, eds., *The Handbook of Texas,* I, 351–52.

2. Charles W. Ramsdell, "Some Problems in Writing the History of the Confederacy," *Journal of Southern History,* II (1936), 135; Nancy Head Bowen, "A Political Labyrinth: Texas in the Civil War—Questions in Continuity" (Ph.D. dissertation, Rice University, 1974), 68, 193–94; Nancy Head Bowen, "A Political Labyrinth: Texas in the Civil War," *East Texas Historical Journal,* XI (Fall, 1973), 3–11; Edward Berry Weisel, "City, County, State: Intergovernmental Relations in Texas, 1835–1860" (Ph.D. dissertation, Rice University, 1975), 291; John Moretta, "Pendleton Murrah, Confederate Texans and States' Rights in the Lone Star State, 1863–65" (paper presented to the Houston Area Southern Historians Seminar meeting at Rice University, April 14, 1993), 5; Marten, *Texas Divided,* 33–105, 175–80.

movement, most Texans had naively believed that there would be, as one Confederate zealot recalled, "no war, no taxes, or hardships—just an increase in happiness, boundless prosperity, & complete freedom from all Yankee interference." When this promise of secession died, rudimentary southern nationalism disintegrated against the more powerful persistence of localism—a force that antebellum constitutional provincialism had spawned and pro-slavery views about state sovereignty and states' rights had enshrined. The refusal to alter traditional ideas regarding the purpose of a central government in a time of national crisis handicapped the southern war effort. When mobilization of men and resources necessary for success on the battlefield proved more demanding than most southerners ever imagined, intense animosities and recriminations arose within Confederate ranks.[3]

When the first Confederate shots hit Fort Sumter, the Texas unionists contemplated running former Whig and Know-Nothing James W. Throckmorton—who among their ranks stood second only to Sam Houston—for the governorship. Their platform would have endorsed a prompt "reconstruction" through adoption of the Crittenden Compromise, but the rapid pace of events ruined their plans. President Abraham Lincoln called up 75,000 state militia to crush the southern rebellion, four more slave states in the upper South seceded from the Union, and, as a North Texas unionist lamented, "the military spirit [took] possession of our entire population." Subsequently, the Dallas convention of the Southern Rights wing of the Texas Democratic party became the only evidence in the state of orchestrated political activity. Announced before arrival of news of the surrender of Fort Sumter as an assembly of "the supporters of the Confederate States" who would put behind them "old partisan issues," the poorly attended convention made no nominations for governor, congressional office, or Confederate presidential electors. Without any attempt by Texas unionists to organize, the belief prevailed that separate political parties were no longer necessary because the only issue was unity in the face of northern aggression. Moreover, the delegates knew that many secessionists were former Whigs, Know-Nothings, Union (or Independent) Democrats—men who had supported at one time or another the so-called prewar Opposition. Nevertheless, behind the facade of a new nonpartisan and independent politics lurked considerable memories of past electoral battles.[4]

---

3. Edward H. Cushing to Guy M. Bryan, June 1, 1865, in Guy M. Bryan Papers, BTHC.
4. Thomas Lewellin to Elisha M. Pease, April 20, 1861, and Benjamin H. Epperson to Elisha M.

The first Confederate Texas gubernatorial election had elements of a rematch, for the two main contenders, Governor Edward Clark and Francis R. Lubbock, had in 1859 vied against one another for the lieutenant governorship. Clark had been a wavering Democrat who had earlier jumped to the Know-Nothings and then returned to the Democratic fold only to abandon it again before being carried to victory by Sam Houston's coattails on the Union Democratic, or Opposition, ticket. Houston decisively defeated his Democratic rival for the governorship by 8,727 votes, but Clark defeated Lubbock for the lieutenant governorship by only 1,133 votes. Subsequently, in the midst of the secession crisis, when Governor Houston refused to take the oath of allegiance to the Confederacy, Clark in effect elevated himself to the vacant office by taking the oath—an action many Texas unionists interpreted as a direct affront to Houston. Lubbock, a zealous pro-slavery Democrat from Harris County (Houston), had favored southern filibustering during the 1850s and had been a delegate to the 1860 national Democratic convention in Charleston. He, along with Thomas J. Chambers, a wealthy political gadfly from East Texas, challenged Clark's bid to continue as governor in the August, 1861, election. Chambers, who possessed large land claims dating from the Texas Revolution, was an egotistical and litigious man who throughout his life, according to his biographer, had "an unfailing ability to make enemies." However, like Lubbock, Chambers had ardently supported secession. All three gubernatorial candidates promised to wage vigorously war upon the North and work harmoniously with Confederate authorities.[5]

Because Lubbock's margin of victory over Clark was a remarkably slim 124-vote plurality, standard accounts of the 1861 election have attributed Clark's defeat to his many alleged liabilities: former Know-Nothing connections, failure to campaign aggressively, inroads into his support by Chambers' candidacy in counties east of the Trinity River, and lack of organization in some important populous counties, namely Bexar (San

---

Pease, May 22, 1861, in Pease-Graham-Niles Collection, AHC; *Texas State Gazette* (Austin), April 13, 1861; Lubbock, *Six Decades in Texas,* 324; Bowen, "A Political Labyrinth," 22–24 (unless otherwise specified, this citation appearing subsequently is to Bowen's dissertation); Ledbetter, "Confederate Texas," 46–49.

5. Ralph A. Wooster, "Texas," in *The Confederate Governors,* ed. W. Buck Yearns (Athens, 1985), 195, 200; Llerena Beaufort Friend, "The Life of Thomas Jefferson Chambers" (M.A. thesis, University of Texas at Austin, 1928), 43; Amelia Edith Huddleston Barr, *All the Days of My Life: An Autobiography* (New York, 1913), 226–27; Bowen, "A Political Labyrinth," 26–28, 33; Friend, *Sam Houston,* 338–39; Justin Whitlock Dart, Jr., "Edward Clark, Governor of Texas March 16 to November 7, 1861" (M.A. thesis, University of Houston, 1954), 26.

Antonio), Galveston (Galveston), Harris (Houston), and Travis (Austin). Moreover, as governor, Clark had annoyed diverse groups of voters by his advocacy of financial relief for railroads, proclamation against commercial intercourse with the North, and hesitation in removing from office many holdover Houston "submissionist" appointees. Perhaps his greatest disadvantage had stemmed from his cooperation with Confederate officials in mobilizing Texas troops for duty far from home.[6]

In light of Clark's two-time apostasy as a Democrat and last-minute embrace of the secessionist movement and the Confederacy, it could be hypothesized that in his contest for the governorship with Lubbock and Chambers, Clark would receive votes primarily from men who had cast Opposition ballots in 1859 for Houston and had voted for disunion in the February, 1861, secession referendum. One could also predict that Clark would stand virtually no chance of winning votes from former Democrats, who not only recalled his vacillations and defections from their ranks, but also could hardly be expected to repudiate directly their votes against him and their ballots for Lubbock in the 1859 lieutenant governor's contest. In addition, one could safely hypothesize that Clark would obtain few, if any, votes from anti-secessionists, who denounced his opportunistic ascension to the governorship as a betrayal of Houston. When Clark stood up to swear his allegiance during the Confederate oath-taking ceremonies at the state capitol, the spit from a female unionist in the gallery hit the Ordinance of Secession lying on the podium.[7]

An analysis of popular voting behavior confirms the supposition that Lubbock's victory over Clark was closely associated with antebellum voting patterns (see table 16). Clark predictably garnered virtually no support from men who had voted in the 1859 governor's race for Hardin R. Runnels, the incumbent Democrat whom Houston defeated. Clark also received negligible support from 1860 anti-Breckinridge fusionists, who were primarily adherents of the Constitutional Union ticket of John Bell and Edward Everett. Nor did Clark attract the votes of Texans who had voted against secession in the February, 1861, statewide referendum. In short, Runnels Democrats, Bell-Douglas fusionists, and anti-secessionists voted against Clark. His total overwhelmingly contained former 1859 Houston

6. Fredericka Ann Meiners, "The Texas Governorship, 1861–1865: Biography of an Office" (Ph.D. dissertation, Rice University, 1974), 21–24, 52–53, 76–77; Dart, "Edward Clark," 123; Bowen, "A Political Labyrinth," 28–29, 32–36, 43 n. 30.

7. Marten, *Texas Divided,* 24.

men who subsequently had voted for Breckinridge and then had either voted for secession or sat out the referendum balloting altogether.

Although Clark fared better than either Lubbock or Chambers at the hands of former 1860 Southern Rights Democrats and 1861 secessionists, two key factors caused Clark's defeat. First, the small unionist constituency was able to decide the outcome when former secessionists divided their votes among Clark, Lubbock, and Chambers. The majority of antisecessionists who went to the polls and voted in the gubernatorial contest cast ballots for Lubbock. The state's most prominent unionist, Sam Houston, voted Lubbock, even though Houston in the heat of the 1859 governor's race had unkindly characterized the Harris County planter as having "all the attributes of a dog" except "fidelity." Houston and his followers were obviously not anxious to vote for a zealous secessionist such as Lubbock, but they were apparently loath to vote for Clark.[8]

Secondly, Lubbock won because he outdistanced his opponents among previous nonvoters, especially men who, for one reason or another, had not voted for governor in 1859 or for president in 1860. The evidence further suggests that most of the new voters, including previously ineligible voters who were apparently drawn into the political arena by the 1861 governor's race (and by the February secession referendum), were nonslaveholders (see table 17). Although fewer than half the Texas voters who owned no slaves turned out and voted in the 1861 governor's race, the preponderance of nonslaveholders who participated favored Lubbock. This is significant, because the planter elites who engineered secession were dependent on nonslaveholder support for continuing the war and defining the goals of the Confederacy.

At first glance, the 1861 gubernatorial election appears to have caused considerable polarization of Texas voters along economic class lines. According to the estimates of the voting behavior of small, medium, and large slaveholders, the 1860 presidential election and the secession referendum had revealed a tendency for slaveholder voter preferences to be correlated with the extent of slaveownership (see table 9). In other words, the more slaves that a planter owned, the greater had been his desire to protect his investment in slave property from possible federal government interference and, therefore, the greater had been the likelihood that he turned out and voted for Breckinridge and secession. In the 1861 governor's race the vast

8. Sam Houston to Francis R. Lubbock, August 9, 1862, in Williams and Barker, eds., *The Writings of Sam Houston*, VIII, 316; Sam Houston quoted in Hamilton, *"My Master,"* 42.

TABLE 16

ESTIMATED RELATIONSHIPS BETWEEN VOTING IN THE 1861 GUBERNATORIAL
ELECTION AND VOTING IN PREVIOUS THREE BALLOTS

(in percentages of the 1861 electorate)

The 1859 and 1861 Gubernatorial Elections   (Actual $N = 116$)

	Percentage Having Voted Democratic	Percentage Having Voted Opposition	Percentage Having Not Voted for Governor	Percentage Having Been Ineligible to Vote	Totals
1861 Lubbock Voters	7	5	8	1	20
1861 Clark Voters	0	19	1	0	20
1861 Chambers Voters	6	5	0	1	13
1861 Voters Not Voting for Governor	12	5	22	8	47
Totals	26	34	31	10	100

The 1860 Presidential and 1861 Gubernatorial Elections   (Actual $N = 121$)

	Percentage Having Voted So. Rights Democratic	Percentage Having Voted Bell-Douglas Fusion	Percentage Having Not Voted for President	Percentage Having Been Ineligible to Vote	Totals
1861 Lubbock Voters	10	3	7	0	20
1861 Clark Voters	19	0	1	0	20
1861 Chambers Voters	5	5	1	2	13
1861 Voters Not Voting for Governor	11	6	27	3	47
Totals	45	14	36	5	100

(continued)

majority of Texas slaveholders split their votes between Chambers and Clark, whereas only a paltry 5 percent of them voted for the winning candidate, Lubbock (see table 17). While the antebellum preferences of slaveholders for Breckinridge and secession were predictable considering their economic self-interest, the lack of their support for Lubbock was more an artifact of the three-way 1861 gubernatorial contest than an aversion to a candidate who championed the concerns of Texas nonslaveholders.

In the Deep South during the antebellum period and Civil War years, resentment of slaveholder wealth and power by poor whites and yeoman farmers never evolved into a serious anti-slavery or anti-slaveholder move-

TABLE 16

(continued)

The 1861 Secession Referendum and 1861 Gubernatorial Election   (Actual $N = 121$)

	Percentage Having Voted For Secession	Percentage Having Voted Against Secession	Percentage Having Not Voted in Referendum	Totals
1861 Lubbock Voters	10	5	6	20
1861 Clark Voters	15	0	5	20
1861 Chambers Voters	9	3	1	13
1861 Voters Not Voting for Governor	9	6	31	47
Totals	43	14	43	100

Source: For the sources for the 1859 gubernatorial, 1860 presidential, and 1861 secession referendum election returns, see tables 1 and 7 above. The 1861 gubernatorial returns are taken from the *Texas Senate Journal: Ninth Legislature,* comp. and ed. by James M. Day (Austin, 1963), 6–8. The number of adult white males in each county, a necessary substitute measure for the number of "qualified voters" whose names were recorded on largely lost or destroyed county "jury lists" for these years, was estimated by straight-line interpolations from 1860 and 1870 federal census data: See *Eighth Census, 1860: Population,* table 1, and *Ninth Census, 1870: Population,* tables 2 and 24. Because the 1870 census did not give separate totals for white and black males over twenty-one years of age, it was assumed here that the proportion of white adult males was the same as the overall proportion of whites of all ages and of both sexes in each county.

Note: The cell entries in the above contingency tables represent the percentage of 1861 adult white males and not the conventional percentage of ballots cast. Thus, in the first table above, if the percentage of 1861 adult white males voting for Lubbock (20 percent) is added to the percentages for Clark (20 percent) and for Chambers (13 percent), the sum equals the turnout for the 1861 gubernatorial election. For a further discussion of the procedures followed in constructing the above tables, see the note to table 5 above. The equations used to generate the internal cell entries were weighted by the number of adult white males in order to ensure that sparsely populated counties would not be overrepresented in the analysis. In the first table above the actual number of counties (or cases) equals 116; for the second and third, $N = 121$. Logically but not statistically impossible estimates which fell outside the 0 to 100 percent range were arbitrarily set at their respective minimum or maximum limits, and the values of the remaining estimates were then adjusted according to the restraints of the marginal values of the contingency table.

ment at the ballot box. In Texas, where antebellum economic debates had taken place within a strong consensus on the slavery issue, serious conflicts of interests in the 1850s between men who owned slaves and men who owned no slaves had been exceptionally rare and had never shaped statewide partisan voting alignments. Many anti-Breckinridge fusionist convictions had been based on the same craving for the security of southern institutions that had prevailed in the ranks of Southern Rights Democracy. Many others had couched their unionism in conditional terms. For example, before Lincoln's election, many Bell-Douglas supporters believed that, if the federal government refrained from actually attacking the institution of slavery, it would be "absurd" for the North and South "to cut each other's throats for niggers." However, by early 1861 the small but vocal minority who put the

TABLE 17

ESTIMATED RELATIONSHIPS BETWEEN
SLAVEOWNERSHIP AND VOTING, 1861–1864

The August 1861 Gubernatorial Election

	Percent for Lubbock	Percent for Clark	Percent for Chambers	Percent Not Voting
All Slaveholders	5	37	39	19
Slaveholders by Number of Slaves Owned				
Large (over 20)	0	33	47	19
Medium (4 to 20)	1	38	43	18
Small (1 to 3)	10	37	32	21
Nonslaveholders	24	16	6	54
All Voters[a]	20	20	13	47

The November 1861 Confederate Congressional Elections

	Percent for Winning Candidates	Percent for Losing Candidates	Percent Not Voting
All Slaveholders	28	40	32
Slaveholders by Number of Slaves Owned			
Large (over 20)	50	50	0
Medium (4 to 20)	29	44	27
Small (1 to 3)	23	33	44
Nonslaveholders	15	12	73
All Voters[a]	18	18	64

The 1863 Gubernatorial Election

	Percent for Murrah	Percent for Chambers	Percent for All Others	Percent Not Voting
All Slaveholders	24	33	10	33
Slaveholders by Number of Slaves Owned				
Large (over 20)	42	33	10	14
Medium (4 to 20)	20	37	6	37
Small (1 to 3)	21	26	5	47
Nonslaveholders	14	6	0	80
All Voters[a]	16	11	1	71

The 1863 Confederate Congressional Elections

	Percent for Incumbents	Percent against Incumbents	Percent Not Voting
All Slaveholders	28	35	37
Slaveholders by Number of Slaves Owned			
Large (over 20)	50	45	5
Medium (4 to 20)	29	37	34
Small (1 to 3)	23	31	46
Nonslaveholders	9	7	84
All Voters[a]	13	13	74

TABLE 17

(continued)

The 1864 Supreme Court Chief Justice Election

	Percent for Roberts	Percent for Bell	Percent Not Voting
All Slaveholders	48	1	51
Slaveholders by Number of Slaves Owned			
Large (over 20)	100	0	0
Medium (4 to 20)	52	1	47
Small (1 to 3)	34	2	64
Nonslaveholders	13	8	79
All Voters[a]	21	6	73

[a] Actual, not estimated statewide percentages of adult white males.

Source: For the source for the 1861 gubernatorial election returns, see table 16 above. The 1861 and 1863 Confederate congressional returns are the MSS Election Returns for 1861 and 1863, RG 307, TSL. For the voting returns for the 1863 governor's race, see *Texas Senate Journal: Tenth Legislature,* comp. and ed. by James M. Day (Austin, 1964), 35–37. The 1863 returns used here include the "informal" votes from Angelina, Jack, Mason, Smith, and Wood Counties. The source for the voting returns for the 1864 Supreme Court chief justice election is [Pendleton] Murrah, "Proclamations and Letters Sent by State Department, 1863–1865," 128–30, RG 301, TSL. For the source of the information on slaveholders, see table 4 above.

Note: "Small" slaveholders are arbitrarily defined here as slaveholders having 1 to 3 slaves in 1860; "Medium" as owning 4 to 20 slaves; and "Large" as holding over 20 slaves. Given these definitions and assuming that slaveholders were primarily adult white men, Texas small slaveholders represented approximately 9.3 percent of state's adult white male population in 1860, and medium and large slaveholders constituted 9.9 percent and 2.1 percent, respectively. Lacking data on the size of slaveholder holdings after 1860, it was necessary to assume that these proportions remained the same for the Civil War years. For a discussion of the "backwards" regression procedure used to generate the above estimates, see table 4 above. Actual $N = 116$.

preservation of the Union before the protection of slavery increasingly argued that slaveholders would dominate a separate southern nation and rule nonslaveowners oppressively. The subsequent outbreak of war brought home the possibility to many nonslaveholders that the Confederate cause could become a "rich man's war and a poor man's fight." Nevertheless, Lubbock's election to the governorship in 1861 with disproportionate support of nonslaveholders did not represent the phenomenon that many zealous Confederate nationalists called at the time "Helperism"—a dangerous conflict of interest between plain folk and planters.[9]

A second look at the estimates of voting behavior suggests that Chambers drew off anti-Houston slaveholder votes that otherwise would have gone to Lubbock (see tables 16 and 17). In other words, without Chambers in the

9. *Daily Ranchero* (Corpus Christi), January 21, 1860; Campbell, *A Southern Community in Crisis,* 147–79, 209; Alvy L. King, *Louis T. Wigfall, Southern Fire-eater* (Baton Rouge, 1970), 117; George Brown Tindall, *America: A Narrative History* (2nd ed.; New York, 1988), 636; Campbell, *An Empire for Slavery,* 210, 213–14; Martin D. Hart [and twenty-three other signers], "Address to the People of Texas. . . ." *The Intelligencer. Extra* (Austin), February 6, 1861, Texas Broadside Collection, BTHC; *Alamo Express* (San Antonio), February 19, 1861.

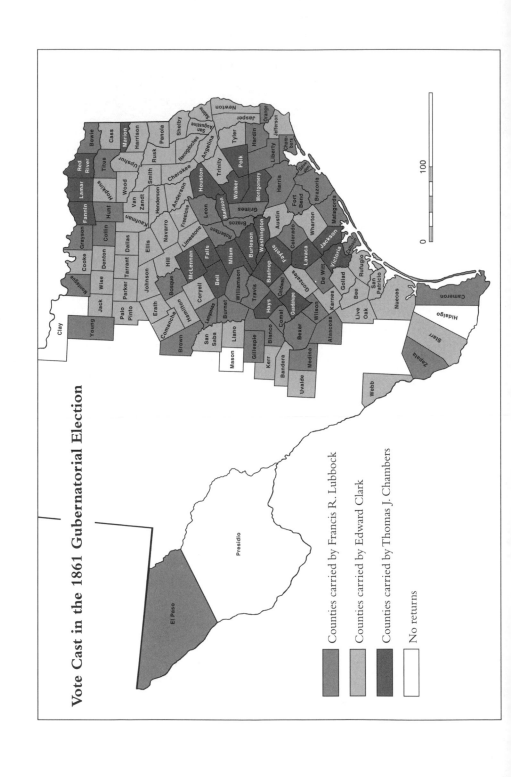

Vote Cast in the 1861 Gubernatorial Election

Counties carried by Francis R. Lubbock

Counties carried by Edward Clark

Counties carried by Thomas J. Chambers

No returns

0   100

race, Lubbock would have won the executive office by a wider margin and with greater slaveholder support. Chambers captured almost half the votes cast by 1859 Democrats who went to the polls in 1861. His candidacy not only cut into traditionally Democratic areas in the central or "western" counties with substantial European immigrant populations, but was also bolstered by slaveholder attraction to candidacies of men from the "eastern" part of the state. Although antebellum Texas was more socially and economically diverse than the distinction between "eastern" and "western" Texas suggested, politicians customarily divided state offices as much as possible on both sides of the Trinity River. Neither this atavistic geographic division nor other simplistic sectional rivalries outweighed the basic loyalties upon which the state's political cohesion depended. Nevertheless, in the 1861 gubernatorial race only Lubbock hailed from west of the Trinity River (from the city of Houston), and he was thus considered the "western" candidate.[10]

The estimates of voting also reveal that almost as many nonslaveholders had voted against Lubbock as had voted for him. Taken in combination with the estimate that Texas nonslaveholders voted for secession at a rate of two to one, the quantitative evidence supports the conventional wisdom that class conflict was sharply circumscribed in Texas by ties of kinship, mutual economic interests, including an extensive slave-hire system, and, perhaps most important, by the powerful notion that all members of the white race shared an equal superiority over black African slaves.[11]

Because of Lubbock's hairbreadth margin of votes over Governor Clark, historians may never dispel the notion that Lubbock achieved his victory fraudulently. (The election was the closest gubernatorial race ever in Texas history.) References immediately after the election to rumors of illegal votes for Lubbock boiled down to charges of vote fraud in Bexar County (San

10. Meinig, *Imperial Texas,* 46–56. On the importance of sectionalism in antebellum Texas politics, see Frederic L. Paxson, "The Constitution of Texas, 1845," *Southwestern Historical Quarterly,* XVIII (1915), 393; Griffin, "Intrastate Sectionalism," 142–60; Floyd F. Ewing, Jr., "Origins of Unionist Sentiment on the West Texas Frontier," *West Texas Historical Association Year Book,* XXXII (October, 1956), 21–29; Moneyhon, *Republicanism in Reconstruction Texas,* 12–17.

11. David M. Potter, *The Impending Crisis, 1848–1861* (New York, 1979), 458–59; Emory M. Thomas, *The Confederate Nation, 1861–1865* (New York, 1979), 8–11; Campbell, *An Empire for Slavery,* 209–30; Randolph B. Campbell, "Research Note: Slave Hiring in Texas," *American Historical Review,* XCIII (February, 1988), 107–14; Susan Jackson, "Slavery in Houston: The 1850s," *Houston Review,* II (Summer, 1980), 79. On the powerful appeal of "herrenvolk democracy," or the equal superiority of all who belong to the master race, see Pierre L. van den Berghe, *Race and Racism: A Comparative Perspective* (New York, 1967).

Antonio). Here Clark's supporters pointed with justification to a specific irregularity in the reported vote, but they also circulated flimsy complaints that Lubbock's men had unfairly manipulated the county's Mexican Texan vote. Lubbock's boast years later that he knew that he had won the election "when the soldier vote came in" led to suspicions that perhaps he had unfairly benefited from votes cast by Texans at military camps. (Because certifications of voting returns received by the secretary of state's office and tallies reported in the newspapers did not list a separate "soldier vote," Lubbock's knowledge of how soldiers voted was probably by word of mouth.) The state legislature resolved the undisputed Bexar County irregularity by rejecting the vote reported from Camp Magruder, a local army encampment, because no voting precinct had been established there. However, speculation still lingers regarding the likelihood of vote fraud in San Antonio and Lubbock's manipulation of the soldier vote.[12]

The quantitative findings suggest that Lubbock's 736-vote margin over Clark in Bexar County was about 633 votes more than it would have been had the county merely mimicked the statewide trends established by prior voting patterns in 1859 and 1860 (see tables 18 and 19). The county's vote was as follows: Lubbock 1,025; Clark 289; and Chambers 17. Clark's political liabilities, however, could have easily accounted for Lubbock's unusual success in Bexar County. Clark's policies after becoming governor had fluctuated too much to reassure any faction, especially in anti-secessionist San Antonio, and given Clark's Know-Nothing antecedents, his Bexar County supporters might understandably have complained that "every Mexican was provided with a Lubbock ticket." Although mobilizing voters by promising money, personal favors, patronage, and the like included illegal behavior, in San Antonio these types of election practices involved men legally entitled to vote and, in the case of the Bexareños, men whose intent was most likely not misrepresented. Governor Clark accepted without protest the "official" Bexar County vote as decided by the legislative count that excluded the irregular ballots from Camp Magruder.[13]

Of the six Texas counties that reported election returns with notations that votes from soldier encampments were included, Lubbock carried four and Clark carried two (see table 19). More important, among the six coun-

---

12. Bowen, "A Political Labyrinth," 37–38; Wooster, "Texas," 198; *Texas Senate Journal: Ninth Legislature,* 6; Lubbock, *Six Decades in Texas,* 324.

13. Bowen, "A Political Labyrinth," 26–27, 30–32, 37–38; Wallace E. Oakes to Edward Clark, August 27, 1861, in Governors' Papers: Edward Clark, RG 301, TSL; Wooster, "Texas," 198.

ties, Lubbock carried Bexar, Calhoun, and Galveston by larger margins than Clark commanded in Austin and Denton. This implies, though of course it does not prove, that Lubbock fared better than Clark among the state's enlisted men. Governor Clark's earnest compliance with Confederate requests for troops to be sent to faraway Virginia probably cost him votes among soldiers with an instinctive "Texas-first" mentality.[14]

Incomparably larger margins for Lubbock over Clark occurred outside Bexar County, but in most of these instances the voting returns can be explained without postulating fraud (see table 19). For example, the uncommonly large Lubbock advantages in two sparsely settled frontier counties were spurious: the inclusion of votes from neighboring unincorporated counties (Coleman and Clay, respectively) pushed turnout levels in Brown and Montague counties above 100 percent. In Caldwell, Blanco, Madison, Burleson, Bastrop, Walker, and Bosque Counties, Chambers' candidacy attracted many votes that otherwise would have gone to Clark. In other words, in these counties Chambers ran far above his predicted levels of support, whereas Clark's totals were considerably below his expected support.[15] In Chambers' home county, which was created and named in his honor in the late 1850s, his and Clark's unpopularity among local Democrats contributed to Lubbock's success. In Atascosa, Young, and Leon Counties, the surprising weakness of Clark's candidacy, rather than any unusual turnout for Lubbock, contributed to Lubbock's uncommonly large margins over Clark. However, the extraordinarily capricious outcome in Harris County (Houston), which was Lubbock's home county, must be placed under suspicion of fraud.

Voter turnout in Harris County in the 1861 gubernatorial election soared to a remarkable 95 percent of the county's adult white male population. By way of comparison, turnout in the county six months earlier in the secession referendum had been 55 percent; in the 1859 gubernatorial election it had reached 68 percent. Yet far more significantly, Clark would have carried Harris County by a handful of votes over Lubbock if the county's voting patterns had mirrored the trends established by all Texas counties between 1859 and 1861. As a resident of the county, Lubbock might have been

14. Bowen, "A Political Labyrinth," 32.
15. Based on the equations used to predict the county results in the 1861 gubernatorial race in table 18 above, the above-expected turnout for Chambers and the below-expected turnout for Clark, respectively, are for Caldwell, 15 and −30 percent; Blanco, 21 and −12 percent; Madison, 19 and −34 percent; Burleson, 20 and −21 percent; Bastrop, 19 and −17 percent; Walker, 17 and −19 percent; and Bosque, 22 and −12 percent.

TABLE 18

Outlier Counties in the 1861 Gubernatorial Election

(in percentages of 1861 county electorates)

Abnormally High Support for Lubbock and Clark

County	Residual Values Above Expected Turnout For Lubbock (%)	County	Residual Values Above Expected Turnout For Clark (%)
Brown	67	Uvalde	34
Harris	50	Panola	28
Montague	41	Karnes	25
Blanco	25	Jasper	24
Gillespie	21	Comanche	23
Chambers	18	Bandera	22
		Live Oak	19
		Newton	19
		Upshur	17
		San Augustine	17

Abnormally Low Support for Lubbock and Clark

County	Residual Values Below Expected Turnout For Lubbock (%)	County	Residual Values Below Expected Turnout For Clark (%)
Starr	−18	Madison	−34
Henderson	−17	Caldwell	−30
Coryell	−16	Montague	−27
Refugio	−16	Young	−26
		Atascosa	−24
		Burleson	−21
		Polk	−19
		Walker	−19
		Washington	−19
		Bastrop	−17
		Jack	−17
		Leon	−17
		Montgomery	−17
		Webb	−17

Source: For the sources of the 1859 gubernatorial, 1860 presidential, and 1861 gubernatorial election returns used in this table, see tables 1, 7, and 16 above. For the procedure used to estimate potentially eligible voters in 1861, see table 16 above.

Note: The residual values or scores above are the differences between the actual percentages of the county electorates voting for Lubbock and Clark, on one hand, and the corresponding estimated or predicted levels of support for them, on the other. The predicted levels for this table are based on voting in the 1859 gubernatorial and 1860 presidential elections. Outliers are arbitrarily defined here as having residual values falling at least two standard errors above or below the respective regression lines. The 1861 gubernatorial returns were analyzed by multiple regressions, taking the percentages of eligible voters favoring Lubbock and Clark as the dependent variables. The independent variables,

TABLE 18

(*continued*)

analyzed separately for Lubbock and Clark were (1) the proportions of the 1861 electorate that had voted for Runnels and Houston in 1859 and for Breckinridge and the Bell-Douglas fusion ticket in 1860, and (2) all first-order interactions among these four variables. To avoid multicollinearity, the 1859 and 1860 nonvoting percentages were not used. All variables were weighted by the adult white male population. For the equation predicting the "percentage Lubbock," $R^2 = .16$; standard error $= .08$; and actual $N = 121$. For the equation predicting "percentage Clark," $R^2 = .40$; standard error $= .08$; and actual $N = 121$.

expected to carry it by a sizable margin, but he received an exceptionally large eleven hundred votes more than his estimated level of support and a net advantage of 1,334 votes over Clark, who ran below his predicted level of support. The evidence thus strongly suggests that Lubbock won the Texas governorship because of amazing, if not fraudulent, efforts for him in his own bailiwick.

Clark's supporters accepted the Harris County results without making any insinuations of fraud. Virtually no clues exist to explain how Lubbock's neighbors and friends managed to mobilize for him such a large percentage of the county's possible electorate. Because the relative size of activities on Lubbock's behalf in his home county dwarf exertions made for him in Bexar, Galveston, and Travis Counties, grave doubt is cast on the conventional wisdom that the remnants of the Democratic party organization in these three counties were "the key" to Lubbock's statewide success. A better explanation for his victory lies in the puzzling, and thus highly suspicious, accomplishments and efforts in just Harris County by Lubbock's political friends, including Edward H. Cushing of the Houston *Telegraph*.[16]

Another enigmatic aspect of the 1861 campaign was the extent to which the gubernatorial candidates were able to attract voters behind their candidacies without formal party organizations. In response to the Know-Nothing threat of the mid-1850s, the Texas Democrats had perfected and refined their organization and, therefore, were always better organized in the late antebellum period than their opponents. To assume that some residual organizational influence of the Democratic party carried over into the war years is reasonable. It certainly had played a role in the secessionist movement. During the war, however, the vital function of party leaders to have ballots printed for distribution at the polling places was apparently sacrificed in many areas to the new nonpartisan dispositions. For example, surviving 1861 election tickets from Angelina and Nacogdoches Counties simply list contending candidates for each office. Ballots printed in this form compelled voters to "scratch" (i.e., draw a line through with a pen or pencil)

16. Bowen, "A Political Labyrinth," 32, 38.

TABLE 19

LARGEST NET GAINS FOR LUBBOCK AND CLARK
IN TERMS OF VOTER SUPPORT ABOVE OR BELOW PREDICTED LEVELS

(in percentages of 1861 county electorates)

Residual Net Gains Greater Than 18 Percentage Points for Lubbock

County	Net Gain for Lubbock over Clark (%)	Estimated Size of 1861 Electorate
Brown	70	66
Montague	68	190
Harris	57	2,341
Caldwell	48	696
Blanco	38	309
Madison	35	379
Chambers	34	233
Atascosa	33	394
Young	33	196
Gillespie	29	683
Burleson	29	891
Leon	28	1,036
Bastrop	27	1,086
Washington	25	2,019
Titus	24	1,660
Brazos	23	475
Walker	21	1,138
Bosque	19	427

Residual Net Gains Greater Than 18 Percentage Points for Clark

County	Net Gain for Clark over Lubbock (%)	Estimated Size of 1861 Electorate
Panola	42	1,237
Uvalde	42	174
Starr	32	751
Karnes	30	374
Comanche	29	147
Jefferson	28	542
Smith	27	1,973
Jasper	27	528
Bandera	26	109
Van Zandt	25	764
Newton	23	460
Medina	23	473
San Patricio	22	157
Anderson	21	1,581
Wise	21	692
Henderson	21	802
Freestone	19	795
Tarrant	19	1,311

TABLE 19

(continued)

Residual Net Gains for Lubbock or Clark in Counties with Large Soldier Encampments

County	Net Gain for Lubbock (%)	Net Gain for Clark (%)	Estimated Size of 1861 Electorate
Austin [Herbert]		8	1,609
Bexar [Picket]	18		3,516
Calhoun [Van Dorn]	11		766
Cameron [Brown]	0	0	1,969
Denton [Buck Creek and Scullyville]		1	1,153
Galveston [Central Wharf and Burleson Guards]	11		2,324

Source: For the sources of the returns for the 1859 and 1861 gubernatorial, and 1860 presidential election returns, see tables 1, 7, and 16 above.

Note: The above percentages represent the net gain (in terms of shares of estimated 1861 potentially eligible voters) for Lubbock over Clark and vice versa due to idiosyncratic county voting behavior above or below the statewide trends estimated by the equations. On the calculation of the residual net gains, see table 13 above. On the rejection by the state legislature of a separate vote count reported from Camp Magruder in Bexar County, see *Texas Senate Journal: Ninth Legislature,* comp. and ed. by James M. Day (Austin, 1963), 6. The military votes cast elsewhere at established precincts were unfortunately not tallied separately but were included in the aggregate totals in the county reports of returns sent to the secretary of state's office. See the MSS Election Returns for 1861, RG 307, TSL.

the names of candidates for whom they did not want to vote. Although a small clique of former Breckinridge Democrats had met in early June at the end of the legislative session to decide who should run for seats in the state senate, the motivation for the meeting had sprung from concerns that pluralities of votes might elect unreliable men unless there was a unification of effort behind preselected candidates. There is no evidence that this meagerly attended "Democratic party" meeting or caucus either planned or printed "partisan" tickets.[17]

Historical accounts have assumed that throughout the state Lubbock's organizational influence far exceeded that of Clark and Chambers. Lubbock's putative organizational advantage, however, was far less evidenced by his proficiency in mobilizing former anti-Houston Democrats than by the ability of his voter coalition to shape the outcomes in the lieutenant governor's race and in the Confederate congressional elections (see table 20). Dallas mayor John M. Crockett, who feared "the uprising of Jayhawk-

---

17. Buenger, *Secession and the Union,* 32–34, 138–140; Louise Horton, *Samuel Bell Maxey: A Biography* (Austin, 1974), 19. Even the *Texas State Gazette* (Austin), a longstanding Democratic party organ, apparently waffled on endorsing either Clark or Lubbock. See Bowen, "A Political Labyrinth," 44 n. 42. There is no indisputable evidence that both Lubbock and Clark ran as "Democrats." Cf. Allan Coleman Ashcraft, "Texas, 1860–1866: The Lone Star State in the Civil War" (Ph.D dissertation, Columbia University, 1960), who claims that Lubbock and Clark ran in 1861 under the Democratic party label (96).

TABLE 20

ESTIMATED RELATIONSHIPS BETWEEN VOTING IN THE 1861 GUBERNATORIAL ELECTION AND VOTING IN THE LIEUTENANT GUBERNATORIAL AND CONGRESSIONAL ELECTIONS

(in percentages of the 1861 electorate)

The August 1861 Gubernatorial and Lieutenant Gubernatorial Elections   (Actual N = 120)

	Percentage Voting for Lubbock	Percentage Voting for Clark	Percentage Voting for Chambers	Percentage Not Voting for Governor	Totals
Crockett Voters	16	11	9	0	36
Foscue Voters	2	7	1	1	11
Voters Voting for Other Candidates	2	0	0	0	2
Voters Not Voting for Lt. Governor	0	2	2	46	50
Totals	20	20	12	47	99

The August 1861 Gubernatorial Election and the November 1861 Congressional Election
(Actual N = 119)

	Percentage Having Voted for Lubbock	Percentage Having Voted for Clark	Percentage Having Voted for Chambers	Percentage Having Not Voted for Governor	Totals
Voters Voting for Winning Candidates	9	3	1	5	18
Voters Voting for Losing Candidates	0	6	4	8	18
Voters Not Voting for Congressional Candidates	12	11	7	34	64
Totals	21	20	12	47	100

Source: The source for the 1861 lieutenant gubernatorial returns is *Texas Senate Journal: Ninth Legislature,* comp. and ed. by James M. Day (Austin, 1963), 6–8. For the source of the 1861 congressional-election returns, see table 16 above.
Note: The actual number of counties or cases equals 120 for the first table and 119 for the second table.

ers and the insurrection of the negroes" in his North Texas region, would have won the 1861 lieutenant governor's race even if every ballot cast for Lubbock had failed to declare a choice for the second spot on the ticket. Yet the rate at which Lubbock men voted for Crockett surpassed the rates at which Clark or Chambers men voted for either Crockett or any of his opponents. This finding, combined with significant rates of "drop-off" voting (the tendency, here, to vote for governor, but not for lieutenant governor) by Clark and Chambers men, suggests that Lubbock's forces might have been better organized, but it does not prove that exclusively "Lubbock and Crockett" ballots were widely circulated at the polls. It was more likely that one or two of Crockett's four opponents in the lieutenant governor's race were simply left off many generalized or nonpartisan ballots that listed all candidates running for each office. Although the exclusion of some candidates from these ballots would not have precluded literate voters from writing in their choice for lieutenant governor, voters probably found a less satisfactory printed selection of lieutenant gubernatorial candidates on exclusively Clark or Chambers ballots.[18]

Estimates of voting patterns between the August governor's race and subsequent balloting in the November Confederate presidential and congressional elections also illustrate the more disciplined behavior of Lubbock voters. All candidates for Confederate presidential electors were, of course, pledged to vote for Jefferson Davis and Alexander H. Stephens. Most 1861 ballots for presidential electors and members of Congress were apparently similar to the old "party strips" in the sense that they listed a single congressional candidate plus only eight (two at-large and six district) electors.[19] Defeated congressional candidates in 1861 shared a rather astonishing characteristic: they received, according to the estimates of voting, virtually no votes from former Lubbock supporters. Over half the total votes attained by losing candidates came from former Clark and Chambers men, while the remainder of support for the losing candidates came from men who had not voted in the August gubernatorial election. On the other hand, former Lubbock supporters cast half the votes received by the successful congressional candidates, whereas only sightly over one-fifth of their collective total vote came from Clark and Chambers voters. Previous nonvoters cast the balance of the votes for winning candidates.

These findings refute the commonly held notion that results in the highly contested 1861 congressional races depended exclusively on the "personal popularity" of the self-announced candidates. Nor did only rival Democrats run in the 1861 congressional races. The runner-up candidate in the Sixth District, Benjamin H. Epperson, was an unsuccessful Whig candidate for governor, a steadfast member of the Opposition, one of the Bell-Douglas fusion ticket's electors, and an anti-secessionist. John A. Wilcox, the win-

18. John M. Crockett to Francis R. Lubbock, March 14, 1862, in Governors' Papers: Francis R. Lubbock, RG 301, TSL. On Lubbock's presumably superior organizational strength, see Bowen, "A Political Labyrinth," 32–33.
19. Records of the Secretary of State, RG 307, MSS Election Returns for 1861, TSL.

ning candidate in the First District, was a former Know-Nothing who also voted for the fusion ticket in 1860.[20] Although enthusiasm for the Confederate cause still submerged voter concerns with specific issues in the fall of 1861, an extraordinary unanimity of the choices of former Lubbock voters determined the results in the congressional races. The quantitative evidence thus suggests that either some network representing ties to Governor-elect Lubbock had been at work in the congressional elections or the summertime political divisions had persisted into the fall balloting for Confederate officeholders.

The congressional races were competitive in all of the state's six Confederate districts except for the Third District, which stretched from Houston and Galveston northwest through Waco into the western "Cross-Timbers" frontier (see table 21). Here, Peter W. Gray, a state district court judge who had represented Harris County (Houston) in the Texas Secession Convention, easily defeated A. P. Wiley, a prominent Walker County (Huntsville) attorney. Former secessionist voters overwhelmingly preferred Gray to Wiley, even though at the 1859 Democratic state convention Wiley had championed and Gray had decried the reopening of the African slave trade (see table 22). Given a choice between two secessionists, it is not surprising that the evidence suggests that the district's small percentage of former anti-secessionist voters sat out the balloting in the congressional race. Only after the war did both Gray and Wiley reject their secessionist pasts and become Republicans.[21]

The Fifth District, stretching westward from Harrison County to Palo Pinto County, was the only other congressional district where the winner won a majority of the votes cast (see table 21). Malcolm D. Graham, a former Democratic state attorney general and secessionist delegate from Rusk County (Henderson), defeated Harvard-educated Richard B. Hubbard, a former United States district attorney for the Western District of Texas. At the outbreak of the war Hubbard, a secessionist who fifteen years later became governor, had stated that he did "not think that it [would] be good *policy* for Texas troops to leave the state." In spite of Hubbard's

20. Wilfred Buck Yearns, *The Confederate Congress* (Athens, 1960), 45; Buenger, *Secession and the Union,* 55, 77, 137.

21. Fornell, *The Galveston Era,* 227–28; Dallas *Herald,* February 13, 1861; Timmons, "Texas on the Road to Secession," II, 767–93; *Weekly Austin Republican,* May 19, 1869; Moneyhon, *Republicanism in Reconstruction Texas,* 62.

TABLE 21

VOTING RESULTS IN THE 1861 SECESSION REFERENDUM AND GUBERNATORIAL AND CONGRESSIONAL ELECTIONS, BY CONGRESSIONAL DISTRICT

(in percentages of 1861 congressional district electorates)

	Secession Referendum			1861 Gubernatorial Vote				1861 Congressional Vote		
	Percentage Voting For	*Percentage Voting Against*	*Percentage Not Voting*	*Percentage Voting for Lubbock*	*Percentage Voting for Clark*	*Percentage Voting for Chambers*	*Percentage Not Voting*	*Percentage for Winning Candidates*	*Percentage for Losing Candidates*	*Percentage Not Voting*
First District	35	13	53	23	14	8	56	16	18	67
Second District	48	22	30	23	12	24	40	14	22	65
Third District	51	7	42	27	17	16	40	26	9	65
Fourth District	46	3	51	12	32	11	45	12	28	60
Fifth District	51	8	41	15	36	6	44	19	18	63
Sixth District	31	28	42	19	17	12	52	18	18	63
All Districts	43	14	43	20	20	13	47	18	18	64

Source: For the sources for the 1861 secession referendum returns, see table 7 above. For the sources for the 1861 gubernatorial and congressional races, see tables 16 and 17 above.

TABLE 22

ESTIMATED VOTING PREFERENCES OF FORMER SECESSIONIST AND UNIONIST VOTERS FOR WINNING CONGRESSIONAL CANDIDATES IN 1861

(by percent)

Congressional District Number and Winning Candidates	Secessionists			Unionists			Voters Not Casting a Vote in the 1861 Secession Referendum		
	Percentage Voting For	*Percentage Voting Against*	*Percentage Not Voting*	*Percentage Voting For*	*Percentage Voting Against*	*Percentage Not Voting*	*Percentage Voting For*	*Percentage Voting Against*	*Percentage Not Voting*
1st Wilcox	18	30	51	[27–49]	0[a]	[51–73]	5	19	76
2nd Herbert	24	23	57	14	15	71	0[a]	[21–23]	[77–79]
3rd Gray	41	4	56	0[a]	0[a]	100[a]	14	21	64
4th Sexton	0[a]	[45–53]	[47–55]	[80–90]	[10–20]	0[a]	26	6	69
5th Graham	38	25	37	15	9	75	0[a]	[8–11]	[89–92]
6th Wright	25	4	70	27	16	58	8	30	62
All Winning Candidates	26	19	56	21	7	71	9	21	70

[a] Estimates falling outside the range of 0 to 100 percent have been set to their logical limits.

Source: For the sources of the 1861 secession referendum returns and the 1861 congressional election returns, see tables 7 and 17 above.

Note: The actual number of cases for the regression estimation of the relationships between voting patterns in the February, 1861, secession referendum and the November, 1861, congressional election for the first district was 32; for the second district, 19; for the third district, 21; for the fourth district, 16; for the fifth district, 12; and for the sixth district, 17.

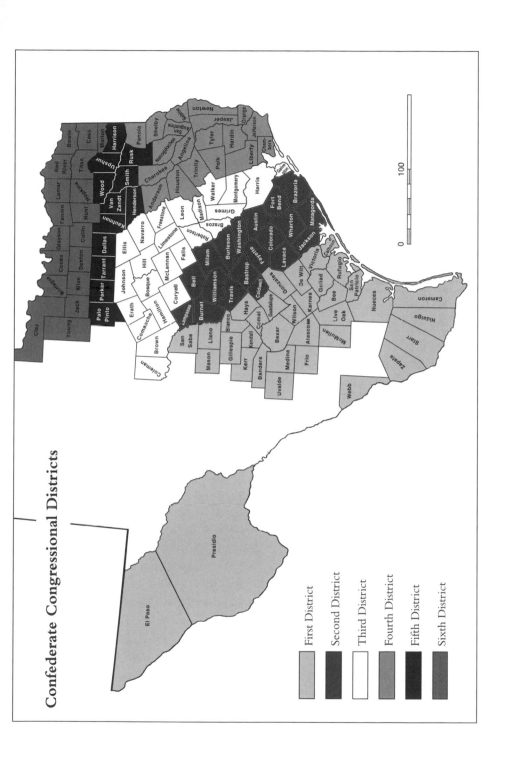

Confederate Congressional Districts

First District
Second District
Third District
Fourth District
Fifth District
Sixth District

"Texas-first" position, both former secessionist and anti-secessionist voters similarly split their votes in favor of Graham (see table 22).[22]

In the remaining congressional districts where winners garnered only a plurality of the votes cast, anti-secessionist votes decided the outcome in the First District and probably shaped the result in the Fourth District. In the First District (Bexar County and the Rio Grande valley) former fusionist leader John A. Wilcox, a nonslaveholder who endorsed secession only after Lincoln's election and then represented Bexar County in the secession convention, defeated two other secessionist delegates, William H. Steward from Gonzales County and Edward R. Hord from Starr County. The evidence suggests that anti-secessionists who turned out and voted in the congressional race in the First District went *en bloc* for Wilcox.[23]

In the Fourth District, which centered around Angelina County in extreme eastern Texas, wealthy planter Franklin B. Sexton, the former president of the 1860 state Democratic convention, defeated five challengers, of whom only one shared with him his not having been a delegate at the secession convention. The evidence suggests that Sexton, who had been among those chosen by the secessionist convention before the outbreak of war to represent Texas in the newly formed Confederacy, was the only victorious candidate to receive virtually no support from former secessionist voters. He unexplainably managed to win by attracting the support of many who had not voted in the February secession referendum and by running disproportionately well among the district's tiny anti-secessionist constituency.[24]

Because of the large proportion of anti-secessionists residing in the band of northern counties along the Red River, Princeton-educated Benjamin H. Epperson, who had advised Governor Houston to accept President Lincoln's offer of military assistance to keep Texas in the Union, came close to winning a congressional seat in the Sixth District. Only after the outbreak of war did Epperson become a reluctant Confederate, calling for southern unity in "opposition to Lincoln's policy of coercion." The admission by Epperson's supporters that his main opponent, Lamar County attorney Wil-

22. Peters, "Texas: Annexation to Secession," 305; Richard B. Hubbard to Edward Clark, May 13, 1861, in Governors' Papers: Clark; Webb, Carroll, and Branda, eds., *The Handbook of Texas*, I, 856–57.

23. Buenger, *Secession and the Union*, 54–55; Wallace, "San Antonio During the Civil War," 24–26; Webb, Carroll, and Branda, eds., *The Handbook of Texas*, II, 909.

24. Buenger, *Secession and the Union*, 127; Franklin B. Sexton to James Harper Starr, May 26, 1865, in James Harper Starr Papers, BTHC; Lubbock, *Six Decades in Texas*, 307; Webb, Carroll, and Branda, eds., *The Handbook of Texas*, II, 594.

liam B. Wright, was better organized probably accounted to some extent for Epperson's defeat, but hostility of the district's secessionists to his "submissionist" stance during the secession crisis ensured, in the end, Wright's victory. (Wright should not be confused with George W. Wright, who was one of three Lamar County delegates who had voted "no" at the Texas Secession Convention.) In the Second District, stretching inland from Matagorda Bay to south-central Texas, secessionists and anti-secessionists divided their votes almost evenly between the winner—wealthy landowner Claiborne C. Herbert of Colorado County—and three others.[25]

In Texas no organized opposition to Jefferson Davis and Alexander H. Stephens existed in the balloting for president and vice-president of the Confederacy. In the competition for the honor of being one of Texas' eight Confederate presidential electors, at least one newspaper had expressed concern that, although electors should be chosen on merit, deference should nevertheless be shown to old party divisions. Elected from Texas to cast votes for president and vice-president of the Confederate States of America were Hamilton P. Bee, Elisha E. Lott, Fletcher S. Stockdale, Henry R. Latimer, John D. Stell, F. I. Jennings, Nathaniel Terry, and A. M. M. Upshaw. Only Stell and Terry had been elected delegates to the Texas Secession Convention. The influential *Texas State Gazette* had endorsed all of the winners. The paper's editor, John Marshall, had been one of the most powerful figures in the extreme pro-slavery faction of the Texas Democratic party in the late antebellum period. More significantly, Marshall had been a behind-the-scenes Lubbock supporter in the previous August election.[26]

The light vote in the 1862 elections for the uncontested state offices of comptroller and treasurer and for five contestants running for associate justice of the state supreme court masked the extent of political activity caused by new controversial issues. Combined with difficulties ranging from Indian incursions to the vexing problems of county and state finances was a burgeoning disenchantment with the Confederate authorities over conscription, martial law, and impressment. Outmoded ideas about state sovereignty increasingly clashed with the Richmond government's need to fight a war

---

25. Ralph A. Wooster, "Ben H. Epperson: East Texas Lawyer, Legislator, and Civic Leader," *East Texas Historical Journal*, V (March, 1967), 33–34; Buenger, *Secession and the Union*, 77–79; Webb, Carroll, and Branda, eds., *The Handbook of Texas*, I, 568–69, II, 938–39; Robert N. Taylor to Benjamin H. Epperson, November 20, 1861, in Benjamin H. Epperson Papers, BTHC.

26. *Standard* (Clarksville), October 26, 1861; Bowen, "A Political Labyrinth," 32, 44–45 n. 42; Dart, "Edward Clark," 120–21; *Texas State Gazette* (Austin), November 2, 1861; Records of the Secretary of State, RG 307, MSS Election Returns for 1861, TSL.

that demanded, and resulted in, considerable centralization of effort. A consensus on white supremacy or hatred of the North could not cloak discordant and disparate feelings in Texas by 1863. In the state legislature, divisions occurred between Confederate nationalists and Texas-firsters, between cotton interests and non–cotton interests, and between slaveholders and non-slaveholders. Governor Lubbock alienated many planters and exponents of limited government by advocating restrictions on planting cotton, by favoring impressment of slaves for work on military fortifications, and by arguing for assumption by the state of the burden of providing for soldiers' families. In reacting to Confederate demands, especially for enforcement of the conscription acts, martial law, and cotton regulations, Lubbock wound up cooperating to such an extent with Confederate authorities that widespread criticism was unavoidable. His decision not to run again for the governorship stemmed less from his announced wish to join the ranks of fighting men than from his unspoken desire to make a dignified exit rather than suffer an embarrassing political defeat. When Lieutenant Governor Crockett announced that he too would not seek another term, he astonishingly proposed adoption of a constitutional amendment dispensing with wartime elections. In all likelihood planter displeasure over his support at a crucial moment of a bill restricting cotton planting had caused him to doubt his chances for reelection.[27]

The absence of political parties was a source of weakness to both the Confederate and Texas governments. Nonpartisan or "no-party" politics precluded the channeling of ties of loyalty, patronage, and self-interest into a responsible organization. In the Confederate Congress from 1861 to 1863 no significant partisan patterns of voting surfaced and, consequently, the Davis administration was never able to summon party loyalty or discipline in support of its policies. While some scholars have uncovered evidence of parties emerging in the Confederacy by 1863 and have pointed to the popularity of former Whigs, especially in Alabama, in the coalescing opposition to Davis, in Texas no correlation existed between pre-1860 political affiliations, on the one hand, and the attitudes of the state's leaders toward Davis and the Richmond government, on the other. The salience of Texas' own Senator Louis T. Wigfall among the ranks of Davis' most violent opponents

27. [F. R.] Lubbock, *Proclamations and Letters Sent by Executive and State Departments, 1861–1863,* RG 301, TSL; Bowen, "A Political Labyrinth," 48–117, 122–23; Meiners, "The Texas Governorship," 185–86, 198–99, 203, 216–17, 250–51, 390; Wooster, "Texas," 201–207; *Texas State Gazette* (Austin), June 24, 1863.

exemplified the lack of any pattern of opposition to Davis. Wigfall had been a former anti-Houston Democrat and rabid disunionist. Texas' other Confederate senator, Williamson Simpson Oldham of Travis County (Austin), had also been a fire-eating secessionist. He too became critical of the Davis administration, especially as the war continued. On the other hand, Congressman Wilcox, a former Know-Nothing and leading supporter in 1860 of the anti-Breckinridge fusionist ticket, became one of Davis' most loyal and spirited defenders.[28]

In the 1863 Texas gubernatorial and congressional elections, the Davis administration was the major issue, but candidates continued to run for office as individuals, not as adherents to any faction or party. Although the two main contenders in the gubernatorial race, the three-time loser Chambers and the lesser-known Harrison County attorney Pendleton Murrah, tried to avoid being identified, respectively, as "anti-Davis" (or "anti-administration") and "pro-Davis" (or "pro-administration"), popular opinion saddled them with these labels, and not without substantial justification. Confederate military authorities in Shreveport, Louisiana (ironically, as events would prove), considered Murrah the administration candidate. Seeking to aid his candidacy by avoiding acts that could possibly turn discontented voters to Chambers, they stipulated that they would not impress slaves and cotton in East Texas until after the election.[29]

Chambers was perhaps more of a Texan than a Confederate in 1863. Deeming it unwise to send more fighting men beyond the state's boundaries while the Texas coast remained undefended, he denounced martial law and repeatedly insisted on subordination of military commanders to civil authority. Appealing to planter interests, Chambers argued against restrictions on the cultivation of cotton. Yet he also favored repeal of what he termed "an odious" draft exemption law. His credibility suffered from his self-serving allegations that a statewide newspaper "editorial oligarchy" was conspiring against him to elect Murrah and that President Davis had dishonorably declined to respect his pleas for an army commission. Chambers' defeat indicated a fundamental resolve and willingness of Texans to continue to work as closely as possible with the Confederate government, despite their

28. Richard E. Beringer, "The Unconscious 'Spirit of Party' in the Confederate Congress," *Civil War History*, XVIII (1972), 312–33; John H. Reagan, *Memoirs: With Special Reference to Secession and the Civil War*, ed. Walter Flavius McCaleb (New York, 1906), 161–62; Ezra J. Warner and W. Buck Yearns, *Biographic Register of the Confederate Congress* (Baton Rouge, 1975), 257–58.

29. Yearns, *Confederate Congress*, 52; Bowen, "A Political Labyrinth," 126–29, 136–37.

extensive grumbling about Confederate policies that they perceived as not in the best interests of either themselves or their state.[30]

Because Chambers, in going down for defeat for the final time as a gubernatorial candidate, polled about 42 percent of the ballots cast, historians have incorrectly assumed that his 1863 total was the largest vote he had ever received. In the 1851 and 1853 gubernatorial elections, Chambers received 2,148 and 2,449 votes, respectively. In 1861 he obtained 13,759 votes, or 756 votes more than his 1863 grand total, which included 548 "informal" votes cast in Angelina, Jack, Mason, Smith, and Wood Counties. Chambers thus obtained fewer votes in his contest with Murrah than he had polled against Lubbock and Clark (see tables 16 and 23). Moreover, the nature of Chambers' support, in terms of the prior choices registered by the voters in 1861, was as bizarre as it was unpredictable. According to the estimates of voting, Chambers managed to win the support of only about one-fourth of the men who had previously cast ballots for him. For every three men who repeated their support for him, two of his former supporters defected to Murrah's column, while the bulk of the 1861 Chambers constituency did not participate in the 1863 balloting. In net results, Chambers' 1863 total vote incongruously included more men who in the previous gubernatorial election had voted against him than had voted for him, while more than a third of his 1863 total was cast by men who, for whatever reason, had not voted in 1861.[31]

The estimates of the relationships between voting patterns in the 1863 governor's race and the 1859 gubernatorial contest reveal, as anticipated, no association with antebellum voter alignments (see table 23). Both former 1859 Houston men and former 1859 Democrats who went to the polls in 1863 divided their votes almost equally between Murrah and Chambers. Murrah, however, like Lubbock in 1861, received disproportionate support from men who had not voted for governor in 1859, and these previous nonvoters provided Murrah with his comfortable margin of victory. Of the 1861 secessionists who subsequently participated in the 1863 gubernatorial election, almost three-fifths of them favored Murrah, whereas former unionists who voted went three to one for Chambers. In terms of prior alignments in the 1861 gubernatorial election, Murrah, who enjoyed Lubbock's

30. Card of T. J. Chambers published in the *Standard* (Clarksville) July 18, 1863; Houston *Tri-Weekly Telegraph*, June 26, 1863; Friend, "The Life of Thomas Jefferson Chambers," 169–75; Wooster, "Texas," 209; Bowen, "A Political Labyrinth," 119–20, 130–31.

31. Bowen, "A Political Labyrinth," 137.

Vote Cast in the 1863 Gubernatorial Election

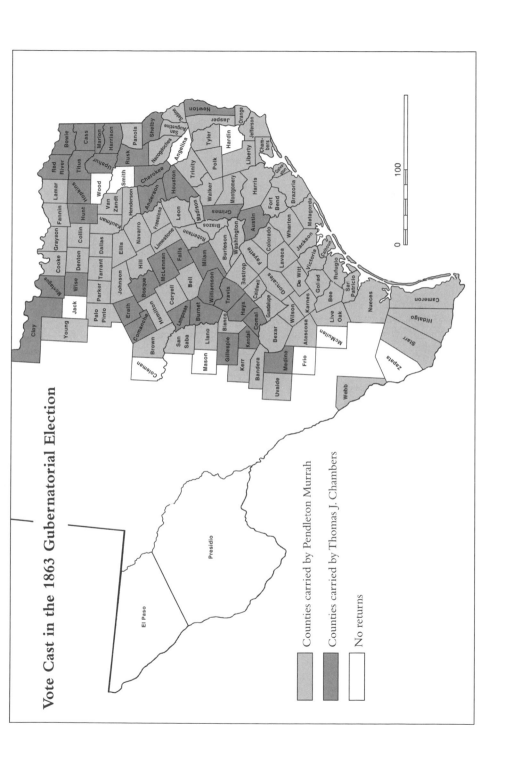

Counties carried by Pendleton Murrah

Counties carried by Thomas J. Chambers

No returns

TABLE 23

ESTIMATED RELATIONSHIPS BETWEEN VOTING IN THE 1863
GUBERNATORIAL ELECTION AND VOTING IN THREE PREVIOUS BALLOTS

(in percentages of 1863 electorate)

The 1859 and 1863 Gubernatorial Elections (Actual N = 116)

	Percentage Having Voted Democratic	Percentage Having Voted Opposition	Percentage Having Not Voted for Governor	Percentage Having Been Ineligible to Vote	Totals
Murrah Voters	3	6	6	1	16
Chambers Voters	3	7	1	1	11
Voters Voting for Other Candidates	0	1	0	0	1
Voters Not Voting for Governor	18	18	23	12	71
Totals	24	32	30	14	100

The 1861 Secession Referendum and 1863 Gubernatorial Elections (Actual N = 117)

	Percentage Having Voted for Secession	Percentage Having Voted Against Secession	Percentage Having Not Voted in Referendum	Percentage Having Been Ineligible to Vote	Totals
Murrah Voters	10	1	5	0	16
Chambers Voters	6	3	3	0	11
Voters Voting for Other Candidates	1	0	0	0	1
Voters Not Voting for Governor	24	9	33	5	71
Totals	41	13	41	5	100

(continued)

endorsement, triumphed because he carried the bulk of 1861 Lubbock men who turned out and voted. Chambers carried, as he had in 1861, the slaveholder vote, whereas nonslaveholders favored Murrah at a rate of more than two to one (see table 17).

None of the quantitative findings conflict with the commonly accepted notion that Chambers' candidacy in 1863 attracted a diverse protest vote that not only reflected resistance to conscription and annoyance with impressment, but also expressed the convictions of outspoken Texas-firsters and also the hopes of quiescent reconstructionists.[32] Nor do the results un-

32. *Ibid.*, 139–40.

TABLE 23

(continued)

The 1861 and 1863 Gubernatorial Elections   (Actual N = 117)

	Percentage Having Voted for Lubbock	Percentage Having Voted for Clark	Percentage Having Voted for Chambers	Percentage Having Not Voted for Governor	Percentage Having Been Ineligible to Vote	Totals
Murrah Voters	7	4	2	3	0	16
Chambers Voters	2	2	3	4	0	11
Voters Voting for Other Candidates	0	1	0	0	0	1
Voters Not Voting for Governor	10	12	7	37	5	71
Totals	19	19	12	45	5	100

Source: For the sources for the 1859, 1861, and 1863 gubernatorial election returns, see tables 1, 16, and 17 above. For the source for the 1861 secession referendum returns, see table 7 above.

cover heretofore unrecognized patterns in the balloting for governor and lieutenant governor. However, the finding that over one-third of the ballots cast for Chambers expressed no choice for lieutenant governor suggests that, assuming that friends of the candidates distributed exclusively Chambers or Murrah ballots, the Murrah campaign made a more practical or sensible effort (see table 24). Otherwise, Texans cast tickets with every conceivable combination of pairing between an "easterner"—Murrah or Chambers—on the one hand, and one of the four "western" lieutenant gubernatorial candidates, on the other.

Of the candidates running for lieutenant governor, Stephen H. Darden, an anti-secessionist who subsequently fought at Sharpsburg (Antietam), was nearest to being perceived as "anti-administration." However, in his second-place finish, Darden fared better at the hands of Murrah supporters than among Chambers men. The winner in the lieutenant governor's race, Fletcher S. Stockdale, was known to be in opposition to Chambers and was the only candidate untainted by either Know-Nothingism or support on the eve of the war for Sam Houston. Stockdale's margin of victory, however, depended on votes he received on ballots cast against Murrah. It was also "every man for himself" in the simultaneously held congressional races.[33]

All six of Texas' Confederate congressmen were up for reelection in

33. *Standard* (Clarksville), July 18, 1863; Bowen, "A Political Labyrinth," 127–28, 132–34.

TABLE 24

ESTIMATED RELATIONSHIPS AMONG VOTING IN THE ELECTIONS OF 1863
AND THE 1861 CONFEDERATE CONGRESSIONAL ELECTION

(in percentages of 1863 electorate)

The 1863 Gubernatorial and Lieutenant Gubernatorial Elections   (Actual *N* = 120)

	Percentage Voting for Murrah	*Percentage Voting for Chambers*	*Percentage Voting for Others*	*Percentage Not Voting for Governor*	*Totals*
Stockdale Voters	7	3	1	0	11
Darden Voters	5	2	0	0	7
Gentry Voters	3	1	0	0	4
Kitrell Voters	2	1	0	0	4
Voters Not Voting for Lieutenant Governor	0	4	0	71	74
Totals	16	11	1	71	100

The 1863 Gubernatorial Election and the 1863 Confederate Congressional Elections
(Actual *N* = 114)

	Percentage Voting for Murrah	*Percentage Voting for Chambers*	*Percentage Voting for Others*	*Percentage Not Voting for Governor*	*Totals*
Voters Voting for Incumbents	5	5	0	3	13
Voters Voting for Challenges	7	5	1	0	13
Voters Not Voting for Congressional Candidates	4	1	0	69	74
Totals	16	11	1	71	100

(continued)

1863. Half of them suffered humiliating defeats. Every race was competitive, and the combined voting totals for challengers slightly exceeded the number of votes cast for incumbents (see table 25). Gray's defeat in the Third District at the hands of Anthony M. Branch, a reluctant secessionist and trusted friend of Sam Houston, stemmed from Gray's ill-advised defense of the exemption clauses in the conscription laws, including the unpopular slave-overseer exemption, or "20-Negro law." One of the most perceptive of influential men in the district believed that Branch "carried almost to a man" the poorer classes. During the campaign, Gray had accused Branch's supporters, of whom the most prominent was Gray's former rival for the con-

TABLE 24

(continued)

The 1861 and 1863 Confederate Congressional Elections (Actual $N = 112$)

	Percentage Having Voted for Winning Candidates in 1861	Percentage Having Voted for Losing Candidates in 1861	Percentage Having Not Voted for Congressional Candidates in 1861	Percentage Having Been Ineligible to Vote in 1861	Totals
1863 Voters Voting for Incumbents	2	1	10	0	13
1863 Voters Voting for Challengers	3	5	6	0	13
1863 Voters Not Voting for Congressional Candidates	11	11	45	5	74
Totals	20	20	13	47	100

Source: The source for the 1863 lieutenant gubernatorial election returns is *Texas Senate Journal: Tenth Legislature,* comp. and ed. by James M. Day (Austin, 1964), 35–37. The returns used here include the "informal" votes from Angelina, Jack, Mason, Smith, and Wood Counties. For the source for the 1861 and 1863 congressional and gubernatorial returns, see tables 16 and 17 above.

gressional seat in 1861, of trying to stir up the poor against the rich by advocating "leveling" agrarian doctrines.[34]

In a very close race in the Fifth District, John R. "Jack" Baylor, a daring but mean-spirited Indian fighter, narrowly defeated Graham, the incumbent, who had approved of most of the Davis administration's measures but had denounced the imposition of martial law by military authorities. Baylor had served briefly, when dreams of Confederate westward expansion were still possible, as the self-appointed "governor" of Arizona. The result was perhaps more of a victory for Baylor than a defeat for Graham. The election hinged on voter belief that President Davis had unjustly deprived Baylor, a lieutenant colonel in the 2nd Texas Mounted Rifles, of a command because Confederate-Indian diplomacy could not accommodate Baylor's invidious treatment of Indians. In the Sixth District Wright lost his reelection bid to Simpson H. Morgan, a Clarksville lawyer and the president of the Memphis, El Paso, and Pacific Railroad Company, who campaigned against special taxes on agricultural products. Wright, who had also served with Morgan on the railroad's directorship, had championed the popular cause of ex-

34. Warner and Yearns, *Biographical Register of the Confederate Congress,* 106–107; Webb, Carroll, and Branda, eds., *The Handbook of Texas,* I, 206; Baggett, "The Constitutional Union Party," 256–61, table 2; Bowen, "A Political Labyrinth," 141, 144–47; William P. Ballinger, diary entry for August 5, 1863, "Diary 1862–1864" [typescript copy #1], in William Pitt Ballinger Diary and Papers, BTHC; Peter W. Gray, quoted in Bowen, "A Political Labyrinth," 147.

TABLE 25

VOTING RESULTS IN THE 1863 GUBERNATORIAL AND CONGRESSIONAL ELECTIONS, BY CONGRESSIONAL DISTRICT

(in percentages of the 1863 congressional district electorates)

	1863 Gubernatorial Race				1863 Congressional Races			
	Percentage Voting for Murrah	Percentage Voting for Chambers	Percentage Voting for Others	Percentage Not Voting	Percentage Voting for Incumbents	Percentage Voting for Challengers	Percentage Voting for Winners	Percentage Not Voting
First District	17	8	0	74	15	9	{15}	76
Second District	19	15	0	66	18	13	{18}	69
Third District	21	11	0	68	11	18	{18}	71
Fourth District	16	12	1	71	15	14	{15}	71
Fifth District	14	11	6	69	16	17	{16}	68
Sixth District	11	13	1	75	10	15	{13}	75
All Districts	16	11	1	71	13	13	{15}	74

Source: For the sources for the 1863 gubernatorial and congressional election returns, see table 17 above.

empting from the draft all militia units engaged in frontier defense. Both men generally embraced the policies of the Richmond government. Personalities more than issues apparently shaped the outcome in the Sixth District.[35]

The reasons for the defeat of Gray, Graham, and Wright baffled and embarrassed many contemporaries of the period. For historians writing generations later, the results are still burdensome to interpret, especially with regard to the dominant pro-administration–versus–anti-administration issue. Of the three incumbents whom the voters returned to office, only Herbert from the Second District (a band of counties along the Colorado River, including the city of Austin) was notoriously anti-administration. Herbert, who was killed after the war by an assassin's bullet, had failed to support any administration measures and had once even warned that if the Richmond government continued the draft, Texas might have to secede from the Confederacy. His colleague from the Fourth District, Sexton, who was an admirer of President Davis and had voted for most administration measures, denounced Herbert's counsel as "foolish." Sexton did, however, express reservations about the legality of the conscription acts, vote against giving Davis power to revoke the right of *habeas corpus,* and object to military impressment of slaves. To some extent Sexton won reelection by falsely associating his challenger with a regressive tax policy. Wilcox, the former 1860 fusionist whom voters reelected from the First District, was also one of the administration's most ardent supporters, but he may have ensured his reelection by serving with General John B. Magruder, Confederate commander of the Texas District, between sessions of Congress. When Wilcox subsequently died before Congress assembled, his unexpired term was filled by Stephen H. Darden, who was seated in Congress on November 21, 1864, after he won the special replacement election in the First District.[36]

The quantitative findings are helpful, however, in ruling out some tentative explanations for the defeat of Gray, Graham, and Wright. For example, the estimated relationships between voting patterns in the 1863 congressional races and the simultaneously held gubernatorial election reveal no association between anti-Murrah ballots and a tendency to vote against

35. Warner and Yearns, *Biographical Register of the Confederate Congress,* 19–20, 103–104, 180–81, 264; Yearns, *Confederate Congress,* 240; Dallas *Herald,* November 7, 1860; *Standard* (Clarksville), July 26, 1863; *McKinney Messenger,* February 3, 1865; Bowen, "A Political Labyrinth," 158–59 n. 75.

36. Bowen, "A Political Labyrinth," 141, 148–149; Webb, Carroll, and Branda, eds., *The Handbook of Texas,* I, 800, II, 257–58; Yearns, *Confederate Congress,* 69, 243; Warner and Yearns, *Biographical Register of the Confederate Congress,* 69, 117–18, 217–18, 257–58.

incumbents (see table 24). Nor did congressional challengers run disproportionately well among nonslaveholders or, for that matter, among slaveholders (see table 17). When one analyzes the 1863 congressional races in terms
of voting patterns in the previous 1861 congressional elections, it is amazing
that any incumbent escaped defeat: incumbents managed collectively to
capture only 10 percent of the men who had voted initially for them in
1861. Even more embarrassingly, most of their previous supporters who
subsequently voted in the 1863 races cast ballots against their reelection. On
the other hand, one-fourth of the men who had voted for losing congressional candidates in 1861 repeated a vote against incumbents in 1863, while
only 5 percent of them switched over to support a congressman against
whom they had initially voted. As a group, incumbents were competitive
only because collectively they outdistanced their challengers among previous nonvoters: about 80 percent of their combined total votes came from
men who had not voted in the 1861 congressional races.

Electoral volatility and unpredictability thus were the hallmarks of the
1863 Texas congressional elections. The large numbers of men absent from
Texas by virtue of their serving in the Confederate army contributed to the
instability in voting patterns between 1861 and 1863. Estimates of the number of Texans who saw military service range from sixty thousand to an
inflated high of ninety thousand, and the numbers of Texas soldiers out of
state at any given time during the war are exceedingly difficult to determine.
In February, 1863, Governor Lubbock claimed that Texas had 68,500 men
in actual service, including some 6,500 state troops. In August, at the time
of the election, newspaper accounts rhetorically spoke of the state's "sixty
thousand disfranchised citizens—gallant soldiers." Throughout the Civil
War no provisions in the law allowed Texas soldiers stationed out of state to
vote in state and local elections by absentee ballot. In the analysis presented
here of voting behavior between the pair of wartime congressional elections, men at home in 1861 but subsequently outside Texas in 1863 were
necessarily dropped into the category of "choosing" not to vote in 1863.
While this procedure does not vitiate the estimates of voter transition probabilities, the inability of incumbents to mobilize their previous supporters
must be interpreted as partially reflecting the extent to which soldiers were
effectively disfranchised.[37]

37. Ralph A. Wooster, "Statehood, War, and Reconstruction," in Donald W. Whisenhunt, *Texas:
A Sesquicentennial Celebration* (Austin, 1984), 112; Oates, "Texas Under the Secessionists," 187; Rupert
N. Richardson, Adrian Anderson, and Ernest Wallace, *Texas: The Lone Star State* (6th ed.; Englewood
Cliffs, N.J., 1993), 214; *Standard* (Clarksville), July 26, 1863 (quotation).

Although isolated by the summer of 1864 from the eastern Confederacy and the Richmond government, Texas was not swept over by Union forces. Military considerations, nevertheless, generated inevitable clashes between Governor Murrah and Confederate authorities in the Trans-Mississippi Department over conscription policy, impressment of slaves, regulation of cotton purchases, and competition for specie and supplies. Murrah recognized that by questioning or attacking unpopular Confederate policies dictated by military necessity, he risked encouraging local discontentment to a hazardous degree. Murrah's dilemma arose from his need to steer clear of the Scylla of sycophantic compliance with the actions of the Confederate authorities and the Charybdis of squarely placing Texas concerns ahead of Confederate interests and priorities. By 1865 Murrah had become overtly hostile to the Richmond government, especially regarding conscription and the cotton trade.[38]

The August, 1864, state elections became the focus of considerable political intrigue when Judge James H. Bell announced his intention to run for the chief justiceship of the Texas Supreme Court. Bell never reconciled himself to the fact that his state was at war with the United States government. Elected in 1858 to the court as an associate justice on the Opposition ticket by a narrow 421-vote margin over his Democratic opponent, Bell was an ardent unionist who capitulated to secession only after Texas joined the Confederacy. As the only unionist to serve on the state supreme court during the war, he had dissented in a case upholding the constitutionality of the first Confederate conscript law. Believing with considerable justification that Bell was a dangerous reconstructionist who would "sustain the Federals at the first good opportunity," Lieutenant Governor Stockdale coordinated a unification among anti-Bell factions behind the candidacy of Oran M. Roberts. Although on "sick leave" from service in the Confederate army, Roberts was well known as the former president of the Texas Secession Convention and as Bell's former colleague on the high court. Before the war the two men had squared off in a historic debate over secession in the state capitol.[39]

Bell's political enemies acknowledged that his candidacy would attract votes in the old unionist strongholds in the German-immigrant settlements

38. Bowen, "A Political Labyrinth," 228, 235–36; Wooster, "Texas," 209; Meiners, "The Texas Governorship," 317, 319, 346, 355–56; Moretta, "Pendleton Murrah," 9–51.

39. Sinclair, "Crossroads of Conviction," 106–109; Bowen, "A Political Labyrinth," 266–70 (quotations on 269); Roberts, "The Political, Legislative, and Judicial History of Texas," 91–92.

along the lower Brazos River and north of San Antonio. In addition, they conceded that he would gain influential support in the northern wheat-growing areas, but they also feared that Bell would make inroads every-where into the ranks of disaffected and war-weary secessionists. By the summer of 1864 his legal opinions on martial law and the conscript law were not necessarily political liabilities in the midst of bitterness toward Confederate policies that many Texans denounced as "military despotism." Bell privately confided that he expected support from those who had lost respect for the zealous secessionists who, in his words, had "led the way to the quicksands," but his chances of winning would depend on driving a wedge between rabid Confederate diehards and more flexible Texas-firsters. The latter group included so-called diplomats, who were willing to consider more pragmatic, although carefully unstated, options ranging from a shift toward Texas independence to a negotiated reconciliation with the Union. Because Bell's loyalty to the Confederate cause was suspect, his candidacy failed to pose a genuine challenge to Roberts. Virtually every newspaper in the state printed letters from writers claiming that northerners would cheer a victory for Bell.[40]

For an off-year state election the chief justice race polled a sizable vote—an indication perhaps of the significance that voters attached to the out-come. Bell lost by a lopsided margin that, at first glance, seemed to reflect the over three-to-one rate at which Texans in 1861 had favored secession. Estimates of relationships between voting patterns in the secession referendum and the 1864 judicial election suggest that nearly all former unionists who ventured to the polling places in 1864 cast ballots for Bell and, in net terms, they constituted two-thirds of his support (see table 26). Only a trifling fraction (about 3 percent) of the 1861 secessionists favored his candidacy, and he predictably received virtually no backing from 1861 Clark men or former Murrah voters. In terms of prior voting in the 1863 gubernatorial election, Bell captured over one-fifth of the Chambers men, who, in turn, were mostly those who made up the unionist bloc of voters within the 1863 anti-Murrah coalition. Bell garnered only a handful of the large number of men who had not voted, for whatever reasons, in the Murrah-Chambers contest.

40. Thomas Smith to Oran M. Roberts, May 25, 1864, in Oran M. Roberts Papers, BTHC; James Madison Hall, "A Journal of the Civil War Period by James Madison Hall, 1860–1866," entry for January 15, 1864, in James Madison Hall Papers, BTHC; James H. Bell to Benjamin H. Epperson, April 13, 1864, in Epperson Papers; Bowen, "A Political Labyrinth," 272–73, 287; *Reporter* (Tyler), July 17, 1864 [newspaper clipping in Box 2M405 in Roberts Papers]; Galveston *News,* July 27, 1864.

TABLE 26

ESTIMATED RELATIONSHIPS BETWEEN VOTING IN THE 1864 JUDICIAL ELECTION
AND VOTING IN THREE PREVIOUS ELECTIONS

(in percentages of 1864 electorate)

The 1861 Secession Referendum and the 1864 Judicial Election   (Actual N = 110)

	Percentage Having Voted for Secession	Percentage Having Voted Against Secession	Percentage Having Not Voted in Referendum	Percentage Having Been Ineligible to Vote	Totals
Roberts Voters	18	0	3	0	21
Bell Voters	1	4	1	0	6
Voters Not Voting for Judicial Candidate	21	9	36	7	73
Totals	40	13	40	7	100

The 1861 Gubernatorial Election and the 1864 Judicial Election   (Actual N = 110)

	Percentage Having Voted for Lubbock	Percentage Having Voted for Clark	Percentage Having Voted for Chambers	Percentage Having Not Voted for Governor	Percentage Having Been Ineligible to Vote	Totals
Roberts Voters	7	6	4	4	0	21
Bell Voters	3	0	1	2	0	6
Voters Not Voting for Judicial Candidate	9	13	7	37	7	73
Totals	19	19	12	43	7	100

The 1863 Gubernatorial Election and the 1864 Judicial Election   (Actual N = 110)

	Percentage Having Voted for Murrah	Percentage Having Voted for Chambers	Percentage Having Voted for Others	Percentage Having Not Voted for Governor	Percentage Having Been Ineligible to Vote	Totals
Roberts Voters	10	4	1	6	0	21
Bell Voters	0	3	0	3	0	6
Voters Not Voting for Judicial Candidate	6	4	0	61	2	73
Totals	15	11	1	70	2	100

Source: For the source for the 1861 and 1863 gubernatorial and 1864 judicial election returns, see table 17 above; for the 1861 secession referendum returns, see table 7 above.

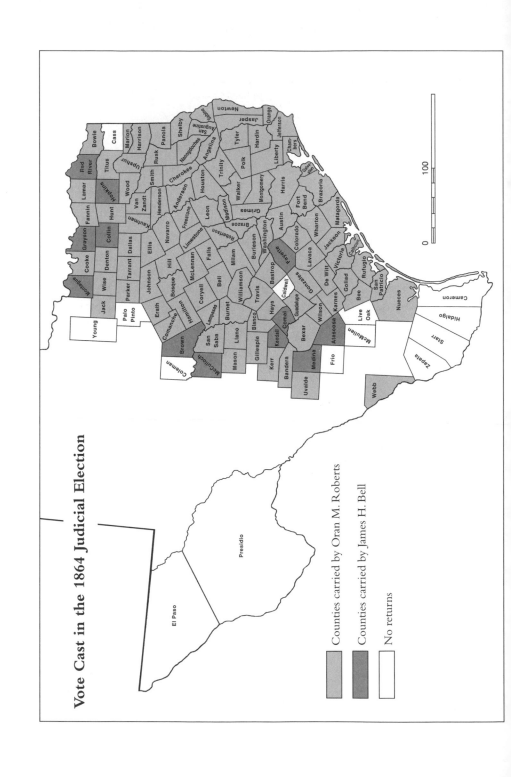

Vote Cast in the 1864 Judicial Election

Counties carried by Oran M. Roberts

Counties carried by James H. Bell

No returns

The 1864 result thus offered no surprises. Texans adhered to the rebellion they had embarked upon in February of 1861. In this last important state-wide election held before the arrival of federal troops, Texans voted to ratify their calamitous 1861 decision for dissolution of the American Union in one final display of enthusiasm for the mangled and dismembered Confederacy. Whereas Texas slaveholders had voted for secession at a rate of approximately sixteen to one, they voted in 1864 against Bell at a rate of almost fifty to one (see table 17). Although nonslaveholders favored Roberts over Bell at a rate slightly below their two-to-one approval of secession, nothing in the quantitative findings contradicts the widely held assessment by historians that Bell's defeat represented a final show of quixotic fervor for the Confederate cause. The anti-secessionist remnants of Houston's 1859 coalition would have been the only basis in 1864 for any reconstructionist, or "peace party," movement.[41]

To a considerable extent the electoral roots of Reconstruction in Texas can be traced back to the 1864 judicial election. Although Bell expressed surprise that "under all the circumstances" so many men had "dared to vote" for him, he was perhaps prone in the wake of his humiliating defeat to exaggerate the extent to which his fellow Texans shared his views. Of the 7,000-some votes that he received, approximately 4,500 had been cast by unionists who had stayed in Texas throughout most of the war and had not actively opposed the Confederate state government. Only about 1,000 votes in Bell's total could have possibly been cast by disenchanted or demoralized ex-secessionists willing to seek peace or reunion with the North. Had the war dragged on through the summer of 1865, Bell would have run against Murrah in the gubernatorial election scheduled for August on a reconstructionist platform advocating a separate peace with the federal government and gradual emancipation of the state's slaves. It was rumored that Chambers would most likely have also campaigned for the governorship, although on a more equivocal peace platform. When federal troops occupied Texas, Bell accepted, just as his antagonists had warned, one of the most important posts in the Reconstruction government. Although the goal was not apparent in the summer of 1865, rewarding men like Bell who had led the old anti-secessionist movement was the very first step in the creation of the Texas Republican party.[42]

41. Bowen, "A Political Labyrinth," 273–76.

42. James H. Bell to Benjamin H. Epperson, October 19, 1864, and February 22, 1865, in Epperson Papers; William P. Ballinger to Guy M. Bryan, February 16, 1865, in Bryan Papers; Moneyhon, *Republicanism in Reconstruction Texas,* 24–25.

4
FROM THE DOLLAR OATH TO
MILITARY REGISTRATION, 1865–1868

President Johnson's policy is Hell on union men and death to the nigger in this section.

—Freedmen's Bureau agent at Sherman to
William H. Sinclair, October 6, 1866

To exalt the common African with his thick skin, wooly head, his super-stition and silly notions, to a level or perfect state of equality with the proud race of Anglo-Saxon blood, is an attempt to place a libel upon the great and original purposes of God himself.

—*Harrison Flag* (Marshall), March 30, 1867

In the summer of 1865 the overriding issue in national politics was how to reunite the defeated Confederacy with the American Union. Moving politics from beneath, however, were two divisive questions that came to form the essence of the political debates over Reconstruction: Which group of white men (either former "rebels" or southern "loyalists") would control the former Confederate state governments? And—a far more crucial and consequential question—what would be the place of the newly freed slaves in postwar southern society? The answers separated men into polarized political camps. How one visualized the roles of former slaves and white unionists in the new order of things placed him on a spectrum of opinion ranging from rejection to acceptance of unprecedented change.[1]

Located on the far right side of this spectrum at the war's end were reactionaries or extreme conservatives who wanted to re-create as quickly as possible the Texas government and society "again as in the 'olden time.'" Most were former secessionists who believed that the honorable cause for which the South had fought had intensified the tragic grandeur of its efforts

---

1. McPherson, *Ordeal by Fire,* 497.

on the battlefield. Although they realized that the war had destroyed slavery, a few clung to the chimera of gradual emancipation. They believed that the North might allow planters to exercise over their "ignorant and helpless" blacks a new form of guardianship—a protective care recognized under the law, conveyed in some manner, and deemed to have a monetary value.[2]

For Texas slaveholders, the prospect of unqualified abolition posed a staggering financial loss. The buying, selling, and hiring of slaves legally lasted in Texas until the arrival of federal troops in Galveston on June 19, 1865—the date referred to forever after by Texas blacks as "Juneteenth." A prominent East Texas planter complained that the "high handed and unlawful act" of emancipation deprived him of "all the capital" that he had invested over the past decades in "that species of property." On the eve of the war Harrison County planters had owned an average of $48,000 of property, but only an average of $9,000 of property, mostly land, a decade later. If in a reconstructed Texas the former valuable bondsmen would have to be paid for their labor, then, according to postwar conservatives, new controls over blacks would have to be established to guarantee dependable sources of labor at harvest time, and also to regulate year-round the black population. Zealousness in restricting black freedom now replaced antebellum zealousness in defending slavery.[3]

A revitalized postwar opposition party to the Democrats was thus destined to be recruited exclusively from segments of the electorate which were open to the possibility of changes in constitutional theory as well as in racial attitudes. This initial reliance on moderate white voters dictated from the outset that any radicalization of northern requirements for Texas readmission to the Union, especially escalating demands that some semblance of justice be given to former slaves, would steadily redefine the political spectrum and place the overwhelming number of the white population in the conservative camp. When Republican radicals staked out new ground on the political left by redefining requirements for southern loyalty, policies that former Confederates had initially perceived as unlawful and revolutionary, such as the uncompensated abolition of slavery, easily became acceptable when the issue was whether to give former slaves full civic and political rights. The unfolding endorsement of legal equality for former slaves and

2. S. Wright to Andrew J. Hamilton, December 6, 1865, in Governors' Papers: Andrew J. Hamilton, RG 301, TSL; Ramsdell, *Reconstruction in Texas*, 46; *Texas Republican* (Marshall), June 16, 1865.
3. Campbell, *An Empire for Slavery*, 240–41, 388, table 26; Hall, "A Journal of the Civil War Period," entry for May 29, 1865, in Hall Papers.

their dramatic registration as legal voters by the army sparked another stage in the revolution that had begun with emancipation. The inclusion of blacks into Texas electoral politics eventually rendered Republicans vulnerable to Democratic appeals based on racist contentions, but even by the end of 1865 conservative endorsement of President Andrew Johnson's undemanding policies of Reconstruction had fractured the antebellum unionism that formed the core of an inchoate Texas Republican party.

Although the northern triumph logically stood to benefit Texans who had either registered their opposition to secession at the ballot box in February of 1861 or suffered subsequently under Confederate rule, restoring the old prewar Opposition party was fraught with difficulties. Just as no unanimity on a plan of action existed among Texas unionists after Abraham Lincoln's election to the presidency in 1860, no consensus on a strategy for formulating a program of reunion existed among them in 1865 or, for that matter, in subsequent years. Antebellum unionism had encompassed a wide range of behavior. Among Texans who voted against secession were some who believed that disunion and war had been forced on them after the outbreak of hostilities in the spring of 1861. They showed their devotion to the southern cause by voluntarily enlisting in the Confederate army. In time, their sacrifices on the battlefield made them embrace a cause which conviction alone could never have done. At the other extreme, many Texas anti-secessionists fled their homes and families to join the Union army or "laid in the bush" in opposition to Confederate authority. Wartime experiences of antebellum unionists often shaped, but did not unfailingly predict, their positions after the war on Reconstruction issues.[4]

In sharp contrast to anti-secessionists who subsequently, although often reluctantly, had served the Confederacy were the unionist refugees. Due to their experience in exile in the North or service in the Union army, they understood that any immediate and uncontested restoration of Texas to the Union would require concessions by former Confederates regarding the rights of the freedmen. In addition, the returning refugees assumed that anti-secessionists and men who could prove their wartime loyalty to the Union would benefit politically more from the northern victory than unrepentant Confederates. This "extreme & radical" group of unionist refugees included Andrew J. Hamilton, a former United States congressman from West Texas whom Lincoln had appointed military governor during

---

4. Moneyhon, *Republicanism in Reconstruction Texas*, 21–41; James W. Throckmorton to Benjamin H. Epperson, January 21, 1866, in Epperson Papers.

the war. President Johnson reappointed him as provisional governor at the end of the war. When escorted in late July by federal troops to the state capitol, Hamilton had, however, hardly established himself as Sam Houston's heir to the prewar Opposition's leadership.[5]

The welcoming speech given by George W. Paschal, the well-known unionist editor and lawyer, exposed just how perplexing it would prove to change the racial views of many presumedly compassionate Texas loyalists. Paschal, who during the war had endured slander, jail, mobbing, and poverty, must have disappointed many in his audience at a flag-raising ceremony in downtown Austin by his condescending remarks to several hundred ex-slaves who had gathered at the back of the crowd. He questioned what possible interest they could have in the "old flag," reminding them that it "was never [their] emblem of liberty." After lecturing them on how they must now find a way to compensate for their "cursed awkwardness" that had "generally ruined" their former masters, Paschal concluded by telling them to go home and prepare themselves "to do better work for less pay."[6]

Even before the end of the war, disagreements among Texas tories over the inevitable redefinition of the relationship between blacks and whites had foreshadowed ominous postwar factionalism in their ranks. Former district court judge and Travis County planter John Hancock, like Hamilton, had also resigned a seat in the state legislature rather than take an oath of allegiance to the Confederacy, but he had, unlike Hamilton, voluntarily departed the South for the North to plead against a military invasion of Texas and to campaign for George B. McClellan in the 1864 presidential race. By the summer of 1865 the split between Hamilton and Hancock supporters was a recurring topic in the correspondence of prominent prewar unionists. James W. Throckmorton, an old-line Whig and Houston supporter who had acquiesced to secession only after it occurred and then subsequently served the Confederacy as Indian commissioner, favorably described Hancock as "a Copperhead Democrat," but viewed Hamilton along with most of the other returned exiles as "radical abolitionists."[7]

5. William P. Ballinger, diary entry for May 30, 1865, in Ballinger Diary and Papers; William P. Ballinger to Guy M. Bryan, June 17, 1865, in Bryan Papers; Moneyhon, *Republicanism in Reconstruction Texas,* 26–28; Marten, *Texas Divided,* 129–30.

6. James P. Hart, "George W. Paschal," *Texas Law Review,* XXVIII (November, 1949), 23–42; Frank Brown, "Annals of Travis County and of the City of Austin [from the earliest to the close of 1875]" (typescript in AHC), chap. 24, p. 41; *Southern Intelligencer* (Austin), August 11, 1865; Marten, *Texas Divided,* 64–66, 153–54.

7. Webb, Carroll, and Branda, eds., *The Handbook of Texas,* II, 763–64; James W. Throckmorton

On the day after the disintegrating Confederate forces west of the Mississippi River had capitulated to Union authorities, Governor Pendleton Murrah set aside—ironically, in light of General Gordon Granger's later-to-be-celebrated proclamation—the date of June 19 for holding an election for delegates to a state convention to reconstruct Texas into the Union. When this gimmick to avoid military occupation failed, Hancock obtained, before the arrival of federal troops, Democratic offers of support in the unreasonable belief that he might be allowed to run for governor in the regular August election. After President Johnson appointed Hamilton as provisional governor, Hancock's prewar unionist supporters hoped to use their influence to control appointments for provisional local governments. However, private statements by Throckmorton boded ill for the embryonic Opposition or Republican party movement. He had no intention of allowing his cooperation with Hamilton, whom he personally despised, to render him "abolitionized" or an accomplice "in the further humiliation & degradation of our people."[8]

In filling local offices, Hamilton had difficulty finding competent men who either were true loyalists or, if not, at least exhibited some sympathy toward the former bondsmen and white unionists. He exaggerated the number of former nonslaveholders who would be "fast friends" of Reconstruction because he convinced himself that they resented the "designing" slaveholders who had misled them during the secession crisis. Nevertheless, by the end of August the most-populated counties had newly appointed governments, more than eighty counties had at least a functioning crew of officials, and newly appointed chief justices and county clerks had initiated the process of voter registration. Although Hamilton's appointments, which approached nearly 3,000 in the fall of 1865, generated few complaints from former Confederates, he took seriously the question of whom he should allow to participate in rebuilding the state government.[9]

to Benjamin H. Epperson, August 6, 1865 [copy], in James W. Throckmorton Papers and Letter Book, BTHC; William P. Ballinger to Guy M. Bryan, June 17, 1865, in Bryan Papers.

8. Moneyhon, *Republicanism in Reconstruction Texas,* 29–30; Dallas *Herald,* June 8, 1865; James W. Throckmorton, quoted in Moneyhon, *Republicanism in Reconstruction Texas,* 29; Edward H. Cushing to Elisha M. Pease, June 12, 1865, in Pease-Graham-Niles Collection; James W. Throckmorton to Benjamin H. Epperson, January 21, 1866 [copy], and Benjamin H. Epperson to James W. Throckmorton, June 18 and 24, 1865, in Throckmorton Papers and Letter Book.

9. Andrew J. Hamilton, quoted in Nora Estelle Owens, "Presidential Reconstruction in Texas: A Case Study" (Ph.D. dissertation, Auburn University, 1983), 102, and in John Pressley Carrier, "A Political History of Texas During the Reconstruction, 1865–1874" (Ph.D. dissertation, Vanderbilt University, 1971), 7; John Conger McGraw, "The Texas Constitution of 1866" (Ph.D. dissertation, Texas

Hamilton's requirement for voter-registration officers to keep separate lists for all who had taken the general amnesty oath and a subset of these oath takers who were entitled to vote did not represent a modification of President Johnson's policies. Separate lists were necessary. If a prospective registrant fell into one of the *fourteen exceptions* of the May 29 Amnesty Proclamation, he had to file, after taking the general amnesty oath as a prerequisite first step toward full clemency, for a special presidential pardon. In addition, because an oath taker also had to meet the legal qualifications for voting under the state laws immediately in force before secession, citizenship and residency requirements could also preclude him from being placed on the voting rolls.[10]

However, by allowing voter registration officers to question those desiring amnesty about their motivations or intentions, Hamilton moved beyond President Johnson's almost mechanical granting of clemency. Evidence of rejections for "false swearing" is extremely rare, but a few insincere oath takers were rejected in Fannin County. Hamilton genuinely tried to prevent false or insincere oaths—a potential abuse that he warned could stall the process of reunification. Under discretionary powers granted him, he refused to recommend for executive clemency, in his words, "any man that I would not be willing to pardon myself were the power mine." Unlike most provisional governors, Hamilton never hesitated to inform Johnson of the uncooperative, if not altogether disloyal, sentiment that pervaded Texas. However, after the president began receiving letters of support from former secessionists, including many who initially had shared the widespread attitude that taking the oath meant swearing "that a white man smells worse than a nigger," he increasingly discounted Hamilton's counsel. Local practices also blunted Hamilton's desire to monitor the process of voter registration.[11]

County officials largely disregarded Hamilton's orders regarding voter registration. All they required, according to many loyalists, was the payment

---

Technological College, 1959), 29; William L. Richter, *Overreached on All Sides: The Freedmen's Bureau Administrators in Texas, 1865–1868* (College Station, 1991), 13.

10. Moneyhon, *Republicanism in Reconstruction Texas,* 25; Ramsdell, *Reconstruction in Texas,* 57–58, 61–62; Frances Dora Ryan, "The Election Laws of Texas, 1827–1875" (M.A. thesis, University of Texas at Austin, 1922), 44–45.

11. Moneyhon, *Republicanism in Reconstruction Texas,* 23–24, 30–31; Andrew J. Hamilton to Andrew Johnson, October 21, 1865, quoted in Michael Perman, *Reunion Without Compromise: The South and Reconstruction* (London, 1973), 125; *Daily Ranchero* (Matamoros), September 24, 1865; David Ryan Smith, "Reconstruction and Republicanism in Grayson, Fannin, and Lamar Counties, Texas, 1865–1873" (M.A. thesis, University of Texas at Austin, 1979), 29.

of "the almighty dollar" as a fee "or as a bribe." Even when officials actually administered the oath, many newly sworn men declared afterwards that they regarded it as "enforced & not binding"—enforced because they could not vote unless they took it and not binding because support for the United States Constitution now included what they believed amounted to the unlawful sanction of emancipation. Few attempts were made to exclude from the voting lists men who fell within the prohibited classes, and local officials, if they made these determinations, often discriminated in favor of former Confederates. For example, Oran M. Roberts, who had served as president of the Texas Secession Convention, was placed on the voting list in Smith County solely because he took the amnesty oath, whereas in Williamson County officials effectively disfranchised a loyalist because, after requiring him to secure an executive pardon before placing him on the voting list, they failed to process his application by election day. Of far greater irritation to Governor Hamilton were reports that unionists who had fled the state during the war and foreign-born Texans who had served in the Union army were being denied registration because of their failure to meet residency requirements or their inability to produce their discharge papers.[12]

Acting under presidential pressure to speed up the process toward Reconstruction, which he would otherwise have delayed, Hamilton in mid-November ordered the required election for delegates to a state constitutional convention. Most of the potentially qualified voters were by then apparently on the voting lists, although the calculations used to decide that a majority was registered remain unclear. The number of white men who would have been entitled to vote under antebellum laws was at this time claimed to be about 80,000, but with the advantage of hindsight obtained by extrapolations between the 1860 and 1870 federal censuses, and assuming that about three-fourths of the number of Texas adult white males would have been qualified to vote under the laws in force immediately before secession, the actual number of potentially eligible voters was probably closer to 90,000 (see Appendix). If, as Hamilton believed, "less than half of

---

12. James Jeffreys and forty-seven others to Andrew J. Hamilton, December 11, 1865, in Governors' Papers: Hamilton; Gilbert D. Kingsbury to his "Friend Webster," January 16, 1866, "Letters 1858–1872," in Kingsbury Papers; Gilbert D. Kingsbury, "Lectures on Texas: Third Lecture," 9, in Kingsbury Papers; "The State of Texas, County of Smith, Certificate of Having Taken Oath: Certificate #286," September 15, 1865, in Roberts Papers; P. H. Adams to Andrew J. Hamilton, May 7, 1866, in Governors' Papers: Hamilton; McGraw, "The Texas Constitution of 1866," 48–49. Roberts clearly fell into one of the fourteen exceptions. Cf. Lelia Bailey, "The Life and Public Career of O. M. Roberts, 1815–1883" (Ph.D. dissertation, University of Texas at Austin, 1932), 148–49.

the registered voters" participated in the selection of delegates, then voter turnout in the January, 1866, election could have been as low as 22,500. Contemporaries of the period blamed voter apathy and the severely cold weather for the disappointingly low turnout.[13]

Hamilton unsuccessfully tried to ban from candidacy, and thus from the convention, those included within the exceptions to the amnesty proclamation who had not yet received their special pardons. The Texans who went to the polls in early January of 1866 to select delegates had voted, however, with little regard for the legal status of the candidates. Assuming that the president would automatically pardon all elected delegates, most voters aspired "to be consistent" by electing, in their words, the same men "who engineered us *out*" to "engineer us *back*." When the convention assembled the following month, a group of conservative anti-Hamilton pre-war unionists held the balance of power between two antagonistic groups of delegates. Former secessionists, who had campaigned, for the most part, on the necessity of maintaining all political power in the hands of white men, constituted the first group; the second and much smaller group was made up of pro-Hamilton loyalists, who were easily distinguishable, if not defined, by their concerns, in the words of a northern observer, "for the good of the negro."[14]

Within the convention the presence of unpardoned ex-Confederates, the legality of secession, and the status of black Africans and their descendants drew heated debate. With the conservative "white-washed rebel" Throck-morton presiding, the convention declared that, because of the outcome of the Civil War, the act of secession was invalid and slavery was at an end. The delegates, however, failed to ratify or endorse the Thirteenth Amendment, which was then already part of the United States Constitution, and avoided stating that secession was essentially wrong from the beginning, or

13. *Standard* (Clarksville), December 3, 1865; Ramsdell, *Reconstruction in Texas,* 85–86; McGraw, "The Texas Convention of 1866," 51–67; *The American Annual Cyclopedia and Register of Important Events* (14 vols.; New York, 1861–1864), VIII, 729; Andrew J. Hamilton, quoted in the *Journal of the Texas State Convention, Assembled at Austin, February 7, 1866, Adjourned April 2, 1866* (Austin, 1866), 21. The assumption that only three-fourths of the adult white males would have been qualified to vote is based on the only instance in the late antebellum period of a state census of qualified voters: "Census of the State of Texas for 1858," in *The Texas Almanac for 1859,* 208–11. Correction of underenumeration problems in the 1858 state census would easily boost the percentage of adult white males who were qualified to vote in that year to 75 percent.

14. McGraw, "The Texas Constitution of 1866," 55; *Executive Record Book* [Gov. Andrew J. Hamilton], 132–33, RG 301, TSL; Owens, "Presidential Reconstruction," 123–24; Moneyhon, *Republicanism in Reconstruction Texas,* 32–33; S. Wright to Andrew J. Hamilton, January 23, 1866, in Governors' Papers: Hamilton; Benjamin C. Truman, quoted in the New York *Times,* March 11, 1866.

null and void *ab initio*. When they barred criminal penalties against anyone
for the consequences of actions carried out in compliance with orders under
Confederate authority, Hamilton, in one of his angriest speeches ever, accused them of "legislating wholesale robbery and murder." He was also
upset at the delegates for ignoring his advice on formulating a new status for
the ex-slaves. The convention went no further than to protect blacks in
their legal right to own property, and allow them to enter into contracts,
sue and be sued, and testify in cases involving only themselves or other
blacks. Failure to allow blacks to testify on an equal basis with whites meant
that, as under the old slave system, authorities could establish no crime in a
situation where "every negro in a vast congregation" had recognized an
escaping horse thief but blacks were the only witnesses. Moreover, and
ominously for the future, the convention constitutionally empowered the
legislature to institute a coercive labor system aimed at the freedmen.[15]

The resulting constitution, although containing a few progressive ad-
vances toward modernizing Texas government, was a victory for the conservative delegates, who had favored submitting, but not consenting, to the
bare minimum requirements for restoration. The convention accomplished
the goals of the extremely influential but still unpardoned Oran Roberts,
whose rallying cry had called for "the *Certain* formation of a white Man's
Gov[ernmen]t" that would "keep Sambo from the polls." Ironically, the
Hamilton, or "Radical," unionists, who had fought in the convention for
Johnson's original, although subsequently discarded, suggestion to grant
limited black suffrage based on property and literacy qualifications, wound
up bitterly opposed to the president and his policies. A loyalist refugee from
South Texas denounced the convention as a "farce," claiming that it was
"as much a Secession Convention in Sentiment as the one [in Austin] in
Jan. 1861." He and other dissident Texans hoped that the actions of the
convention would play into the hands of the radical Republicans in Congress, who were locked in a bitter battle with the president over Reconstruction policy.[16]

15. William Alexander, quoted in Owens, "Presidential Reconstruction," 133; Ramsdell, *Recon-
struction in Texas,* 96–97, 99–101, 105; Andrew J. Hamilton, quoted in the *Southern Intelligencer* (Austin),
May 24, 1866; Carrier, "A Political History of Texas," 65–66; Moneyhon, *Republicanism in Reconstruction
Texas,* 38; *Weekly State Gazette* (Austin), May 19, 1866; Charles A. Frazier, quoted in *Flake's Daily
Bulletin* (Galveston), February 25, 1866.

16. McGraw, "The Texas Constitution of 1866," 155; Oran M. Roberts, quoted *ibid.,* 142; Kings-
bury, "Lectures on Texas," 25, 28, Kingsbury Papers, BTHC; Dan T. Carter, *When the War Was Over:
The Failure of Self-Reconstruction in the South, 1865–1867* (Baton Rouge, 1985), 36; San Antonio *Express,*
May 24, 1866.

NATIONAL
Democratic Ticket

For Governor,
GEN. SAM HOUSTON.

For Lieut.-Gov.
EDWARD CLARK.

For Congress, 2nd District
A. J. HAMILTON.

For Commissioner Land Office.
S. CROSBY.
F. M. WHITE.

For State Senator,

For Representative.

For Floater,

**1859 Union Democratic,
or Opposition, ticket**

*Courtesy Texas Broadside Collection,
Eugene C. Barker Texas History Collections,
the Center for American History,
the University of Texas at Austin*

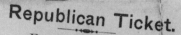

Republican Ticket.

For the Constitution.

For Governor,
GEN. EDMUND J. DAVIS

For Lieutenant Governor,
HON. J. W. FLANAGAN.

For Comptroller,
HON. A. BLEDSOE.

For Commissioner of the Land Office,
HON. JACOB KUECHLER.

For State Treasurer,
HON. GEO. W. HONEY.

For Congress, 3d District,
GEN. W. T. CLARK.

For Senator —17th Senatorial District.
W A SAYLOR.

For Representatives,
GEO T HASWELL
JOHN MITCHELL
CHARLES W GARDINER

For Sheriff,
J D NUNNELEY

For District Clerk,
W K HOMAN

For Justice of the Peace

**1869 Republican, or Radical, ticket showing
distinctive backing for ease of identification
by illiterate freedmen**

*Courtesy Orr Family Papers, Box C, Austin History Center,
Austin Public Library*

Hardin R. Runnels

*Courtesy Prints and Photographs Collection, the Center for American History,
the University of Texas at Austin [CN 01719]*

Sam Houston
Courtesy Prints and Photographs Collection, the Center for American History,
the University of Texas at Austin [CN 01469A]

Edward Clark
Courtesy Prints and Photographs Collection, the Center for
American History, the University of Texas at Austin

Francis R. Lubbock
*Courtesy Prints and Photographs Collection, the Center for American History,
the University of Texas at Austin [CN 00912B]*

Thomas J. Chambers
Courtesy Prints and Photographs Collection, the Center for American History, the University of Texas at Austin [CN 00452]

Pendleton Murrah
Courtesy Prints and Photographs Collection, the Center for
American History, the University of Texas at Austin [CN 01065]

Andrew J. Hamilton
*Courtesy Prints and Photographs Collection, the Center for American History,
the University of Texas at Austin [CN 01000]*

James W. Throckmorton
Courtesy Prints and Photographs Collection, the Center for American History,
the University of Texas at Austin [CN 03386]

Elisha M. Pease

*Courtesy Prints and Photographs Collection, the Center for American History,
the University of Texas at Austin [CN 03883]*

Edmund J. Davis
*Courtesy Prints and Photographs Collection, the Center for American History,
the University of Texas at Austin [CN 03434]*

Believing that the new southern state governments brought into existence by Johnson's policies had merely restored to leadership the same kind of men, and often the same men, who had governed during the late antebellum period, congressional Republicans refused to seat representatives from states that had completed well ahead of Texas the process outlined by the president. Then they created a Joint Committee on Reconstruction that heard overwhelming evidence regarding mistreatment of former slaves and loyalists throughout the South. The same month that the Texas constitutional convention convened, a former army officer, whose patrols had regularly been ambushed outside the town of Marshall, testified to the contempt with which community leaders regarded the Freedmen's Bureau, a government agency helping the ex-slaves make the transition from slavery to free laborers. In late 1865 in this northeastern area of Texas, where the army and the Freedmen's Bureau proved unable to establish order beyond the limits of the county seats, another bureau official claimed that "blacks are frequently beaten unmercifully, and shot down like wild beasts, without any provocation, followed with hounds, and maltreated in every way."[17]

In April, when the state constitutional convention adjourned, Congress, in response to increasing reports of violence against black and white loyalists, passed over Johnson's veto a revolutionary Civil Rights Act. The bill guaranteed citizenship and fundamental civil rights, short of suffrage, to the former slaves. Then, in the second week of June, by a straight party-line vote, Congress passed the Fourteenth Amendment. When ratified, this amendment, besides eliminating any question as to the constitutionality of the Civil Rights Act, prevented from holding state or national office anyone who had taken an oath of loyalty to the Constitution and subsequently aided the Confederacy. Not surprisingly, when Texans went to the polls in late June to vote for state and local officials, the overwhelming majority of them regarded Johnson as their only hope to protect them from, in Throckmorton's words, "the hell hounds of radicalism" who had caused an unconstitutional expansion of federal authority and blacks' rights.[18]

Preparations for the June election had originated at the constitutional convention. According to Throckmorton, the "Secession party" delegates,

17. Campbell, *A Southern Community in Crisis*, 257; Richter, *Overreached on All Sides*, 46–48; Foner, *Reconstruction*, 119; Inspector General William E. Strong, quoted in Gregg Cantrell, "Racial Violence and Reconstruction Politics in Texas, 1867–1868," *Southwestern Historical Quarterly*, XCIII (1990), 333–34.

18. Foner, *Reconstruction*, 239–61; James W. Throckmorton to Benjamin H. Epperson, January 21, 1866 [copy], in Throckmorton Papers and Letter Book.

in order to "convince the Gen[era]l Government of their earnest desire for an early restoration as well as their loyalty," decided to support anti-Hamilton unionists. This marriage of convenience witnessed the self-styled "Conservative Unionists" (or Democrats) give the gubernatorial nomination to Throckmorton because he also opposed extending additional rights to the freedmen. The isolated and discontented "Union Republicans," after they failed to get Hamilton to accept their nomination, chose Elisha M. Pease, a former Democratic governor and a steadfast unionist. Pease endorsed *ab initio,* federalism, and justice for the ex-slaves. He criticized the new state constitution for failing to share the public school fund with blacks and grant them equal testimony privileges in the courts. He hedged, however, on the issue of black suffrage, admitting that if Congress demanded it, he would acquiesce if literacy tests qualified the new voters. Holding to these extremely unpopular, although in hindsight relatively moderate, positions and lacking an organization in most counties in eastern Texas, Pease and his supporters knew that his candidacy was doomed.[19]

Convinced that a vote for the "Pease-Hamilton party" was a vote in favor of congressional Republicans who "openly proclaimed social and political equality with the negro," Texans voted four to one for Throckmorton. The Austin *Weekly State Gazette* expressed its gratitude that Pease's defeat had successfully restrained the "hand of miscegenation filth seized from the [Charles] Sumner sewer." For the Texas loyalists, however, the results were disastrous, for many of them at every level of government were now, in their words, "forced to give way to rebels" or even worse to "Union men–at–heart" types who as a matter of expediency had chosen during the war to run with "the dogs of treason." In scores of local elections the victorious Conservative Unionist candidates had put forth service to the Confederacy as their only claim for votes. Overall, Texas government was, just as congressional Republicans had anticipated, virtually restored to pre-war circumstances rather than reconstructed. Loyalists and freedmen had no illusions of being accorded justice and consideration from most county gov-

---

19. Moneyhon, *Republicanism in Reconstruction Texas,* 42–43; James W. Throckmorton to Benjamin H. Epperson, April 17, 1866 [copy], in Throckmorton Papers and Letter Book; Ramsdell, *Reconstruction in Texas,* 106, 108, 111–12; Winkler, ed., *Platforms of the Political Parties in Texas,* 97; Carrier, "A Political History of Texas," 85–88, 91–93; Benjamin Hillon Miller, "Elisha Marshall Pease: A Biography" (M.A. thesis, University of Texas, 1927), 114; Edmund J. Davis to Elisha M. Pease, July 14, 1866, cited in Ronald N. Gray, "Edmund J. Davis: Radical Republican and Reconstruction Governor of Texas" (Ph.D. dissertation, Texas Tech University, 1976), 95–96; John H. Potts to Elisha M. Pease, July 7, 1866, in Governors' Papers: Pease; Owens, "Presidential Reconstruction," 133.

ernments, most district judgeships, and the newly elected legislature. Consequently, after the results of the election were known, many blacks and loyalists were, according to Brevet Brigadier General Edgar M. Gregory, the head of the Texas Freedmen's Bureau, either "trembling for their lives" or "preparing to leave the state."[20]

Throckmorton's election represented more than a landslide victory for President Johnson's policies. It cemented a new and enduring association between many anti-secessionists and secessionists—men formerly divided in 1861. The quantitative evidence confirms that Throckmorton's candidacy forged this new alliance among the masses of voters as well as among elites. Of the 1861 anti-secessionists who in 1866 turned out and voted for governor, half of them most likely favored Throckmorton (see table 27).

Further analysis of the 1866 vote reveals that the defections from the anti-secessionist ranks were limited to a particular geographical area: the bulk of former anti-secessionists in the Conservative Unionist (commonly called "Conservative") party column was from the old Whig areas of North Texas. Here, especially among many transplanted whites of Appalachian origin, a potent Negrophobia had blended naturally with a dislike of wealthy East Texas slaveowners to produce a powerful "conditional unionism"—a desire to forgo secession until "the commission of an overt act" by the new Lincoln administration. Even if Benjamin H. Epperson, a staunch unionist and close friend of Throckmorton, had not withdrawn as the candidate for lieutenant governor on the Pease ticket and thus kept the northern counties represented on the Union Republican ballot, the outcome would not have changed. Pease failed to win 40 percent or more of the vote in any North Texas county in the Second District, which included seven counties that had voted in 1861 against secession and which was also the home of Throckmorton. The only county east of the Brazos River that failed to give Throckmorton a majority was Wood County (north of Tyler). Here, the Pease victory was an aberration accomplished by A. P. Shuford, an attorney and prominent prewar unionist who had thrown the weight of

20. *Weekly State Gazette* (Austin), May 19 (first quotation) and June 16 (third quotation), 1866; Moneyhon, *Republicanism in Reconstruction Texas,* 44–46; James W. Throckmorton to Benjamin H. Epperson, May 30, 1866 [copy] (second quotation), in Throckmorton Papers and Letter Book; Miller, "Elisha Marshall Pease," 123; M. Kreisle to Joseph J. Reynolds, November 3, 1869 (fourth quotation), Microfilm Reel #21, COCADT, RG 393, NA; Kingsbury, "Lectures, Reports and Writings," II, 36 (sixth quotation) and 39 (fifth quotation) and "Lectures on Texas," 29, in Kingsbury Papers; Campbell, *A Southern Community in Crisis,* 258–59; John L. Haynes to Charles Griffin, April 30, 1867, "List of District Judges of the State of Texas," Microfilm Reel #6, COCADT, RG 393, NA; Edgar M. Gregory, quoted in Ramsdell, *Reconstruction in Texas,* 134.

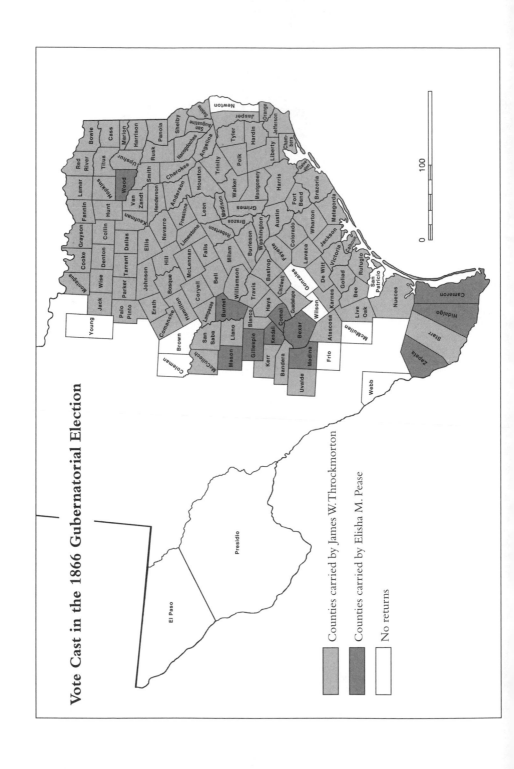

Vote Cast in the 1866 Gubernatorial Election

Counties carried by James W. Throckmorton

Counties carried by Elisha M. Pease

No returns

his influence behind the Union Republicans in the columns of his Quitman newspaper.[21]

Pease's strength came largely from foreign-born Texans residing in the western central and extreme southern regions of the state (see table 28). As anticipated, the relationships between place-of-birth variables and voting patterns in the 1866 governor's race suggest that German Texans and Mexican Texans, who as "outsiders" and, for the most part, nonslaveholders, had been lukewarm to the Confederate cause, either voted for Pease or sat out the balloting altogether. However, at the hands of all prewar nonslaveholders, Pease lost by more than a two-to-one margin. This sobering result destroyed once and for all the illusion of a prewar anti-secessionist alliance with a postwar expanded loyal yeoman class.[22]

Although most German Texans were in the ranks of the Union Republican or radical Unionist party before the formation of the Conservative Union party, their refusal to vote in the 1866 gubernatorial race for Throckmorton, a former Know-Nothing who genuinely disliked foreigners, further explains their virtual absence from his column. Throckmorton's opposition at the end of the war to schemes to promote immigration from the North and Europe had prompted him privately to accuse "sour krauts" and "swindling Yankees" of being potential "d—m—d negro worshiping skunks" who would mongrelize Texas society at the expense of "the genteel and ennobling qualities of kindness" which he believed were embodied only in "southern blood." Throckmorton's nativistic response to the foreign elements which he observed in the ranks of the Texas radicals could have possibly reinforced his own conservative stance in the postwar period.[23]

The weakness of Pease's candidacy in East Texas was due to the predictable absence from the Union Republican constituency of nearly all former secessionists (see table 27). Nor did Pease win significant support from either 1861 Edward Clark supporters or 1863 Murrah voters. Although Pease captured as many anti-secessionist voters as the Democrats or Conservative

21. Sam Houston, quoted in Gallaway, ed., *Dark Corner of the Confederacy,* 73; Ramsdell, *Reconstruction in Texas,* 111–12; William Curtis Nunn, *Texas Under the Carpetbaggers* (Austin, 1962), 7; Owens, "Presidential Reconstruction," 134; McGraw, "The Texas Constitution of 1866," 206–207; Wooster, "Ben H. Epperson," 35; Moneyhon, *Republicanism in Reconstruction Texas,* 47; A. P. Shuford to Charles Griffin, May 14, 1867, Microfilm Reel #7, COCADT, RG 393, NA; Michael Fellman, *Inside War: The Guerrilla Conflict in Missouri During the American Civil War* (New York, 1989), 7.

22. Marten, *Texas Divided,* 106–27 (quotation on p. 107).

23. James W. Throckmorton to Benjamin H. Epperson, January 21, 1866 [copy], in Throckmorton Papers and Letter Book; Carrier, "A Political History of Texas," 27; *Texas Demokrat* (Houston), December 8, 15, and 29, 1865, and January 5 and 19, 1866.

TABLE 27

ESTIMATED RELATIONSHIPS BETWEEN VOTING IN THE 1866
GUBERNATORIAL ELECTION AND VOTING IN THREE PREVIOUS ELECTIONS

(in percentages of the 1866 electorate)

The 1866 Gubernatorial Election and the 1861 Secession Referendum (Actual $N = 114$)

	Percentage Having Voted for Secession	Percentage Having Voted Against Secession	Percentage Having Not Voted in Secession Referendum	Percentage Having Been Ineligible to Vote	Totals
Throckmorton Voters	27	5	9	1	41
Pease Voters	0	5	5	0	10
Voters Not Voting for Governor	11	3	24	10	49
Totals	38	12	38	11	100

The 1861 and 1866 Gubernatorial Elections (Actual $N = 112$)

	Percentage Having Voted for Lubbock	Percentage Having Voted for Clark	Percentage Having Voted for Chambers	Percentage Having Not Voted for Governor	Percentage Having Been Ineligible to Vote	Totals
Throckmorton Voters	6	14	11	8	2	41
Pease Voters	3	0	0	7	0	10
Voters Not Voting for Governor	9	4	0	27	9	49
Totals	18	18	11	42	11	100

The 1863 and 1866 Gubernatorial Elections (Actual $N = 113$)

	Percentage Having Voted for Murrah	Percentage Having Voted for Chambers	Percentage Having Voted for Others	Percentage Having Not Voted for Governor	Percentage Having Been Ineligible to Vote	Totals
Throckmorton Voters	9	6	1	25	0	41
Pease Voters	0	3	0	8	0	10
Voters Not Voting for Governor	6	2	0	34	7	49
Totals	15	11	1	67	7	100

TABLE 27

(continued)

The 1866 Gubernatorial and 1864 Judicial Elections (Actual $N = 110$)

	Percentage Having Voted for Roberts	Percentage Having Voted for Bell	Percentage Having Not Voted in the 1864 Judicial Race	Percentage Having Been Ineligible to Vote	Totals
Throckmorton Voters	12	1	28	0	41
Pease Voters	0	5	5	0	10
Voters Not Voting for Governor	8	0	37	4	49
Totals	20	6	70	4	100

Source: For the source for the secession referendum returns, see table 7 above. For the source for the 1861 and 1863 gubernatorial and the 1864 judicial election returns, see tables 16 and 17 above. The 1866 gubernatorial election returns are taken from the MSS Election Returns for 1866, RG 307, TSL.

Note: On the procedures used to generate regression estimates of voting transition probabilities between pairs of elections, see table 2 above.

Unionists, voters who had supported Francis Lubbock in 1861 and Thomas J. Chambers in 1863 went, respectively, two to one into Throckmorton's column. Pease, however, predictably captured most of the small number of former supporters of James H. Bell, the prewar unionist turned reluctant Confederate whom voters had defeated in 1864 as a reputed "reconstructionist" candidate for chief justice of the state supreme court. Conversely, nearly all of the former 1864 anti-Bell or Roberts men who subsequently turned out and voted in the 1866 gubernatorial election favored Throckmorton.

The quantitative evidence provides a few additional clues to the collective identity, in prior and future political terms, of many Pease voters. The finding that half the Pease voters were previous Bell voters is consistent with the estimates that the bulk of the Pease supporters had not participated in the two wartime gubernatorial elections. In addition, men who had not voted, for whatever reasons, in either the 1864 judicial election or the 1861 secession referendum cast the other half the votes received by the Union Republicans. This estimate reflects the extent to which rebels intimidated foreign-born voters during the secession crisis and resulting civil war. More difficult to explain is the finding that a large proportion of the Pease men were subsequently not on the voter-registration lists, and thus disfranchised, during Congressional Reconstruction (see table 33 below).

Many Pease supporters subsequently either were denied registration as

TABLE 28

THE SOCIAL BASIS OF SUPPORT FOR THROCKMORTON AND PEASE

(by percent)

Estimated Relationships between Former Slaveownership and Voting Patterns in the 1866 Gubernatorial Election (Actual N = 112)

	Percent for Throckmorton	Percent for Pease	Percent Not Voting
All Ex-slaveholders	[81–83]	0[a]	[17–19]
Ex-Slaveholders by Number of Slaves Owned			
Large (over 20)	100[a]	0[a]	0[a]
Medium (4 to 20)	[85–88]	0[a]	[12–15]
Small (1 to 3)	73	1	26
Pre-1865 Nonslaveholders	29	13	58
All Voters[b]	41	10	49

Estimated Relationships Between Religious Affiliation and Voting Patterns in the 1866 Gubernatorial Election (Actual N = 89)

Religious Affiliation	Percent for Throckmorton	Percent for Pease	Percent Not Voting
All Other Churches	66	0	33
Baptist	60	8	32
Presbyterian	54	8	37
Methodist	48	5	47
Nothingarian	41	11	48
Disciples of Christ	31	20	49
Episcopalian	8	2	91
Roman Catholic	0[a]	[0–3]	[97–100]
Lutheran	0[a]	100[a]	0[a]
All Voters[b]	41	10	49

Estimated Relationships Between Birthplace and Voting Patterns in the 1866 Gubernatorial Election (Actual N = 105)

Place of Birth	Estimated Number of Adult Males	Percent of Adult White Males for Throckmorton	Pease	No Candidate	Percent of Disfranchised Black Adult Males
Texas	80,188	41	21	10	28
Georgia, Alabama, Mississippi, and Louisiana	35,789	7	0[a]	27	67
All Other States	40,178	[33–43]	[0–4]	[53–63]	0[a]
Germany	5,402	0[a]	[25–63]	[37–75]	0[c]
Mexico	4,727	0	[4–24]	[76–96]	0[a]
All Other Foreign Countries	2,532	0[a]	0[a]	[60–100]	[0–40]
All Places	168,816	29[b]	7[b]	36[b]	28[b]

TABLE 28

(continued)

voters under the Congressional Reconstruction Acts or refused, for whatever reasons, even to try to register to vote. Although the Pease coalition, unlike the initial postwar opposition to the Democrats in other ex-Confederate states, never attracted many former Whigs and Know-Nothings, many in the ranks of the Texas Union Republicans in 1866 could have been prewar or Confederate officeholders who believed that they would have difficulty passing any loyalty test formulated by Republicans in Congress and, therefore, voted for Pease. Knowing that a Throckmorton victory would be repugnant to northern Republicans, they hoped that a Pease administration could spare them from possible disfranchisement and prohibition from holding public office. The Pease camp repeatedly argued that the Conservatives, by refusing to grant blacks more justice and qualified suffrage, were in effect the ones pursuing the very course that would result in Congress singling out certain groups of white men for legal castigation. The immediate postwar situation was—according to Bell, who was now a candidate on the Pease ticket for the Texas Supreme Court—analogous to the secession crisis: the reactionaries, if again elected, would provoke black suffrage and white disfranchisement, "just as they accomplished the abolition of slavery while they denounced [in 1861] Mr. Pease and myself as abolitionists."[24]

Bell's argument was similar to the one made by John H. Reagan, the former postmaster general of the Confederacy, who from a Massachusetts jail cell wrote his renowned "Fort Warren" letter "To the People of Texas." Reagan bluntly asserted that a limited form of black suffrage was the only way to avoid further undesirable radical changes. Texas conservatives so censured him for this suggestion that upon his subsequent release he avoided politics until, paradoxically, his opposition to Congressional Reconstruction rehabilitated his reputation and political career. Nevertheless, Reagan's logic might have appealed to many pragmatic or apprehensive ex-Confederates who supported Pease in the hope that, by avoiding unnecessary confrontation with northern Republicans, they might enhance their chances of having or extending a career in local or state politics.[25]

Given the political uncertainty of the times, few contemporaries of the period foresaw that the 1866 campaign forged a political realignment of the white electorate that would last throughout Reconstruction. A more depressing observation, in terms of trying to envision what might have been a constructive response by Texas whites to military defeat and black emancipation, is found in the results of the simultaneous referendum balloting in the June election on the ratification of the 1866 state constitution. Voters approved the newly drafted constitution by a narrow majority. The entire revised constitution was essentially voted on and carried by a vote of 28,119 to 23,400.[26]

The choice on the bottom of the ballot allowing voters to vote either "for the amendments" or "against the amendments" attracted little attention and was not a partisan issue. Indeed, at the time of the election precisely what was being voted on and what would be the consequence of a victorious no-vote were unclear. The convention regarded as irrevocable its actions regarding secession, Confederate debt repudiation, and the freedmen. However, it submitted to the voters for approval as a single package the amendments extending terms of state officers and giving them salary increases, changing court jurisdictions to improve efficiency, requesting the

24. Moneyhon, *Republicanism in Reconstruction Texas*, 81; *Texas State Gazette* (Austin), August 1, 1866; McGraw, "The Texas Constitution of 1866," 216–17; Albert H. Latimer [and twenty-two other signees], "To the People of Texas" (Austin, n.d.), Texas Broadside Collection, BTHC; James H. Bell, quoted in the *Southern Intelligencer* (Austin), June 21, 1866.

25. Reagan, *Memoirs*, 286–95.

26. McGraw, "The Texas Constitution of 1866," 203.

governor to petition the United States government for frontier protection, and providing for a possible division of the state. Moreover, the convention resolved that these amendments, which were a subset of all the changes made by the convention, "shall present the whole Constitution as proposed to be amended." This procedure pleased the conservative delegates in the convention because voters would be forced to accept the major Reconstruction amendments or live under the 1845 Texas Constitution as it existed just before secession.[27]

The Dallas *Herald* stressed the dangers of defeating the amendments and having the antebellum state constitution remain in force. Because blacks were citizens after passage of the Civil Rights Act over President Johnson's veto, they would be able to receive under the 1845 Constitution a distribution of the school fund and, although unable to vote, would be qualified to run for public office. The only argument that the *Herald* had heard against the amendments was that increasing the salaries of judges and other state offices would, in the unlikely absence of the passage of a proposed ten-dollar occupation tax on doctors and lawyers, unduly tax "the people generally." Fainter criticism arose over the new constitution's generous arrangements, on one hand, for potential state aid to railroad corporations and closefisted provisions, on the other, for state funds for supporting public schools. Otherwise, one can search in vain in the historical record for additional reasons for voting against the amendments. Nevertheless, the small margin by which the amendments passed suggests that some unarticulated motivation for the large no-vote must have existed among the masses of voters.[28]

Although the evidence supports the claim that the counties in the Houston-Galveston commercial hub "saved" the 1866 Constitution from defeat by their "heavy" yes-vote, nothing sustains the affiliated notion that "areas with poor communications generally voted negatively." In terms of the regularity and speed of mail and stagecoach arrivals, communications were better in the counties in extreme eastern Texas, where the amendments suffered a lopsided defeat, than in the Rio Grande valley region,

27. Ramsdell, *Reconstruction in Texas,* 106; McGraw, "The Texas Constitution of 1866," 196–97; Resolution of the 1866 state constitutional convention passed on March 27, 1866, quoted in Roberts, "The Political, Legislative, and Judicial History of Texas," 154; *Journal of the [1866] Texas State Convention,* 297–300.

28. Dallas *Herald,* June 16 and May 12, 1866; James R. Arnold, letter to the Nacogdoches *Chronicle* reproduced as a broadside, May 22, 1866, in Edwards (Peyton Forbes) Family Papers, BTHC; Carrier, "A Political History of Texas," 98; Smith, "Reconstruction and Republicanism," 52.

where voters favored adoption by a large margin, or on the western frontier, where voters divided equally over adoption. An additional sifting of the evidence, however, uncovers a clear pattern in the voting on the 1866 constitutional amendments.[29]

Opposition to the new constitution was extraordinarily strong in the old small-slaveholding and pro-secessionist areas east of the Trinity River, especially in the so-called "red lands" region around the old colonial town of Nacogdoches (see tables 29 and 31). Here, in the counties sandwiched between the more cosmopolitan centers of Houston and Galveston to the south and Marshall and Jefferson to the north, the wartime supporters of defeated gubernatorial candidates, Clark and Chambers, voted heavily against the amendments (see table 30). It remains a mystery why voters in this area chose to ignore forceful arguments made by conservatives that approval of the amendments would counteract the newly enacted Civil Rights Act, thwart a possible continuation of military rule, and avoid a call for a new convention that would likely promote more unpopular changes. A potently reactionary, perhaps even pathological, resentment of the rights conferred on the emancipated slaves by the 1866 Constitution and its allowance, although highly unlikely, for legislative action in the future to let "Sambo into the Court House" far outweighed other objections, such as the unpopularity of salary increases for state officials. In this provincial area of East Texas there prevailed unequaled by other regions an anti-administration sentiment during the final years of the war, an extreme bitterness at its end over defeat, and during Reconstruction the "most intense hatred" by white Texans toward the federal government, occupying soldiers, northerners, and the freedmen.[30]

29. McGraw, "The Texas Constitution of 1866," 204.

30. Oran M. Roberts, "San Augustine and the Red Lands of East Texas: Their Early Settlement by an Intelligent Population, with Their Influence upon the Public Affairs of Texas, Both in Peace and War" (typescript in BTHC), 3–4; Carrier, "A Political History of Texas," 99; Galveston *Daily News,* April 19, 1866; Gallaway, ed., *Dark Corner of the Confederacy,* vii; Jefferson *Jimplecute,* April 28, 1866, quoted in McGraw, "The Texas Constitution of 1866," 199; Owens, "Presidential Reconstruction," 129–30; Ramsdell, *Reconstruction in Texas,* 112; and William E. Strong, quoted in Richter, *Overreached on All Sides,* 20. Idiosyncratic voting behavior above and below estimated statewide trends produced the largest percentage net gains, in terms of shares of potentially eligible voters, against the constitutional amendments in the following counties: Tyler (65 percent), Anderson (47 percent), Rusk (43 percent), San Augustine (43 percent), Panola (42 percent), Shelby (41 percent), Angelina (40 percent), Nacogdoches (38 percent), Limestone (37 percent), and Liberty (34 percent). The statewide trends are based on voting patterns in the 1863 and 1866 gubernatorial elections. For the equation predicting the percentage voting for the amendments, $R^2 = .49$, standard error $= .07$, and actual $N = 102$. For the equation predicting the percentage voting against the amendments, $R^2 = .43$, standard error $= .07$, and

TABLE 29

VOTER PARTICIPATION IN THE 1866 REFERENDUM
ON THE CONSTITUTIONAL AMENDMENTS, BY REGION

(in percentages of the 1866 regional electorates)

Region	Percentage Voting "For the Amendments"	(Difference Between Regions[a])	Region	Percentage Voting "Against the Amendments"	(Difference Between Regions[a])
Galveston-Houston Hub	35	(+11)	East Texas	33	(+14)
North Texas	29	(+5)	Western Frontier	25	(+4)
Elsewhere	26	(+1)	North Texas	24	(+4)
Western Frontier	25	(0)	Elsewhere	21	(0)
East Texas	24	(−1)	Galveston-Houston Hub	12	(−9)
Rio Grande Valley	22	(−3)	Rio Grande Valley	2	(−20)
All Texas	25		All Texas	21	

[a] The difference between regions was obtained by employing a "dummy," or nominal, variable that coded the absence or presence of the geographical characteristic (or location) of the counties. For a discussion of the regression procedure used and listings of counties included in each region, see table 3 above.
Source: The votes cast in 1866 for and against adoption of the constitutional amendments are taken from the MSS Election Returns for 1866, RG 307, TSL.

For different reasons than those held by rustic East Texas Confederate diehards, a smaller group of radical unionists also found the 1866 Constitution unpalatable. Not surprisingly, the no-vote coalition contained many Pease voters and former anti-secessionists—many of whom were, of course, the same voters (see tables 27 and 30). Most former anti-secessionists who voted on the constitutional amendments predictably voted against adoption. In spite of Pease's support for the amendments and the absence of any convincing evidence that the Union Republicans or radicals publicly opposed approval, the constitutional amendments fared worse among Pease supporters than among Throckmorton voters: Pease men were evenly split over adoption, whereas Throckmorton adherents voted in favor of the amendments at a rate of five to four. The Pease men who voted against the amendments thus constituted a small group totaling approximately 4,850 voters. They represented a beleaguered, although hardly homogeneous,

actual $N = 102$. The finding that opposition, for example, in Tyler County to the amendments profited from a 65-percentage-point advantage over the margin of support against the amendments which would have occurred had Tyler County behaved in the same way as all other Texas counties, was calculated by subtracting the below-expected turnout in the county for the amendments from the above-expected turnout in the county against the amendments.

TABLE 30

ESTIMATED RELATIONSHIPS BETWEEN VOTING IN THE 1866
CONSTITUTIONAL REFERENDUM AND VOTING IN FOUR PREVIOUS BALLOTS

(in percentages of the 1866 electorate)

The 1866 Constitutional Referendum and the 1861 Secession Referendum   (Actual $N = 106$)

	Percentage Having Voted for Secession	Percentage Having Voted Against Secession	Percentage Having Not Voted in Secession Referendum	Percentage Having Been Ineligible to Vote	Totals
Voters Voting For the 1866 Constitution	16	3	4	0	23
Voters Voting Against the 1866 Constitution	9	4	7	0	20
Voters Not Voting in the 1866 Referendum	13	5	27	11	57
Totals	38	12	38	11	100

The 1861 Gubernatorial Race and the 1866 Referendum Election   (Actual $N = 104$)

	Percentage Having Voted for Lubbock	Percentage Having Voted for Clark	Percentage Having Voted for Chambers	Percentage Having Not Voted for Governor	Percentage Having Been Ineligible to Vote	Totals
Voters Voting For the 1866 Constitution	7	4	6	6	1	23
Voters Voting Against the 1866 Constitution	0	10	4	6	0	20
Voters Not Voting in the 1866 Referendum	11	4	1	30	10	57
Totals	18	18	11	42	11	100

(continued)

radical white constituency. Although most of them believed that the conservatives were ignoring the reality of military defeat and desiring to keep blacks in a permanent state of peonage, bordering on reenslavement, through passage of harsh labor laws, others in their ranks harbored a malevolence toward former Confederates that far eclipsed any concerns that they might have had for the welfare of the ex-slaves.[31]

Radical fears were confirmed when Hamilton's elected successor, Throckmorton, downplayed stories of violence against loyalists and blacks, calling the reports exaggerations, possibly even outright falsehoods. The

31. McGraw, "The Texas Constitution of 1866," 200–203.

TABLE 30

(continued)

The 1863 Gubernatorial Race and the 1866 Referendum Election   (Actual N = 105)

	Percentage Having Voted for Murrah	Percentage Having Voted for Chambers	Percentage Having Voted for Others	Percentage Having Not Voted for Governor	Percentage Having Been Ineligible to Vote	Totals
Voters Voting For the 1866 Constitution	8	1	1	13	0	23
Voters Voting Against the 1866 Constitution	0	8	0	12	0	20
Voters Not Voting in 1866 Referendum	7	2	0	41	7	57
Totals	15	11	1	67	7	100

The 1866 Referendum Election and the 1866 Gubernatorial Election   (Actual N = 105)

	Percentage Having Voted for Throckmorton	Percentage Having Voted for Pease	Percentage Having Not Voted for Governor	Totals
Voters Voting For the 1866 Constitution	20	4	0	23
Voters Voting Against the 1866 Constitution	16	4	0	20
Voters Not Voting in 1866 Referendum	5	2	50	57
Totals	41	10	50	100

Source: For the source for the secession-referendum returns, see table 7 above; for the 1861 and 1863 gubernatorial-election returns, see tables 16 and 17 above; for the 1866 gubernatorial-election returns, see table 27 above; and for the votes cast in the 1866 constitutional referendum, see table 29 above.

new governor demanded the dismantlement of the Freedmen's Bureau, the agency which documented in the immediate postwar years hundreds of killings of blacks by whites for reasons ranging from disputing labor-contract settlements to not laboring in the manner desired by their employers. Judging blacks to be the "most inferior of God's creatures that wear the forms of men," Throckmorton believed that unless coerced, the "nigs" would not work productively or take care of themselves in their new freedom. From the moment he took office in August of 1866 to his ouster a year later as an impediment to Congressional Reconstruction, Throckmorton never doubted that "voluntary restoration" was the only viable way to reconstruct Texas. He blamed all of the state's difficulties on the Republicans or, once

TABLE 31

ESTIMATED RELATIONSHIPS BETWEEN FORMER SLAVEOWNERSHIP
AND VOTING ON THE 1866 CONSTITUTIONAL AMENDMENTS

(by percent)

	Percentage For Constitutional Amendments	Percentage Against Constitutional Amendments	Percentage Not Voting in 1866 Referendum
All Ex-slaveholders	43	36	21
Ex-Slaveholders by Number of Slaves Owned			
Large (over 20)	77	23	0
Medium (4 to 20)	44	39	18
Small (1 to 3)	34	36	29
Pre-1865 Nonslaveholders	18	15	67
All Voters[a]	23	20	57

[a] Actual, not estimated, statewide percentages of adult white males.

Source: For the source of the votes cast for and against the 1866 constitutional amendments, see table 29 above. For the source of the information on slaveholders, see table 4 above.

Note: Former "small" slaveholders are arbitrarily defined here as having held 1 to 3 slaves before June 19, 1865; "medium" as having held 4 to 20 slaves; and "large" as having held more than 20 slaves. Given these definitions and assuming that slaveholders were primarily adult white men, Texas small slaveholders represented approximately 9.3 percent of the state's adult white male population in 1860, and medium and large slaveholders constituted 9.9 percent and 2.1 percent, respectively. Lacking data on the size of slaveholder holdings after 1860, it was necessary to assume that these proportions remained the same for the period immediately after the end of the Civil War. For a discussion of the "backwards" regression procedure used to generate the above estimates, see table 4 above. Actual $N = 104$. In terms of just those voters who went to the polls and voted (as opposed to the entire electorate), the estimates above suggest that former slaveholders were divided 54 percent to 46 percent in favor of the amendments, whereas former nonslaveholders were almost identically divided, with 55 percent voting for and 45 percent voting against.

when complaining to local military authorities, entirely on "the presence of Colored troops." Failing to understand the extent of northern disillusionment that led to his removal, he accurately surmised in the wake of vacating the governor's mansion that he was "more popular with the people of Texas than any man ever was."[32]

The actions of the Eleventh Legislature confirmed northern Republican distrust of Governor Throckmorton's administration. Believing that military defeat and unqualified emancipation had already humiliated Texas enough, the lawmakers, following Throckmorton's exhortations, took no action on the Thirteenth Amendment and rejected the Fourteenth. They

32. Owens, "Presidential Reconstruction," 159–60; Campbell, *A Southern Community in Crisis,* 267–68; Barry A. Crouch, "A Spirit of Lawlessness: White Violence; Texas Blacks, 1865–1868," *Journal of Social History,* XVIII (Winter, 1984), 217–32; James W. Throckmorton to Benjamin H. Epperson, December 10 (first quotation) and January 21 (third quotation), 1866, and September 5 (fifth quotation), 1867 [copies], and James W. Throckmorton to Louis T. Wigfall, December 30 (second quotation), 1867 [copy], and James W. Throckmorton to Samuel P. Heintzelman, September 25 (fourth quotation), 1866 [copy], in Throckmorton Papers and Letter Book.

sent the arch conservative Oran Roberts to the United States Senate, proscribed the rights of white loyalists, gerrymandered many old unionist counties into districts with secessionist counties, and eliminated the districts of two Union Republican judges. The legislators wrote an elaborate and excessively harsh series of labor, vagrancy, and apprentice laws ruthlessly designed to virtually reenslave the blacks. The laws, collectively known as the Texas Black Codes and worded in nondiscriminatory language to evade a challenge to their legality posed by the Fourteenth Amendment, were as severe as those passed earlier by any other former Confederate state.[33]

At the time of the drafting of the Black Codes and against a backdrop of unpunished crimes increasingly committed against blacks, the northern Republican victories in the off-year 1866 congressional elections raised the spirits of many Texas loyalists and freedmen. Edmund J. Davis, an antisecessionist who during the war led the Union invasion of the lower Rio Grande and who had recently returned from the highly publicized Philadelphia Southern Loyalist Convention, announced that Congress would soon wrench control from the president over Reconstruction. Texas, he asserted, could anticipate an election, based on universal manhood suffrage, for delegates to another constitutional convention. His predictions proved correct. When Congress began enacting its own Reconstruction plans, it spectacularly changed the entire course of southern politics. Reconstruction subsequently proceeded under military control and with changes in voter registration that enfranchised the masses of former slaves and disfranchised most of the South's antebellum officeholders.[34]

Passed over Johnson's veto on March 2, 1867, the First Reconstruction Act divided the former Confederate states, except Tennessee, into five military districts and declared the existing civil governments in these states to be only provisional. Congress combined Texas with Louisiana into the Fifth Military District under the command of General Philip H. Sheridan. After Texans, through a convention chosen by manhood suffrage, drafted and ratified a constitution that included black suffrage, and when a new legislature adopted the Fourteenth Amendment, Congress would readmit the

33. "Message of Gov. Throckmorton, Austin, Aug. 18, 1866" (typescript in Throckmorton Papers and Letter Book); Moneyhon, *Republicanism in Reconstruction Texas,* 49–51; McGraw, "The Texas Constitution of 1866," 221–23; Carrier, "A Political History of Texas," 136–40, 164–66; James M. Smallwood, *Time of Hope, Time of Despair: Black Texans During Reconstruction* (Port Washington, N.Y., 1981), 130–31; Barry A. Crouch, "'All the Vile Passions': The Texas Black Code of 1866," *Southwestern Historical Quarterly,* XCVII (1993), 13–34.

34. Edmund J. Davis to Elisha M. Pease, November 24, 1866, in Pease-Graham-Niles Collection.

state's representatives. The supplementary Reconstruction Act of March 23 provided that an eligible voter must swear that before the war he had never held a state office or had taken an oath to support the United States Constitution and afterwards engaged in rebellion against the Union or given aid to its enemies. The act also required the army to register eligible voters and set the process in motion for the election of delegates to a constitutional convention. In a subsequent act passed on July 19, Congress granted the district military commanders the power to remove and appoint civil officials. Texas Republicans thus acquired the means to secure the patronage required in the process of party building. By the end of July, General Sheridan had removed Throckmorton and appointed Pease as provisional governor.[35]

The advent of Congressional Reconstruction shocked and angered Texas conservatives. Disregarding the four years of Civil War just ended, the Conservatives, or Democrats, now charged the northern Republicans with unleashing with "fanatical malignity" a "stupendous revolutionary scheme." Although the initial news from Washington prompted a temporary decline in violence against blacks, Freedmen's Bureau agents throughout the state continued to chronicle the many "sad complaints" of the freedmen and the routine "fearful state of things" in their respective districts. Nevertheless, inspired Pease supporters (whom, if southern by birth or long residence, the Conservatives derogatorily called "scalawags") and African Texan leaders (contemptuously called "nigs" or "niggers") along with a small, but often influential, group of newly arrived northerners (mostly former or current United States soldiers or officers whom Conservatives called "carpetbaggers") held mass meetings of blacks and formed secret local Union Leagues for mobilizing the black Republican electorate. White violence against blacks rapidly escalated and then reached its highest levels for 1867 when a biracial meeting on July 4 in Houston organized an unabashed Texas Republican party.[36]

Republican fortunes depended squarely on the leadership of the most

35. Special Order No. 105, Fifth Military District, quoted in the Dallas Herald, August 8, 1867; Smallwood, Time of Hope, Time of Despair, 132–33; Moneyhon, Republicanism in Reconstruction Texas, 68; Gray, "Edmund J. Davis," 102–103.

36. Oran M. Roberts, quoted in Bailey, "The Life and Public Career of O. M. Roberts," 199–200; Ramsdell, Reconstruction in Texas, 149; Campbell, A Southern Community in Crisis, 275; Cantrell, "Racial Violence and Reconstruction Politics," 344–46; William H. Horton to Joel T. Kirkman, June 19, 1867, Microfilm Reel #6, BRFAL, RG 105, NA; Alwyn Barr, Black Texans: A History of Negroes in Texas, 1528–1971 (Austin, 1982), 41; Smallwood, A Time of Hope, Time of Despair, 136; Harrell Budd, "The Negro in Politics in Texas, 1867–1898" (M.A. thesis, University of Texas at Austin, 1925), 13.

stouthearted of the freedmen. Black leaders were commonly the first to brave harassment when approaching the registration tables. The freedmen often had to ignore jeers and insults of angry whites in the street. In one instance within a courthouse they had to avoid white onlookers who showed their displeasure with the registration process by urinating on the floor. Republican hopes also hinged on excluding from the voting lists every unqualified ex-Confederate. The task of registering voters to participate in the election of delegates to a constitutional convention fell upon Sheridan's subordinate and close friend, Brevet Major General Charles Griffin. Like Sheridan, Griffin was a strong supporter of Congressional Reconstruction. In April, when Throckmorton was still in office, Griffin had initiated a registration directive providing for a division of the state into fifteen enrolling districts made up of county boards which in turn consisted of three registrars chosen "irrespective of color." Procedure required the local boards to move about the county to facilitate registration, keep lists of the total number of black and white registrants, record the reason for anyone whom they denied registration, and state whether they had registered all loyal voters and if not, why not. The process of registration entailed canvassing about 196,000 square miles within 126 Texas counties, which military authorities believed contained approximately 82,000 white and 42,000 black potential registrants. Griffin denied that problems had arisen in some counties in finding competent registrars who could take the required "ironclad oath" that they had never voluntarily aided the Confederacy. The oath was the "test oath" prescribed by the Act of Congress of July 2, 1862. (The vast majority of Texas white men in 1867 would not have been able to take this oath.) Griffin sanguinely anticipated an early election for convention delegates.[37]

Conservatives criticized Griffin's broad interpretation of ambiguous disfranchisement provisions of the Congressional Reconstruction laws, especially the stipulation that barred from registration former "executive and judicial officers of the state" who had held office before February 1, 1861, and then later supported the rebellion. Registration often hinged on the

37. Margaret Swett Henson and Deolece Parmelee, *The Cartwrights of San Augustine: Three Generations of Agrarian Entrepreneurs in Nineteenth-Century Texas* (Austin, 1993), 259–60; Richter, *Overreached on All Sides,* 149; Charles Griffin to Philip H. Sheridan, March 30, 1867 [copy], Microfilm Reel #1, and *Oath of Office* ["Form that must be sworn, signed, and returned to Headquarters 5th Military District at Austin"], Microfilm Reel #7, COCADT, RG 393, NA; Moneyhon, *Republicanism in Reconstruction Texas,* 70; Charles Griffin to James W. Throckmorton, April 4, 1867, Throckmorton Papers and Letter Book; and Circular No. 16, May 16, 1867, reprinted in the Dallas *Herald,* June 15, 1867.

definitions of "judicial" or "executive" officers. Griffin's explanation in a secret memorandum in May included every civil officer who had served on the federal or state level, from eminent congressmen and governors to lowly road overseers and deputy sheriffs. In late September, shortly after Griffin's death, which had been the result of a disastrous malaria epidemic, local boards reopened registration to add whites who could qualify under a new directive—one that allowed loyalists who had held office during the war years to avoid military duty to take the oath to that effect, and thus register. During a second reopening of registration in late January of 1868, the new commander of the Fifth Military District, General Winfield S. Hancock, a Democrat with presidential pretensions, issued a general order to all Texas registrars instructing them to ignore Griffin's controversial May memorandum. In practice, however, the local registration boards relied upon their own judgment in interpreting the law. They continued, for the most part, to determine loyalty under Sherman and Griffin's earlier guidelines and instructions. Decisions of the local boards were final unless appealed.[38]

When the August registration totals, compiled before the two subsequent reopenings, were first made public in late November, 1867, the low rate of white registration surprised Conservatives. They escalated their complaints about biased decisions of the boards. However, the actual extent of disfranchisement will remain a mystery, not only because Texas was one of five states that did not tabulate numbers of rejected applicants, but also because of the impossibility of discovering the number of white men who did not try to register but who, if they had tried, would have been rejected. Contemporaries of the period rarely made estimates in their localities of the size of groups comprising both rejected applicants and those whom boards would have rejected had they been faced with making determinations. The county judge of Burleson County (on the Brazos River northwest of Houston) believed that his county's "disfranchised class" was approximately sixty men—an estimate that represented just less than 6 percent of the county's adult male population. Extrapolations made here between data in the 1860 and 1870 federal censuses place the number of adult white males in Burleson County and Texas in 1868 at 1,112 and 126,939, respectively (see the Appendix). Had Burleson County been a microcosm of the entire state, the

---

38. Moneyhon, *Republicanism in Reconstruction Texas,* 70–71; Carrier, "A Political History of Texas," 225–28 (quotation on 226); Richter, *Overreached on All Sides,* 205–206; Betty Jeffus Sandlin, "The Texas Reconstruction Constitutional Convention of 1868–1869" (Ph.D. dissertation, Texas Tech University, 1970), 25–27; and Ramsdell, *Reconstruction in Texas,* 195–96.

number of men effectively disfranchised statewide would have been close to 7,000—an estimate in line with the 7,500 claimed at the time by the Republicans.[39]

The initial registration figures showed 57,368 whites registered throughout the state. By the close of the extended registration on January 31, 1868, the white total rose slightly to 60,445, but fell short by 900 of the total vote cast in the 1866 Throckmorton-Pease contest. With the exceptions of Trinity County (northeast of Huntsville), where many whites were "stricken off" the voting lists, and Jack County (on the northwestern frontier), where white registration dramatically increased, the relative positions of counties ranked by their registration rates changed little between August and the end of January. On the eve of the election of delegates to a new constitutional convention, local boards had registered less than half the adult white male population. When they reopened registration lists in 1869, the percentage of the Texas adult white males who were registered climbed to slightly more than 60 percent. This increase suggests that whites had been in 1867 and 1868 somewhat underregistered—a situation that does not mean, however, that biased decisions by local boards had suppressed earlier levels of registration to a greater extent than white indifference or opposition to the registration process itself. Estimates of voting patterns between the 1866 governor's race and subsequent voting in elections supervised by military authorities in 1868 and 1869 suggest that as high as 12,694 men who voted in the Throckmorton-Pease contest were not, for whatever reason, on the voter registration lists by the end of January, 1868. At the time of the 1869 election, as many as 5,187 of them had not been issued voter-registration certificates (see tables 33 and 37 below).[40]

County-by-county registration data tell more about the registration than statewide totals do. Although analyzing county-by-county statistics cannot

39. A. W. McGuire [?] to James W. Throckmorton, May 2, 1867 [copy], Microfilm Reel #8, COCADT, RG 393, NA; Austin *Republican,* November 27, 1867; Carrier, "A Political History of Texas," 229; Forrest G. Wood, "On Revising Reconstruction History: Negro Suffrage, White Disfranchisement, and Common Sense," *Journal of Negro History,* LI (April, 1966), 106; "Number of White and Colored Voters Registered in Each of the States Subject to the Reconstruction Acts of Congress, with Other Statistics Relative to the Same Subject," *Senate Executive Documents,* Doc. 53, 40th Cong., 2nd Sess., Serial 1317, pp. 1–12.

40. United States Army, Fifth Military District, State of Texas, General Order No. 73, *Tabular Statement of Voters (White and Colored) Registered in Texas at Registration in 1867, and at Revision of the Lists in 1867–'68–'69; Showing Also the Number (White and Colored) Stricken Off the Lists. Tabular Statement of Votes (White and Colored) Cast at Election Held in the State of Texas, Under the Authority of the Reconstruction Acts of Congress* (hereinafter cited as *Tabular Statement of Registration and Voting*), Austin: April 16, 1870, pp. 2–5; Ryan, "The Election Laws of Texas," 58.

resolve the question of unfairness or laxness in allowing whites to register, it is, nevertheless, possible to probe more systematically the issue of disfranchisement by taking into account the expected, or "normal," level of white registration for each county at each of the three times when military authorities made the voting lists public. The expected level of registration among adult white males is based here on four critical characteristics of each county: its rate of voter turnout in the 1866 Throckmorton-Pease election, the percentage of its adult white male population who were United States citizens in 1870, the foreign-born percentage of its population in 1870, and the black percentage of its population in 1870 (see table 32).

When the level of white registration is regressed upon these four variables, the resulting equation produces a predicted level of registration that is a weighted linear composite of the independent variables. Because the sole purpose of using a regression equation as it is employed here is to predict a particular level at which adult white males turned out to register and received voting certificates, the high degree of multicollinearity that exists between the citizenship and immigrant percentages poses no problem: in the case of "predicting" registration levels, as opposed to "explaining" them by determining which factors best account for the variation in registration rates, the relative magnitudes of the coefficients are ignored. The predicted levels of registration express whatever sources of variance in white registration are due to prior voter turnout in the 1866 governor's race, to the extent to which the racial composition of the county influenced whites to register, and to the absence of adult males from the voting lists due to their status as immigrants or aliens. Therefore, if the predicted levels are subtracted from the actual white registration levels, the remainders, or residual values, should express sources of variance other than those due to prior turnout and the presence of blacks, immigrants, and aliens. Counties with the highest residual values must be suspected of being localities where whites were more assertive in trying to register or local registration boards were more lax in the awarding of registration certificates, or some combination of the two. On the other hand, counties with the lowest values must be considered as places where whites were more apathetic or embittered about the enrolling process or where local boards were more rigorous in their examination of prospective registrants.

The most important observation to be made from the data on actual and predicted levels of white registration is that no support exists for the conventional wisdom that white disfranchisement was, except for a handful

TABLE 32

MILITARY REGISTRATION AND DISFRANCHISEMENT:
ACTUAL AND PREDICTED LEVELS OF WHITE-VOTER REGISTRATION
IN TEXAS COUNTIES IN 1867, 1868, AND 1869, BY REGION

(in percentages of adult white males)

County	Percentage of Adult White Males Registered			Residual Values for Percentage of Adult Males Registered[a]		
	1867	*1868*	*1869*	*1867*	*1868*	*1869*
East Texas						
Lower Trinity River, including the Beaumont-Woodville Area						
Chambers	58	62	80	22	25	30
Hardin	52	53	71	7	8	14
Jasper	58	65	85	1	6	10
Jefferson	31	34	57	−12	−9	0
Newton	27	47	75	—	—	—
Orange	37	44	86	−5	2	32
Polk	47	51	77	−4	−2	7
Trinity	65	45	73	11	−10	5
Tyler	37	38	50	−6	−5	−6
Northeastern East Texas, including the Marshall-Jefferson Area						
Bowie	59	61	70	7	7	0
Cass	74	79	93	20	23	23
Harrison	73	78	95	20	22	21
Henderson	60	60	65	5	4	−4
Hopkins	65	63	70	8	5	0
Marion	43	42	71	−0	−3	10
Panola	62	62	68	14	12	4
Rusk	62	59	74	12	7	7
Smith	50	53	62	−6	−6	−12
Titus	65	65	72	13	12	5
Upshur	67	69	87	13	13	16
Van Zandt	55	53	69	0	−2	2
Wood	62	63	57	10	11	−8
Central East Texas, including the Nacogdoches-Hemphill Area						
Anderson	66	74	94	7	12	16
Angelina	59	63	82	5	8	15
Cherokee	77	82	98	20	23	25
Houston	57	67	96	−1	6	20
Nacogdoches	64	59	70	13	7	4
Sabine	68	68	100	18	16	34
San Augustine	64	69	86	10	13	14
Shelby	63	64	80	5	5	7

(continued)

TABLE 32

(continued)

County	Percentage of Adult White Males Registered			Residual Values for Percentage of Adult Males Registered[a]		
	1867	*1868*	*1869*	*1867*	*1868*	*1869*
Galveston-Houston Commercial Hub						
Austin	43	51	57	−6	−1	−11
Brazoria	36	39	57	−16	−17	−18
Brazos	32	39	66	−13	−7	5
Colorado	57	60	98	−1	−2	21
Fort Bend	32	40	66	−26	−22	−15
Galveston	26	27	48	−0	−0	9
Grimes	45	50	68	−7	−5	−4
Harris	40	44	53	−8	−7	−12
Liberty	56	56	79	2	−1	7
Madison	53	53	71	4	2	6
Montgomery	63	64	81	−3	−5	−5
Walker	33	40	66	−18	−14	−6
Washington	43	44	61	−3	−5	−4
Wharton	65	74	94	−8	−5	−5
North Texas						
Collin	51	52	57	−0	0	−6
Cooke	49	51	58	−6	−4	−9
Dallas	36	36	52	−16	−16	−13
Denton	64	64	70	9	8	3
Fannin	55	54	62	−1	−3	−7
Grayson	39	41	47	−9	−8	−9
Hunt	48	48	62	−2	−3	−0
Kaufman	47	48	70	−13	−13	−3
Lamar	66	65	72	10	8	1
Red River	71	73	80	8	7	−1
Tarrant	54	57	84	−2	0	17
Rio Grande Valley						
Cameron	8	10	21	7	7	9
El Paso	39	42	68	—	—	—
Hidalgo	11	10	15	−13	−17	−21
Kinney	8	7	6	—	—	—
Maverick	5	5	9	—	—	—
Nueces	27	28	46	1	−1	6
Presidio	6	6	12	—	—	—
San Patricio	42	48	55	—	—	—
Starr	3	4	10	−3	−5	−8
Webb	5	5	23	—	—	—
Zapata	17	16	19	11	8	2

TABLE 32

(continued)

	Percentage of Adult White Males Registered			Residual Values for Percentage of Adult Males Registered[a]		
County	*1867*	*1868*	*1869*	*1867*	*1868*	*1869*
Western Frontier						
Bandera	51	64	85	10	22	32
Brown	85	99	100	—	—	—
Comanche	56	61	81	−10	−6	3
Erath	63	68	83	−3	1	5
Gillespie	55	57	69	14	13	14
Hamilton	80	78	89	6	2	2
Jack	26	44	77	−14	4	25
Kerr	46	48	70	0	1	12
Llano	49	48	69	0	−1	9
Mason	77	84	98	33	37	40
Montague	82	83	100	20	20	26
Palo Pinto	27	33	57	—	—	—
Parker	53	58	85	−11	−8	8
San Saba	61	63	61	4	5	−8
Uvalde	56	61	67	21	26	21
Wise	46	60	83	−15	−2	10
Elsewhere						
Austin-Bastrop-Georgetown Area						
Caldwell	53	54	78	−3	−5	4
Bastrop	56	56	70	−3	−7	−8
Blanco	43	46	53	−9	−7	−11
Burleson	52	52	69	−1	−3	−0
Burnet	47	48	54	−0	1	−5
Fayette	55	58	68	10	10	6
Hays	45	48	68	2	4	11
Milam	61	61	66	13	12	3
Travis	28	29	41	−17	−17	−20
Williamson	56	60	75	−3	−0	3
San Antonio Area						
Atascosa	56	54	72	9	6	12
Bexar	33	38	52	−11	−9	−7
Blanco	43	46	53	−9	−7	−11
Comal	62	62	69	19	16	12
Gonzales	72	74	86	—	—	—
Guadalupe	60	60	77	3	−0	2
Karnes	44	51	68	−8	−4	1
Kendall	49	48	61	4	−1	1
Medina	46	52	64	4	7	8
Wilson	41	42	64	—	—	—
Matagorda Bay and South Central Area						
Bee	40	41	53	−4	−7	−8
Calhoun	30	34	51	−9	−7	−3
De Witt	55	56	64	12	12	7

(continued)

TABLE 32

(continued)

County	Percentage of Adult White Males Registered			Residual Values for Percentage of Adult Males Registered[a]		
	1867	1868	1869	1867	1868	1869
Matagorda Bay and South Central Area (continued)						
Goliad	56	59	73	4	5	6
Jackson	63	75	89	15	25	23
Lavaca	65	66	81	9	7	9
Live Oak	42	42	63	0	−0	11
Matagorda	40	40	50	−13	−17	−24
Refugio	28	28	32	−15	−16	−24
Victoria	42	47	55	−2	1	−6
Waco and North Central Area						
Bell	36	36	50	−12	−12	−10
Bosque	35	36	47	−10	−10	−10
Coryell	55	56	70	6	7	10
Ellis	46	49	65	−4	−2	2
Falls	42	40	56	−3	−7	−6
Freestone	43	44	78	−8	−9	10
Hill	42	41	52	−3	−4	−4
Hood	50	53	83	—	—	—
Johnson	48	49	72	−8	−8	4
Lampasas	51	52	83	−10	−10	10
Leon	57	61	97	9	12	33
Limestone	41	41	53	−3	−3	−4
McLennan	46	49	64	−1	2	1
Navarro	38	44	48	−10	−5	−14
Robertson	39	38	53	−7	−10	−11
Statewide						
All Counties	46	48	61	0	0	0

[a] A dash has been entered where incomplete or missing data prevented computation of residual values.

Note: The percentages of adult white males who were registered in each county in 1867, 1868, and 1869 were computed by dividing the respective numbers of registered voters by estimates of the adult male populations in 1867, 1868, and 1869. Straight-line extrapolations made on data in the 1860 and 1870 federal censuses generated the size of the potential white electorate in each Texas county for these three years. The percentages of adult white males who were registered were regressed upon the percentage foreign-born in 1870, the percentage black in 1870, the percentage of adult males who were United States citizens in 1870, and the turnout rate of potentially eligible voters in the 1866 gubernatorial election. Statewide, voter turnout in 1866 equaled 52.2 percent, the black component of the Texas population in 1870 was 30.9 percent, the percentage of adult males who were citizens in 1870 was 89.5 percent, and the foreign-born constituted 7.6 percent of the total population. The equations, run separately for each year, were weighted by the respective estimate of the potential white electorate. For the equation predicting the percentage of white adult males who were registered in 1867, $R^2 = .59$, standard error $= .07$, and actual $N = 115$; for 1868, $R^2 = .61$, standard error $= .07$, and actual $N = 115$; and for 1869, $R^2 = .58$, standard error $= .08$, and actual $N = 115$.

Source: White registration data are taken from United States Army, Fifth Military District, State of Texas, General Order No. 73, *Tabular Statement of Voters (White and Colored) Registered in Texas at Registration in 1867, and at Revision of the Lists in 1867–'68–'69; Showing Also the Number (White and Colored) Stricken Off the Lists. Tabular Statement of Votes (White and Colored) Cast at Election Held in the State of Texas, Under the Authority of the Reconstruction Acts of Congress* (hereinafter cited as *Tabular Statement of Registration and Voting*) (Austin: April 16, 1870), pp. 2–5. Data in the 1870 federal census were used to estimate the size of the potential electorate in each Texas county. For the numbers of adult male citizens, foreign-born persons, and black persons in 1870, see U.S. Census Bureau, *Ninth Census, 1870: Population,* tables 2, 5, and 24. For the source of the 1866 gubernatorial election returns, see table 27 above.

of counties, "spread fairly evenly over the state."[41] On the lower parts of the Brazos and Colorado Rivers and within the nexus of the Galveston-Houston commercial hub were localities, with the exception of peripheral Madison County, with unexpectedly low percentages of their adult white male populations on the registry lists. White registration was also demonstrably low in a group of counties centered around McLennan (Waco) in north Central Texas, although McLennan itself and neighboring Coryell were exceptions. On the other hand, in the East Texas "red lands" region around Nacogdoches, where opposition to the 1866 constitution had been especially intense and brutalities against the freedmen were common occurrences, the numbers of whites granted voter certificates were higher than would be expected. With the exceptions of Smith (Tyler), Marion (Jefferson), and Van Zandt Counties, the regression equation similarly underpredicted rates of white registration in counties constituting the entire northeastern part of the state. The explanation for this regional variation in white registration rates remains elusive.

In 1868 all the counties within the Galveston–Houston commercial hub, with the exception again of Madison, had black majorities registered, whereas in the Nacogdoches area, similar circumstances existed in only Houston, Newton, and San Augustine Counties. One could thus hypothesize that whites residing in predominately black counties despaired of registering because they knew that they had, in the face of solid black voting blocs, little chance of carrying local offices for Conservative or anti-Republican candidates. This explanation for variations in white disfranchisement throughout the state must, however, be embraced cautiously, because the residual values for all Texas counties contain all of the information on the ways that the percentage of black people in a county's population fails to predict the rates at which whites were converted into registrants. Nor can dissimilar rates of growth in the adult white male population explain the variation from one region to another in the levels of white disfranchisement, because the rate at which whites were registered is calculated here from estimates of the *potential* white electorate. The estimates thus had already incorporated information on declines or increases in the white population.[42]

41. Carrier, "A Political History of Texas," 233.
42. *Tabular Statement of Registration and Voting,* 2–5. A few counties in extreme northeastern Texas, such as Bowie, Harrison, and Rusk, also had white minorities registered in 1868, but have positive residuals for the percentage of adult white males registered (see table 32 above).

Reports from voter registrars in the Galveston-Houston area offer a few explanations why in this region many potential white registrants were not on the voting lists by the end of January, 1868. Apathy in Burleson County stemmed partly from "sullenness" and partly from the belief that there would soon be no difference between those who were registered and those who were not. This conviction hinged on the assumption that, once the work of the new constitutional convention became public, the overwhelming majority of whites would flock to the anti-Republican camp. In Brazoria County the local board had denied registration to twelve white applicants when statewide totals were first promulgated, but approximately two-thirds of the county's whites had not even tried to register. "False pride," indifference, disgust at the sight of a black board member at the registration tables, and "a dislike to accept what many consider[ed] humiliating terms" had kept them away.[43]

Why did not similar sentiments in the counties in extreme northeastern Texas keep whites away from the registration tables? Perhaps in this region the higher levels of unchecked white violence against blacks and the relative lack of effective Union League organization encouraged local whites to register. Or perhaps whites with "pliant consciences" justified making false oaths before local boards in order to prevent affairs from falling into the hands of blacks and scalawags. One thing is clear: on the eve of the constitutional convention election in this region—an area where the army and Freedmen's Bureau agents often exercised scant control outside the county seats—white disfranchisement was nominal and hardly severe.[44]

To the same extent that conservatives exaggerated the number of whites denied registration, they insisted that the number of blacks registered was excessive—a charge echoed by historians for generations. Both the qualitative and quantitative evidence, however, offer little support for this complaint. The Dallas *Herald* claimed that black registration should have totaled no more that 35,000—an approximation which fell 7,000 below the initial estimate made by military authorities. If the researcher (1) assumes that the wartime legislatures levied taxes on slaves in the same manner as in 1860,

43. M. H. Addison to Jesse Stancel, August 8, 1867 (first quotation), and Hennell Stevens to Commanding General, District of Texas, October 3, 1867 (third quotation), Microfilm Reel #7, COCADT, RG 393, NA; Galveston *Daily News,* July 1, 1867 (second quotation); Ramsdell, *Reconstruction in Texas,* 193–94.

44. D. W. Steele to Charles Griffin, August 27, 1867, Microfilm Reel #7, COCADT, RG 393, NA; Campbell, *A Southern Community in Crisis,* 268; Richter, *Overreached on All Sides,* 47, 112–13, 166–67.

(2) factors in the best estimates of the number of slaves "refugeed" to Texas during the war (for safekeeping when Union troops overran neighboring southern states), and (3) extrapolates from data in the 1860 and 1870 censuses, but acknowledges problems caused by the underenumeration of blacks in the latter census, then the best estimate of the number of adult black males in Texas in 1868 is about 56,500 (see Appendix).[45]

Thus, by the end of January, 1868, local boards throughout the state had registered about 89 percent of the black adult males, or 49,550 freedmen. This figure revealed considerable Republican success, often in the face of white violence and intimidation, in mobilizing the freedmen to register. Black majorities existed, however, in only 33 of 126 counties, and, more significantly, for determining the calculus of electoral politics, the total number of white registrants outnumbered blacks by 10,895. Texas was one of five unreconstructed states in which whites were a majority of registrants. Moreover, the disparity between the white and black populations was increasing in the postwar period due to the heavy immigration of whites. The Conservative press confidently predicted that, in spite of the current "unsettled" nature of state politics, demography would eventually make Texas solidly Democratic.[46]

A common charge made by Conservatives, or Democrats, was that blacks had been "registered with little regard to age." Although Collin County (north of Dallas) had registered on the eve of the constitutional convention referendum only 76 percent of its potentially eligible freedman—a percentage below the statewide rate—former governor Throckmorton accused the local board of registering "every Negro 16 years old & upward." At the same time in Galveston County (Galveston) virtually all the potentially eligible blacks were registered, but when evidence demonstrated that officials had allowed a seventeen-year-old black male to register, the president of the local board arrested him for violating his oath. Authorities brought the young man before the board, made him surrender his certificate, and placed him in the custody of the chief of police. No evidence exists to suggest that local boards knowingly registered more blacks than were legally qualified. To the contrary, local registration boards frequently stuck to the letter of the law. For example, they routinely barred from registration any

45. Houston *Weekly Telegraph,* December 3, 1867; Dallas *Herald,* December 21, 1867; Ramsdell, *Reconstruction in Texas,* 196; Charles Griffin to Philip H. Sheridan, March 30, 1867 [copy], Microfilm Reel #1, COCADT, RG 393, NA.

46. *Tabular Statement of Registration and Voting,* 5; *The Harrison Flag* (Marshall), February 29, 1868; Moneyhon, *Republicanism in Reconstruction Texas,* 71.

black man who had not yet adopted a surname. In one instance, a local board refused registration to some two hundred blacks who were born in Africa because the United States government had not naturalized them. The board eventually permitted the African-born men, who were "considered among the most industrious and reliable of the colored population," to register, but not until after the balloting for or against calling a convention and the simultaneous election of convention delegates.[47]

The balloting was held on five consecutive days, February 10 to 14, in only the county seats, where troops had been instructed to stay away from the polls unless needed to restore order. The self-styled "Conservatives," a coalition that included virtually all Democrats and others unwilling to accept any ex-slave as their equal before the law, abandoned the idea of boycotting the election. The requirement that a majority of registered voters had to approve a convention call had initially dictated the boycott strategy. The Conservatives now called for white Texans to register, if possible, and vote against holding a convention and for delegates who favored creating a constitution without black suffrage. While the Conservatives hoped to prevent the "Africanization of the state," the Republicans endorsed the Congressional Reconstruction Acts, including black suffrage and white disfranchisement. The two sides thus stood for antithetical convictions and beliefs. This situation proved to be a prescription for white intimidation and terrorization of blacks.[48]

Contrary to the widely held notion that the election "passed off more quietly than might have been expected," attacks on the freedmen during the campaign and the election, and reprisals upon them immediately afterward, were the most murderous, brutal, and extensive of the entire 1867–1868 period. In Wood County assailants killed and wounded several people at a Republican rally for the party's candidate for the convention. In Harrison County the Conservative press played down an assassination attempt of a Republican candidate and supported local planters who refused to hire blacks who belonged to the "diabolical" Republican party Union League. In San Augustine County (east of Nacogdoches) attackers armed with

47. John Hancock to Winfield S. Hancock, December 23, 1867, quoted in Carrier, "A Political History of Texas," 227–28; James W. Throckmorton, quoted in Sandlin, "The Texas Reconstruction Constitutional Convention," 24; William Parker to Charles Griffin, June 24, 1867, and Julius Schutze to Charles Griffin, April 10, 1867, and Hennell Stevens to Commanding General, District of Texas, October 3, 1867, Microfilm Reel #7, COCADT, RG 393, NA; Hennell Stevens to Elisha M. Pease, January 23, 1868, in Governors' Papers: Pease; Sibley, Travelers in Texas, 142–43.

48. Dallas Herald, February 8, 1868; Carrier, "A Political History of Texas," 235–41.

"Knives, Pistols, and Shot guns" broke the windows of the polling place, shot one black voter, and threatened others. In Bastrop County (southeast of Austin) a hostile crowd harassing black voters forced authorities to suspend the balloting. After the balloting in Smith County, blacks who "took too much interest in the late election" were systematically singled out for retribution.[49]

Despite widespread intimidation, Republican mobilization of the freedmen had been a success. Texas blacks flocked to the polls and voted in large enough numbers to validate the holding of the constitutional convention. They also boldly discounted the advice of moderate Republicans by electing nine members of their own race as delegates to the convention. On the days of the election when blacks arrived en masse to vote, many county seats had the look of what one observer called an "African settlement." In Travis County a group of Webberville blacks, dramatically led by their leader holding a sword and the national flag, came to the polls armed and on horseback. Blacks residing in county seats often housed their counterparts who had traveled from the countryside to vote. To the disgust of Conservatives in Harrison County, blacks were "marched by the platoons" from the surrounding farms to the polling place. Upon their arrival, the local postmaster handed their leaders "Radical" ballots stamped on the back with "the United States Post Office stamp" so that the illiterate among their followers would be able to identify them as genuine Republican tickets.[50]

The call for a convention passed by a vote of 44,683 for to 11,441 against, with 51 percent of the registered voters—just enough to ensure a convention—participating in the referendum election. White registrants avoided the polls in droves: over two-thirds of them sat out the referendum balloting. The turnout showed that most Texas whites did not consider that they had a genuine voice in the election or that they simply did not care. The pro-Conservative press was forced to acknowledge that the Republicans had, in effect, won by default. Of the whites who voted, only 7,750 favored

49. Ramsdell, *Reconstruction in Texas,* 198; Cantrell, "Racist Violence and Reconstruction Politics," 349; Moneyhon, *Republicanism in Reconstruction Texas,* 77–78; *Harrison Flag* (Marshall), January 4 and February 15, 1868; William Phillips to Elisha M. Pease, February 10, 1868, quoted in Sandlin, "The Texas Reconstruction Constitutional Convention," 35; Albert A. Metzner to J. P. Richardson, February 21, 1868, Microfilm Reel #13, and Gregory Barrett, Jr., to J. P. Richardson, April 21, 1868, Microfilm Reel #10, BRFAL, RG 105, NA.

50. *Weekly Austin Republican,* December 18, 1867; *Flake's Daily Bulletin* (Galveston), March 7, 1868; John P. Osterhout, quoted in Randy J. Sparks, "John P. Osterhout, Yankee, Rebel, Republican," *Southwestern Historical Quarterly,* XC (1986), 134; Moneyhon, *Republicanism in Reconstruction Texas,* 78; *Harrison Flag* (Marshall), February 15, 1868.

calling a convention, whereas 10,623 voted against holding it. The comparable figures for the blacks who voted were 36,933 in favor and only a paltry 818 against. More than three-fourths of the black registrants participated in the referendum election. Moreover, in only a handful of counties had fraud and intimidation played a role in reducing the black vote or misrepresenting black voter intentions.[51]

Almost half the black votes cast against calling a convention emanated from Anderson (Palestine), Cherokee (Rusk), and Panola (Carthage) Counties. Most of the 393 black votes cast against a convention in these three adjoining counties in extreme northeast Texas were fraudulent. In Anderson County the presiding officer of the election, with the help of one member of the registration board, opened the ballot boxes at night and changed the results. They allegedly disposed of 276 votes cast for the Republican candidates and added in roughly this number for their opponents, resulting in the election of two Conservative delegates from Anderson and Henderson Counties. In Cherokee County an extraordinarily low percentage of black registrants turned out to vote and most of them were, according to a local Republican, "forced to vote contrary to their wishes." Few blacks voted also in Panola County, where lynchings of freedmen were so commonplace that the local Freedmen's Bureau agent admitted that "it would have been a waste of time" for him to investigate them. Among Panola County blacks who turned out and voted, almost half of them incongruously voted against holding a convention and against two of their own race, Mitchell Kendall and Wiley Johnson, for delegates. Nonetheless, Kendall and Johnson, along with a scalawag and a carpetbagger, were elected convention delegates on the Republican ticket solely on the strength of the united black vote in neighboring Harrison County (joined with Panola for the purpose of electing delegates). The assumption that in Panola County a "good many negroes" freely voted the Conservative ticket is ludicrous.[52]

More ominous for Texas Republicans than intimidation of black voters or Union League disorganization was the disappointingly few whites who

51. *Tabular Statement of Registration and Voting*, 6–9; *Harrison Flag* (Marshall), February 22, 1868.

52. William V. Tunstall to Joseph J. Reynolds, March 26, 1868, in Governors' Papers: Pease; John H. Morrison to HFMD, June 23, 1869, Microfilm Reel #3, and John H. Morrison and others to HFMD, December 6, 1869, Microfilm Reel #24, COCADT, RG 393, NA; W. W. Waddell to Joseph J. Reynolds, October 5, 1869, Microfilm Reel #10, COCADT, RG 393, NA; Richter, *Overreached on All Sides,* 166–67; Brevet Captain Charles Rand, quoted in James Smallwood, "When the Klan Rode: White Terror in Reconstruction Texas," *Journal of the West,* XXV (October, 1986), 6; *Harrison Flag* (Marshall), February 22, 1868; Secretary of State, MSS Election Returns for 1868, RG 307, TSL; Campbell, *A Southern Community in Crisis,* 285–86.

voted for calling a convention. It is estimated here that most of the 7,750 whites favoring a convention were, not surprisingly, former 1861 anti-secessionists or 1866 Pease voters (see table 33). Yet only about two-fifths of the 1866 Pease constituency had turned out and voted for calling a convention. (By way of comparison, 75 percent of the 1868 black registrants had voted for holding a convention.) The remainder of whites voting "yes" in 1868 consisted of as high as 1,200 former Throckmorton supporters and as high as 2,600 men who had not voted in the 1866 governor's race. The bottom line, however, was that the Republicans had not been able to maintain their hold on the 1866 Union Republicans who had voted for Pease. This was a distressing sign for a party that had to expand its support among whites in order to build a successful biracial coalition.

With the election to the state constitutional convention of twelve Conservative and seventy-eight Republican delegates, including among the latter sixty-four scalawags, nine blacks, and six carpetbaggers, the Republicans had an opportunity to dominate the convention and write a constitution that would win support among white moderates and conservatives. Although the party's showing among white voters had been discouraging, its leaders hoped that, once Americans settled the issues of race and Reconstruction, the reassertion of antebellum economic and geographical divisions would cleave many repoliticized white Texans into the anti-Democratic column. This scenario was, however, extremely optimistic. In the spring of 1868 many things militated against the ability of the Texas Republicans to construct a viable broad-based and biracial coalition to challenge the Democrats.[53]

Republican party disadvantages were numerous. Military removals of local officials hostile to Congressional Reconstruction had proceeded slowly, leaving Republicans with only superficial power in many counties and, overall, in firm command of less than one-fifth of the state's officeholders. Moreover, many military-appointed officials, although often undisputed loyalists, were not always sympathetic toward the aspirations of the freedmen. In many counties the judicial system offered blacks virtually no protection for their "life, limb or property." In a few instances, even the detachments of soldiers stationed in the county seats were indifferent or even unfriendly to scalawags and freedmen. Former Confederate use of

53. Sandlin, "The Texas Reconstruction Constitutional Convention," 36–42; Ramsdell, *Reconstruction in Texas*, 200–201; Edmund J. Davis to Elisha M. Pease, March 8, 1868, in Governors' Papers: Pease.

TABLE 33

ESTIMATED RELATIONSHIPS BETWEEN VOTING ON 1868 CONSTITUTIONAL
CONVENTION AND VOTING IN TWO PREVIOUS BALLOTS

(in percentages of 1868 white adult males)

The 1861 Secession and 1868 Convention Referenda   (Actual N = 120)

	Percentage Having Voted for Secession	Percentage Having Voted Against Secession	Percentage Having Not Voted in Referendum	Percentage Having Been Ineligible to Vote	Totals
Voters Voting For Holding a Convention	0	3	3	0	6
Voters Voting Against Holding a Convention	5	1	3	0	9
Voters Registered But Not Voting	18	6	8	2	34
Adult White Males Not Registered	13	2	23	13	51
Totals	36	12	37	15	100

The 1866 Gubernatorial Election and the 1868 Convention Referendum   (Actual N = 116)

	Percentage Having Voted for Throckmorton	Percentage Having Voted for Pease	Percentage Having Not Voted in the 1866 Governor's Race	Percentage Having Been Ineligible to Vote	Totals
Voters Voting For Holding a Convention	1	4	2	0	6
Voters Voting Against Holding a Convention	9	0	0	0	9
Voters Registered But Not Voting	25	2	7	0	34
Adult White Males Not Registered	6	4	37	4	51
Totals	41	10	46	4	100

Source: For the source for the 1861 secession referendum returns, see table 7 above. For the source of the 1866 gubernatorial returns, see table 27 above. The votes cast by white men in 1868 for and against holding a convention and the number of white voters registered under the authority of the Congressional Reconstruction Acts are taken from *Tabular Statement of Registration and Voting,* 6–9.

Note: The marginal values of the above tables reflect the detail that no voting on holding a convention occurred in Bee, Hamilton, and Presidio Counties.

intimidation and savagery against blacks remained largely unchecked and essentially unpunished. Outrages against the freedmen were still so frequent in many areas that, in the words of one East Texas scalawag, "little note is made of it."[54]

The problem of persistent factionalism within the Texas Republican party also was an interminable liability. In the fall of 1867 a serious split had arisen within the Pease administration over the multidimensional and, at times, confusing issue of *ab initio*—the question of whether the acts of all legislatures meeting in Texas after secession, including the acts of the Eleventh Legislature in 1866, were invalid from the start. At stake was more than the collection of back taxes on land owned by Texas tories, or the validity of land grants to corporations, or railroad reimbursement of money borrowed from the state school fund. *Ab initio* now entailed in a willingness to rectify past injustices as interpreted by both persecuted unionists and former slaves, along with a commitment to the political goals of the latter. To a large degree, the story of the inability to reconcile this basic disagreement between radical and more moderate Texas Republicans would shape the future of their party almost as much as the vitality of racism and conservatism among their Democratic opponents.[55]

54. Moneyhon, *Republicanism in Reconstruction Texas,* 80–81; Jesse A. Asberry to HFMD, April 10, 1867, Microfilm Reel #3, COCADT, RG 393, NA; George W. Whitmore to Elisha M. Pease, March 18, 1868, in Governors' Papers: Pease.

55. Carrier, "A Political History of Texas," 173; Moneyhon, *Republicanism in Reconstruction Texas,* 72–75.

5
THE STILLBIRTH OF TWO-PARTY POLITICS: THE 1869 GUBERNATORIAL RACE

"Submit to everything, agree to nothing" *is my idea. I think Jack Hamilton is the best of his party, and I think the constitution is as good as we can get from the Rads*—**but neither you or I approve it. . . . I** *want to see our true men* **do nothing.**

—former Confederate congressman Franklin B. Sexton
to Oran M. Roberts, August 6, 1869

The poor Negroes were forced to vote against their own wills. . . . I never saw such a scene in all my life.

—A. M. Attaway, Republican candidate for County Clerk
of Falls County, to Nathan Patten, December 6, 1869

When the state constitutional convention assembled in the summer of 1868, the Republican delegates proved that they lacked a unifying interest. The Republicans, or "the niggers and their white allies" as the Dallas *Herald* insultingly described them, disagreed over the following matters: the doctrine of *ab initio,* or the legality of wartime and postwar legislation; the division of the state into two or three states; the extent to which former secessionists and ex-Confederates should be disfranchised; and the degree to which the law should be favorable to the civil rights of the freedmen. After two months in session, the delegates exhausted funds allotted for the convention's expenses and adjourned the convention without completing its primary task. In early December, after the holding of the 1868 presidential election, in which Congress barred Texas from participating, the convention reconvened. The national Republican party's triumph in electing Ulysses S. Grant, who campaigned promising moderation and a retreat from Reconstruction, neither brought harmony to the contending Texas Republican factions nor afforded them greater protection from intimidation and violence.[1]

While the delegates debated, the reorganized Texas Democrats began a methodical attack upon Republican leaders and key parts of their fledgling party organization, including the Freedmen's Bureau schools, local registration boards, and pro-Republican newspapers. Motivated by apprehension about the potential political power of blacks, groups dedicated to preserving white supremacy, such as the Ku Klux Klan and Democratic party clubs, escalated the level of violence against loyalists and freedmen. The files of the commander of the Military District of Texas and the reports of the Freedmen's Bureau were soon full of complaints of atrocities, outrages, and murders. At times "a virtual state of war" broke out in some counties, although blacks were essentially the only victims of these disorders. White terrorism touched the convention itself with the brutal murder by a white mob of carpetbagger delegate George W. Smith, who had been an officer in the Union Army before becoming a merchant in Jefferson (Marion County) and an earnest friend of the local freedmen.[2]

When the convention finally finished its work in early February of 1869, divisions in Republican ranks had crystallized. Edmund J. Davis, a former district judge in South Texas who had raised the 1st Texas Cavalry for the Union army, led the radical faction—a combination, for the most part, of blacks and West Texans. Davis was among those who had, in the words of one of many white Texans who despised him, "led armies to sack & pillage their own state." Aligned with Davis were James P. Newcomb, a San Antonio unionist who had fled to Mexico after Confederates destroyed his *Alamo Express* newspaper office, and Morgan C. Hamilton, another prewar unionist, but a newcomer to politics, who now controlled the state's influential Union League associations. Provisional Governor Elisha M. Pease, who had reservations about building a party dependent upon black votes, led the moderate faction. Supporting him were former provisional secretary

1. Dallas *Herald,* September 5, 1868; Richard R. Moore, "Reconstruction," in Pen Proctor and Archie P. McDonald, eds., *The Texas Heritage* (St. Louis, 1980), 99; Ramsdell, *Reconstruction in Texas,* 200–60; Moneyhon, *Republicanism in Reconstruction Texas,* 82–103; Carrier, "A Political History of Texas," 249–326; Sandlin, "The Texas Reconstruction Constitutional Convention," 43–214.

2. Charles Virgil Keener, "Racial Turmoil in Texas, 1865–1874" (M.S. thesis, North Texas State University, 1971), 72–76; Moneyhon, *Republicanism in Reconstruction Texas,* 94–95; Smallwood, *Time of Hope, Time of Despair,* 141; Smallwood, "When the Klan Rode," 11; Carrier, "A Political History of Texas," 295–96; Richter, *Overreached on All Sides,* 235–36. The issue of violence united all Republican delegates and generated two convention reports; see *Journal of the Reconstruction Convention Which Met at Austin, Texas, June 1, A.D. 1868* (Austin, 1870), 193–203, 500–505.

of state James H. Bell and former military and provisional governor Andrew J. Hamilton, who was the younger brother of Morgan C. Hamilton. Each faction formed its own executive committee and state organization, and each sent a delegation headed by one of the Hamiltons to Washington to vie for the recognition and patronage of the Grant administration and the national Republican party.[3]

The constitution drafted by the quarreling Republicans revealed, however, a consensus on fundamental principles. It acknowledged the supremacy of the United States Constitution and guaranteed the equality of all persons before the law. It thus theoretically guaranteed full and equal citizenship to African Texans. The old stipulations against their right to vote, hold office, serve on juries, and testify in courts of law were eliminated. The new constitution established a public school system for all Texas children, without regard to their race or color, and supplied adequate measures to finance it. The constitution provided for a properly empowered legislature and an excellent judicial system above the county level. It increased the executive authority of the governor, thus giving him the chance to build political power through his control of patronage. To deal with the problem of lawlessness, it empowered the governor to establish a state police force. Although most scholars have subsequently considered the Constitution of 1869 a progressive frame of government, at the time it fell squarely outside the traditional conceptions of southern statecraft and the radical faction of the Texas Republicans initially regarded it as unsatisfactory.[4]

Wanting an extensive political reorganization that would have transcended the agenda outlined by Republican moderates, the radicals in early 1869 would have divided the state and demanded greater restrictions on the suffrage of former Confederates. In addition, the radicals would have insisted upon an *ab initio* declaration that would have brought into question many additional actions of the Texas government as it existed both during and after the war. When lobbying in Washington against the new constitution, the radicals protested that it would allow railroad corporations to repay the school fund with worthless Confederate warrants and would acknowledge the transfer of lands unfairly sold during the war by Confederate auc-

3. Moneyhon, *Republicanism in Reconstruction Texas,* 82–103; James W. Throckmorton to Benjamin H. Epperson, April 17, 1866 [copy], in James W. Throckmorton Papers and Letterbook; Sandlin, "The Texas Reconstruction Constitutional Convention," 215–34.

4. Carrier, "A Political History of Texas," 317–26; Moore, "Reconstruction," 99; Sandlin, "The Texas Reconstruction Constitutional Convention," 213–14. The entire Constitution of 1869 is in Gammel, comp., *Laws of Texas,* VII, 395–430.

tioneers. They also feared that the provision allowing all men to vote except those disqualified from holding certain offices or positions by the Fourteenth Amendment would restore the Democratic party to power before true Republicans (as opposed to an expedient Hamilton-Pease-Bell alliance with Democrats or Conservatives) could obtain a firm grip on state and local government. They argued that division of the state would help solve the problem of widespread lawlessness, protect loyalists in the western counties, and provide additional safeguards for black rights.[5]

The radical Republicans soon realized that President Grant's apparent nonchalance in taking sides in Texas affairs reflected the conservative drift nationwide that had precipitated his indecision over the future course of Reconstruction policy. They quickly adjusted to the new political realities by moving in a moderate direction. They pursued a party reunification movement, endorsed the new constitution, and chose Davis as their gubernatorial candidate at a June convention in Houston. Although the moderate Republicans still held a share of federal patronage and seemed to have the support of Grant's military commander in Texas, Brevet Major General Joseph J. Reynolds, the radicals outmaneuvered them. In early July the national Republican committee recognized the radicals as the Republican party of Texas. Grant then postponed the holding of the constitutional referendum from July until late November, thus giving the radicals more time to organize their forces against Andrew J. Hamilton, the leader of the moderate or conservative Republicans who had earlier in the year "nominated himself" for the governorship. Hamilton's subsequent accommodation with the Democrats caused General Reynolds to do an about-face and favor the radicals. In September Grant, who had been Reynolds' friend since their days at West Point, wholeheartedly embraced the Texas radicals and commanded Reynolds to oversee for them voter registration, federal patronage, and officeholder appointments. Pease, upset with the course of events, resigned the governorship.[6]

Historians have exaggerated Reynolds' subsequent role in helping Davis

5. "Memorial to the Senate and House of Representatives of the United States, Washington, D.C., March 11, 1869," quoted in *Flake's Daily Bulletin* (Galveston), March 27, 1869; Carrier, "A Political History of Texas," 275–78, 328–29; Moneyhon, *Republicanism in Reconstruction Texas,* 105–108; Sandlin, "The Texas Reconstruction Constitutional Convention," 217–22.

6. New York *Times,* November 29, 1869; William Gillette, *Retreat from Reconstruction, 1869–1879* (Baton Rouge, 1979), 99–100; Gray, "Edmund J. Davis," 150–76; Moneyhon, *Republicanism in Reconstruction Texas,* 104–17; Elisha M. Pease to Joseph J. Reynolds, September 30, 1869, Microfilm Reel #26, COCADT, RG 393, NA.

to win the governorship. Davis' supporters wanted Reynolds to postpone the election until the Union League associations had more time to organize or until at least half the three thousand provisional local officeholders were removed and Davis men put in their places. Otherwise, they predicted "a sham reconstruction" of Texas "after the fashion of Georgia and Virginia." Reynolds, however, neither delayed the election until 1870 nor removed any of the pro-Hamilton local officeholders targeted for replacement by radicals. Startled by the repercussions of his political advice to Grant, Reynolds apparently tried to soften his influence in the hope of furthering Republican party harmony. Although he appointed many new voter registrars, who were mostly Davis men, and usually assigned at least one army officer to each local board, scant evidence exists to support the allegation, made at the time by Hamilton and repeated for generations, that the radicals successfully used the revision of the voting lists to advance their cause through a wholesale rejection of otherwise qualified white applicants.[7]

During the 1869 revision of registration the local boards possessed the same prerogatives they had held under former orders. When the ten-day registration period closed—just four days before the actual balloting—nearly all the adult black males in the state had been issued registration certificates, and the percentage of adult white males registered jumped from its previous level of 48 percent to 61 percent. Of the 135,553 men registered, 56,810 were black and 78,743 were white. Because the additions and removals from the voting lists during the revision resulted in the registration of more whites than blacks, the white percentage of all registrants increased from 55 percent to 58 percent—a result that hardly augured well for Davis and the radicals.[8]

The registration revision left largely unchanged the basic geographical pattern of white disfranchisement established in 1868 (see table 32 above). In central and lower East Texas, with the peculiarity of Tyler County, where "secessionists" were allegedly "excluded without exception," the numbers of whites granted certificates were unexplainably far above the

7. Ramsdell, *Reconstruction in Texas*, 281; Nunn, *Texas Under the Carpetbaggers*, 18–19; Morgan C. Hamilton and others to Joseph J. Reynolds, November 8, 1869, Microfilm Reel #26, and Edmund J. Davis to Joseph J. Reynolds, November 10, 1869 [telegram], Microfilm Reel #20, COCADT, RG 393, NA; Moneyhon, *Republicanism in Reconstruction Texas*, 116–17; Carrier, "A Political History of Texas," 390–92; Gray, "Edmund J. Davis," 175–76.

8. *Tabular Statement of Registration and Voting*, 2–5. Figures for black and white registrants in 1869 are incorrectly reported in Gray, "Edmund J. Davis," 176, and in Carrier, "A Political History of Texas," 390.

statewide average. For instance, the percentage of adult white males registered in Sabine and Cherokee Counties reached a remarkable 100 percent and 98 percent, respectively, or 34 and 25 percentages points, respectively, above what one would predict, given prior turnout in the 1866 gubernatorial election and the presence or absence of blacks, immigrants, and aliens in the two counties. Joining most of East Texas as an area where white disfranchisement was nominal and extraordinarily mild was, except for San Saba and Palo Pinto Counties, the sparsely settled western frontier region. However, as in 1867 and 1868, many counties in the Houston-Galveston commercial hub and in North Texas still had, for whatever reasons, low rates of their white adult males converted into registrants. And, as previously, thousands of otherwise qualified whites had refused even to try to register.[9]

The pinpointing of individual counties for apparent underregistration or overregistration cannot solve the issue of unfair rejections of white applicants, but it can help to corroborate accusations that Reynolds encouraged particular boards to suppress white registration. For example, Bexar County (San Antonio), along with other "populous and important" counties, is often singled out as the supreme illustration of how the radicals took unethical advantage of the registration revision to advance their cause. Most complaints involved proof of United States citizenship. Immigrants who had their discharge papers from the Union army or who had resided in the Republic of Texas six months before the acceptance of the Constitution of 1845 were not compelled to produce their naturalization papers, but the San Antonio board apparently required immigrants who arrived subsequently to so prove their citizenship. Sworn affidavits claimed that Newcomb, whom Reynolds had allowed to remain as president of the local board and who subsequently became secretary of state in the Davis administration, was "entirely blind to all considerations of justice." At one point Reynolds found it necessary to overrule the rejection of some 100 registrants by the Bexar County board. Nevertheless, had the registration process in Bexar County progressed in the same manner as in all the other counties, only about an additional 200 white men would probably have joined the 1,586 of their counterparts who received registration certificates signed by Newcomb's board (see table 32 above).[10]

9. H. C. Pedigo to Elisha M. Pease, October 1, 1867, in Governors' Papers: Pease.

10. Ramsdell, *Reconstruction in Texas,* 280–281; Affidavit signed by C. Nuñez, August Kramvitz, and Epistacio Mondragón, October [?], 1869, Microfilm Reel #36, COCADT, RG 393, NA; Smallwood, *Time of Hope, Time of Despair,* 146–47; Keener, "Racial Turmoil in Texas," p. 67; James P. Newcomb to HFMD, December 2, 1869 [Register #3, p. 146], Microfilm Reel #4, and George P.

Far better instances of probable suppression of white registration in other populous counties, according to the findings presented here, are Travis (Austin) and Harris (Houston), although both had low registration rates in 1867 and 1868 and fewer individual complaints emanated from these counties in 1869 than from Bexar. The Travis County board allegedly stuck to the ruling that all men whom it had rejected at previous registrations were to be refused again without the benefit of any reconsideration of their circumstances. Even a few previously rejected unionists who had held antebellum and wartime official positions were among those automatically rejected again. On the other hand, in heavily populated Fayette (La Grange), Harrison (Marshall), and Galveston (Galveston) Counties, whites were ostensibly overregistered. One observer called the revision in Galveston County "ridiculous" because the most "Conservative Rebs" rejected by the old board were allowed to register.[11]

Manuscript materials in the U.S. Army's Office of Civil Affairs also help to clarify the issue of the fairness of the 1869 revision. In most counties there arose no complaints at all regarding the registration process. The rabidly anti-Republican Dallas *Herald* at the close of the local registration reported that it had not heard a word of criticism, but rather "a universal expression of satisfaction" in the entire process. Yet the evidence presented here shows that white registration in Dallas County (Dallas) was uncommonly low, suggesting that either apathy was commonplace or complaints from rejected applicants should more likely than not have arisen. Throughout the state, surviving lists of applicants refused registration often contain justifications that, at least on the surface, were logical and clear-cut. Questionable decisions often hinged on determining whether "aid or comfort" had been freely given, rather than given under duress, to the enemies of the United States. Appeals and complaints about the registration process were not limited to Hamilton partisans. Davis supporters, for example, were distressed that men whose names were currently before Congress for removal of their disabilities were frequently refused registration. One revealing complaint came from a few freedmen who begged not to serve as "challengers" at the registration tables, because they "would be afraid to challenge any [white]

Douglas to Joseph J. Reynolds, November 21, 1869, Microfilm Reel #21, and Frank W. Petmeckey to Charles E. Morse, November 20, 1869, Microfilm Reel #26, and Horibrook Thompson to HFMD, November 20, 1869, Microfilm Reel #38, COCADT, RG 393, NA.

11. Brown, "Annals of Travis County and the City of Austin," chap. 28, p. 19, AHC; L. F. Harris to HFMD, November 18, 1869, Microfilm Reel #21, and William E. Parker to Joseph J. Reynolds, November 24 [telegram] and 26, 1869, Microfilm Reel #21, COCADT, RG 393, NA.

person & be subject to persecution in the future." Their fears were justified. In 1868 white terrorists killed three blacks who served as members of county registry boards, and other black registrars were fired upon, assaulted, and threatened so often that authorities had lost count.[12]

With the close of registration, the stage was set for the Texas voters to participate concurrently in two actual elections: a referendum on the ratification of the proposed state constitution and a selection, should the constitution be approved, of state and local officials. Military authorities limited the four days of balloting (from November 30 through December 3) to only county seats—a voting requirement of the 1868 election incorporated subsequently in the new constitution. The more than six hundred federal troops dispatched for the election, usually a half dozen soldiers at each county seat, were ordered to stay away from the courthouses or polling places unless called upon by the local registration boards to keep the peace. The weather was uncooperative: a cold front accompanied in some areas with ice and freezing winds swept over the state.[13]

Democratic party leaders did not oppose the new constitution, but neither did they want the responsibility for its passage. While labeling it "objectionable" because it violated the "old Democratic principles," they nevertheless wanted it adopted because it would eliminate what they commonly called "the sway of the bayonet." Or as the Republicans elaborated, the Democrats wanted the federal troops removed as soon as possible because "then they expect to Rule to their hearts [sic] content."[14]

12. Dallas *Herald*, November 27, 1869; Austin Daily *Republican*, November 24, 1869; "List and Cause of Rejection of 128 Persons Refused Registration in Harris County, Texas [November 16 to 26, 1869]," Microfilm Reel #31, and J. A. H. Cleveland to E. E. Sellers, December 9, 1869 [copy], Microfilm Reel #21, and William H. Russell to H. Clay Wood, January 20, 1870, Microfilm Reel #30, C. J. Stockbridge to Charles E. Morse, November 27, 1869, Microfilm Reel #27, and H. W. Forbet to Charles E. Morse, November 26, 1869, Microfilm Reel #31, COCADT, RG 393, NA. On the murders of black voter registrars by white attackers in Brazos, Burleson, and Hopkins Counties, see Barry A. Crouch, *The Freedmen's Bureau and Black Texans* (Austin, 1992), 118–21; L. Shoemaker to Elisha M. Pease, June 23, Microfilm Reel #32, and DeWitt C. Brown to Acting Assistant Adjutant General, June 12, 1868 [Register for Volume 2, p. 52], Microfilm Reel #3, BRFAL, RG 105, NA. For the plight of other blacks who served as voter registrars, see Randolph B. Campbell, "The Burden of Local Black Leadership during Reconstruction: A Research Note," *Civil War History*, XXXIX (June, 1993), 148–53; James P. Shenton, ed., *The Reconstruction: A Documentary History of the South After the War, 1865–1877* (New York, 1963), 131; Samuel R. Peacock to Charles E. Morse, May 28, 1868, Microfilm Reel #7, COCADT, RG 393, NA; Richter, *Overreached on All Sides*, 206–207.

13. General Orders, No. 174, October 1, 1869, HFMD [signed by H. Clay Wood], Microfilm Reel #23, COCADT, RG 393, NA; Robert W. Shook, "Federal Occupation and Administration of Texas, 1865–1870" (Ph.D. dissertation, North Texas State University, 1970), 401; Moneyhon, *Republicanism in Reconstruction Texas*, 122; *State Gazette* (Austin), December 3, 1869.

14. *For Lieut.-Governor. Fellow-Citizens of Texas*, [signed by] Wells Thompson, August 2, 1869,

Almost two-thirds of the state's adult black males and slightly under one-third of their white counterparts participated in the 1869 election. A lopsided vote of 72,366 to 4,928 ratified the new constitution. Black registrants voted overwhelmingly in favor of ratification, 36,496 to 879 (see table 34). The report of returns contains only one internal inconsistency: For Jack County it shows "3" blacks registered to vote in 1869, but "4" blacks voting in favor of ratifying the constitution. The number of blacks in the county voting for the constitution was thus arbitrarily set to "3," and the county's white total voting in favor was raised from "110" to "111." Accordingly, throughout the state 37,375 blacks voted in the 1869 ratification referendum, whereas 37,751 blacks had participated in the 1868 referendum on calling a convention. Viewed in another way, in only the Texas counties where elections were held, black registrants failing to turn out and vote in 1869 and 1868 totaled 18,422 and 11,699, respectively. In spite of a net addition of 7,260 blacks to the voting lists during the revision of registration, 376 fewer African Texans voted in 1869 than had voted in 1868, and the percent of registered black voters who turned out to vote tumbled from 76 to 66 percent. North Texas claimed a disproportionate share of the dozen counties where there occurred the largest percentage declines in black voting (see table 35).[15]

Among the white registrants who bothered to go to the polls, the constitution met approval by a vote ratio of about nine to one (see table 34.A). The constitution failed, however, to receive the support of the majority of white registered voters because essentially half of them, including a very small portion who were stricken off the voting lists, did not participate in the ratification balloting. Moreover, the whites who had voted initially against a convention call did not necessarily return to vote as a group in favor of adoption of the constitution. The transition probabilities of voting between 1868 and 1869 suggest that most of the whites who voted against holding a convention subsequently did not vote in the ratification referendum. Although a few of the whites who cast no-votes in 1868 were stricken off the voting lists during the revision of registration, the rest of them were probably demoralized by Ulysses S. Grant's election to the presidency and decided to let the radicals carry the new constitution by default.

Texas Broadsides Collection, BTHC; Matthias Ward and others to Joseph J. Reynolds, August 31, 1869, Microfilm Reel #12, COCADT, RG 393, NA.

15. *Tabular Statement of Registration and Voting,* 1–9. *Cf.* Moneyhon, *Republicanism in Reconstruction Texas,* 124, who slightly exaggerates the decline in the number of blacks failing to return to the polls in 1869.

The miserably cold weather in extreme northern Texas might have played a role in suppressing black turnout, but other factors presumably kept blacks away from the polls, especially in adjacent Collin, Cooke, and Hunt Counties, where there existed a legacy of wartime brutality. None of the 270 registered blacks in Collin County (north of Dallas) turned out to vote in the 1869 election. This incredible detail cannot be adequately explained by assuming that the freedman whom a journalist saw on election day trading a Davis ballot for "an old pair of boots" represented a "widespread" phenomenon. The Collin County region was the scene of the prolonged and bloody Lee-Peacock feud sparked by hatred between "tried and true Southerners" who established a conclave of the Ku Klux Klan, on one side, and Confederate army deserters and scalawags, on the other. Klan activities, which had allegedly touched the life "of almost every Negro" in this region of North Texas, along with strong prewar unionist and scalawag support for Hamilton, presumably accounted for the decline in black voting.[16]

Democratic party strategy in the 1869 gubernatorial election dictated supporting Hamilton for two basic reasons. Congress would have voided the election to the Texas governorship of an "unreconstructed" prewar officeholder, and running a Democratic ticket against Hamilton would have divided the anti-Davis vote. The latter scenario became an actual possibility. Hamilton Stuart, the editor of the Galveston *Civilian* who had been a prewar unionist and reluctant Confederate, headed up, without the approval of the Texas Democratic State Committee, an unadulterated Democratic ticket. Given these circumstances, Democratic leaders accepted Hamilton as a lesser evil. They explained to their rank and file that his election, and the resulting avoidance of delay in Texas readmission to the Union, would represent "the shortest road to the ultimate triumph of the Democratic party in the state." Support for Hamilton Stuart's candidacy virtually dissolved. In 1872 Governor Davis appointed Stuart to the board of administrators of the still nonexistent "University of Texas."[17]

Although Hamilton campaigned as a Republican and denied that he

16. Stambaugh and Stambaugh, *A History of Collin County*, 74; C. L. Sonnichsen, *I'll Die Before I'll Run: The Story of the Great Feuds of Texas* (Lincoln, 1988), 21–34 (quotation on 22); Smallwood, *Time of Hope, Time of Despair*, 132; A. Bledsoe to Joseph J. Reynolds, July 1, 1869, Microfilm Reel #10, COCADT, RG 393, NA; Richard B. McCaslin, "Wheat Growers in the Cotton Confederacy," 538.

17. Marten, *Texas Divided*, 43–44; Moneyhon, *Republicanism in Reconstruction Texas*, 119–20; Dallas *Herald*, October 16, 1869; Carrier, "A Political History of Texas," 370–73; Ashbel Smith and others to Oran M. Roberts, February 12, 1869, in Roberts Papers; Fornell, *The Galveston Era*, 147; J. J. Lane, "History of the Educational System of Texas," in *A Comprehensive History of Texas*, ed. Dudley G. Wooten (2 vols.; Dallas, 1898), II, 448.

TABLE 34

ESTIMATED RELATIONSHIPS BETWEEN VOTING IN THE 1868 CONVENTION
REFERENDUM AND VOTING IN THE 1869 RATIFICATION REFERENDUM, BY RACE

(in percentages of white and black registrants)

Estimated Voting Patterns of White Registrants in 1868 and 1869   (Actual $N = 121$)

	Percentage Having Voted for Convention	Percentage Having Voted Against Convention	Percentage Having Not Voted in the 1868 Referendum	Percentage Having Been Unregistered to Vote	Totals
1869 White Voters Voting For Ratification	6	6	10	23	45
1869 White Voters Voting Against Ratification	0	0	5	0	5
1869 White Voters Registered But Not Voting	3	6	35	3	47
Former Voters "Stricken Off" Voting Lists	1	1	1	0	3
Totals	10	13	52	25	100

Estimated Voting Patterns of Black Registrants in 1868 and 1869   (Actual $N = 120$)

	Percentage Having Voted for Convention	Percentage Having Voted Against Convention	Percentage Having Not Voted in the 1868 Referendum	Percentage Having Been Unregistered to Vote	Totals
1869 Black Voters Voting For Ratification	47	1	3	14	65
1869 Black Voters Voting Against Ratification	1	0	1	0	2
1869 Black Voters Registered But Not Voting	17	0	16	0	33
Former Voters "Stricken Off" Voting Lists	0	0	1	0	1
Totals	65	1	20	14	100

Source: For the source for the number of white and black voters registered under the authority of the Congressional Reconstruction Acts, and for the source for the votes cast in 1868 by white and black registrants for and against a convention call and for and against ratification of the 1869 Constitution, see *Tabular Statement of Registration and Voting,* 2–9.

Note: The marginal values of the above tables reflect the detail that no vote on the convention was held in Bee, Hamilton, and Presidio Counties and that military authorities closed the polls during the ratification election in Milam and Navarro Counties. The 1,803 white registrants in these five counties were thus excluded from the analysis. The

TABLE 34

(continued)

percentages in the first table were necessarily based on the voting behavior of the 76,940 white registrants who lived elsewhere. Likewise, the marginal values of the table estimating black voting patterns are based on counties other than the five mentioned above and excluding Webb County (Laredo), where no blacks were registered. The percentages in the second table are thus based on the voting behavior of the 55,783 black registrants who lived in counties where elections were successfully held in both 1868 and 1869. In both tables, the estimates confirm the commonsense realization that whites and blacks "stricken off" the voting lists could not by definition also have been added to the lists of registered voters.

intended to lead the Democratic party back to power, he was vulnerable to Davis' charge that he had "sold out to the rebels." To many white Republicans, the Hamilton coalition with the anti-Davis forces had proved disappointing when a fair division of local offices met with Democratic resistance. Ferdinand Flake, an influential conservative Republican newspaper editor, concluded that behind the determination of the Democrats to support Hamilton, there lurked the goal to elect only their men to Congress, install a Democrat as lieutenant governor, and "save the legislature." Moreover, typical of the basic, if often the exclusive, appeal of many candidates on the Hamilton ticket were outmoded, but unyielding, avowals "to be a white man, and [the wish] to be the equal of white men only."[18]

A razor-thin margin favoring Davis foiled Democratic ambitions. With little financial assistance and the backing of no more than a small fraction of the more than one hundred newspapers in the state, but with black leaders working tirelessly to mobilize the masses of freedmen, Davis won the gubernatorial election by fewer than 800 votes out of nearly 80,000 cast. (Davis received 39,838 votes; Hamilton, 39,055; and Hamilton Stuart, 445.) By similar margins the radicals swept the races for the other principal state executive offices, and their ticket won three of four congressional seats. Davis and the radicals had, in fact, engineered a stunning triumph. His hometown newspaper, the *Nueces Valley* (Corpus Christi), praised him for having "almost singlehanded, canvassed the State, and by his pluck, nerve & indomitable energy carried it in a struggle apparently hopeless."[19]

18. Edmund J. Davis, quoted in Moneyhon, *Republicanism in Reconstruction Texas,* 163; Ferdinand Flake, quoted *ibid.*, 121; "To the Voters of Hopkins County [by J. M. Ashcroft]," November 11, 1869 [unidentified newspaper clipping], Microfilm Reel #31, COCADT, RG 393, NA.

19. U.S. Army, Fifth Military District, State of Texas, General Order No. 19, *Tabular Statement, Showing the Number of Votes Cast in Each County For and Against the Constitution, and for State Officers. Tabular Statement, Showing Number Votes Cast in Each County for Members of Congress. Tabular Statement, Showing the Votes Cast in Each District for Senators and Representatives. Statement, Showing Vote by Counties for Clerks of District Courts, Sheriffs, and Justices of the Peace* [hereinafter cited as *Tabular Statements of Voting in 1869]*, (Austin: February 1, 1870), 2–8; Smallwood, *Time of Hope, Time of Despair,* 146; Carrier, "A Political History of Texas," 387; *Nueces Valley* (Corpus Christi), November 12, 1870, quoted in Gray, "Edmund J. Davis," 178.

A large increase in black-voter turnout in the 1869 election occurred significantly in and around the Twentieth Subdistrict established by the Freedmen's Bureau. This area encompassed Grimes and Brazos Counties on the lower Brazos River. In the latter county the Ku Klux Klan had murdered six blacks, including two prominent political leaders, and had severely wounded two other freedmen. Although just one of many incidents of recurring violence that the army and local authorities had been powerless to prevent, this so-called Millican riot in the summer of 1868 was one of the worst instances of Klan brutality in Texas during Reconstruction. It received broad attention because a black community had tried to defend itself against intimidation by hooded Klansmen. Feeling indignant about the assertiveness of the freedmen and fearing a further erosion of white supremacy, whites murdered the community's leaders. Among the dead was George E. Brooks, a Methodist minister, federal voter registrar, and leader of the local Republican Union League. Brooks was also an agent for The Free Man's Press, an African American newspaper whose publisher avoided putting its name on wrapping papers because otherwise mailings "might be confiscated on the road." Although there undoubtedly were many "incalculable ramifications" of the killing of the Brazos County freedmen, an immediate decline in black political participation was not among them. In Brazos and Grimes Counties 750 more blacks voted in 1869 than in 1868, and 675 more blacks voted than previously in the surrounding counties of Madison, Robertson, Leon, and Burleson (see table 35). This behavior of black voters does not square with accounts of the disturbance by historians who exaggerate the extent to which "disorder infused the Millican black colony" and anxiety spread throughout neighboring freedmen communities.[20]

The radical victory was flawed only by Davis' failure to win significant white support. Because election officials tabulated racial breakdowns of the vote only for and against the proposed constitution, deriving the actual minimum number of white men who favored Davis in each county is impossible. It is possible, however, to estimate Davis' strength among white voters in every county, and thus in the entire state, by subtracting the number of blacks who voted in the constitutional referendum from Davis'

20. Moneyhon, *Republicanism in Reconstruction Texas*, 312; "Records of Criminal Offenses Committed in the State of Texas," Vol. 3 (13), Microfilm Reel #32, BRFAL, RG 105, NA; *Free Man's Press* (Austin), August 1, 1868; Crouch, *The Freedmen's Bureau and Black Texans*, 103–27 (quotation on p. 126); Robert A. Calvert and Arnoldo De León, *The History of Texas* (Arlington Heights, Ill., 1990), 138.

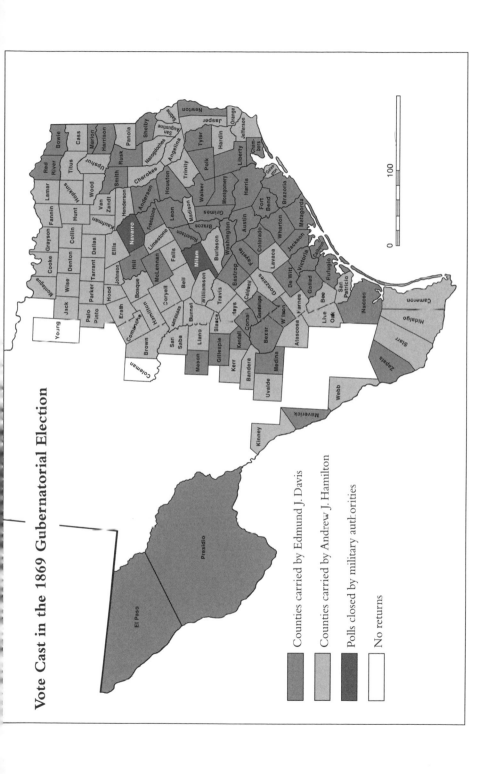

Vote Cast in the 1869 Gubernatorial Election

Counties carried by Edmund J. Davis

Counties carried by Andrew J. Hamilton

Polls closed by military authorities

No returns

TABLE 35

DECLINES AND INCREASES IN BLACK-VOTER PARTICIPATION, BY COUNTY

(in percentages of registered blacks)

Counties with Declines in Numbers of Blacks Voting in 1869

County	Decline in Black Voting Expressed as a Percentage of 1869 Registered Blacks	Decline in Black Voting Expressed as a Percentage-Point Drop Between Percentages of Registered Blacks Voting in 1868 and 1869[a]	Decrease in the Number of Blacks Voting Between 1868 and 1869
Collin	70	74	190
Bell	42	47	108
Dallas	40	43	160
Cooke	39	39	35
Hunt	38	39	59
Burnet	38	39	21
Lamar	37	39	297
Hardin	33	33	15
Denton	31	31	22
Kaufman	29	34	55
Fannin	26	27	121
Angelina	23	25	32
Tyler	23	18	53
Van Zandt	22	27	32
Falls	21	29	196
Travis	20	28	203
Nacogdoches	19	26	105
Cameron	18	32	22
Hopkins	18	19	52
Smith	17	22	223
Caldwell	16	22	73
Comal	16	15	13
Wharton	15	17	123
Bosque	15	22	13
Guadalupe	15	26	78
Tarrant	14	20	30
Hays	14	21	27
Upshur	13	21	113
McLennan	13	19	144
Karnes	11	16	5
Trinity	10	13	20
Gonzales	10	15	71
Lavaca	10	13	44
Williamson	10	17	21
Brazoria	9	16	124
Matagorda	9	14	53
Coryell	9	15	4
Victoria	8	11	33
Jackson	7	14	19
Kendall	7	21	2
Fort Bend	6	16	84

TABLE 35

County	Decline in Black Voting Expressed as a Percentage of 1869 Registered Blacks	Decline in Black Voting Expressed as a Percentage-Point Drop Between Percentages of Registered Blacks Voting in 1868 and 1869[a]	Decrease in the Number of Blacks Voting Between 1868 and 1869
Orange	5	12	3
Johnson	3	4	3
Bastrop	3	13	30
Sabine	2	10	4
Rusk	2	9	24
Harrison	1	9	30
Washington	1	15	41

Counties with Increases in Numbers of Blacks Voting in 1869

County	Increase in Black Voting Expressed as a Percentage of 1869 Registered Blacks	Increase in Black Voting Expressed as a Percentage-Point Rise Between Percentages of Registered Blacks Voting in 1868 and 1869[a]	Increase in the Number of Blacks Voting Between 1868 and 1869
Grayson	35	34	139
Madison	34	10	89
Nueces	34	3	26
Robertson	29	21	343
Leon	27	13	192
Brazos	26	8	310
Newton	24	20	43
Calhoun	23	6	44
Grimes	22	−4	440
Goliad	21	12	34
Limestone	20	3	75
Liberty	18	8	63
Jefferson	17	9	20
Cherokee	15	14	108
Wood	14	18	33
Fayette	11	−3	127
Anderson	10	−2	100
Freestone	10	0	101
Colorado	9	−5	124
San Augustine	9	−4	35
Montgomery	9	0	74
Houston	8	−3	83
Polk	8	6	69
Panola	8	7	48
Henderson	7	10	19
Walker	7	−10	95
Parker	6	−3	5

(continued)

TABLE 35

(continued)

County	Increase in Black Voting Expressed as a Percentage of 1869 Registered Blacks	Increase in Black Voting Expressed as a Percentage-Point Rise Between Percentages of Registered Blacks Voting in 1868 and 1869[a]	Increase in the Number of Blacks Voting Between 1868 and 1869
Austin	6	−10	76
Harris	6	−13	128
Marion	5	−16	69
Cass	5	−1	31
Hill	5	−6	8
Ellis	5	3	19
Burleson	5	−4	33
Galveston	4	−13	47
Shelby	4	−3	16
Chambers	3	−12	3
Atascosa	3	9	1
Bexar	3	−10	13
Bowie	2	−5	8
Red River	2	−5	22
Wilson	1	−21	1

[a] Many counties recording increases in the number of blacks voting between 1868 and 1869 also exhibited drops in the percentages of black registered voters who went to the polls between these two years. This seemingly incongruous circumstance is explained by the additional numbers of blacks placed on the voter registration lists after 1868.

Source: For the sources for the votes cast by blacks in 1868 for and against a convention call and in 1869 for and against ratification of the constitution, and the number of black voters registered in 1868 and 1869 under the authority of the Congressional Reconstruction Acts, see table 34 above.

Note: Throughout the state between 1868 and 1869 the percentage of registered black voters who went to the polls dropped from 76 percent to 66 percent. Yet only 375 fewer blacks voted in 1869 than had voted in 1868—a figure representing less than 1 percent of the 56,810 blacks registered in 1869. The decline in black voting is thus best expressed as a percentage of the registered blacks in 1869. Total black registration increased between 1868 and 1869 by 7,260.

total vote. Although this method assumes that all blacks who participated in the referendum balloting also cast ballots for Davis (which is not an actual likelihood), the resulting total of 4,935 white men nevertheless strongly suggests the minimum strength of Davis among all Texas white registrants (see table 36).[21]

According to the estimates of the relationships between voting patterns in the 1866 and 1869 gubernatorial elections, Davis won virtually no support from the group of whites added to the voting lists during the revision of registration before the election (see table 37). His support from white

21. Andrew J. Hamilton to HFMD, December 21, 1869 [Register 4, p. 373], Microfilm Reel #4, COCADT, RG 393, NA. In his *Republicanism in Reconstruction Texas,* Moneyhon uses the statewide, rather than individual county, voting totals to generate an estimate of the minimum strength of Davis among Texas white voters (124, 275–76 n. 50).

voters came exclusively from the ranks of whites who had either voted in 1866 for Pease or favored in 1868 a call for a constitutional convention. The quantitative findings suggest that Davis garnered about 43 percent of the 1866 Pease total, or approximately 5,172 votes—an estimate very much in line with the 4,935 white votes calculated by subtracting the number of blacks who voted in the constitutional referendum from Davis' total vote in each county and then summing the remainders. Not surprisingly, the bulk of the white votes cast for Davis came from counties with large concentrations of German Texans and Mexican Texans. Because the white-voter majority was destined to increase considerably in the constantly growing Anglo-Texan population, Davis' inability to win meaningful white support outside the western and southern parts of the state would be the most crucial problem that the Texas Republicans would have to face in devising strategies for winning subsequent elections.[22]

In retrospect, Hamilton exaggerated the degree to which Democrats and white conservatives would put aside their animosity to his wartime unionism and subsequent Republicanism. If only half of the 1866 Throckmorton men who had subsequently obtained their voter registration certificates had turned out and voted for Hamilton, he would easily have defeated Davis. Apathy in the ranks of the anti-Davis forces, in the end, undermined Hamilton's chances of victory. The anti-radical Tri-Weekly State Gazette (Austin) aptly concluded that a Hamilton victory had been "possible, but tossed away" because "the election [was] lost by the white registered voters not turning out."[23]

Before Reynolds' announcement of the official results, the 1869 election produced an avalanche of allegations of fraud from all across the state. Foremost among the still unresolved issues surrounding the controversial Davis-Hamilton contest is the extent to which voting irregularities, especially intimidation of black voters by the anti-Davis forces or chicanery on the part of the radical Republicans or United States military authorities, might have shaped the outcome. Most current scholarship holds that abstentions by old-guard Democrats, rather than their disfranchisement per se, determined the outcome to a far greater extent than duplicity or fraud, and that only small percentages of blacks were probably kept from casting ballots for the Davis, or radical, ticket by some variety of intimidation. Historians, however, have reached no consensus on whether Davis' victory would have

22. The Austin Record, January 12, 1870, reported that Davis captured only about 3,992 white votes.
23. Tri-Weekly State Gazette (Austin), December 10, 1869.

TABLE 36

ESTIMATES OF WHITE SUPPORT OF DAVIS' CANDIDACY AND BLACK SUPPORT OF HAMILTON'S CANDIDACY

(in percentages of 1869 registered white or black voters)

	White Support of Davis			Black Support of Hamilton	
County	Estimated Percentage of Registered Whites Voting for Davis	Corresponding Number of White Ballots for Davis	County	Estimated Percentage of Registered Blacks Voting for Hamilton	Corresponding Number of Black Ballots for Hamilton
Medina	80	226	Williamson	60	226
Kendall	55	107	San Saba	53	8
Gillespie	54	264	Sabine	45	112
El Paso	48	334	Coryell	40	18
Zapata	44	31	Tarrant	32	69
Comal	42	305	San Augustine	32	121
Maverick	40	20	Orange	29	17
Nueces	37	161	Panola	28	157
Bexar	35	553	Jasper	27	82
Hill	33	227	Falls	25	234
Refugio	33	56	Hardin	24	11
Kerr	28	46	Brazoria	22	291
Wilson	28	86	Ellis	19	72
Blanco	25	33	Hood	16	4
Presidio	25	17	Burnet	13	7
Cameron	24	159	Hunt	12	19
Calhoun	23	81	Titus	12	65
Guadalupe	23	185	Cherokee	11	77
Mason	20	34	Wise	10	1
Van Zandt	17	127	Bell	9	23
De Witt	16	100	Jefferson	9	10

County			County		
Smith	16	195	Johnson	9	8
Matagorda	14	23	Madison	8	20
Victoria	13	54	Montgomery	8	63
Webb	13	23	Robertson	8	99
Goliad	12	48	Travis	8	78
Tyler	12	39	Washington	6	160
Atascosa	9	40	6 Other Counties	0–5	122
San Patricio	9	7			Total: 2,074
Angelina	8	42			
Hidalgo	8	7			
Starr	8	10			
Trinity	8	32			
Wood	8	51			
Caldwell	7	40			
Fort Bend	7	20			
Rusk	7	101			
Freestone	6	50			
Jackson	6	14			
Nacogdoches	6	54			
36 Other Counties	0–5	746			
		Total: 4,935			

Source: The 1869 gubernatorial returns are taken from United States Army, Fifth Military District, State of Texas, General Order No. 19, *Tabular Statement, Showing the Number of Votes Cast in Each County For and Against the Constitution, and for State Officers. Tabular Statement, Showing Number Votes Cast in Each County for Members of Congress. Tabular Statement, Showing the Votes Cast in Each District for Senators and Representatives. Statement, Showing Vote by Counties for Clerks of District Courts, Sheriffs, and Justices of the Peace* (hereinafter cited as *Tabular Statements of Voting in 1869*)(Austin: February 1, 1870), 1–46. For the source for the racial breakdown of the vote cast for and against ratification of the 1869 Constitution, see table 34 above.

Note: The estimates of white support of Davis and black support of Hamilton are based on the racial divisions of the vote cast in the constitutional referendum. The estimates of Radical white voters in each county were computed by subtracting the number of blacks who voted in the constitutional referendum from the total vote cast for Edmund J. Davis. Conversely, estimates of the minimum number of black ballots for Andrew J. Hamilton were computed by first subtracting the number of white ballots cast in the constitutional referendum from the total number of votes received by Hamilton, and then limiting the number of black votes cast for him to as many as were left over after subtracting the vote cast for Davis from the number of blacks voting in the referendum election. The method assumes a racially polarized vote (which was not likely), but it yields estimates that suggest the respective minimum strength of Davis among white voters and of Hamilton among black

(continued)

TABLE 36

(continued)

voters. See Carl H. Moneyhon, *Republicanism in Reconstruction Texas* (Austin, 1980), note 50, on pp. 275–76. Racial breakdowns of the voters who participated in the 1869 election for state and local offices were rarely tabulated by election officials. Nevertheless, the racial divisions of the vote for and against the proposed constitution represent for the vast majority of counties excellent surrogate measures of the actual numbers of whites and blacks who voted in the 1869 election. The slightly better accuracy that could be had by using extant poll lists would not be worth the huge investment of time and effort required. The manuscript poll lists reveal the name of every legally registered individual who deposited a ballot in the election. Many election officials made separate columns on their poll lists for "white" and "colored" voters, whereas others simply entered a "w" or "c" opposite each name. The actual ballots, which were numbered and deposited in the ballot boxes in the same order in which voters came forward and voted, have apparently not survived. See "Returns of Elections, 1869 [unarranged]," E4850, The 5th Military District, and the Department of Texas, 1867–1870, *Records of the U.S. Army Continental Commands, 1821–1920,* RG 393, NA. The total number of votes cast in the referendum election equaled the number of ballots cast in the governor's race in only 8 counties. In 52 counties the total vote cast in the governor's race fell below the total vote in the referendum, whereas in the remaining 64 counties the vote in the governor's race was higher. In net results, 1,041 more Texans participated in the gubernatorial election than in the constitutional referendum. The largest disparity between the voting totals occurred in Freestone County, where 271 more men managed to vote in the gubernatorial contest than in the referendum balloting. The next largest disparities occurred in El Paso, Rusk, and Galveston Counties, with 228, 218, and 171 more votes, respectively, polled in the governor's race than in the referendum.

been overturned if military authorities had ordered a new election in Milam (northeast of Austin) and Navarro (southeast of Dallas) Counties.[24]

In Milam County the polls were closed due to disturbances on the second day of the balloting; in Navarro County a breakup of the preelection revision of voter registration had occurred. After a Milam County white man shot and wounded a United States army officer escorting about one hundred freedmen to the county seat of Cameron—described by one traveler as "a poor dilapidated town on a sand hill"—a crowd of about 150 to 175 white men from nearby Port Sullivan stormed the polls to prevent the blacks from voting. In Navarro County acts of intimidation against the board of registrars were at the root of the difficulties. After a disfranchised Corsicana merchant by the name of McEntee boasted that he would control "more nigger votes" than any "damned radical" and "whip into voting right" the blacks that he could not "coax into voting right," the president of the registration board left the county with the lists of registered voters and their sworn oaths in his saddlebags. He later claimed that the feelings of hatred against him were due to his father, John H. Lippard, who was a candidate on the Davis ticket for the Twentieth District senatorial seat.[25]

Because throughout the state Davis fared poorly at the hands of white voters and mobilized the overwhelming majority of black votes through the efforts of the Union League, one can easily calculate projected results for Milam and Navarro Counties. In 1870 the black component of the population in Milam and Navarro was one-third and one-fourth, respectively. In 1869 registered blacks in Milam County barely outnumbered their counterparts in Navarro County: 507 blacks and 829 whites were registered in the former; 506 blacks and 664 whites were registered in the latter. If every registered black and white voter had turned out and voted along undivided racial lines, Hamilton's majority over Davis in the two counties would have been 480 votes.[26]

24. Moneyhon, *Republicanism in Reconstruction Texas,* 104–28; Carrier, "A Political History of Texas," 327–404; Gray, "Edmund J. Davis," 175–81.

25. John H. [Benham?], Jr., to Charles E. Morse, December 9, 1869, Microfilm Reel #39, and C. H. Bostnick to Joseph J. Reynolds, December 8, 1869, Microfilm Reel #39, and L. B. Lippard to John B. Johnson, November 22, 1869, Microfilm Reel #27, and John B. Johnson to HFMD, December 9, 1869 [Register #3, p. 640], Microfilm Reel #4, COCADT, RG 393, NA; Dr. G. C. McGregor, quoted in Lelia M. Batte, *History of Milam County, Texas* (San Antonio, 1956), 72; report of M. P. Hunnicutt to John B. Johnson, December 2, 1869, Microfilm Reel #27, and L. B. Lippard to Joseph J. Reynolds, December 20, 1869, Microfilm Reel #38, COCADT, RG 393, NA.

26. *Ninth Census, 1870: Population,* table 2; *Tabular Statement of Registration and Voting,* 2–5. *Cf.* Moneyhon, *Republicanism in Reconstruction Texas,* 124, who assumes that blacks were in the majority in both Milam and Navarro Counties.

TABLE 37

ESTIMATED RELATIONSHIPS BETWEEN VOTING IN THE 1869 GUBERNATORIAL ELECTION AND VOTING IN TWO PREVIOUS BALLOTS

The 1866 and 1869 Gubernatorial Elections (in percentages of 1869 adult males; actual $N = 105$)

	Percentage Having Voted for Throckmorton	Percentage Having Voted for Pease	Percentage Having Been Whites Not Voting in 1866	Percentage Having Been Blacks Unable to Vote in 1866	Percentage Having Been Whites Ineligible to Vote	Percentage Having Been Blacks Not Yet Adults	Totals
1869 Hamilton Voters	12	0	7	2	0	0	21
1869 Davis Voters	0	3	0	18	0	0	21
1869 Voters Not Voting for Governor	14	1	6	9	0	0	30
Adult Males Not Registered	0	3	20	0	4	0	27
Totals	26	7	32	30	4	0	100

The 1868 Convention Referendum and the 1869 Gubernatorial Election   (in percentages of 1868–69 registered voters; actual $N = 121$)

	Percentage Having Been Whites For Convention	Percentage Having Been Whites Against Convention	Percentage Having Been Whites Not Voting	Percentage Having Been Whites Added to Lists	Percentage Having Been Blacks For Convention	Percentage Having Been Blacks Against Convention	Percentage Having Been Blacks Not Voting	Percentage Having Been Blacks Added to Lists	Totals
1869 Hamilton Voters	0	4	9	13	3	0	0	0	29
1869 Davis Voters	5	0	0	0	18	1	1	6	30
1869 Voters Not Voting for Governor	1	4	21	1	6	0	7	0	40
Former Registrants "Stricken Off"	0	0	1	1	0	0	0	0	2
Totals	6	8	30	15	27	1	8	6	100

Note: The slow growth rate in the adult black male population in the late 1860s reflects the migration of many of the formerly "refugeed" slaves out of Texas after the war. For the procedures used to estimate the number of adult black males in 1868 and 1869 and to compensate for the "underenumeration" problems in the 1870 federal census, see the Appendix.

Source: For the sources for the number of white and black voters registered under the authority of the Congressional Reconstruction Acts and for the votes cast in 1868 by white and black registrants for and against a convention call, see table 34 above. For the source of the 1869 gubernatorial returns, see table 36 above; for the 1866 gubernatorial returns, see table 27 above.

The pivotal question is not whether Hamilton would have carried Milam and Navarro Counties, but whether he would have picked up enough additional votes to offset his statewide margin of defeat. Because Hamilton lost by 783 votes, the hypothetical outcome formulated here would not have overturned Davis' victory. In other words, had military authorities held a new election in the two counties, the probability of its changing the statewide result would have been, barring massive intimidation of black voters, extremely remote. Nevertheless, Hamilton claimed that the uncounted votes from the two counties "would almost certainly" have given him the governorship. His adherents illogically prophesied that new elections would have given him a one-thousand-vote majority. After authorities declined to order a new election, Hamilton's supporters charged that he was fraudulently "counted out"—a charge uncritically repeated by Texas historians for over a century.[27]

Discussion of the refusal of military officials to order a new election in Milam and Navarro Counties is often linked to the most powerful and enduring myth about the 1869 election, namely, that General Reynolds, the commander of the Fifth Military District, "never made public" the manuscript returns and that they either "have never been found" or mysteriously—and thus suspiciously—have disappeared.[28] The manuscript returns are in the National Archives, where they are grouped by county, but not in any readily apparent order. Random inspections of voting totals written on thousands of separate slips of certified returns for state and local offices reveal no discrepancies with the county voting totals that military authorities in February, 1870, officially reported.[29]

Reynolds, moreover, had judiciously decided to forgo holding new elections in the two counties. After the election he learned from William J. Parrish, the newly appointed Navarro County sheriff, that "negro whipping" had sharply risen. Seeking revenge against the freedmen for the

27. Andrew J. Hamilton to Joseph J. Reynolds, December 21, 1869, Microfilm Reel #31, COCADT, RG 393, NA; Ramsdell, *Reconstruction in Texas,* 284–85 and 285 n. 1; *Weekly Austin Republican,* January 6, 1870.

28. Richardson, Anderson, and Wallace, *Texas: The Lone Star State,* 234. See also Ernest Wallace, *The Howling of the Coyotes: Reconstruction Efforts to Divide Texas* (College Station, 1979), 134; William L. Richter, *The Army in Texas During Reconstruction, 1865–1870* (College Station, 1987), 254 n. 51; Gray, "Edmund J. Davis," 180; Connor, *Texas: A History,* 221; John Anthony Moretta, "William Pitt Ballinger: Public Servant, Private Pragmatist" (Ph.D. dissertation, Rice University, 1986), 260–61.

29. "Returns of Elections, 1869 [unarranged]," E4850, Fifth Military District 1867–1870, *Records of the U.S. Army Continental Commands, 1821–1920,* RG 393, NA; and *Tabular Statements of Voting in 1869,* 1–46.

breakup of the preelection registration, a mob of whites had taken blacks to the courthouse in Corsicana and pistol-whipped them in public. Sheriff Parrish, who had served in an Illinois regiment during the war, freely admitted that fear for his safety prevented him from thwarting this atrocity. The county's assessor-collector, Andrew Hanson, who was one of the defeated radical candidates for the state legislature, made a similar admission, claiming that his life was also "not safe yet" in the wake of the registration debacle.[30]

Milam County's notorious reputation for lawlessness influenced Reynolds' refusal to schedule a new election. In 1867 Governor Pease had requested that troops be sent to the county because it was practically in a state of rebellion due to the disloyalty of most of its white citizens. In the summer of 1869 a "perfect reign of terror" had followed the cold-blooded murder of United States Army captain George Haller. (Haller was killed because he had undertaken the task of investigating the murder of five freedmen near Cameron.) For months after his assassination, blacks were afraid to talk or even be seen during the day with United States officers. Local white officials admitted that they were "painfully aware" that they were "powerless" to protect blacks from violence. Nothing in the correspondence of the Fifth Military District suggests that the situation had changed in the months following the 1869 election. To the contrary, the reports from the county were disturbing. Davis supporters accused the same Port Sullivan throng of white men who had rushed the polls to prevent blacks from voting of trying to force "the greater portion of the Republicans" into hiding or leaving the county. In March, 1870, shortly before the small detachment of federal troops abandoned Milam County, the local commanding officer reported that it was still unsafe for "any person connected with the Army" to venture alone outside the county seat.[31]

Is it possible that Davis would still have defeated Hamilton if a fair and

30. William J. Parrish to Andrew Hanson and J. H. Lippard, December 29, 1869, Microfilm Reel #38, and Andrew Hanson to Morgan C. Hamilton, December 18, 1869, Microfilm Reel #38, and Morgan C. Hamilton to HFMD, January 7, 1870, [Register 4, p. 821], Microfilm Reel #4, COCADT, RG 393, NA.

31. James Oakes to Elisha M. Pease, October 2, 1867, in Governors' Papers: Pease; Brevet Major W. O. Connell to Theodore J. Wint, August 1, 1869, Microfilm Reel #18, and unidentified and undated statement of a civil officer of Milam County in William A. Cory to Theodore J. Wint, June 30, 1869, Microfilm Reel #9, and J. M. Thurmond to Charles E. Morse, December 12, 1869, Microfilm Reel #18, and Brevet Major Lynde Catlin to H. Clay Wood, March 14, 1870, Microfilm Reel #30, COCADT, RG 393, NA. On the Haller episode, see reports of William A. Cory to Charles E. Morse, July 5, 1869, Microfilm Reel #9, COCADT, RG 393, NA.

free election had taken place in all counties other than Milam and Navarro? Besides looking at counties where sharp declines in black voting occurred between 1868 and 1869, a straightforward way of checking for possible vote fraud is to isolate counties reporting returns out of line with what one might expect, given the racial mix of their voter registrations or racial divisions of their votes cast simultaneously for and against adoption of the 1869 Constitution. The use of ecological regression equations is an even more sophisticated, and arguably better, method for identifying counties where voting irregularities might have occurred. Because the key to Davis' victory lay in mobilizing the votes of the freedmen, knowledge of previous black and white patterns of registering and voting in the 1868 referendum on calling a constitutional convention constitutes a well-specified equation predicting the vote in the subsequent gubernatorial race (see table 37).

A county having a positive residual in table 38 means that, given the proportions of the county's black and white voters who, respectively, voted for a convention, voted against a convention, registered but failed to vote, were added to the registration lists between 1868 and 1869, or were not registered in 1868, and given the statewide relationships between black and white voter turnout for and against a convention call, rates of registering but failing to vote, and extent of not registering to vote, on the one hand, and the Davis or Hamilton vote, on the other, the county favored Davis or Hamilton at a rate much higher than it would have had it behaved in the same way as all Texas counties. Residual values for Davis and Hamilton sum to a more robust measure of a county's idiosyncratic voting behavior; they are referred to here as the "residual net gain" benefiting the candidate who ran unusually well despite winning or losing. To understand the meaning of a residual net gain or loss, consider, for example, counties where Hamilton ran surprisingly well, by either winning by a larger than expected margin or managing to run, although in a losing effort, far better than anticipated. (In the same counties, Davis could have attracted lower than predicted support regardless of whether he carried the county or lost it.) In terms of the analysis presented here, one could thus characterize Hamilton's performance as having profited from an unexpected advantage due to the subtraction of the percentage of the electorate that Davis received below his predicted level from the percentage Hamilton received above his predicted level. The resulting net gain for Hamilton is his unpredictable vote margin over or above the margin of support he otherwise would have had in the county had the county merely behaved in the same way as all Texas counties behaved between 1868 and 1869.

Many explanations other than vote fraud in the 1869 election could account for the idiosyncratic behavior of counties that have voting results out of line with what one might anticipate, given declines in black turnout, racial breakdowns of votes cast for and against the 1869 Constitution, or largest percentage swings away from predicted vote margins based on previous voting in the 1868 referendum (see tables 38 and 39). If not, the counties must be scrutinized more thoroughly because they remain under suspicion of being localities where voting irregularities occurred.

Both Davis and Hamilton ran very well where they resided, namely, the Corpus Christi and Austin areas, respectively. The abnormally high levels of turnout for Hamilton in Williamson and Travis Counties and for Davis in Nueces, De Witt, and Calhoun Counties are thus not surprising (see table 38). Although Williamson County (north of Austin) had the highest estimated percentage of black registrants voting for Hamilton, no complaints by radicals regarding the fairness of the outcome have yet been found. Hamilton's lopsided victory in the county, which had favored his candidacy for the United States Congress in 1859 and had voted against secession in a statewide referendum in 1861, must, therefore, be taken at face value.[32]

Other counties, like Williamson, where Hamilton ran far better than the statewide trends would have predicted, but also where Davis' supporters made virtually no complaints regarding the results, are Jack, Erath, Brazoria, Bandera, and Blanco (see table 39). Only Brazoria County (south of Houston) among this group was located far from the western frontier. It also was unsurpassed among all Texas counties in having the largest estimated raw number of its black registrants voting for Hamilton (see table 36). Although Davis' victory was never in doubt in Brazoria County, his shallow 169-vote majority was far below normal in this coastal region commonly referred to throughout the late nineteenth century as "Senegambia," an allusion to the area's large black population. By way of comparison, carpetbagger William T. Clark, the successful radical candidate for Congress, defeated his Democratic opponent in Brazoria County by 821 votes.[33]

The robust Hamilton vote in Brazoria County reflected an intramural Republican battle in the Twelfth District senatorial race. Running on the Hamilton ticket was Andrew P. McCormick, a scalawag who had received

---

32. For the sources for the Williamson County vote in the 1859 congressional and 1861 secession referendum elections, see Appendix.

33. *Tabular Statements of Voting in 1869,* 7. A representative racial characterization of the area can be found in the Austin *Statesman,* February 3, 1876.

TABLE 38

OUTLIER COUNTIES IN THE 1869 GUBERNATORIAL CONTEST

(in percentages of 1869 county electorates)

Abnormally High Turnout for Hamilton and Davis

County	*Above Expected Turnout for Hamilton* (%)	County	*Above Expected Turnout for Davis* (%)
Jack	24	Hill	18
San Saba	23	Medina	16
Bandera	23	Gillespie	15
Williamson	15	Mason	13
San Augustine	14	Nueces	11
Sabine	11	Newton	10
Falls	11	Red River	10
Blanco	11	De Witt	10
Brazoria	11	Henderson	9
Cooke	11	Calhoun	9
Montague	10	Kerr	9
Travis	8	Guadalupe	9
Orange	7	Kendall	9
		Wilson	9
		El Paso	8

Abnormally Low Turnout for Hamilton and Davis

County	*Below Expected Turnout for Hamilton* (%)	County	*Below Expected Turnout for Davis* (%)
Brown	−18	Erath	−20
Mason	−16	Sabine	−19
Uvalde	−16	Williamson	−18
Comanche	−13	Jack	−15
El Paso	−13	Falls	−15
Hill	−12	Brazoria	−15
Polk	−11	Burnet	−13
Trinity	−11	Jasper	−12
Chambers	−11	Blanco	−10
Medina	−11		
Jackson	−10		
Newton	−9		
Gillespie	−8		
Hardin	−8		
Matagorda	−8		
Refugio	−8		
Wharton	−8		
Wilson	−7		

TABLE 38

(continued)

Source: The residual values were generated by the equations which were used to construct the second contingency table in table 37 above.

Note: The residual values or scores above are the differences between the actual percentages of the county electorates voting for Hamilton and Davis, on one hand, and the corresponding estimated or predicted levels of support for Hamilton and Davis, on the other. The predicted levels for this table are based on voting in the 1868 constitutional convention referendum. Outliers are arbitrarily defined here as having residual values falling at least two standard errors above or below the respective regression lines. The voting returns were analyzed by multiple ecological regressions, taking the percentages of potentially eligible voters favoring Hamilton and Davis in the 1869 gubernatorial election as the dependent variables. The independent variables, analyzed separately for the Hamilton and Davis percentages, were the proportions of the 1869 electorate consisting of (1) blacks voting against calling a constitutional convention, (2) blacks voting for holding a convention, (3) whites voting against a convention, (4) whites voting for a convention, (5) blacks registered in 1868 but not voting in the convention referendum, (6) whites registered in 1868 but not voting in the convention referendum, (7) blacks added to the registration lists between 1868 and 1869, and (8) whites added to the registration lists between 1868 and 1869. To avoid multicollinearity, the percentage of the 1869 electorate constituting whites who were not registered at the time of the 1869 gubernatorial election was not used. All variables were weighted by the adult male population. For the equation predicting the Hamilton percentage, R^2 = .62; standard error = .04; and actual N = 119. For the equation predicting the Davis percentage, R^2 = .84; standard error = .04; and actual N = 119.

an appointment as the county's chief justice during Presidential Reconstruction and afterwards had been elected as a delegate to the constitutional conventions of 1866 and 1868–1869. McCormick mounted a spirited, but unsuccessful, challenge to Davis supporter George T. Ruby of Galveston. Ruby, a mulatto carpetbagger who had arrived in Texas in 1866 as an agent of the Freedmen's Bureau, was the powerful and skillful leader of the Union League. Ruby later became one of Davis' most important supporters, and Governor Davis subsequently appointed McCormick to a district judgeship. The conventional wisdom that many blacks in Brazoria County freely voted for Hamilton should thus be allowed to stand.[34]

Neither Hamilton's supporters nor subsequent accounts by historians challenged the uncommonly high level of support for Davis in the central Texas "hill country" region. Here, high concentrations of German Texans caused contemporaries of the period to anticipate Davis' strong showing in Medina, Gillespie, Mason, Kerr, and Kendall Counties (see table 38). On the Davis ticket for land office commissioner was Jacob Kuechler, a German-born scientist and socialist who had raised in 1862 a short-lived unionist volunteer company in Gillespie County (Fredericksburg). Joining him on the radical ticket for representative to Congress was Edward Degener, a former member of the 1848 German National Assembly at Frankfurt

---

34. Budd, "The Negro in Politics," 33–34; *Weekly Austin Republican,* April 28, 1869; Webb, Carroll, and Branda, eds., *The Handbook of Texas,* II, 104; Eric Foner, *Freedom's Lawmakers: A Directory of Black Officeholders During Reconstruction* (New York, 1993), 187; Campbell, "Grass Roots Reconstruction: The Personnel of County Government in Texas, 1865–1876," *Journal of Southern History,* LVIII (1992), 115.

TABLE 39

NET GAINS FOR HAMILTON AND DAVIS IN TERMS OF
VOTER SUPPORT ABOVE OR BELOW PREDICTED LEVELS

(in percentages of 1869 county electorates)

Residual Net Gains Greater Than 18 Percentage Points for Hamilton

County	Net Gain for Hamilton over Davis (%)	Estimated Size of 1869 Electorate
Jack	39	186
Williamson *(Georgetown)*	33	1,319
Sabine	31	682
San Saba	28	278
Falls *(Marlin)*	26	2,108
Erath	26	403
Brazoria	26	1,865
San Augustine	23	815
Bandera	23	163
Blanco	20	256
Burnet	18	716

Residual Net Gains Greater Than 18 Percentage Points for Davis

County	Net Gain for Davis over Hamilton (%)	Estimated Size of 1869 Electorate
Hill *(Hillsboro)*	29	1,515
Medina	26	460
Gillespie	23	728
El Paso *(San Elizario)*	22	1,097
Newton	18	477
Refugio	18	597

**Residual Net Gains for Hamilton or Davis in Counties Having Allegations
of Voting Irregularities**

Intimidation of Black Voters

County	Net Gain for Hamilton (%)	Net Gain for Davis (%)	Estimated Size of 1869 Electorate
Anderson *(Palestine)*		4	2,099
Coryell	13		807
Dallas *(Dallas)*		5	2,924
Denton *(Denton)*		1	1,563
Ellis *(Waxahachie)*	2		1,757
Colorado *(Columbus)*		2	2,531
Cherokee *(Rusk)*	1		2,409
Falls *(Marlin)*	26		2,108
Hood	6		595
Jasper	13		791

TABLE 39

(continued)

County	Net Gain for Hamilton (%)	Net Gain for Davis (%)	Estimated Size of 1869 Electorate
Johnson *(Cleburne)*	3		1,093
Kaufman *(Kaufman)*	1		1,451
Lamar *(Paris)*	1		3,277
McLennan *(Waco)*	1		3,006
Nacogdoches *(Nacogdoches)*		4	1,910
Panola *(Carthage)*	10		1,979
Rusk *(Henderson)*		4	3,459
Sabine	31		682
San Augustine	23		815
Tarrant *(Fort Worth)*	11		1,372
Walker *(Huntsville)*	2		2,355
Wharton		11	995

Other Election Irregularities Imputed to Pro-Hamilton Supporters

County	Net Gain for Hamilton (%)	Net Gain for Davis (%)	Estimated Size of 1869 Electorate
Anderson *(Palestine)*		4	2,099
Burnet	18		716
Cameron *(Brownsville)*		7	3,201
Cherokee *(Rusk)*	1		2,409
Fannin *(Bonham)*	3		2,755
Lamar *(Paris)*	1		3,277
Starr *(Rio Grande City)*	0	0	1,256
Robertson *(Owensville)*	7		2,513
Washington *(Brenham)*	0	0	5,277
Webb		5	793
Wood *(Quitman)*	5		1,354
Zapata		3	368

Other Election Irregularities Imputed to Pro-Davis Supporters

County	Net Gain for Hamilton (%)	Net Gain for Davis (%)	Estimated Size of 1869 Electorate
El Paso *(San Elizario)*		22	1,097
Hill *(Hillsboro)*		29	1,515
Bexar *(San Antonio)*		3	3,551

Source: For allegations of fraud in the above counties, see Ricky Floyd Dobbs, "'A Slow Civil War': Resistance to the Davis Administration in Hill and Walker Counties, 1871" (M.A. thesis, Baylor University, 1989), 16–22; Ronald N. Gray, "Edmund J. Davis: Radical Republican and Reconstruction Governor of Texas" (Ph.D. dissertation, Texas Tech University, 1976), note 103 on p. 181; James M. Smallwood, *Time of Hope, Time of Despair: Black Texans during Reconstruction* (Port Washington, N.Y., 1981), 145–46; Edmund J. Davis to HFMD, December 13, 1869, Microfilm Reel #39, Andrew J. Hamilton to HFMD, December 21, 1869 [Registrar 4, p. 373], Microfilm Reel #4, James G. Tracy to HFMD, December 11, 1869 [Registrar 4, p. 822], Microfilm Reel #4, Joseph Conrad to Charles E. Morse, January 21, 1870, Microfilm Reel #34, James Brown and B. F. Boydstun to Charles E. Morse, December 27, 1869,

(continued)

TABLE 39

(continued)

Microfilm Reel #32, and Mary E. Coffee to Joseph E. Reynolds, January 28, 1870, Microfilm Reel #28, COCDADT, NA; Cruise Carson to Edmund J. Davis, January 12, 1870, Edward Hall to Edmund J. Davis, April 9, 1870, and James Bryden to Edmund J. Davis, January 23, 1870, Governors' Papers: Edmund J. Davis, STL.

Note: The percentages above represent the net gains (in terms of shares of estimated 1869 potentially eligible voters in each county) for Davis and Hamilton due to idiosyncratic county voting behavior above or below the statewide trends estimated by the equations described in table 38 above. For example, the finding that Hamilton benefited in Falls County from a 26-percentage-point advantage was calculated by subtracting the 15 percentage points which Davis received *below* his predicted level from the 11 percentage points Hamilton received *above* his predicted level (or 11% minus −15% = 26%). In other words, Hamilton in Falls County profited from an unexplained vote margin over and above the margin of support he would have had in the county had the county merely behaved in the same way as all Texas counties between the 1868 referendum balloting and the 1869 governor's race.

am Main. During the war, civil authorities imprisoned Degener on charges of treason, and Kuechler narrowly escaped death when Confederate soldiers massacred his party of German unionists fleeing from Texas via Mexico to the North. Degener's two sons, Hugo and Hilmer, who accompanied Kuechler were killed at this so-called Battle of the Nueces.[35]

After failing to get a new election ordered in Milam and Navarro Counties, Hamilton narrowed his allegations of radical Republican chicanery to Bexar (San Antonio), El Paso (present-day El Paso), and Hill (Hillsboro) Counties. Among the nineteen counties where Davis received an estimated one-fifth or more of the ballots cast by white men, only Hill County is demographically anomalous (see table 36). Located in the "blacklands" of the north-central part of the state, Hill County neither contained significant concentrations of foreign-born Texans (as did Medina, Kendall, Gillespie, El Paso, Zapata, Comal, Maverick, Bexar, Kerr, Wilson, Blanco, Presidio, Guadalupe, and Mason Counties) nor shared geographical proximity to Davis' home in South Texas (as did Nueces, Refugio, Cameron, and Calhoun Counties). Moreover, unlike the above named counties, Hill had a flourishing clandestine Ku Klux Klan outfitted in "masks, gowns and tall hats" that compelled local blacks "to whip each other until they could hardly stand." The county also had a distinctive reputation in the postwar period for "the vicious persecutions and murders of Union men and their families."[36]

Davis carried Hill County because he received about 270 more votes

35. Jordan, *German Seed in Texas Soil,* 54–59, 182–85; Frank W. Heintzen, "Fredericksburg, Texas, During the Civil War and Reconstruction" (M.A. thesis, St. Mary's University of San Antonio, 1944), 29, 99; Webb, Carroll, and Branda, eds., *The Handbook of Texas,* I, 482, II, 290; Carrier, "A Political History of Texas," 45, 253; Marten, *Texas Divided,* 115–17; Kamphoefner, "Texas Germans and Civil War Issues," 17–18.

36. Harrison Holt to John B. Johnson, September 3, 1869, Microfilm Reel #27, COCADT, RG 393, NA; Richter, *Overreached on All Sides,* 191.

than he would have attracted had the county behaved as all Texas counties between 1868 and 1869 (see tables 38 and 39). When combined with the finding that Hamilton received about 180 votes below his predicted level of support, Davis should have lost Hill County to Hamilton by a margin of around 300 votes. If radical election managers in any county had stuffed the ballot box by adding many Davis tickets and extracting a smaller number of Hamilton ballots, the pattern of abnormal support for Davis would resemble that of Hill County. Here, the extent of discounted Hamilton ballots and the higher than predicted voter turnout offset the amount of inflated Davis strength.

The most recent scholarly analysis of Hill County during Reconstruction accepts the 1869 result without question, arguing that white support for Davis was "particularly strong in and around Hillsboro." Hamilton and his supporters, however, claimed that the Hill County vote was "a deliberate fraud" because the ballot boxes had been taken away before the polls closed and then subsequently returned. Only one member of the registry board apparently counted the votes. The historical literature on the 1869 election has overlooked the detail that indictments handed down in early 1872 by a federal grand jury confirmed that the voters' intentions were, one way or another, fraudulently misrepresented. The same group of Hill County radical Republicans who tampered with the ballot box in 1869 was subsequently proven to have stuffed it in the 1871 congressional elections.[37]

Davis received his largest estimated number of votes among white men in Bexar and El Paso Counties. Both were localities where Hamilton claimed voting irregularities had cost him votes (see table 36). In Bexar County, unlike in Hill County, the victory of the radical ticket was not surprising, especially given the size of the county's Tejano population and the strength of prewar anti-secessionist sentiment in San Antonio. The probable percentage of Bexar County's registered whites who favored Davis was not out of line with the percentage of whites who probably voted for

37. Ricky Floyd Dobbs, " 'A Slow Civil War': Resistance to the Davis Administration in Hill and Walker Counties, 1871" (M.A. thesis, Baylor University, 1989), 58; Andrew J. Hamilton to Joseph J. Reynolds, December 21, 1869, Microfilm Reel #31, COCADT, RG 393, NA; Dallas *Herald,* January 15, 1870; *Weekly Austin Republican,* December 22, 1869; Ramsdell, *Reconstruction in Texas,* 284. William Hooper and William L. Booth engineered the fraudulent election giving Davis 322 and Hamilton 173 votes in Hill County. See the testimony of George S. Chambers and George R. Hart, in "D. C. Giddings vs. W. T. Clark," *House Miscellaneous Documents,* Doc. 163, 42nd Cong., 2nd Sess., Serial 1526, pp. 152–55; *Tri-Weekly Statesman* (Austin), February 3, 1872. In the 1871 congressional election the ballot box was again stuffed with Republican ballots, but the Republican candidate, William T. Clark, failed to carry the county. *Cf.* Ellis Bailey, *A History of Hill County, Texas: 1836–1965* (Waco, 1966), 122.

him in neighboring Comal, Wilson, and Blanco Counties. Nor was Davis' margin of victory over Hamilton in Bexar County unusually large (see tables 36 and 39). In short, the quantitative evidence does not support the allegation that the radicals benefited from a fraudulent outcome in Bexar County. However, the same evidence demands that the result in El Paso County be placed under suspicion of possible vote fraud.

Issues touching on civic and political equality for African Americans had counted for little in El Paso, the outermost western county on the Chihuahua–to–Santa Fe trail. With only two of the county's four registered blacks participating in the 1869 balloting, the 336 votes polled by Davis had to have been cast primarily by Mexican Texans. Hamilton received only 122 votes, although his supporters subsequently obtained affidavits from hundreds of men who swore that they had voted for him. Local Anglo radicals described these men as "ignorant Mexicans" who "have been bought and cannot read." If the El Paso County vote had merely reflected the statewide voting trends between 1868 and 1869, then Hamilton would have carried the county by a narrow margin (see tables 38 and 39). Historical accounts agree that during the late sixties and early seventies El Paso County elections were usually "characterized by fraud, vote purchasing, ballot stuffing, bribery, intimidation, or tampering by corrupt election officials," but scholars have reached no consensus over the extent to which the actual intentions of the county's voters were misrepresented.[38]

The chief players in the tramontane balloting in 1869 in El Paso included the Reverend Antonio Borajo, an influential Catholic priest who felt his position challenged by the European and Anglo elite; W. W. Mills, a prominent anti-secessionist who had married Hamilton's daughter after the war; Louis Cardis, a recent Italian immigrant who had served as a captain in Garibaldi's army; and Albert J. Fountain, a former Union army officer from California via New York, whose life was, in the words of his biographer, "one of the most colorful and amazing careers in the history of the American West." These men were swept up by Republican factionalism, personal quarrels, and unanticipated events, but the struggle that configured El Paso politics throughout the Reconstruction period was the effort to secure ownership of the salt deposits at nearby Guadalupe Peak. When Fountain de-

---

38. Frank R. Diffenderfer to Edward Degener, January 5, 1870, [Register 3, p. 191], Microfilm Reel #4, and W. M. Pierson's endorsement on a letter by Frank R. Diffenderfer to HFMD, December 19, 1869, [Register 3, p. 189], Microfilm Reel #4, COCADT, RG 393, NA; W. H. Timmons, *El Paso: A Borderlands History* (El Paso, 1990), 156; De León, *They Called Them Greasers*, 56.

cided to run on the Davis ticket for the state legislature solely on the promise
to acquire the salt flats for all El Pasoans, his feud with Mills, who was
running for the legislature as a conservative Republican candidate in the
camp of his father-in-law, became public.[39]

Immersion in the deluge of accusations surrounding the 1869 election
results in El Paso County discloses a remark that goes to the heart of the
fraud issue. The commanding officer at Fort Bliss wrote that Fountain and
another had confided to him that they had "procured the alteration of
ballots fraudulently . . . but that the Board of Registrars were in no way
responsible for it." Because of this comment and other evidence, the best
hypothesis is that Fountain's ally, Father Borajo, masterminded the alterations of Hamilton ballots in the hands of many Spanish-speaking voters who
arrived in the county seat of San Elizario, twenty miles below El Paso, to
vote on the first day of the election. The modifications, or "scratchings,"
which were made mostly with a blue crayon pencil, changed many votes
for county as well as state offices.[40]

El Paso conservatives subsequently charged that the "cool, calculated and
deliberate" alterations made "clear through" many Hamilton ballots could
not possibly have been made in the street or in a crowd, but were fabricated
after the board of registrars allowed the radical faction to tamper with the
ballot box. The anti-radical faction also claimed that the actual vote in their
county should have been "about 278 for Hamilton and 182 for Davis."
Generated by the analysis of voting patterns throughout the state between
1868 and 1869, the estimated El Paso County outcome in the Davis-
Hamilton race yields a narrow 269-to-245-vote victory for Hamilton.
Therefore, the statistical findings produced here suggest that Hamilton received about 147 fewer votes than he would have received if El Paso
County had merely mimicked the statewide trends. Fountain, Borajo, and
the radicals might easily have altered, or to use the favorite word of the
conservatives, "disfigured," as many as 154 Hamilton tickets.[41]

39. Sonnichsen, *Pass of the North*, 173–94; A. M. Gibson, *The Life and Death of Colonel Albert Jennings
Fountain* (Norman, 1965), 4.

40. Sonnichsen, *Pass of the North*, 186; H. C. Merriam's comments written on back of Albert H.
French's affidavit, December 4, 1869, Microfilm Reel #28, COCADT, RG 393, NA; Gaylord J. Clarke
to W. W. Mills, December 7, 1869, quoted in W. W. Mills, *El Paso, A Glance at Its Men and Contests for
the Last Few Years. The Election Fraud, the Marshes, Williams, Pearson, Verney, Stine, and Fountain, the
Infamous* (Austin, 1871), 11; affidavit of José María Gonzáles, December 15, 1869, Microfilm Reel #28,
COCADT, RG 393, NA.

41. Affidavit of José María Gonzáles, December 15, 1869, Microfilm Reel #28, COCADT, RG
393, NA; Gaylord J. Clarke, quoted in W. W. Mills, *El Paso, A Glance*, 11–12; affidavit of Albert H.
French, December 4, 1869, Microfilm Reel #28, COCADT, RG 393, NA.

In spite of the corroborating statistical evidence presented here of electoral fraud in El Paso County, the actual extent to which the voters' intentions were violated remains problematical. Fountain and Borajo cleverly capitalized on genuine and widespread distrust of Mills's designs on the nearby salinas, where the salt had historically been free for the taking. Moreover, Fountain's subsequent efforts to keep the salt beds in the hands of all citizens and out of the grasp of rapacious groups of Anglos were honorable and sincere. Nevertheless, a second look at the 1869 voting returns suggests that his election to the Texas senate was achieved by an additional subtlety, perhaps even by outright guile.[42]

Cardis, whose murder eight years later in 1877 triggered the bloody "El Paso Salt War," repeatedly accused Fountain of having "crept" in 1869 into the legislature by a "trick." The Davis ticket in El Paso and in neighboring Presidio County mysteriously listed Jesus Lujan in Fountain's place for state senator. Lujan, a disfranchised member of a prominent Tejano family, had vigorously aided the Confederacy in his capacity as a county commissioner during the war. Fountain thus received not one vote in the county of his residence for the office that he won only because of votes cast for him in counties other than El Paso and Presidio. Lujan's popularity presumably helped Borajo's operatives distribute Davis tickets or, perhaps more important, write in Lujan's name over that of James B. Thomas, who was the conservative senatorial candidate listed on the Hamilton ballot. So successful was this ploy that Thomas, who was Fountain's principal challenger, received less than 10 percent of the ballots cast in El Paso and Presidio Counties, which were in the extreme western end of the Thirtieth Senatorial District. If Thomas had won the same number of votes that Hamilton polled in El Paso County, Fountain would have lost the senatorial race.[43]

If one moves the 154 controversial "disfigured" El Paso County ballots into Hamilton's column, subtracts from Davis' column the undeniably fraudulent Hill County votes generously estimated at approximately 200 ballots, and adds into the statewide totals the hypothetically generated 480-vote majority for Hamilton in Milam and Navarro Counties, then Hamilton would have been elected with about a 205-vote margin of victory. (The adjusted vote would equal 39,689 votes for Hamilton and 39,484 votes for

42. Sonnichsen, *Pass of the North*, 186.

43. *Ibid.*, 186; Louis Cardis, quoted in Timmons, *El Paso*, 160; W. W. Mills, *Forty Years at El Paso, 1858–1898* (El Paso, 1962), 10–11 n. 17; William P. Bacon to Albert H. French, January 2, 1868, Microfilm Reel #28, COCADT, RG 393, NA; and *Tabular Statements of Voting in 1869*, pp. 3, 22.

Davis.) This adjustment in the balloting, however, fails to take into account the number of black votes lost to Davis because of physical intimidation and economic coercion exercised against the freedmen. If a fair and free election had taken place in all areas of the state, Davis still would have won.

An examination of the primary and secondary sources uncovers at least twenty-two counties stigmatized by allegations of varying degrees of intimidation of black voters during the 1869 election (see table 39). Statements by military authorities regarding fraud were less frequent, although arguably more credible, than charges leveled by Davis' supporters. According to the company commander at the post of Nacogdoches, "hundreds of colored voters" in his corner of northeastern Texas "were, by open threats, and violence and other influences," prevented from voting. Although Davis in a losing cause ran better in Nacogdoches County than expected, one cannot say the same for the surrounding counties of Jasper, Panola, Sabine, and San Augustine, where Hamilton defeated him by unpredictably large margins.[44]

Davis lost Sabine County by a lopsided 336–5 vote. Black and white registration figures were 249 and 427, respectively. Assuming that blacks voting in the constitutional referendum cast complete tickets (and did not "scratch" gubernatorial candidates from their ballots), the freedmen in Sabine County favored Hamilton over Davis at an extraordinary rate of twenty-six to one. In San Augustine County, where registered blacks slightly outnumbered registered whites, Davis managed to poll only 157 votes out of a total of 490 cast. With 309 blacks on the registration lists in Jasper County and 185 of them participating in the referendum balloting, Davis managed to garner only 13 votes. In Panola County, 220 of the county's 569 registered blacks participated in the constitution's ratification election, but Davis won only 63 votes.[45]

Davis used the rhetoric of fraud to characterize the results in San Augustine, Jasper, and Sabine Counties and demanded an investigation of the returns from Panola County, where over three-fifths of the registered blacks had failed to turn out and vote in the constitutional referendum. Curiously, however, his supporters provided him virtually no details regarding the

44. Joseph Conrad to Charles E. Morse, January 21, 1870, and Edmund J. Davis to Joseph J. Reynolds, December 14, 1869, Microfilm Reel #34, COCADT, RG 393, NA.

45. The atypical 100 percent registration rate for Sabine County's adult white males suggests that false swearing during voter registration was common among the county's ex-Confederates. On the other hand, this extraordinary white adult registration rate could be an artifact of underenumeration problems in the 1870 federal census. Comparable white adult registration rates in 1869 for San Augustine, Jasper, and Panola Counties were 86, 85, and 68 percent, respectively.

intimidation of black voters in these counties. Since the arrival in the region of federal soldiers, dislike of the Freedmen's Bureau agents and the army's role in Reconstruction had been pervasive, even though many occupying troops in this region were "butternuts" from Illinois, who had little sympathy for the freedmen. Perhaps the activities of outlaw gangs and the Ku Klux Klan were not more violent in this area than elsewhere throughout northeastern Texas, but no one questions the prevalence during this period of secretive white terrorist groups that murdered, intimidated, and defrauded the freedmen with impunity.[46]

In San Augustine County in early 1868 during the election on calling a constitutional convention and selecting delegates, "rebels" had assaulted the polling place. Apparently inspired by a justice of the peace's injunction to "go ahead" and "drive those damn Yankees out," the rioters broke windows, shot one black voter, threatened others, and forced the black member of the registration board into hiding. Only the interference of "respectable citizens" spared remaining election managers, including the Freedmen's Bureau agent, from violence and enabled the election to proceed, although without the black member of the board. In spite of this incident, blacks courageously turned out and voted in sufficient numbers to carry the county for convention delegates on the "Union [Republican] Ticket."[47]

A historical account published in the 1930s celebrates the exploits during this time of a Klan-type organization that consisted of some two hundred men. They were allegedly led by I. D. Thomas, Jr., the son of the wealthy planter-merchant I. D. Thomas, county clerk of San Augustine County from his election in 1869 until his resignation on March 5, 1873. His son's self-styled Invisible Empire allegedly staged relentless nightly raids in San Augustine and neighboring Sabine counties, administering a "good flogging" to "obnoxious" black leaders and driving away those "whose minds had been inflamed by Yankee emissaries." This white terrorism presumably increased during the time of the 1869 balloting, when the same narrator

46. Edmund J. Davis to Joseph J. Reynolds, December 14, 1869, Microfilm Reel #34, COCADT, RG 393, NA; Frank Holsinger, April 5, 1866, Register of Letters Received (Feb. 25, 1866 to Aug. 30, 1867), p. 181, Microfilm Reel #3, BRFAL, RG 105, NA; Smallwood, "When the Klan Rode," 4–13; Richter, *Overreached on All Sides*, 44, 47, 114, 262–64; McPherson, *Ordeal by Fire*, 20.

47. William Phillips to Elisha M. Pease, February 10, 1868, quoted in Sandlin, "The Texas Reconstruction Constitutional Convention," 35; affidavit of Albert A. Metzner, June 19, 1868, and Albert A. Metzner to C. P. Richardson, February 21, 1868, Microfilm Reel #13, BRFAL, RG 105, NA; Richter, *Overreached on All Sides*, 171–72.

declares the blacks to have become "inspired with a wholesome respect for the white population."[48]

The plight of James Lowrie, the Freedmen's Bureau agent in Jasper County, captures the flavor of the times in this area during Congressional Reconstruction. Lowrie had been shot in the thigh by unknown assailants on a summer night in 1867. While recuperating, he caused a crisis by arresting Sheriff J. K. P. Truett for killing a freedman. (Truett had stabbed the freedman in the lung with a large pocket knife at a political meeting.) Claiming that only President Andrew Johnson could order troops to detain their sheriff, crowds of local whites went berserk, and rabble-rousers called for an armed attack upon an occupying force of soldiers. After mollifying a mob by letting the sheriff go free, Lowrie was himself "arrested" and subjected to a kangaroo-court proceeding that evaluated his "crimes." Without constant troop support, Lowrie was subsequently ineffective as a bureau agent. During the following summer he fled the county to avoid assassination. A military report on Lowrie's predicaments concluded that most whites still viewed the freedmen as "legitimate plunder" and labor settlements would again be unfair in the region. A similar report a year later characterized the area as a "district where Emancipation has never reached."[49]

The best hypothesis regarding the suppression of the black vote in Jasper, Sabine, San Augustine, and Panola Counties is that the weakness of local Republican party Union League organizations, the inability of military authorities or county officials to force whites to play by the rules, and the lack of leadership among the smattering of white Republicans rendered blacks in these counties—much more so than elsewhere in northeastern Texas— unable to protect their lives, property, and contractual rights, much less defend the integrity of their franchise. Without any foundation upon which to mobilize their support for Davis and the radical ticket, black voters in these counties were understandably reluctant to assert their right to vote. Predictably, immediately after General Reynolds announced the victory of Davis, white terrorist groups retaliated throughout the region against blacks known to have voted for Davis. In response to daily reports of outrages of

48. George Louis Crocket, *Two Centuries in East Texas: A History of San Augustine County and Surrounding Territory from 1685 to the Present Time* (Dallas, 1932), 347 (first and third quotations), 348 (second quotation) and 349 (fourth and fifth quotations); *Registers of Elected and Appointed State and County Officials, 1867–1885,* Microfilm Reel #5, p. 525, RG 307, TSL.

49. James Lowrie to Joel T. Kirkman, September 13, 1867, Microfilm Reel #13, BRFAL, RG 105, NA; Richter, *Overreached on All Sides,* 175–76, 275–76; Smallwood, *Time of Hope, Time of Despair,* 145.

this sort, the commander at Nacogdoches reported that he was making "no attempts" to arrest and punish the offenders because local civil officers were "afraid to act" and the small number of troops at his disposal prevented him from rendering assistance.[50]

Burnet, Coryell, and Tarrant are other counties where Davis supporters used the rhetoric of fraud and Hamilton received uncommonly high voter support (see table 39). Hamilton carried Tarrant County (Fort Worth) by a majority of 514 votes. Perhaps, as alleged, Hamilton supporters swindled many freedmen out of their votes by crossing out Davis' name and substituting Hamilton's name on radical tickets. Davis, however, ran ahead of radicals running for county offices. Because factionalism split the small group of white radicals in Tarrant County, some doubt must fall on the veracity of statements made to military authorities regarding possible fraud in the gubernatorial race. Scalawags Hiram S. Johnson and Benjamin F. Barkley provided weak and discredited leadership to the Davis forces. The former was a onetime Freedmen's Bureau agent in Trinity County whom the army had dismissed from the service with a loss of all his pay; the latter was a physician-lawyer and a wartime-victimized unionist who, nonetheless, repeatedly failed during the postwar period to win the confidence of the local commanders of occupying troops. Johnson and Barkley most likely contributed as much, if not more, to Hamilton's strong showing in Tarrant County as did frauds committed against the county's black voters.[51]

Coryell County (Gatesville), located in north-central Texas on the legendary Chisholm Trail, failed to give Davis a single vote. A local military commander blamed the lopsided result on ex-sheriff William W. Hammack, who, although under indictment for allowing the lynching of prisoners in his jail, still exercised along with others in his family a powerful influence at the time of the balloting. While it might have been true, as alleged, that the small group of freedmen in the county was "either kept away from the polls by fear or made to vote as Hammack dictated," abnormally large margins for Hamilton characterized this entire region of the state.[52]

50. Joseph Conrad to Charles E. Morse, January 21, 1870, Microfilm Reel #34, COCADT, RG 393, NA.

51. A. G. Walker to Joseph J. Reynolds, December 14, 1869, and T. C. Tupper's report on the state of affairs in Tarrant County, January 26, 1870, Microfilm Reel #38, COCADT, RG 393 NA; Richter, *Overreached on All Sides*, 192–94, 206.

52. Lieutenant J. H. Sands to Charles E. Morse, January 20, 1870, Microfilm Reel #40, COCADT, RG 393, NA.

To the west of Coryell County lay a string of a dozen counties extending along the northwestern frontier of settlement, including Jack, San Saba, Erath, and Burnet. All are also "flagged" here by the statistical analysis for exceptionally large margins for Hamilton (see table 39). In these twelve adjoining counties, Davis polled a scant 39 votes out of 1,129 votes cast. The handful of Burnet County freedmen who claimed that their radical tickets were deliberately never counted might have been telling the truth, but this irregularity alone would scarcely begin to explain Hamilton's unpredictably large margin of support over Davis. In all these counties, including Coryell, because of their geographical contiguity, small percentages of blacks, and shared ranching and cattle culture, it is reasonable to accept at almost face value Hamilton's unusual success.[53]

The absence of abnormally large residual net gains favoring either Hamilton or Davis in a particular county does not necessarily prove that the election was free from vote fraud. A case in point is Lamar County, located on the Red River in extreme North Texas. Here, the intimidation of black voters failed to benefit Hamilton because of factionalism among the county's white voters. Most white citizens in the county, including even some "mortified Democrats," suspected that a familial clique of local Hamilton men had tampered with the ballots. The chicanery involving the ballot box apparently could have been "proved by circumstantial testimony as strong as ever hung any man," but it extended to only a couple of local races and not to the governor's race. The quantitative evidence presented here provides no support for the frequently quoted allegation that a palpable "leak" in the ballot box drained away as many as "500 votes" from Davis' column (see table 39). The evidence merely confirms that the popular revulsion in the white community against the Micajah L. Armstrong family deprived Hamilton of many white votes. Before the election Davis had blamed many of the bad conditions in Lamar County on the Armstrong family and its confidants, especially George Armstrong, John S. Bland, and G. W. DeWitt. The poor showing by Hamilton, however, must not be allowed to obscure another peculiarity: Lamar County had the largest decline in the state in the number of blacks voting between 1868 and 1869 (see table 35).[54]

53. Mary E. Coffee to Joseph J. Reynolds, 28 January 1870, Microfilm Reel #28, COCADT, RG 393, NA. The string of twelve counties on the northwestern frontier includes Brown, Burnet, Comanche, Erath, Hamilton, Jack, Lampasas, Llano, Montague, Palo Pinto, San Saba, and Wise.

54. Richard Peterson to Edmund J. Davis, December 24, 1869, and John H. Fowler to Edmund J. Davis, December 10, 1869, Microfilm Reel #38, COCADT, RG 393, NA: John H. Fowler to Edmund J. Davis, January 25, 1870, in Governors' Papers: Edmund J. Davis, RG 301, TSL; [Petition of over one

In effect, the "fraud imbroglio" had made inconsequential the intimidation of blacks prior to the election. Described during the war by an aristocratic female refugee from Louisiana as "the dark corner" of the Confederacy, Lamar County after the war became inundated by Klan klaverns and outlaw gangs. The streets of Paris, the county seat, literally "rang with gunfire, night and day." In the spring of 1868, DeWitt C. Brown, the local Freedmen's Bureau agent whom the Klan marked for death, reported in disbelief that several white "young ladies" had entered the freedmen's school building and "actually shit over the floor, and upon the benches, and in the water bucket." After Cullen M. Baker's nefarious gang ambushed his farm, Brown retreated to Paris, where he waited in vain for the troops that the army had promised him. Outlaws and Klansmen poured into town, "wanting to be the first to shoot down the hated bureau agent." Tired of narrowly escaping assassination on many occasions, Brown finally resigned his post after his horse was shot from under him, and he returned to Ohio. While he had been in office, he helped tabulate the deaths of some of the twenty-three freedmen in the county whom whites had murdered since the end of the war.[55]

In Lamar County almost three hundred fewer blacks voted in 1869 than had voted in 1868. On the eve of the 1869 election, the freedmen were still mistreated with impunity and balked at reporting any of the injuries that they suffered "for fear of their very lives." Conservatives instructed blacks to join so-called Democratic Clubs or endure the consequences. To Thomas E. Younger, a Davis canvasser and black schoolteacher from Marion County, disheartened local blacks confided their dread of having their crops destroyed if they voted the radical ticket. Whites had told them that the military would soon leave the state, and they would thus be left without any protection and "murder & bloodshed would follow as it had in the

hundred citizens of Lamar County] to Joseph J. Reynolds, n.d., and W. B. Minoa, Joseph Ballinger, and eleven other citizens of Lamar County to Joseph J. Reynolds, n.d., Microfilm Reel #38, COCADT, RG 393, NA: U. Trulock to Edmund J. Davis, January 18, 1870, in Governors' Papers: Davis; Smith, "Reconstruction and Republicanism," 86; Edmund J. Davis to Morgan C. Hamilton, November 25, 1869, Microfilm Reel #38, COCADT, RG 393, NA.

55. San Antonio *Daily Express,* January 8, 1870; (first quotation); Gallaway, ed., *Dark Corner of the Confederacy,* 237 (second quotation); Richter, *Overreached on All Sides,* 279 (third quotation)–280 (sixth quotation); DeWitt C. Brown, quoted in William L. Richter, " 'The Revolver Rules the Day!': Colonel DeWitt C. Brown and the Freedmen's Bureau in Paris, Texas, 1867–1868," *Southwestern Historical Quarterly,* XCIII (1990), 314 (fourth and fifth quotations); DeWitt C. Brown to Ulysses S. Grant, April 5, 1869, Microfilm Reel #21, COCADT, RG 393, NA; Citizens of Lamar County to Edmund J. Davis, January 3, 1870, in Governors' Papers: Davis; Smallwood, *Time of Hope, Time of Despair,* 142.

past." A subsequent investigation by the state legislature regarding the Eleventh District (Lamar and Fannin Counties) senate race found that many Lamar County blacks had avoided the polls in 1869 because it was easier for them to give up their right to vote rather than cope with white retaliation.[56]

Elsewhere in North Texas, in the adjoining counties of Dallas (Dallas), Denton, Ellis (Waxahachie), and Kaufman, Brevet Brigadier General George P. Buell, commander of the 15th Infantry, believed that few "Union men of any color" had been free to vote as they wished. Although these counties do not have idiosyncratic voting patterns favoring Hamilton, they, except for Ellis County, exhibit, like many other North Texas counties, large declines in the numbers of black registrants voting between 1868 and 1869 (see table 35). The quantitative findings thus do not impugn the sworn testimony of radicals who described how blacks in Dallas County had "their houses shot into" as warnings against voting the Davis ticket, how a mob in Denton County during the election drove away Davis campaign workers, and how black voters in Kaufman County had their Davis ballots taken away from them at the polls.[57]

A large decline in black voting and an uncommonly large degree of voter support for Hamilton prove radical allegations of vote fraud in Falls County (Marlin). Located in east central Texas and named for the falls on the Brazos River, Falls County had been a favorite "home" for slaveholding refugees during the Civil War. The influx of at least a 1,870 blacks for "safekeeping" during wartime presumably weakened their economic bargaining power in the immediate postwar period, but it did not lessen levels of white violence against them. A year and a half after the end of Presidential Reconstruction, Texas Republicans claimed that ex-Confederates were still routinely rob-

---

56. Remarks written by Charles J. Whiting and William Hoffman and dated July 27, 1869, on John A Bagby's letter of June 25, 1869, Microfilm Reel #21, affidavit of Thomas E. Younger, December 18, 1869, Microfilm Reel #23, COCADT, RG 393, NA; Smith, "Reconstruction and Republicanism," 86–87.

57. George P. Buell to Charles E. Morse, telegram received by HFMD on December 18, 1869, affidavit of William W. Lewis, December 20, 1869, Microfilm Reel #23; COCADT, RG 393, NA; "Papers in the Contested Election Case of Grafton vs. Conner," *House Miscellaneous Documents*, Doc. 144, 41th Cong., 2nd Sess., Serial 1433, 1–2; James Brown and B. F. Boydstun to Charles E. Morse, December 27, 1869, Microfilm Reel #32, COCADT, RG 393, NA. The contention that Dallas County during the late 1860s escaped much of the racial violence that afflicted other surrounding areas is found in Christopher LaPlante, "Reconstruction in Dallas County, 1865–1873" (M.A. thesis, University of Texas at Arlington, 1974), 2, and is accepted by Dr. Robert Prince in his *History of Dallas: From a Different Perspective* (Dallas, 1993), 37. For convincing evidence to the contrary, see Smallwood, *Time of Hope, Time of Despair,* 135–36; Richter, *Overreached on All Sides,* 175; James Bentley to Joseph J. Reynolds, December 15, 1869, Microfilm Reel #29, COCADT, RG 393, NA.

bing, assaulting, and killing former slaves. In 1869 blacks constituted almost half the county's population. About 90 percent of the county's black adult males had registered, compared to about 56 percent of their white counterparts. Therefore, with 949 blacks and 600 whites on the Falls County registration lists, Davis should have carried the county easily. After he lost it by 232 votes and noticed that almost 200 fewer blacks voted in 1869 than had voted in 1868, he claimed that the election there was "simply a *farce*."[58]

The two leading "scoundrels" whom Davis blamed for the Falls County atrocity were neither former secessionists nor ex-Confederates. They were Major Clarence Mauck, the U.S. Army commander of the local military post and president of the board of registration, and Benjamin G. Shields, a staunch unionist who had been a U.S. congressman from Alabama and the American chargé d'affaires in Venezuela before settling in the county in the early 1850s. Major Mauck, who saw nothing inappropriate about bringing his private supply of liquor to the election room, enjoyed the company of "General" Shields, who admittedly commanded considerable and well-deserved respect from the freedmen. Shields had courageously, although somewhat dangerously, voiced his opinion during the late antebellum period that slavery was morally wrong and economically moribund. His distinguished reputation and large-slaveholder status combined to safeguard him from physical harm at the hands of zealous secessionists. After the war Shields had been one of the so-called radical unionists at the state constitutional convention assembled in 1866 during Presidential Reconstruction. In 1869 he was an ardent Hamilton supporter and a Republican candidate for Congress until he withdrew from the race shortly before the election.[59]

On the morning of the first day of the four days of balloting in Falls County, black men were overwhelmingly casting what the local newspaper called the "mongrel ticket." Major Mauck closed the polls at noon to allow Shields to talk to the freedmen. Former slave Harry Holmes recalled Shields's warnings about the dangers of voting the red-colored Davis ticket: "We would vote ourselves out of house & home and our old white friends

58. Campbell, *An Empire for Slavery,* 243 (second quotation), 244 (first quotation), 245–46, 264–65; Elisha M. Pease to Joseph J. Reynolds, July 16, 1868, in Governors' Papers: Pease; Edmund J. Davis to Joseph J. Reynolds, December 13, 1869 (third quotation), Microfilm Reel #39, COCADT, RG 393, NA.

59. Edmund J. Davis to Joseph J. Reynolds, December 13, 1869, and Clarence Mauck to Charles E. Morse, December 18, 1869, Microfilm Reel #39, COCADT, RG 393, NA; Moneyhon, *Republicanism in Reconstruction Texas,* 121; *A Memorial and Biographical History of McLennan, Falls, Bell and Coryell Counties, Texas* (1893; rpr. St. Louis, 1984), 482–86; James A. Baggett, "Birth of the Texas Republican Party," *Southwestern Historical Quarterly,* LXXVIII (1974), 8–9 n. 27.

who had been supporting us so long would through [*sic*] us off and we would suffer for it."[60]

Shields's admonishments to the freedmen with Mauck's sanction marked the turning point in the balloting. Throngs of Hamilton supporters subsequently took control of the courthouse lawn. To arriving black voters the crowd relayed, with considerable embellishments, Shields's warnings about voting the radical ticket—that if they did they "would lose their cotton and get shot down in scores." Mauck cavalierly refused to bring a few soldiers to the courthouse to protect blacks from having their ballots scrutinized by the growing crowd of whites. Though throughout the state U.S. Army troops were under orders not to appear at any polling place unless a breach of the peace arose, popular mythology surrounding the 1869 election incongruously holds that soldiers "stationed at the polls probably prevented many Democrats from voting." But in Falls County, in the absence of federal troops, planters "marched up" their employed black laborers, "gave each a Hamilton ticket," and "saw it put into the box." Freedmen testified that red Davis tickets were "torn from [their] hands" and white Hamilton ballots substituted "with threats accompanying them that they must vote them or they would be killed." According to the unsuccessful Davis candidate for county clerk, many blacks did not vote at all but instead went home "in fear and disgust with the Davis ticket in their pockets." In addition, two Davis candidates for district offices testified that they left Falls County during the election because of threats to kill them if they stayed.[61]

There can be little doubt that had the freedmen in Falls County been allowed an untrammeled ballot, the outcome there would have redounded to Davis' benefit. Moreover, the sharp declines in the number of blacks voting between 1868 and 1869 in many North Texas counties, such as Collin and Lamar, suggest that the freedmen surrendered their newly established right to the elective franchise rather than contending with white

60. William Devine to Nathan Patten, December 6, 1869, Microfilm Reel #39, COCADT, RG 393, NA; Falls County *Pioneer* (Marlin), December 8, 1869; and affidavit of Harry Homes [Holmes?], February 5, 1870, Microfilm Reel #39, COCADT, RG 393, NA.
61. William Devine to Nathan Patten, December 6, 1869 (first and third quotations); affidavits of Washington T. Taylor [February 4, 1870], Joseph Quenan [n.d.], Moses Wells [December 10, 1869], and Barry Cotton [December 10, 1869] (fourth quotation), A. M. Attaway to Nathan Patten, December 6, 1869 (fifth quotation), Microfilm Reel #39, COCADT, RG 393, NA; Brief description of Governor Davis' administration contained in "Records of the Governor: 1863 Murrah thu Campbell 1911," (second quotation), RG 301, TSL; affidavits of Jackson Dunn [December 10, 1869] and S. W. Ford [December 10, 1869], and B. F. Scogin's answers to interrogatories, February 4, 1870, Microfilm Reel #39, COCADT, RG 393, NA.

terrorist groups. Intimidation of freedmen also cost Davis many votes in Jasper, Sabine, and San Augustine Counties. Here, in this corner of north-eastern Texas, more traditional evidence corroborates the notion that the franchise of hundreds of black voters went virtually unprotected. Therefore, if one adjusts the final tallies in the 1869 governor's race for the radical-orchestrated chicanery in El Paso and Hill Counties, and if military author-ities had ordered a new election in Milam and Navarro Counties, the addi-tional votes for Hamilton, according to the analysis presented here, would still not have come close to offsetting the gains for Davis created by rectify-ing the instances of intimidation of black voters.

Although Hamilton received a significant number of black votes, esti-mated here at about 2,074 (of which many, but certainly not all, were freely cast for his candidacy), historians have exaggerated the degree to which he won support among the white Republican–unionists who had either sup-ported Pease in 1866 or voted for calling a constitutional convention in 1868 (see tables 36 and 37). Davis probably won less than half the 1866 Pease vote. This does not, however, necessarily mean that Hamilton cap-tured the balance of the former Pease men.[62] According to the estimates of voting, few, if any, former Pease voters subsequently voted for Hamilton. If they failed to vote for Davis, they either sat out the balloting for governor or were among the men who in 1869 were not registered to vote. Hamil-ton's support among whites who had favored a convention call was also negligible. These findings suggest that the behavior of prominent Hamilton men, such as Pease, Bell, and Shields, was a very poor predictor of the behavior of the otherwise anonymous white Texans who in the past had supported Republican causes. Among the masses of white voters the lines were thus rigidly drawn in the Davis-Hamilton contest: nearly all the partic-ipating Pease voters and advocates of calling a constitutional convention favored Davis; essentially all the Throckmorton men and opponents of a convention call who subsequently bothered to vote in the 1869 election cast ballots for Hamilton.

On the other hand, Hamilton benefited extraordinarily from the revision of registration. He won about 87 percent of the ballots cast by white men added after the 1868 election to the registry lists (see table 37). In net results, almost 45 percent of his vote came from the group of whites who had most

---

62. Moneyhon surmises that Hamilton "attracted almost two-thirds of the potential white Repub-lican vote" (Moneyhon, *Republicanism in Reconstruction Texas,* 124). See also Carrier, "A Political History of Texas," 398.

recently been added to the voting lists. Although an equal share of Hamilton's total contained whites who were on the voting lists before 1869, his candidacy attracted only about 30 percent of them. In short, Hamilton's candidacy proved woefully unacceptable to the older segment of white registrants. The reason for this disparity in turnout rates reflects the commonsense conclusion that many whites who registered in 1867 and 1868 could not have foreseen being faced with voting for a set of, in their opinion, unsatisfactory choices (Hamilton and Davis), whereas whites who had little intention of voting in the 1869 election would most likely not have been among those who made an effort to register immediately before its holding.

Because of the multiplicity of local candidates who had run on anti–Davis tickets, the first legislature since 1866 to assemble in Texas comprised a Republican, but not a radical, majority. The subset of moderate or conservative Republican representatives, who were elected, for the most part, on Hamilton tickets, held the balance of power between the Davis radicals and the Democrats. However, in terms of the larger political spectrum, any divisive Republican factionalism was an unaffordable indulgence in a period when unrestrained approval of "Negro equality" could lead to a shallow grave. Democrats reacted with disgust and outrage to the election on the Davis ticket of fourteen blacks. They included in the Senate the Union League leader Ruby, who had built a power base in Galveston as a labor organizer among black dockworkers, and Matthew Gaines, a self-taught former slave from Washington County who spoke up for black agricultural workers. In the House, African Texans included Richard Allen, Goldsteen Dupree, Jeremiah J. Hamilton, Silas Cotton, D. W. Burley, Mitchell M. Kendall, David Medlock, John Mitchell, Henry Moore, Sheppard Mullens, Benjamin F. Williams, and Richard Williams. The pro-Democratic Galveston *Tri-Weekly News* editorialized that their artificial elevation to high political office represented "as vile a collection of ignorance, vice, servility, barbarism and cruelty" as ever witnessed by any civilized society. All of the black members of the Twelfth Legislature received their share of death threats. In 1873 the Ku Klux Klan murdered Dupree while he was campaigning for Governor Davis' reelection.[63]

63. Ann Patton Malone, "Matt Gaines: Reconstruction Politician," in Alwyn Barr and Robert A. Calvert, eds., *Black Leaders: Texans for Their Times* (Austin, 1981), 55–57, 67; Carrier, "A Political History of Texas," 398–401; Galveston *Tri-Weekly News*, January 1, 1870; Alwyn Barr, "Black Legislators of Reconstruction Texas," *Civil War History*, XXXII (December, 1986), 340–52; Foner, *Freedom's Lawmakers*, 5–6, 51, 68, 80–81, 93–94, 125, 147–48, 151–52, 156, 187, 230, 232; William Harley Gandy, "A History of Montgomery County, Texas" (M.A. thesis, University of Houston, 1952), 170.

Under direction of military authorities the Provisional Legislature convened in early March of 1870. Its first task was to comply with the conditions required by Congress for readmission to the Union. The lawmakers ratified the Fourteenth and Fifteenth Amendments to the United States Constitution and selected Morgan Hamilton and James W. Flanagan, an anti-secessionist from Rusk County who had been elected to the lieutenant governorship on the Davis ticket, to serve in the United States Senate. In late March President Grant signed the act restoring Texas to the Union. On April 16, 1870, General Reynolds formally transferred power to the civil government of the state, and the reconstruction of the Lone Star State legally ended.[64]

Davis took the oath as regular governor on April 28 and delivered one of the most remarkable inaugural addresses in the history of the Texas governorship. Events had caused, he proclaimed, a "second annexation of Texas," although this time with the eradication of slavery. Memories, he asserted, were perhaps too recent to agree that "Providence" might have guided this "improvement and progress of the human race." Nevertheless, Davis expressed the hope that reasonable men would band together in acceptance of the new order of things and support a "fresh departure" in politics. After pointing out that it had taken the southern states one hundred years to live up to Thomas Jefferson's promise in the Declaration of Independence of the brotherhood of all men in the new American nation, Davis, who owed his election to the votes cast for him by African Texans and a small number of whites, pledged that his administration would do everything in its power to secure and perpetuate this new dawn of freedom in the Lone Star State.[65]

64. Moneyhon, *Republicanism in Reconstruction Texas,* 128; Gray, "Edmund J. Davis," 186–87, 190–91; Ramsdell, *Reconstruction in Texas,* 290–92.

65. Edmund J. Davis, *Inaugural Address of Gov. Edmund J. Davis to the Twelfth Legislature, April 28, 1870* (Austin, 1870), 3.

Conclusion

Texas was distinctive in vital respects from the ten other states that formed the Confederate States of America. It had been the only southern slave state with an international boundary, a history as an independent republic, and an extensive line of western frontier settlements. In addition, it was home to two considerable ethnic groups—Mexicans and Germans—whose culture and language set them apart from the plantation society of the Old South. Moreover, antebellum Texas contained many Anglo frontiersmen and yeoman farmers who did not share the slaveholders' dream for the future of their state as a dynamic empire based on slavery and cotton agriculture. No southern state during the secession crisis had a governor who was so staunchly an opponent of secession as Sam Houston, the state's most famous resident and leading unionist. Finally, unlike other Confederate states, Texas escaped the physical devastation caused by the military campaigns of the Civil War.

Nevertheless, during the tumultuous period of secession, Civil War, and Reconstruction, most white Anglo-Texans were unable to surmount a destructive relationship with slavery and its legacy. The Lone Star State thus failed to forge a history significantly dissimilar from the other slave states that had cast their lot with the movement for southern independence. Contemporaries of the period and later accounts by historians relied on the term *unionism* to characterize antebellum opposition to the "Southern Rights" Democratic party and secessionist movement. The term was also used to represent antagonism to Confederate nation-building during the Civil War and to identify potential support for granting civic and political rights to former slaves during Reconstruction. Although unionism remains a durable notion in accounts of southern history, it is nonetheless, in many respects, an inadequate description for the political conflict between white Texans that took place throughout these years. Unionism was only minimally based upon any specific ideology and never exemplified a unified or shared agenda. Instead, it represented the failed attempts during these years by various Texans to create, for whatever reasons, a viable and enduring political alternative to the dominant Democratic party.

Until John Brown's raid on the Harpers Ferry arsenal, Texas unionism appeared to be a formidable element in the calculus of late antebellum state politics. In the summer of 1859 the Texas Democrats struggled to downplay the significance of the spectacular comeback victory of Sam Houston over incumbent Governor Hardin R. Runnels. They claimed that the election had been no different from the previous 1857 gubernatorial election, for both elections had featured the same candidates running on nearly the same issues for the same offices. They argued that, although Houston won his rematch with Runnels by temporarily assembling an odd combination of former Whigs, Know-Nothings, and Union Democrats, the controversy between the North and South over slavery had remained unresolved. Influential Democratic party spokesmen confidently pointed out that upon the slavery issue "the heart of Texas" would always beat "true and firm." The subsequent course of state politics proved this prognostication to be correct, but such characterizations of the nature of Houston's political resurrection, and traditional explanations for it by subsequent generations of historians, should not be allowed to stand.[1]

Contrary to the conventional wisdom, Houston's election to the Texas governorship on an independent "Opposition," or Union Democratic, ticket had not depended upon his winning over men who had previously voted against him. His victory hinged on neither capturing a breakaway faction of unionist Democrats nor attracting an extraordinary number of just simply everyday Democrats. But for the indifference in the ranks of the 1857 Runnels voters and, to a lesser extent, the magnetism of Houston's candidacy among new and previous nonvoters, Governor Runnels would have won reelection and thus foiled Houston's political comeback. The disappearance from Runnels' ranks of approximately one-third of the men who had previously voted for him destroyed his chances for reelection. This segment of his former supporters simply sat out, for the most part, the 1859 balloting. Much of their extraordinary apathy can be attributed to the success of Houston and the Opposition in putting Runnels and the regular Democrats squarely on the defensive in every political debate, especially over attempts to reopen the African slave trade or otherwise unnecessarily agitate the slavery issue.

Subsequent events, primarily Brown's raid in October and the breakup in the following year of the national Democratic party into northern and southern factions, destroyed any chance that Governor Houston might have had to build an institutional barrier that could have held latent secessionist sentiment in check. Well over half of Houston's 1859 supporters voted in

1. Galveston *Weekly News*, August 9, 1859.

the 1860 presidential election for the splinter Southern Rights Democratic ticket, which in Texas swept to an easy victory over a John Bell–Stephen A. Douglas combination or "fusion," ticket. In retrospect, Houston's victory had unquestionably attested to the unpopularity of extreme, fire-eating rhetoric at a time when the South had not yet lost its dominion over the national political system. However, Houston's victory to a far lesser extent exemplified the unconditional unionism that could have been safely drawn upon in his beloved Texas under strikingly changed circumstances to thwart the advocates of secession.

Texas secession is best understood as a series of calculated choices by rational men at all levels of the social pyramid. During the winter of 1860–1861 the Texas Democratic party's vision of a South under threat from an imminent revolutionary assault from the North had a wider appeal than to just the state's slaveholders. From the point of view of Democratic ideologues, the creation of a separate, slaveholding confederacy held out the promise of sealing off the Lone Star State from the contagion of abolition. The charm of this argument extended far beyond the planter elite, for Southern Rights Democratic party spokesmen were easily able to present secession to southern-born nonslaveholders as the best way to preserve the stability of the social order. Maintenance of white supremacy and protection from slave violence were themes holding far greater appeal than the traditional American patriotism of Houston and other staunch Texas unionists. That was the brilliance of the pro-slavery Democratic strategy, and it explains why wealthy East Texas planters who engineered the secessionist movement were able to mobilize a mass base for reactionary rebellion and probable war.

Voting irregularities in the secession referendum balloting in February of 1861 occurred in far fewer Texas counties than allegations made by contemporaries of the period would suggest. In Uvalde County, centered around Fort Inge on the southwestern frontier, the excessive influence of its county judge, who supported the Union on principle, resulted in an unpredictably lopsided vote against secession. The county's prior voting patterns combined with the judge's communiqué on the official report of returns, along with the circumstances surrounding his subsequent murder, suggest that the county's 1861 no-vote was the product of vote fraud. The result in Uvalde County, however, was an anomaly, if only because voting irregularities elsewhere typically involved chicanery by secessionists and intimidation of unionists, including many Mexican Texans in South Texas.

For example, had the election in southmost Cameron County (Brownsville) been freely and fairly conducted, the unionist vote would have been much higher. The browbeating of Cameron County unionists was perhaps mild compared with the defilement of the voting process in another South Texas county, Zapata, where a clique of disunionists had threatened citizens with fines if they failed to vote for secession. The county's chief justice subsequently falsified the Zapata County referendum returns by reporting to the Texas Secession Convention a unanimous and grossly inflated secessionist vote. Returns from neighboring Starr and Webb Counties, which like Zapata possessed a history of control and manipulation of the votes of poor and landless Tejanos, are also suspect. Here, the influence of prominent local secessionists, such as the Benavides family in Laredo, shaped the disproportionate votes for secession, but unlike in Zapata County, secessionists did not try to embellish their voting strength.

In Young County (Fort Belknap), on the extreme northwestern frontier, a case of "vote padding" may or may not have violated the voters' intentions. Although it is unlikely that virtually every potentially eligible voter appeared at the county's polling places, the desire of Anglo frontiersmen for security and stability in this region had turned many who otherwise would have been unionists against the federal authorities in charge of the Brazos and Comanche Indian Reservations. An analysis of county voting returns confirms, however, the validity of allegations regarding a silencing of German Texan unionists in Colorado County in the heart of plantation country on the lower Colorado River bottomlands. On the other hand, in many other counties, such as Bexar and Kaufman, where Texas unionists used the rhetoric of fraud to characterize voting outcomes, the quantitative evidence offers no corroboration that likely instances of intimidation and voting irregularities resulted in significantly diminished anti-secessionist totals.

Once Texas joined the newly formed Confederate States of America, the flourishing political party struggles that had characterized its antebellum history did not disappear into a nonpartisan void created by wartime unity. During the war, conflicting opinions regarding compulsory military service, confiscation laws, impressment, and suspension of habeas corpus created tremendous political controversy. New issues and resentments over Confederate policies, taken together with the remembrance of partisan battles that occurred in the years immediately before the outbreak of the war, predictably spilled over into wartime politics. The evidence presented here thus rejects two persistent notions regarding politics in Confederate Texas, namely, that (1) Texans simply forgot all political divisions existing before 1861, and (2) during wartime elections voters merely selected candidates from a parade of personalities marching in lockstep to shared policies and ideologies.

Memories of past struggles between Democrats and their opponents largely determined the voting alignments in the August, 1861, governor's race. Francis R. Lubbock, the former lieutenant governor under Runnels and a vocal supporter of the secessionist movement, successfully challenged the reelection bid of Edward Clark, who was serving out the remaining months of Houston's term in office. In this closest gubernatorial election ever in Texas history, Clark lost to Lubbock by only a handful of votes out of some 58,000 votes cast. The extraordinary voter turnout for Lubbock in his home county of Harris strongly suggests some form of subterfuge by his supporters. Vote fraud in Harris County obviously injured Clark, but his inability to attract statewide votes cast by 1859 Democrats, 1860 anti-Breckinridge fusionists, and 1861 unionists, in effect guaranteed his defeat. Texas unionists evidently never forgave Clark for his betrayal of the dethroned Houston. After former secessionist voters divided their votes among Clark, who was their first choice, Lubbock, and political maverick Thomas J. Chambers, who was their third choice, the small unionist constituency was paradoxically placed in a position to decide the outcome. But for the bloc of former anti-secessionist voters in his column in his race against Governor Clark, Lubbock would have lost the 1861 gubernatorial election.

The apparent creation of an inchoate voting coalition arose when an insignificant number of Lubbock's supporters subsequently voted for unsuccessful congressional candidates in November of 1861. However, after seemingly influencing the results in the congressional races, the coalition forged by Lubbock's candidacy fell apart in 1863. Nor were prewar voting alignments of any consequence at all in determining voter choices in the 1863 gubernatorial and congressional elections. Although many issues in Confederate Texas could have formed the basis of party division, only "anti-administration" and "pro-administration" portrayals of individual candidates gained widespread favor. Annoyance with Confederate cotton impressment and a latent "Texas-first" attitude caused many slaveholders to join with former anti-secessionists and vote in protest for Chambers, the anti-administration gubernatorial candidate, who lost to Pendleton Murrah, a lesser-known pro-administration candidate. This strange alliance of prewar unionists and East Texas slaveholders was understandable in terms of the new polarization of voters caused by wartime circumstances. After the fall of Vicksburg the Texas unionists—admittedly a small group—were, for the most part, quiescent "reconstructionists" who believed that their state should negotiate a separate agreement with President Abraham Lincoln to come back peaceably into the Union. On the other extreme, most Texas slaveholders were now Texas-firsters, who harbored a genuine dislike of Confederate confiscation and impressment laws.

During the Civil War years when Texas secessionists, or Southern Rights, Democrats were themselves politically divided, the votes of former unionists and previous nonvoters often determined voting outcomes. Corralling most of the votes cast by slaveholders or former secessionists was thus not always tantamount to electoral success during the war years. If the ballots of only secessionists had been counted in the 1861 gubernatorial race, Clark would have retained the governorship. Slaveholders had disproportionally cast their votes in 1861 and 1863 against the successful gubernatorial candidates, Lubbock and Murrah, respectively. In addition, victorious congressional candidates as a group in 1861 had failed to capture most of the votes cast by planters.

The outline of the most basic division in the Texas electorate during the Civil War years, the political chasm between those who favored disunion in 1861 and those who did not, remained, nonetheless, intact. In 1864 Oran M. Roberts, a former prime mover of the state's secessionist movement, vanquished James H. Bell, a prewar unionist and reluctant Confederate, in a contest for chief justice of the state supreme court. In effect, the Texas-firsters had joined with pro-administration men and diehard Confederates to thrash soundly a reconstructionist candidate. The votes that Bell received were essentially a mere subset of those cast by men who had opposed secession. At the end of the war the basic division running through the Texas electorate thus remained in essence the same as in February of 1861.

The Texas secessionists by their calamitous decision in 1861 managed to bring about precisely what they had left the Union to prevent: the liberation of the Texas slaves occurred on June 19, 1865, when the commander of the arriving federal occupying forces announced their emancipation. The overwhelming majority of the political issues that fueled the partisanship, and also the violence, of Reconstruction revolved around the issue of what would be the status of former slaves in the postwar world. The political stance that both former secessionists and unionists took concerning the freedmen was largely determined by the extent of their commitment to the principle of white supremacy. The fledgling Texas Republican party had trouble winning the support of white voters, including a few of the state's most illustrious prewar unionists and wartime loyalists. Although unionism often translated into a genuine dislike of ex-Confederates, it did not guarantee support for sharing full civic and political equality with a race that most Anglo Texans had long regarded as primitive and servile.

During Presidential Reconstruction, Provisional Governor Andrew J. Hamilton believed that he could establish a loyal government in Texas consisting of prewar unionist leaders and also many former nonslaveholders. Hamilton hypothesized that the latter now realized how secessionists had tragically misled them in 1861. Distrustful of President Andrew Johnson's assumption that the mere avowal of an oath converted a secessionist into a dependable citizen, Hamilton instructed county registration boards to question applicants in order to discern insincere affirmations of loyalty. Voter enrollment dragged on through the fall of 1865 when Hamilton, citing rising incidences of white terrorism, deflected requests from Washington that he rapidly convene a constitutional convention.

Voter turnout was low in the January, 1866, election of delegates to the state constitutional convention. When the convention finally convened, the presence of unpardoned former Confederates, the question of the legality of secession, and efforts to define the status of black Africans and their descendants drew heated debate. The resulting constitution was a victory for conservative delegates who had favored submitting, but not consenting, to the bare minimum requirements for restoration to the Union. Hamilton's hopes for building a viable egalitarian movement out of the prewar unionist leadership and a postwar expanded loyal yeoman class were fatally undercut when the Democrats, including former secessionist leaders, bestowed their support for the governorship upon James W. Throckmorton, who had resisted secession back in 1861 but now opposed granting freedoms to blacks beyond emancipation. Most voters identified the "Union Republicans," led by former governor Elisha M. Pease, with the Radical Republican elements in Congress who wanted a reconstructed South based on equal civic and political rights for former slaves. Pease's candidacy was therefore doomed from the start, and Throckmorton's easy victory forged a new coalition between many former anti-secessionists and secessionists that would last throughout Reconstruction.

Pease and the Union Republicans captured most of the former supporters of James H. Bell, whom Texans had decisively rejected in 1864 as a reconstructionist candidate for the state supreme court. In addition, Pease won the backing of nearly all German Texan and Mexican Texan voters who had turned out and voted in 1866. He even attracted a handful of pragmatic Anglo racists who knew that the North would not allow ex-Confederates to restrict the freedmen to semi-slavery. However, virtually all former secessionists and prewar slaveholders had studiously avoided voting the Union Republican ticket, and most of them, moreover, were not the least repentant about their involvement in slavery or treason.

Antagonism to the newly drafted constitution was uniquely concentrated in old, small-slaveholding and pro-secessionist pockets east of the Trinity River. Here, wartime supporters of defeated gubernatorial candidates Clark and Chambers had voted heavily against the amendments. Voters in this provincial region centered around the old colonial town of Nacogdoches ignored arguments made by Democrats and conservatives that approval of the amendments would counteract the newly enacted Civil Rights Act, prevent a continuation of military rule, and deflect a call for a new convention that would likely promote more unpopular changes. A resentment of the limited rights conferred on the freedmen by the 1866 Texas Constitution, along with its possible, but unlikely, allowance for future legislative action to grant them voting rights, far outweighed other sundry and minor objections to its approval and almost prevented its adoption. For completely different reasons, a smaller group of radical unionists, who now found themselves in bitter opposition to President Johnson and his policies, also found the new constitution unacceptable.

Reports from Texas of unpunished crimes committed with increasing frequency against the freedmen and the promulgation of the harsh and discriminatory Black Codes merely confirmed fears of northern Republicans that Presidential Reconstruction was an unmitigated failure. At the heart of the new laws were draconian vagrancy and contract provisions that sought to guarantee that ex-slaves would go to work and remain at work for white planters. Governor Throckmorton, along with the overwhelming majority of the state and local officeholders who had been elected with him in 1866, considered the Black Codes benevolent and humane. This was a profound misreading of northern opinion, and they soon found their world turned upon its apex when Congress altered the course of southern politics by passing the First Reconstruction Act in March of 1867.

When the process of voter registration began, African Texans enrolled with enthusiasm and organized local Loyal Union Leagues that quickly gained a powerful voice in Republican party councils. Local boards ultimately registered most black males of voting age. However, the true political strength of the massive anti-Republican opposition remains problematical, because the concurrent disfranchisement of Texas whites will always be an enigma. The numbers of rejected antebellum officeholders were never tabulated, and it is impossible to detect the number of white men among those failing to try to register who, had they applied, would also have been rejected.

Despite the intractable problem of estimating the extent that local boards denied Texas whites registration, the quantitative evidence contradicts a widely held belief that the level of white disfranchisement was, for the most part, equitably extended across the state. Counties in the valleys of the lower Brazos and the Colorado Rivers had unpredictably low percentages of their adult white male populations on the voter registration lists on the eve of the statewide referendum required by Congress on whether to call a new state constitutional convention. A strong aversion to Congressional Reconstruction also kept a disproportionate number of whites away from the registration tables in a group of counties clustered around Waco in north Central Texas. On the other hand, in the East Texas regions where opposition to the 1866 constitution had been especially intense and where chronic and virulent white resistance had frustrated the task of forming Loyal Union League organizations, the numbers of whites granted voter certificates were abnormally high.

Fear of potential black political power resulted in widespread white terrorism directed at critical components of the Republican party organization during the campaign for delegates to the new constitutional convention. Nevertheless, the political mobilization of the freedmen was a success. More foreboding for Republican fortunes than intimidation of its black voter constituency was how few whites voted to call a convention. Added to this disappointment was the persistence of internecine factionalism within the party's own ranks. Texas Republicans relied on the fanciful assumption that once America resolved the issues of race and Reconstruction, the reassertion of antebellum economic and geographical divisions would unify prewar Houston supporters and cause many other white Texans to move instinctively into an anti-Democratic coalition. But by the time of the gubernatorial election in December of 1869, the Republicans had hopelessly divided. Factionalism drove them to field two separate slates of candidates for state offices.

The radicals chose Edmund J. Davis, a prewar unionist who had organized a regiment of federal cavalry in South Texas during the war, on a platform that endorsed the newly drafted constitution, championed the reestablishment of law and order, provided for the financing of public schools, and advocated state subsidization of internal improvements in the newer areas of the state. Conservative and moderate Republicans rallied behind the candidacy of former provisional governor Hamilton. They tried to attract discontented Democrats by agreeing to disregard temporarily black aspirations, including demands for equal educational and economic opportunities, meaningful protection from white violence, and full civic and political rights. By successfully mobilizing the black vote through the efforts of the Loyal Union Leagues, Davis won a narrow victory over Hamilton.

If the final tallies in the 1869 governor's race had been rectified for the vote fraud perpetuated by the Davis radicals in El Paso and Hill Counties, and if military authorities had ordered a new election in Milam and Navarro Counties, many additional votes would have been placed accordingly in Hamilton's column. Yet even such additional votes would not have offset the gains for Davis created by correcting the instances elsewhere of intimidation of black voters. Blacks were kept from voting in large numbers in Falls County, in many North Texas counties, especially in Lamar County, and in the San Augustine–Sabine area of East Texas. These findings thus strengthen revisionist interpretations which reject the notion that Davis and Brevet Major General Joseph J. Reynolds, the military commander of the District of Texas, stole the 1869 election. Although the degree of intimidation of black voters by anti-Davis men far exceeded the extent of radical chicanery, the evidence introduced here is compatible with historical accounts that argue that white-voter apathy was the deciding factor in producing Davis' victory. Many conservatives and Democrats who opposed Davis could not bring themselves to vote for Hamilton, a prewar unionist who had bitterly denounced the former secessionists while serving as provisional governor.

Unfortunately, by 1874 the endeavor to establish an interracial democracy in Texas collapsed; the Republican party failed to become a legitimate statewide alternative to the Democrats. In retrospect, the failure of Davis and the Texas Republicans to achieve their goals was far less remarkable than the fact that Texas blacks stood at the beginning of the 1870s, in the words of W. E. B. Du Bois, for "a brief moment in the sun." For once in Texas history they received, although for only a short and shaky duration, a measure of fairness and justice. That this semblance of black equality did not endure is almost beside the point. Texas was still, as the Republicans claimed, "the arena of civil war." Everywhere on the horizon lurked the possibility of white terrorism against blacks. Moreover, Democratic party spokesmen found no merit whatever in any program endorsed or inaugurated by the Davis government. Very few Anglo Texans acknowledged that a former slave was lawfully a voter with civic and political rights equal to their own. Most white men never regarded the Thirteenth, Fourteenth, and

Fifteenth Amendments to the United States Constitution to be genuine and binding, but confidently anticipated overriding them and nullifying the accomplishments of the Davis administration after a white backlash reinstalled the Democratic party to power.[2]

One must not allow the many reasons given by historians to explain the subsequent success of the so-called redeemer Democrats—the conservative whites who had been so conditioned by slavery that they refused to consider blacks as citizens or even free agents—to obscure a basic no-win situation that engulfed Governor Davis and his supporters in 1870. In the ensuing years, Davis, who was assisted by a divided Republican party that held a small margin in the state legislature, was unable to carry out the two contradictory aims of his administration: to protect blacks in their newly won rights and to win over new white converts to his party. The fact that a small group of some five thousand white Texans, including many of German and Mexican descent, and their newly enfranchised African American allies failed in this quest was far less a function of the weakness of Republican party policies or leadership than of widespread bigotry and violence—traits that precluded fair play and became mainstays of the Texas Democratic party's crusade to restore white supremacy to all levels of government in the reconstructed Lone Star State. In short, the Texas Republicans had no remedy for political extremism and undiluted racism.

From the governorship of Sam Houston to that of Edmund J. Davis, Texas unionism, for whatever reasons embraced or however articulated, proved powerless to either stop the calamitous decision of Texans to secede from the American Union in 1861 or lay a solid foundation for the establishment of a truly biracial democracy based on free labor and equal rights in 1869. After Houston's voter coalition shattered before the counterrevolution of southern independence, what remained and survived of Texas unionism through the Civil War years collapsed once again before the revolution of black freedom. The range of white opinion was simply much too narrow to generate sufficient dissenting or egalitarian sentiment to prevent secession or furnish enough reliable white allies for a political party endorsing racially equal rights after the war. For Texas, the Civil War and its immediate aftermath did not represent a watershed in the state's electoral politics. In the 1870s the countervailing persistence of white racism, the

2. W. E. B. Du Bois, *Black Reconstruction in America: An Essay Toward a History of the Part Which Black Folk Played in the Attempt to Reconstruct Democracy in America, 1860–1880* (New York, 1935), 30; *Daily State Journal* (Austin), April 11, 1871.

political mobilization of previously unregistered whites, and the large migration into the state of ex-Confederates and Democrats from the older South, combined to guarantee a rapid demise of Republicanism in Reconstruction Texas.

Appendix

VOTING RETURNS AND TURNOUT IN SELECTED TEXAS ELECTIONS, 1852–1873

Late Antebellum Period

Election	Ballots Cast for Democrats or Southern Rights Democrats or For Secession	Ballots Cast for "Opposition" Candidates (Whigs, Know-Nothings, Union Democratic, etc.) or Against Secession	Adult White Males Not Voting[a]	Estimated Voter Turnout (%)
1852 Presidential	14,857	5,366	31,603	39.0
1853 Gubernatorial	26,525	9,639	22,108	62.1
1855 Gubernatorial	25,219	18,194	27,751	61.0
1856 Presidential	31,995	16,010	29,605	61.9
1857 Gubernatorial	32,552	23,628	27,876	66.8
1858 Judicial	24,904	25,325	40,273	55.5
1859 Gubernatorial	27,691	36,527	32,730	66.2
1860 Presidential	48,155	15,618	39,621	61.7
1861 Secession Referendum	46,188	15,149	46,524	56.9

Civil War Years

Election	Ballots Cast for Winning or Incumbent Candidates	Ballots Cast for Losing or Challenging Candidates	Adult White Males Not Voting[a]	Estimated Voter Turnout (%)
1861 Gubernatorial and Lieutenant Gubernatorial	21,854	35,548	50,459	53.2
1861 Congressional	39,233	14,627	54,001	49.9
1863 Gubernatorial	18,913	19,400	69,548	35.5
1863 Gubernatorial and Lieutenant Gubernatorial	17,916	14,493	80,903	28.6
1863 Congressional	11,928	17,055	84,329	25.6
1864 Judicial	14,825	15,161	83,326	26.5
	24,127	7,228	84,682	27.0

Presidential Reconstruction

Election	Ballots Cast for Conservative Union or For Constitutional Amendments	Ballots Cast for Union Republican or Against Constitutional Amendments	Adult White Males Not Voting[a]	Estimated Voter Turnout (%)
1866 Gubernatorial and Constitutional referendum	49,277	12,068	60,143	50.5
	28,146	23,682	69,660	42.7

Congressional Reconstruction

Election	Ballots Cast Against Convention or Against Ratification or Against Radicals	Ballots Cast For Convention or For Ratification or For Radicals	Ballots Cast for All Others[b]	Registered Voters	Registered Voters Not Voting	Adult Males Not Registered
1868 Call for Convention	11,441	44,683		109,995	53,871	73,500
1869 Gubernatorial and Ratification Referendum	39,055	39,838	458	135,553	56,202	50,922
	4,928	72,366		135,553	58,259	50,922
1869 Congressional	31,588	38,705	5,898	135,553	59,363	50,922

The Early 1870s

Election	Ballots Cast for Democrats	Ballots Cast for Republicans	Ballots Cast for All Others[b]	Estimated Number of Adult Males Not Voting	Estimated Voter Turnout (%)
1871 Congressional	74,927	50,562	403	82,431	60.4
1872 Presidential and Congressional	67,797	47,912	115	111,616	50.9
	69,991	47,048		110,401	51.5
1873 Gubernatorial	98,906	51,049		96,602	60.8

(continued)

VOTING RETURNS AND TURNOUT IN SELECTED TEXAS ELECTIONS, 1852–1873

(continued)

[a] The estimates of voter turnout before 1867 represent percentages of adult white males, a surrogate measure for legally eligible voters, and were derived by straight-line extrapolations between 1850, 1860, and 1870—the years for which federal census data are available. The estimates of adult white males in 1850 and 1860 (38,934 and 103,394, respectively) were derived by adding 90 percent of the white males 20 to 29 years of age to the number of them who were 30 years of age and over. See *Seventh Census, 1850: Compendium*, table 1, *Eighth Census, 1860: Population*, table 1, and *Ninth Census, 1870: Population*, table 23. The 1870 census reports 132,390 white males in the category of 21 years of age and over. Because the corresponding 1870 figure for black adult males is 5,235 less than the number of black men registered by 1869 under military supervision, it was assumed here that in each county the proportion of black adult males was the same as the overall proportion of blacks of all ages and of both sexes. This arbitrary, but not unrealistic, assumption generated an estimate of the number of adult black males for every county, which, in turn, summed up to a statewide total equal to 6 more blacks than were registered in 1869. See *Tabular Statement of Registration and Voting*, 2–5. While the underenumeration problem is not solved by accepting the higher estimated figure of 56,816 adult black males and merely adding it to 132,390 adult white males to equal an estimated 189,206 adult males in 1870, the upward adjustment made here in the number of adult black males can be justified by additional information that corroborates that Texas blacks were undercounted in the 1870 census. If county tax assessors in 1864 levied taxes for slaves at the same rates at which they did in 1860, then the estimate of Texas' black population in 1864 would be 273,586 (87.76 percent of 273,586 equals the reported 240,099 "Negroes taxed" in 1864). This approximation of the 1864 black population represents 20,111 more blacks than reported in the 1870 census. Assuming that the number of slaves "refugeed" to Texas between 1862 and 1864 for safekeeping when Union troops overran neighboring Confederate states could have easily reached 32,000, and granting the likelihood that many of them left Texas after emancipation, it is, nevertheless, doubtful that their departure (even if combined with losses due to death and migration of other blacks) would have offset the growth rate in the approximately 241,000 nonrefugeed slaves residing in Texas in 1864 and caused a net loss of over 3,000 blacks each year between 1864 and 1870. For the number of slaves taxed in 1860 and 1864, see Records of the Comptroller of Public Accounts, Ad Valorem Tax Division, County Real and Personal Property Tax Rolls (Microfilm edition), 1860 and 1864, TSL. For a discussion of refugeed slaves, see Campbell, *An Empire for Slavery* (1989), 243–46. After 1867 the number of adult males was determined by first accepting the estimate calculated above for the 1864 total black population and then by assuming that the ratio of adult black males to the 1864 estimated black population was essentially the same as the ratio of adult black males to the total black population in 1870. The resulting estimate of 55,538 (20.3 percent of 273,586) black adult males in 1864 was, in turn, used with the 1869 black registration figure of 56,810 to generate a straight-line extrapolation of 56,556 black adult males in 1868. This procedure entails the additional, but reasonably modest, supposition that the fullest possible registration of black voters occurred under the Reconstruction Acts and produces estimates that approximately 87.6 percent of the state's black male population over the age of twenty-one was registered by 1869. Cf. Moneyhon, *Republicanism in Reconstruction Texas*, 71, and note 22 on p. 264. Thus, in the above table the 50,922 men listed under "Adult Males Not Registered" during the 1869 balloting for governor and on ratification of the constitution are exclusively white men. The 1880 census reports 380,376 adult males. The estimates of adult males for the election years between 1870 and 1880 were derived by straight-line extrapolations between 1870 and 1880. See *Tenth Census, 1880: Population*, table 8.

[b] The vote for "All Others" equals ballots marked in the 1869 governor's race for Hamilton Stuart; in the 1869 congressional races, for candidates running as an "Independent" or "Independent Democrat" plus "scattered" returns; in the 1871 congressional races, for Louis W. Stevenson in the third district; and in the 1872 presidential election, the "Regular Democratic" ticket of Charles O'Connor.

Source: With the exception of the 1858 judicial election and the 1861 referendum, the source for the late antebellum election returns is the compilation and evaluation of official and unofficial reports of votes by Texas archivist Paul R. Scott. See his "The Democrats and Their Opposition: A Statistical Analysis of Texas Elections, 1852–1861," (Typescript, Texas A&M University Archives), and his companion machine-readable dataset deposited in the Public Policy Resources Laboratory, Texas A&M University, College Station, Texas. For the source for the 1858 judicial elections, see *Executive Record Book* [Gov. Hardin R. Runnels], 181–84, RG 301, TSL. The 1859 gubernatorial vote includes the "unofficial" vote for Henderson County. The 1860 presidential returns are the official returns which are reproduced in Burnham, *Presidential Ballots*, 764–813. Included here are returns omitted from Burnham's compilation for Atascosa, Bee, and Milam Counties. See MSS

Election Returns for 1860, RG 307, TSL. The 1861 secession referendum returns are taken from Timmons, "The Referendum in Texas," 15–16, table 1. In following Timmons' characterization of the "scattered" returns, the totals against secession in Goliad, Grimes, Hays, Nacogdoches, and San Patricio Counties have been calculated as 41, 10, 116, 105, and 7, respectively, and the secessionist vote in Wood County has been computed as 452. Because the five improperly designated votes cast at the Wallisville precinct in Chambers County were marked "Union," they have been added to the county's total cast against secession. The Brown County vote has been corrected to equal 29 to 0 for secession: see Baum, "Pinpointing Apparent Fraud," 208–209. The few unidentified scattered votes reported by Nueces County have necessarily been disregarded. The "unofficial" or "informal" reports of votes polled in Presidio and Coleman Counties are included in the calculation of the statewide totals, although the accuracy of the report from Presidio County is questionable because the unionist total is identical to the number of the county's adult white males listed in the 1860 federal census. In Presidio County the vote against secession at Fort Davis and Presidio del Norte reportedly was 48 to 0 and 316 to 0, respectively. See Daniel Murphy to Elisha M. Pease, February 25, 1861, Pease-Graham-Niles Collection, AHC. In the case of Coleman County the manuscript returns could be interpreted to read 25 to 2, rather than 13 to 0, for secession: see MSS Election Returns for 1861, RG 307, TSL. The 1861 gubernatorial and lieutenant gubernatorial returns are taken from *Texas Senate Journal: Ninth Legislature*, 6–8. The source for the 1861 and 1863 congressional returns is MSS Election Returns for 1861 and 1863, RG 307, TSL. The source for the 1863 gubernatorial and lieutenant gubernatorial election returns is *Texas Senate Journal: Tenth Legislature*, 35–37. The returns used here include the "informal" votes from Angelina, Jack, Mason, Smith, and Wood Counties. The returns for the 1864 Supreme Court Chief Justice election is [Pendleton] Murrah, "Proclamations and Letters Sent by State Department, 1863–1865," 128–30, RG 301, TSL. The 1866 gubernatorial election returns and the 1866 referendum returns on the constitutional amendments are taken from MSS Election Returns for 1866, RG 307, TSL. The source for the 1868 vote on calling a constitutional convention and the 1869 vote on ratification of the constitution is *Tabular Statement of Registration and Voting*, 6–9. The 1869 gubernatorial and congressional returns are taken from *Tabular Statements of Voting in 1869*, 2–8. The 1871 congressional returns are taken from MSS Election Returns for 1871, RG 307, TSL. The source for the 1872 presidential and congressional returns is Secretary of State, *Report of the Secretary of State of the State of Texas, For the Year 1872* (Austin, 1873), 2–13. The 1873 gubernatorial election returns are taken from MSS Election Returns for 1873, RG 307, TSL.

BIBLIOGRAPHY

PRIMARY MATERIALS

MANUSCRIPT COLLECTIONS

Washington, D.C.

The National Archives

Records of the Adjutant General's Office, 1780s–1917

Case Files of Applications from Former Confederates for Presidential Pardons ("Amnesty Papers"), 1865–1867. Group I: Pardon Applications Submitted by Persons from the South. RG 94. Microfilm Publication M1003

Letters Received by the Office of the Adjutant General, 1861–1870. RG 94. Microfilm Publication M1868.

Records of the Bureau of the Census

Population Schedules of the Eighth Census of the United States, 1860, State of Texas. RG 29. Microfilm Publication M653.

Records of the Bureau of Refugees, Freedmen, and Abandoned Lands

Records of the Assistant Commissioner for the State of Texas, Bureau of Refugees, Freedmen, and Abandoned Lands, 1865–1869. RG 105. Microfilm Publication M821.

Records of the U.S. Army Continental Commands, 1821–1920

Correspondence of the Office of Civil Affairs of the District of Texas, the 5th Military District, and the Department of Texas, 1867–1870. RG 393. Microfilm Publication M1188.

Returns of Elections, 1869 [unarranged]. The 5th Military District, and the Department of Texas, 1867–1870. RG 393. E4850.

Affidavits in Civil Affairs Cases. Department of Texas and the 5th Military District, 1865–1870. Record Group 393. E4851.

Austin, Texas

Archives Division, Texas State Library

Governors' Papers and Records, RG 301

Clark, Edward

Davis, Edmund J.

Hamilton, Andrew J.

Houston, Sam

Lubbock, Francis R.

Pease, Elisha M.

Murrah, Pendleton

Runnels, Hardin R.

Throckmorton, James W.

Records of the Secretary of State, RG 307, Manuscript Election Returns

Registers of Elected and Appointed State and County Officials, 1867–1885, RG 307, Microfilm Edition

Austin History Center, Austin Public Library
>   Brown, Frank. "Annals of Travis County and of the City of Austin (from the earliest times to the close of 1875)." Typescript.
>   Pease-Graham-Niles Collection.

Eugene C. Barker Texas History Collections, Center for American History, University of Texas at Austin
>   Ballinger, William Pitt. Diary and Papers.
>   Bell, James H. Papers.
>   Black, William W. Family Papers.
>   Bryan, Guy M. Papers.
>   Epperson, Benjamin H. Papers.
>   Edwards (Peyton Forbes) Family Papers.
>   Hall, James Madison. Papers.
>   Kingsbury, Gilbert D. Papers.
>   Leyendecker, John Z. Papers.
>   Roberts, Oran M.
>>   Papers.
>>   "San Augustine and the Red Lands of East Texas: Their Early Settlement by an Intelligent Population, with Their Influence upon the Public Affairs of Texas, Both in Peace and War." Typescript of a lecture presented on May 26, 1893, at the University of Texas.
>   Starr, James Harper. Papers.
>   Throckmorton, James W. Papers and Letter Book.
>   White, Francis Menefee. Papers.

Regional Historical Resource Depository, Texas State Library
>   "List of Registered Voters of Galveston, 1853–1873" and "Register of Voters in the City of Galveston, 1865–1872."

Huntsville, Texas
>   Newton Gresham Library, Sam Houston State University
>>   Sexton, Franklin B. Papers.

Weimar, Texas
>   Wilson, J. L. D. Papers. In possession of Jefferson Carroll.

NEWSPAPERS AND BROADSIDES

Alamo Express (San Antonio), 1861
Austin *Record,* 1869
Austin *Republican, Daily Republican,* and *Weekly Republican,* 1867, 1869
Austin *Statesman,* 1876
Daily Ranchero (Corpus Christi), 1860–61
Daily Ranchero (Matamoros, Mex.), 1865
Daily State Journal (Austin), 1871
Dallas *Herald,* 1858, 1861, 1865, 1867–70
Falls County *Pioneer,* 1869
Flake's Daily Bulletin (Galveston), 1866, 1869

Free Man's Press (Austin), 1868
Galveston *News*, 1857, 1864
Galveston *Daily News*, 1866–67
Galveston *Weekly News* and *Tri-Weekly News*, 1861
Houston *Union*, 1870
Houston *Weekly Telegraph*, 1867
Houston *Tri-Weekly Telegraph*, 1863
Harrison Flag (Marshall), 1860, 1867
McKinney Messenger, 1861, 1865
Nacogdoches *Chronicle*, 1866
New York *Times*, 1866, 1869
Reporter (Tyler), 1864
San Antonio *Express* and *Daily Express*, 1866, 1870
Southern Intelligencer (Austin), 1858–59, 1865–66
Standard (Clarksville), 1859, 1865
State Gazette and *Tri-Weekly State Gazette* (Austin), 1869
Texas Baptist, 1861
Texas Demokrat (Houston), 1865–66
Texas Republican (Marshall), 1859, 1865
Texas State Gazette (Austin), 1857, 1860–61, 1869
Tri-Weekly Statesman (Austin), 1872
Weekly Austin Republican, 1867, 1869–70
Weekly State Gazette (Austin), 1865–66
Texas Broadside Collection, Barker Texas History Collections, University of Texas at Austin
    Arnold, James R. "Amendments to the State Constitution. Argument Supporting
        Them." Nacogdoches *Chronicle*, May 22, 1866.
    Chambers, T. J. "To the People of Texas." Galveston, July 10, 1861.
    ———. "To the People of Texas." Austin, February 20, 1863; Republished, Houston,
        June 23, 1863.
    "Common Sense." Dallas County. [Signed by] "One who was at Vicksburg." Septem-
        ber, 1863.
    Hart, Martin D. [and twenty-three other signees]. "Address to the People of Texas.
        . . ." *The Intelligencer. Extra.* (Austin), February 6, 1861.
    Houston, Sam. "Proclamation by the Governor of the State of Texas." [Signed by] Sam
        Houston Austin, February 9, 1861.
    Latimer, Albert H. [and twenty-two other signees]. "To the People of Texas." Austin,
        n.d.
    "An Ordinance to Dissolve the Union Between the State of Texas and the Other States,
        United Under the Compact Styled 'The Constitution of the United States of Amer-
        ica.'" Austin, 1861.
    Thompson, Wells. *For Lieut.-Governor. Fellow-Citizens of Texas.* [Signed by] Wells
        Thompson. August 2, 1869.

GOVERNMENT PUBLICATIONS

Constitutional Convention (Texas). *The Constitution of the State of Texas as Amended by the
    Delegates in Convention Assembled.* Austin, 1866.

————. *Journal of the Texas State Convention, Assembled at Austin, February 7, 1866, Adjourned April 2, 1866.* Austin, 1866.

————. *Journal of the Reconstruction Convention Which Met at Austin, Texas, June 1, A.D. 1868.* Austin, 1870.

Davis, Edmund J., *Inaugural Address of Gov. Edmund J. Davis to the Twelfth Legislature, April 28, 1870.* Austin, 1870.

Secretary of State (Texas). *Report of the Secretary of State of the State of Texas, for the Year 1872.* Austin, 1873.

Texas House Journal: Seventh Biennial Session. Austin, 1857.

Texas Senate Journal: Eighth Legislature. Austin, 1860.

Texas Senate Journal: Ninth Legislature. Edited and compiled by James M. Day. Austin, 1963.

Texas Senate Journal: Tenth Legislature. Edited and compiled by James M. Day. Austin, 1964.

U.S. Army. Fifth Military District. State of Texas. General Order No. 73. *Tabular Statement of Voters (White and Colored) Registered in Texas at Registration in 1867, and at Revision of the Lists in 1867–'68–'69; Showing Also the Number (White and Colored) Stricken off the Lists. Tabular Statement of Votes (White and Colored) Cast at Election Held in the State of Texas, Under the Authority of the Reconstruction Acts of Congress.* Austin: April 16, 1870, pp. 1–9.

U.S. Army. Fifth Military District. State of Texas. General Order No. 19. *Tabular Statement, Showing the Number of Votes Cast in Each County For and Against the Constitution, and for State Officers. Tabular Statement, Showing Number Votes Cast in Each County for Members of Congress. Tabular Statement, Showing the Votes Cast in Each District for Senators and Representatives. Statement, Showing Vote by Counties for Clerks of District Courts, Sheriffs, and Justices of the Peace.* Austin: February 1, 1870, pp. 1–46.

U.S. Bureau of the Census. *Seventh Census, 1850: Compendium.*

————. *Eighth Census, 1860: Statistics.*

————. *Eighth Census, 1860: Agriculture.*

————. *Eighth Census, 1860: Population.*

————. *Ninth Census, 1870: Population.*

————. *Ninth Census, 1870: Statistics.*

————. *Tenth Census, 1880: Statistics.*

U.S. Congress. 40th Cong., 2nd Sess. *Senate Executive Documents,* No. 53 (Ser. 1317).

————. 41st Cong., 2nd Sess. *House Executive Documents,* No. 265 (Ser. 1426).

————. 41st Cong., 2nd Sess. *House Miscellaneous Documents,* Doc. 144, "Papers in the Contested Election Case of Grafton vs. Conner."

————. 42nd Cong., 2nd Sess. *House Miscellaneous Documents,* No. 163 (Ser. 1526).

PUBLISHED COLLECTIONS OF LETTERS AND DOCUMENTS

Denison, George S. "Some Letters of George Stanton Denison, 1854–1866: Observations of a Yankee on Conditions in Louisiana and Texas," ed. James A. Padgett. *Louisiana Historical Quarterly,* XXIII (1940), 1132–1240.

Gammel, Hans Peter Nielson, comp., *Laws of Texas.* 10 vols. Austin, 1898.

Reagan, John H. "A Conversation with Governor Houston." *Quarterly of the Texas State Historical Association,* III (April, 1900), 279–81.

Shenton, James P., ed. *The Reconstruction: A Documentary History of the South after the War: 1865–1877.* New York, 1963.

The Texas Almanac for 1859. Galveston, 1858.

Williams, Amelia W., and Eugene C. Barker, eds. *The Writings of Sam Houston, 1813–1863.* 8 vols. Austin, 1943.

Winkler, Ernest William, ed. *Journal of the Secession Convention of Texas, 1861.* Austin, 1912.

———. *Platforms of the Political Parties of Texas.* Bulletin of the University of Texas, No. 53. Austin, 1916.

AUTOBIOGRAPHIES, MEMOIRS, AND DIARIES

Anderson, John Q., ed. *Brokenburn: The Diary of Kate Stone.* Baton Rouge, 1956.

Barr, Amelia Edith Huddleston. *All the Days of My Life: An Autobiography.* New York, 1913.

Black, Reading Wood. *The Life and Diary of Reading W. Black; A History of Early Uvalde.* Compiled by Ike Moore. Austin, 1934.

Cross, F. M. *A Short Sketch-History from Personal Reminiscences of Early Days in Central Texas.* Brownwood, Tex., 1912.

Gallaway, B. P., ed. *The Dark Corner of the Confederacy: Accounts of Civil War Texas as Told by Contemporaries.* Dubuque, Iowa, 1968.

Lubbock, Francis Richard. *Six Decades in Texas, or Memoirs of Francis Richard Lubbock, Governor of Texas in War-Time, 1861–63; A Personal Experience in Business, War, and Politics.* Edited by C. W. Raines. Austin, 1900.

North, Thomas. *Five Years in Texas; or, What You Did Not Hear During the War from January, 1861, to January, 1866: A Narrative of His Travels, Experiences, and Observations, in Texas and Mexico.* Cincinnati, 1871.

Reagan, John H. *Memoirs: With Special Reference to Secession and the Civil War.* Edited by Walter Flavius McCaleb. New York, 1906.

Roberts, Oran M. "The Experiences of an Unrecognized Senator." *Quarterly of the Texas State Historical Association,* XII (October, 1908), 87–147.

Smithwick, Noah. *The Evolution of a State, or Recollections of Old Texas.* Compiled by Nanna Smithwick Donaldson. Barker Texas History Center Series, No. 5. Austin, 1983.

BOOKS, ARTICLES, AND PAMPHLETS BY CONTEMPORARIES

Brown, John Henry. *History of Texas, From 1685 to 1892.* Vol. II of 2 vols. St. Louis, 1893.

Hamilton, Andrew Jackson. "Origin and Objects of the Slaveholders' Conspiracy Against Democratic Principles, As Well As Against the National Union." New York, 1862.

Hamilton, Jeff. As told to Lenoir Hunt. *"My Master": The Inside Story of Sam Houston.* Dallas, 1940.

Houzeau, Jean-Charles. *La terreur blanche au Texas et mon évasion.* Brussels, 1862.

Lane, J. J. "History of the Educational System of Texas." In *A Comprehensive History of Texas, 1685–1897.* Vol. II of 2 vols. Edited by Dudley G. Wooten, pp. 424–70. Dallas, 1898.

A Memorial and Biographical History of McLennan, Falls, Bell and Coryell Counties, Texas. 1893; rpr. St. Louis, 1984.

Mills, W. W. *El Paso, A Glance at Its Men and Contests for the Last Few Years. The Election Fraud, the Marshes, Williams, Pearson, Verney, Stine, and Fountain, the Infamous.* Austin, 1871.

———. *Forty Years at El Paso, 1858–1898.* El Paso, 1962.

Newcomb, James P. *Sketch of Secession Times in Texas and Journal of Travel from Texas Through Mexico to California, Including a History of the "Box Colony."* San Francisco, 1863.

Olmsted, Frederick Law. *A Journey Through Texas; Or, a Saddle-Trip on the Southwestern Frontier: With a Statistical Appendix*. 1857; rpr. New York, 1978.

Roberts, Oran M. "The Political, Legislative, and Judicial History of Texas for Its Fifty Years of Statehood, 1845–1895." In *A Comprehensive History of Texas, 1685–1897*. Vol. II of 2 vols. Edited by Dudley G. Wooten, pp. 7–325. Dallas, 1898.

Speer, John W. *A History of Blanco County*. Edited by Henry C. Armbruster. Austin, 1965.

Sprague, John T. *The Treachery in Texas, the Secession of Texas, and the Arrest of the United States Officers and Soldiers Serving in Texas*. New York, 1862.

SECONDARY MATERIALS

BOOKS

Acheson, Sam. *35,000 Days in Texas: A History of the Dallas News and Its Forbears* [sic]. New York, 1938.

The American Annual Cyclopedia and Register of Important Events. 14 vols. New York, 1861–64.

Bailey, Anne J. *Between the Enemy and Texas: Parsons's Texas Cavalry in the Civil War*. Fort Worth, 1989.

Bailey, David T. *Shadow on the Church: Southwestern Evangelical Religion and the Issue of Slavery, 1783–1860*. Ithaca, 1985.

Bailey, Ellis. *A History of Hill County, Texas, 1836–1965*. Waco, 1966.

Bailey, Fred Arthur. *Class and Tennessee's Confederate Generation*. Chapel Hill, 1987.

Baker, T. Lindsay. *Ghost Towns of Texas*. Norman, 1986.

Bandera County History Book Committee. *History of Bandera County, Texas*. Dallas, 1986.

Barkley, Mary Starr. *A History of Central Texas*. Austin, 1970.

Barney, William L. *The Secessionist Impulse: Alabama and Mississippi in 1860*. Princeton, 1974.

Barr, Alwyn. *Black Texans: A History of Negroes in Texas, 1528–1971*. Austin, 1982.

Batte, Lelia M. *History of Milam County, Texas*. San Antonio, 1956.

Beringer, Richard E., et al. *Why the South Lost the Civil War*. Athens, 1986.

Boren, Carter E. *Religion on the Texas Frontier*. San Antonio, 1968.

Bowen, David Warren. *Andrew Johnson and the Negro*. Knoxville, 1989.

Buenger, Walter L. *Secession and the Union in Texas*. Austin, 1984.

Burnham, Walter Dean. *Presidential Ballots, 1836–1892*. Baltimore, 1955.

Calvert, Robert A., and Arnoldo De León. *The History of Texas*. Arlington Heights, Ill., 1990.

Campbell, Randolph B. *An Empire for Slavery: The Peculiar Institution in Texas, 1821–1865*. Baton Rouge, 1989.

———. *Sam Houston and the American Southwest*. New York, 1993.

———. *A Southern Community in Crisis: Harrison County, Texas, 1850–1880*. Austin, 1983.

Campbell, Randolph B., and Richard G. Lowe. *Wealth and Power in Antebellum Texas*. College Station, 1977.

Capers, Gerald M. *John C. Calhoun, Opportunist: A Reappraisal*. Gainesville, 1960.

Carter, Dan T. *When the War Was Over: The Failure of Self-Reconstruction in the South, 1865–1867*. Baton Rouge, 1985.

Castañeda, Carlos E. *Our Catholic Heritage in Texas, 1519–1936*. 7 vols. Austin, 1936–1958.

Castro Colonies Heritage Association, Inc. *The History of Medina County, Texas*. Dallas, 1983.

Chabot, Frederick C. *With the Makers of San Antonio*. San Antonio, 1937.

Channing, Steven A. *Crisis of Fear: Secession in South Carolina*. New York, 1974.

Cheshire, Joseph Blount. *The Church in the Confederate States: A History of the Protestant Episcopal Church in Texas*. New York, 1912.

[Comfort Chamber of Commerce]. "Discover Yesterday in the Comfort of Today." Comfort, Tex., 1986.

Connor, Seymour V. *Texas: A History*. Arlington Heights, Ill., 1971.

Creighton, James A. *A Narrative History of Brazoria County*. Waco, 1975.

Crocket, George Louis. *Two Centuries in East Texas: A History of San Augustine County and Surrounding Territory from 1685 to the Present Time*. Dallas, 1932.

Crofts, Daniel W. *Reluctant Confederates: Upper South Unionists in the Secession Crisis*. Chapel Hill, 1989.

Crouch, Barry A. *The Freedmen's Bureau and Black Texans*. Austin, 1992.

Crouch, Barry A., and Donaly E. Brice. *Cullen Montgomery Baker, Reconstruction Desperado*. Baton Rouge, 1997.

Crouch, Carrie J. *Young County: History and Biography*. 1937; rpr. Austin, 1956.

Cummins, Light Townsend, and Bailey, Alvin R., Jr., eds. *A Guide to the History of Texas*. New York, 1988.

Debo, Darrell. *Burnet County History: A Pioneer History, 1847–1979*. Vol. I of 2 vols. Burnet, Tex., 1979.

Degler, Carl N. *The Other South: Southern Dissenters in the Nineteenth Century*. New York, 1974.

De León, Arnoldo. *The Tejano Community, 1836–1900*. Albuquerque, 1982.

———. *They Called Them Greasers: Anglo Attitudes Toward Mexicans in Texas, 1821–1900*. Austin, 1983.

De Shields, James T. *They Sat in High Places: The Presidents and Governors of Texas*. San Antonio, 1940.

Dollar, Charles M., and Richard J. Jensen. *Historian's Guide to Statistics: Quantitative Analysis and Historical Research*. New York, 1971.

Du Bois, W. E. B. *Black Reconstruction in America: An Essay Toward a History of the Part Which Black Folk Played in the Attempt to Reconstruct Democracy in America, 1860–1880*. New York, 1935.

Eaton, Clement. *A History of the Southern Confederacy*. New York, 1961.

Escott, Paul D. *After Secession: Jefferson Davis and the Failure of Confederate Nationalism*. Baton Rouge, 1978.

Eckstein, Stephen Daniel, Jr. *History of the Churches of Christ in Texas, 1824–1950*. Austin, 1963.

Fellman, Michael. *Inside War: The Guerrilla Conflict in Missouri During the American Civil War*. New York, 1989.

Foner, Eric. *Freedom's Lawmakers: A Directory of Black Officeholders During Reconstruction*. New York, 1993.

———. *Reconstruction: America's Unfinished Revolution, 1863–1877*. New York, 1988.

Fornell, Earl Wesley. *The Galveston Era: The Texas Crescent on the Eve of Secession*. Austin, 1961.

Franklin, John Hope. *Reconstruction After the Civil War*. Chicago, 1961.

Friend, Llerena B. *Sam Houston: The Great Designer.* 1954; rpr. Austin, 1979.

Genovese, Eugene. *The Political Economy of Slavery: Studies in the Economy and Society of the Slave South.* New York, 1965.

Gibson, A. M. *The Life and Death of Colonel Albert Jennings Fountain.* Norman, 1965.

Gillette, William. *Retreat from Reconstruction, 1869–1879.* Baton Rouge, 1979.

Goyne, Minetta Altgelt. *Lone Star and Double Eagle: Civil War Letters of a German-Texas Family.* Fort Worth, 1982.

Grayson County Frontier Village. *The History of Grayson County, Texas.* Vol. I of 2 vols. N.p., 1979.

Greer, James K., ed. *A Texas Ranger and Frontiersman: The Days of Buck Barry in Texas.* Dallas, 1932.

Havins, T. R. *Camp Colorado: A Decade of Frontier Defense.* Brownwood, Tex., 1964.

Henderson, Jeff S., ed. *100 Years in Montague County, Texas.* Saint Jo, Tex., 1958.

Henson, Margaret Swett, and Deolece Parmelee. *The Cartwrights of San Augustine: Three Generations of Agrarian Entrepreneurs in Nineteenth-Century Texas.* Austin, 1993.

Hewitt, Phil W. *Land and Community: European Migration to Rural Texas in the 19th Century.* Boston, 1981.

Hinojosa, Gilberto Miguel. *A Borderlands Town in Transition: Laredo, 1755–1870.* College Station, 1983.

Horton, Louise. *Samuel Bell Maxey: A Biography.* Austin, 1974.

Huckabay, Ida Lasater. *Ninety-Four Years in Jack County, 1854–1948.* Waco, 1949.

Huson, Hobart. *Refugio: A Comprehensive History of Refugio County from Aboriginal Times to 1955.* Vol. II of 2 vols. Woodsboro, Tex., 1955.

James, Marquis. *The Raven: A Biography of Sam Houston.* 1929; rpr. Austin, 1988.

Johnson, Frank W. *A History of Texas and Texans.* 5 vols. Chicago, 1916.

Jordan, Gilbert J. *Yesterday in the Texas Hill Country.* College Station, 1979.

Jordan, Terry G. *German Seed in Texas Soil: Immigrant Farmers in Nineteenth-Century Texas.* Austin, 1966.

————. *Immigration to Texas.* Boston, 1981.

Kerlinger, Fred N. *Foundations of Behavioral Research.* 3rd ed. New York, 1986.

King, Alvy L. *Louis T. Wigfall, Southern Fire-eater.* Baton Rouge, 1970.

Landrum, Graham, and Allan Smith. *Grayson County: An Illustrated History of Grayson County, Texas.* Fort Worth, 1967.

Lane, Robert E. *Political Life: Why and How People Get Involved in Politics.* Glencoe, Ill., 1959.

Langbein, Laura Irwin, and Allan J. Lichtman. *Ecological Inference.* Sage University Paper series on Quantitative Applications in the Social Sciences, series no. 17-010. Beverly Hills, 1978.

Lathrop, Barnes F. *Migration into East Texas, 1835–1860: A Study from the United States Census.* Austin, 1949.

Ledbetter, Barbara Neal. *Civil War Days in Young County, Texas.* Newcastle, Tex., 1965.

Lipset, Seymour Martin. *Political Man: The Social Basis of Politics.* Garden City, N.Y., 1963.

Lott, Virgil N., and Mercurio Martinez. *The Kingdom of Zapata.* San Antonio, 1953.

Loveland, Anne C. *Southern Evangelicals and the Social Order, 1800–1860.* Baton Rouge, 1980.

Lucas, Mattie Davis, and Mita Holsapple Hall. *A History of Grayson County, Texas.* Sherman, Tex., 1936.

McPherson, James M. *Ordeal by Fire: The Civil War and Reconstruction.* New York, 1982.

Mantell, Martin E. *Johnson, Grant, and the Politics of Reconstruction.* New York, 1973.

Marten, James. *Texas Divided: Loyalty and Dissent in the Lone Star State, 1856–1874.* Lexington, 1990.

Mathews, Donald G. *Religion in the Old South.* Chicago, 1977.

Meinig, D. W. *Imperial Texas: An Interpretive Essay in Cultural Geography.* 1969; rpr. Austin, 1981.

Moneyhon, Carl H. *Republicanism in Reconstruction Texas.* Austin, 1980.

Montejano, David. *Anglos and Mexicans in the Making of Texas, 1836–1986.* Austin, 1987.

Montgomery, Robin. *The History of Montgomery County.* Austin, 1975.

Moursund, John Stribling. *Blanco County History.* Burnet, Tex., 1979.

Murphy, Du Bose. *A Short History of the Protestant Episcopal Church in Texas.* Dallas, 1935.

Myres, Sandra L., ed. *Force Without Fanfare: The Autobiography of K. M. Van Zandt.* Fort Worth, 1968.

Neighbours, Kenneth Franklin. *Robert Simpson Neighbors and the Texas Frontier, 1836–1859.* Waco, 1975.

Neville, A. W. *The History of Lamar County.* Paris, Tex., 1937.

Nichols, Roy F. *The Disruption of American Democracy.* New York, 1948.

Nunn, William Curtis. *Texas Under the Carpetbaggers.* Austin, 1962.

Oakes, James. *The Ruling Race: A History of American Slaveholders.* New York, 1982.

Perman, Michael. *Reunion Without Compromise: The South and Reconstruction.* London, 1973.

Potter, David M. *The Impending Crisis, 1848–1861.* New York, 1979.

Potter, Mrs. W. R. *History of Montague County, Texas.* 1912; rpr. Saint Jo, Tex., 1957.

Prince, Dr. Robert. *A History of Dallas: From a Different Perspective.* Dallas, 1993.

Procter, Ben H. *Not Without Honor: The Life of John H. Reagan.* Austin, 1962.

El Progreso Club. *A Proud Heritage: A History of Uvalde County, Texas.* Uvalde, Tex., 1975.

Ramsdell, Charles William. *Reconstruction in Texas.* 1910; rpr. Austin, 1970.

Reynolds, Donald E. *Editors Make War: Southern Newspapers in the Secession Crisis.* Nashville, 1966.

Richardson, Rupert Norval. *Texas: The Lone Star State.* New York, 1943.

Richardson, Rupert N., Adrian Anderson, and Ernest Wallace. *Texas: The Lone Star State.* 6th ed. Englewood Cliffs, N.J., 1993.

Richter, William L. *The Army in Texas During Reconstruction, 1865–1870.* College Station, 1987.

————. *Overreached on All Sides: The Freedmen's Bureau Administrators in Texas, 1865–1868.* College Station, 1991.

Rogers, Mary Nixon. *A History of Brazoria County, Texas.* Richmond, Tex., 1965.

Rosenbaum, Robert J. *Mexicano Resistance in the Southwest: "The Sacred Right of Self-Preservation."* Austin, 1981.

Russell, Traylor. *History of Titus County, Texas: Containing Biographical Sketches of Many Noted Characters.* Vol. I of 2 vols. Waco, 1965.

Scarbrough, Clara Stearns. *Land of Good Water—Takachue Pouetsu: A Williamson County, Texas, History.* Georgetown, Tex., 1973.

Sibley, Marilyn McAdams. *Travelers in Texas, 1761–1860.* Austin, 1967.

Silverthorne, Elizabeth. *Ashbel Smith of Texas: Pioneer, Patriot, Statesman, 1805–1886.* College Station, 1982.

Simpson, Colonel Harold B. *Cry Comanche: The 2nd U.S. Cavalry in Texas, 1855–1861*. Hillsboro, Tex., 1979.

Smallwood, James M. *Time of Hope, Time of Despair: Black Texans During Reconstruction*. Port Washington, N.Y., 1981.

Sonnichsen, C. L. *I'll Die Before I'll Run: The Story of the Great Feuds of Texas*. Lincoln, 1988.

———. *Pass of the North: Four Centuries on the Rio Grande*. 1968; rpr. 2 vols. El Paso, 1980.

SPSS-X User's Guide. 3rd ed. Chicago, 1988.

Stambaugh, J. Lee, and Lillian J. Stambaugh. *A History of Collin County, Texas*. Austin, 1958.

Stampp, Kenneth M. *America in 1857: A Nation on the Brink*. New York, 1990.

Takaki, Ronald T. *A Pro-Slavery Crusade: The Agitation to Reopen the African Slave Trade*. New York, 1971.

Tatum, Georgia Lee. *Disloyalty in the Confederacy*. 1934; rpr. New York, 1970.

Thomas, Emory M. *The Confederate Nation, 1861–1865*. New York, 1979.

Thompson, Jerry D. *Mexican Texans in the Union Army*. Southwestern Studies No. 78. El Paso, 1986.

———. *Vaqueros in Blue and Gray*. Austin, 1976.

Timmons, W. H. *El Paso: A Borderlands History*. El Paso, 1990.

Tindall, George Brown. *America: A Narrative History*. 2nd. ed. New York, 1988.

van den Berghe, Pierre L. *Race and Racism: A Comparative Perspective*. New York, 1967.

Wallace, Ernest. *The Howling of the Coyotes: Reconstruction Efforts to Divide Texas*. College Station, 1979.

———. *Texas in Turmoil: The Saga of Texas, 1849–1875*. Austin, 1965.

Waller, John L. *Colossal Hamilton of Texas: A Biography of Andrew Jackson Hamilton, Militant Unionist and Reconstruction Governor*. El Paso, 1968.

Warner, Ezra J., and W. Buck Yearns. *Biographic Register of the Confederate Congress*. Baton Rouge, 1975.

Webb, Walter Prescott. *The Texas Rangers: A Century of Frontier Defense*. Boston, 1935.

Webb, Walter Prescott, H. Bailey Carroll, and Eldon Stephen Branda, eds. *The Handbook of Texas*. 3 vols. Austin, 1952, 1976.

Weyand, Leonie Rummel, and Houston Wade. *An Early History of Fayette County*. La Grange, Tex., 1936.

Wharton, Clarence R. *Wharton's History of Fort Bend County*. San Antonio, 1939.

Whisenhunt, Donald W., ed. *Texas: A Sesquicentennial Celebration*. Austin, 1984.

White, James C. *The Promised Land: A History of Brown County, Texas*. Brownwood, Tex., 1941.

Wiggins, Sarah Woolfolk. *The Scalawag in Alabama Politics, 1865–1881*. University, Ala., 1977.

Winfrey, Dorman H. *A History of Rusk County, Texas*. Waco, 1961.

Winkle, Kenneth J. *The Politics of Community: Migration and Politics in Antebellum Ohio*. New York, 1988.

Wintz, Cary D. *Reconstruction in Texas*. Boston, 1983.

Wisehart, Marion K. *Sam Houston: American Giant*. Washington, D.C., 1962.

Wooster, Ralph A. *The Secession Conventions of the South*. Princeton, 1962.

———. *Texas and Texans in the Civil War*. Austin, 1995.

Wright, Gavin. *Old South, New South: Revolutions in the Southern Economy Since the Civil War*. New York, 1986.

Yearns, Wilfred Buck. *The Confederate Congress*. Athens, 1960.

Yelderman, Pauline. *The Jay Bird Democratic Association of Fort Bend County: A White Man's Union*. Waco, 1979.

ARTICLES AND ESSAYS

Alexander, Thomas B. "Persistent Whiggery in the Confederate South, 1860–1877." *Journal of Southern History*, XXVII (1961), 305–29.

Alexander, Thomas B., *et al.* "The Basis of Alabama's Ante-bellum Two-Party System: A Case Study in Party Alignment and Voter Response in the Traditional Two-Party System of the United States by Quantitative Analysis Methods." *Alabama Review*, XIX (October, 1966), 243–76.

Ashcraft, Allan C. "East Texas in the Election of 1860 and the Secession Crisis." *East Texas Historical Journal*, I (July, 1963), 7–16.

Baggett, James Alex. "Birth of the Texas Republican Party." *Southwestern Historical Quarterly*. LXXVIII (1974), 1–20.

———. "The Constitutional Union Party in Texas." *Southwestern Historical Quarterly*, LXXXII (1979), 233–64.

———. "Origins of Early Texas Republican Party Leadership." *Journal of Southern History*, XL (1974), 441–54.

Bailey, Anne J. "A Texas Cavalry Raid: Reaction to Black Soldiers and Contrabands." *Civil War History*, XXXV (1989), 138–52.

Baker, Robin E., and Dale Baum. "The Texas Voter and the Crisis of the Union, 1859–1861." *Journal of Southern History*, LIII (1987), 395–420.

Barr, Alwyn. "Black Legislators of Reconstruction Texas." *Civil War History*, XXXII (1986), 340–52.

———. "The Making of a Secessionist: The Antebellum Career of Roger Q. Mills." *Southwestern Historical Quarterly*, LXXIX (1975), 129–44.

Baum, Dale. "Chicanery and Intimidation in the 1869 Texas Gubernatorial Race." *Southwestern Historical Quarterly*, XCVII (1993), 37–54.

———. "Pinpointing Apparent Fraud in the 1861 Texas Secession Referendum." *Journal of Interdisciplinary History*, XXII (1991), 201–21.

Baum, Dale, and Robert A. Calvert. "Texas Patrons of Husbandry: Geography, Social Contexts, and Voting Behavior." *Agricultural History*, LXIII (1989), 36–55.

Beringer, Richard E. "The Unconscious 'Spirit of Party' in the Confederate Congress." *Civil War History*, XVIII (1972), 312–33.

Betts, Vicki. "'Private and Amateur Hangings': The Lynching of W. W. Montgomery, March 15, 1863." *Southwestern Historical Quarterly*, LXXXVIII (1984), 145–66.

Boatright, Mody C. "The Myth of Frontier Individualism." *Southwestern Social Science Quarterly*, XXII (June, 1941), 14–32.

Bowen, Nancy Head. "A Political Labyrinth: Texas in the Civil War." *East Texas Historical Journal*, XI (Fall, 1973), 3–11.

Buenger, Walter L. "Secession and the Texas German Community: Editor Lindheimer vs. Editor Flake." *Southwestern Historical Quarterly*, LXXXII (1979), 379–402.

———. "Secession Revisited: The Texas Experience." *Civil War History*, XXX (1984), 293–305.

————. "Texas and the Riddle of Secession." *Southwestern Historical Quarterly*, LXXXVII (1983), 151–82.

Campbell, Randolph B. "The Burden of Local Black Leadership During Reconstruction: A Research Note." *Civil War History*, XXXIX (1993), 148–53.

————. "Carpetbagger Rule in Reconstruction Texas: An Enduring Myth." *Southwestern Historical Quarterly*, XCVII (1994), 587–96.

————. "The District Judges of Texas in 1866–1867: An Episode in the Failure of Presidential Reconstruction." *Southwestern Historical Quarterly*, XCIII (1990), 357–77.

————. "The End of Slavery in Texas: A Research Note." *Southwestern Historical Quarterly*, LXXXVIII (1984), 71–80.

————. "George W. Whitmore: East Texas Unionist." *East Texas Historical Journal*, XXVIII (1990), 17–28.

————. "Grass Roots Reconstruction: The Personnel of County Government in Texas, 1865–1876." *Journal of Southern History*, LVIII (1992), 99–115.

————. "Planters and Plain Folk: Harrison County, Texas, as a Test Case, 1850–1860." *Journal of Southern History*, XL (1974), 369–98.

————. "Research Note: Slave Hiring in Texas." *American Historical Review*, XCIII (1988), 107–14.

————. "Statehood, Civil War, and Reconstruction, 1864–76." In *Texas Through Time: Evolving Interpretations*. Edited by Walter L. Buenger and Robert A. Calvert, pp. 165–96. College Station, 1991.

————. "The Whig Party of Texas in the Elections of 1848 and 1852." *Southwestern Historical Quarterly*, LXXIII (1969), 17–34.

Cantrell, Gregg. "Racial Violence and Reconstruction Politics in Texas, 1867–1868." *Southwestern Historical Quarterly*, XCIII (1990), 333–55.

————. "Sam Houston and the Know-Nothings: A Reappraisal." *Southwestern Historical Quarterly*, XCVI (1993), 327–43.

"The Christianization of Negroes." *Texas Baptist*, March 7, 1961.

Cooper, William J., Jr. "The Politics of Slavery Affirmed: The South and the Secession Crisis." In *The Southern Enigma: Essays on Race, Class, and Folk Culture*. Edited by Walter J. Fraser, Jr., and Winfred B. Moore, Jr., pp. 199–215. Westport, Conn., 1983.

Crewe, Ivor, and Clive Payne. "Another Game with Nature: An Ecological Regression Model of the British Two-Party Vote Ratio in 1970." *British Journal of Political Science*, VI (January, 1976), 43–81.

Crouch, Barry A. "'All the Vile Passions': The Texas Black Code of 1866." *Southwestern Historical Quarterly*, XCVII (1993), 13–34.

————. "Black Dreams and White Justice." *Prologue*, VI (Winter, 1974), 255–65.

————. "Freedmen's Bureau Records: Texas, A Case Study." In *Afro-American History: Sources for Research*. Edited by Robert L. Clarke, pp. 74–94. Washington, D.C., 1981.

————. "A Spirit of Lawlessness: White Violence; Texas Blacks, 1865–1868." *Journal of Social History*, XVIII (Winter, 1984), 217–32.

————. "'Unmanacling' Texas Reconstruction: A Twenty-Year Perspective." *Southwestern Historical Quarterly*, XCIII (1990), 275–302.

Donald, David H. "The Scalawag in Mississippi Reconstruction." *Journal of Southern History*, X (1944), 447–60.

Ellem, Warren A. "Who Were the Mississippi Scalawags?" *Journal of Southern History,* XXXVIII (1972), 217–40.

Elliot, Claude. "Union Sentiment in Texas, 1861–1865." *Southwestern Historical Quarterly,* L (1947), 449–77.

Ewing, Floyd F., Jr. "Origins of Unionist Sentiment on the West Texas Frontier." *West Texas Historical Association Year Book,* XXXII (October, 1956), 21–29.

————. "Unionist Sentiment on the Northwest Texas Frontier." *West Texas Historical Association Year Book,* XXXIII (October, 1957), 58–70.

Flanigan, William H., and Nancy H. Zingale. "Alchemists Gold: Inferring Individual Relationships from Aggregate Data." *Social Science History,* IX (Winter, 1985), 71–91.

Geiser, S. W. "Men of Science in Texas, 1820–1880: II." *Field and Laboratory,* XXVII (January, 1959), 20–48.

Gilligan, Arthur E. "John Robert Baylor." In *Ten Texians in Gray.* Edited by W. C. Nunn. Hillsboro, Tex., 1968.

Glauber, Robert R. "Multicollinearity in Regression Analysis: The Problem Revisited." *Review of Economics and Statistics,* XLIX (February, 1967), 92–107.

Griffin, Roger A. "Intrastate Sectionalism in the Texas Governor's Race of 1853." *Southwestern Historical Quarterly,* LXXVI (1972), 142–60.

Hall, Claude H. "The Fabulous Tom Ochiltree: Promoter, Politician, and Raconteur." *Southwestern Historical Quarterly,* LXXI (1968), 347–76.

Harmon, Dave. "Zapata's Falcon Lake Awash with Memories, Future Promise." Dallas *Morning News,* December 5, 1993, pp. 64A–65A.

Harper, Cecil, Jr. "Slavery Without Cotton: Hunt County, Texas, 1846–1864." *Southwestern Historical Quarterly,* LXXXVIII (1985), 387–405.

Hart, James P. "George W. Paschal." *Texas Law Review,* XXVIII (November, 1949), 23–42.

Henderson, Shuffler R. "Decimus et Ultimus Barziza." *Southwestern Historical Quarterly,* LXVI (1963), 501–12.

Hooper, William T., Jr. "Governor Edmund J. Davis, Ezra Cornell, and the A&M College of Texas." *Southwestern Historical Quarterly,* LXXVIII (1975), 307–12.

"How Texas Was Surrendered: A Military Sketch." *New Jersey Magazine,* May 1, 1867.

Jackson, Susan. "Slavery in Houston: The 1850s." *Houston Review,* II (Summer, 1980), 66–82.

Jordan, Terry G. "Germans and Blacks in Texas." In *States of Progress: Germans and Blacks in America over 300 Years; Lectures from the Tricentennial of the Germantown Protest Against Slavery.* Edited by Randall M. Miller, pp. 89–97. Philadelphia, 1989.

————. "Imprint of the Upper and Lower South on Mid-Nineteenth Century Texas." *Annals of the Association of American Geographers,* LVII (December, 1967), 667–90.

Kamphoefner, Walter D. "German-Americans and Civil War Politics: A Reconsideration of the Ethnocultural Thesis." *Civil War History,* XXXVII (1991), 232–46.

————. "Texas Germans and Civil War Issues: The Evidence from Immigrant Letters." *Journal of the German-Texan Heritage Society,* XIII (Spring, 1991), 16–23.

Klos, George. " 'Our People Could Not Distinguish One Tribe from Another': The 1859 Expulsion of the Reserve Indians from Texas." *Southwestern Historical Quarterly,* XCVII (1994), 599–619.

Kousser, J. Morgan. "Ecological Regression and the Analysis of Past Politics." *Journal of Interdisciplinary History,* IV (1973), 237–62.

————. "Must Historians Regress? An Answer to Lee Benson." *Historical Methods,* XIX (Spring, 1986), 62–81.

————. "A Review Essay: Reconstruction Compared to What?" *Slavery and Abolition,* VII (December, 1986), 290–98.

Ledbetter, Billy D. "Politics and Society: The Popular Response to Political Rhetoric in Texas, 1857–1860." *East Texas Historical Journal,* XIII (Fall, 1975), 11–24.

Lowe, Richard, and Randolph Campbell. "Wealthholding and Political Power in Antebellum Texas." *Southwestern Historical Quarterly,* LXXIX (1975), 21–30.

McAvoy, Thomas T. "The Formation of the Catholic Minority in the United States, 1820–1860." In *Religion in American History: Interpretive Essays.* Edited by John M. Mulder and John F. Wilson, pp. 254–69. Englewood Cliffs, N.J., 1978.

McCaslin, Richard B. "Voices of Reason: Opposition to Secession in Angelina County, Texas." *Locus,* III (Spring, 1991), 177–94.

————. "Wheat Growers in the Cotton Confederacy: The Suppression of Dissent in Collin County, Texas, During the Civil War." *Southwestern Historical Quarterly,* XCVI (1993), 527–39.

McCrary, Peyton. "The Party of Revolution: Republican Ideas About Politics and Social Change, 1862–1867." *Civil War History,* XXX (1984), 330–50.

McCrary, Peyton, Clark Miller, and Dale Baum. "Class and Party in the Secession Crisis: Voting Behavior in the Deep South, 1856–1861." *Journal of Interdisciplinary History,* VIII (1978), 429–57.

McDonald, Archie P. "Secession, War, and Reconstruction in Texas." *Journal of Confederate History,* VII (1991), 33–49.

McGregor, Stuart. "The Texas Almanac, 1857–1873." *Southwestern Historical Quarterly,* L (1947), 419–30.

McKitrick, Eric L. "Party Politics and the Union and Confederate War Efforts." In *The American Party Systems.* Edited by William Nisbet Chambers and Walter Dean Burnham, pp. 117–51. New York, 1967.

McNeir, Agnes Paschal. "Did Texas Secede?" *The Quarterly of the Texas State Historical Association,* V (July, 1901–April, 1902), 168–69.

Malone, Ann Patton. "Matt Gaines: Reconstruction Politician." In *Black Leaders: Texans for Their Times.* Edited by Alwyn Barr and Robert A. Calvert, pp. 49–81. Austin, 1981.

Mann, William L. "Early History of Williamson County." In *Williamson County Centennial 1848–1948,* pp. 5–16. Georgetown, Tex., 1948.

Middleton, Annie. "The Texas Convention of 1845." *Southwestern Historical Quarterly,* XXV (1921), 26–62.

Miller, Lauraine. "The Lost Town of Zapata." *Texas Magazine,* August 15, 1993, pp. 6–14.

Moneyhon, Carl H. "George T. Ruby and the Politics of Expediency in Texas." In *Southern Black Leaders of the Reconstruction Era.* Edited by Howard N. Rabinowitz, pp. 364–78. Urbana, 1982.

————. "Public Education and Texas Reconstruction Politics, 1871–1874." *Southwestern Historical Quarterly,* XCII (1989), 393–416.

Moore, Richard R. "Reconstruction." In *The Texas Heritage.* Edited by Ben Proctor and Archie P. McDonald, pp. 95–107. St. Louis, 1980.

Moretta, John. "William Pitt Ballinger and the Travail of Texas Secession." *Houston Review,* XI (1989), 3–26.

Neighbours, Kenneth F. "Indian Exodus out of Texas in 1859." *West Texas Historical Association Year Book,* XXXVI (October, 1960), 80–97.

Nieman, Donald G. "Black Political Power and Criminal Justice: Washington County, Texas, 1868–1884." *Journal of Southern History,* LV (1989), 391–420.

Norton, Wesley. "The Methodist Episcopal Church and the Civil Disturbances in North Texas in 1859 and 1860." *Southwestern Historical Quarterly,* LXVIII (1965), 317–41.

————. "Religious Newspapers in Antebellum Texas." *Southwestern Historical Quarterly,* LXXIX (1975), 145–65.

Oates, Stephen B. "Texas Under the Secessionists." *Southwestern Historical Quarterly,* LXVII (1963), 167–212.

Olsen, Otto H. "Reconsidering the Scalawags." *Civil War History,* XII (1966), 304–20.

Ownby, Ted. "The Defeated Generation at Work: White Farmers in the Deep South, 1865–1890." *Southern Studies,* XXIII (1984), 325–47.

Paxson, Frederic L. "The Constitution of Texas, 1845." *Southwestern Historical Quarterly,* XVIII (1915), 386–98.

Pitre, Merline. "Richard Allen: The Chequered Career of Houston's First Black State Legislator." *Houston Review,* VIII (1986), 79–88.

Platt, Harold L. "The Stillbirth of Urban Politics in the Reconstruction South: Houston, Texas, as a Test Case." *Houston Review,* IV (1982), 55–74.

Potter, David M. "Jefferson Davis and the Political Factors in Confederate Defeat." In *Why the North Won the Civil War.* Edited by David Donald, pp. 91–114. Baton Rouge, 1960.

Powell, Lawrence N. "Correcting for Fraud: A Quantitative Reassessment of the Mississippi Ratification Election of 1868." *Journal of Southern History,* LV (1989), 633–58.

Ramsdell, Charles William. "The Frontier and Secession." In *Studies in Southern History and Politics,* pp. 61–79. New York, 1914.

————. "Presidential Reconstruction in Texas." *Quarterly of the Texas State Historical Association,* XII (January, 1909), 204–30.

————. "Some Problems in Writing the History of the Confederacy." *Journal of Southern History,* II (1936), 135.

Reynolds, Donald E. "Reluctant Martyr: Anthony Bewley and the Texas Slave Insurrection Panic of 1860." *Southwestern Historical Quarterly,* XCVI (1993), 345–61.

————. "Vigilante Law During the Texas Slave Panic of 1860." *Locus,* II (Spring, 1990), 173–86.

Richter, William L. " 'The Revolver Rules the Day!': Colonel DeWitt C. Brown and the Freedmen's Bureau in Paris, Texas, 1867–1868." *Southwestern Historical Quarterly,* XCIII (1990), 303–32.

Roper, Laura Wood. "Frederick Law Olmstead and the Texas Free-Soil Movement." *American Historical Review,* LVI (1950), 58–64.

Russ, William A., Jr. "Radical Disfranchisement in Texas, 1867–1870." *Southwestern Historical Quarterly,* XXXVIII (1934), 40–52.

————. "Registration and Disfranchisement Under Radical Reconstruction." *Mississippi Valley Historical Review,* XXI (1934), 163–80.

Sharpless, John. "Collectivity, Hierarchy and Context: The Theoretical Framework for the Aggregation Problem." *Historical Methods,* XVII (Summer, 1984), 132–40.

Shook, Robert W. "The Battle of the Nueces, August 10, 1862." *Southwestern Historical Quarterly,* LXVI (1962), 31–42.

————. "Toward a List of Reconstruction Loyalists." *Southwestern Historical Quarterly,* LXXVI (1973), 315–20.

Smallwood, James M. "Charles E. Culver, a Reconstruction Agent in Texas: The Work of Local Freedmen's Bureau Agents and the Black Community." *Civil War History,* XXVII (1981), 350–61.

————. "The Freedmen's Bureau Reconsidered: Local Agents and the Black Community." *Texana,* XI (1973), 309–20.

————. "G. T. Ruby: Galveston's Black Carpetbagger in Reconstruction Texas." *Houston Review,* V (1983), 24–33.

————. "When the Klan Rode: White Terror in Reconstruction Texas." *Journal of the West,* XXV (October, 1986), 4–13.

Smyrl, Frank H. "Texans in the Union Army." *Southwestern Historical Quarterly,* LXV (1961), 234–50.

————. "Unionism in Texas, 1856–1861." *Southwestern Historical Quarterly,* LXVIII (1964), 172–95.

Sneed, Edgar P. "A Historiography of Reconstruction in Texas: Some Myths and Problems." *Southwestern Historical Quarterly,* LXXII (1969), 435–48.

Somers, Dale A. "James P. Newcomb: The Making of a Radical." *Southwestern Historical Quarterly,* LXXII (1969), 449–69.

Sparks, Randy J. "John P. Osterhout, Yankee, Rebel, Republican." *Southwestern Historical Quarterly,* XC (1986), 111–38.

Storey, John W. "Battling Evil: The Growth of Religion in Texas." In *Texas: A Sesquicentennial Celebration.* Edited by Donald W. Whisenhunt, pp. 371–86. Austin, 1985.

Stout, Harry S., and Robert Taylor. "Sociology, Religion, and Historians Revisited: Towards an Historical Sociology of Religion." *Historical Methods Newsletter,* VIII (December, 1974), 29–38.

Thornton, J. Mills, III. "The Ethic of Subsistence and the Origins of Southern Secession." *Tennessee Historical Quarterly,* XLVIII (Summer, 1989), 67–85.

Timmons, Joe T. "The Referendum in Texas on the Ordinance of Secession, February 23, 1861: The Vote." *East Texas Historical Journal,* XI (Fall, 1973), 12–28.

Trelease, Allen W. "Who Were the Scalawags?" *Journal of Southern History,* XXIX (1963), 445–68.

Wood, Forrest G. "On Revising Reconstruction History: Negro Suffrage, White Disfranchisement, and Common Sense," *Journal of Negro History,* LI (April, 1966), 98–113.

Wooster, Ralph A. "An Analysis of the Membership of the Texas Secession Convention." *Southwestern Historical Quarterly,* LXII (1959), 322–35.

————. "An Analysis of the Texas Know-Nothings." *Southwestern Historical Quarterly,* LXX (1967), 414–23.

————. "Ben H. Epperson: East Texas Lawyer, Legislator, and Civic Leader." *East Texas Historical Journal,* V (March, 1967), 29–42.

————. "Statehood, War, and Reconstruction." In *Texas: A Sesquicentennial Celebration.* Edited by Donald W. Whisenhunt, pp. 93–120. Austin, 1985.

————. "Texas." In *The Confederate Governors.* Edited by W. Buck Yearns, pp. 195–215. Athens, 1985.

Wooten, Dudley G. "The Life and Services of Oran M. Roberts." *Texas State Historical Quarterly,* II (1898), 1–21.

THESES, DISSERTATIONS, AND OTHER MANUSCRIPTS

Ashcraft, Allan Coleman. "Texas, 1860–1866: The Lone Star State in the Civil War." Ph.D. dissertation, Columbia University, 1960.

Bailey, Lelia. "The Life and Public Career of O. M. Roberts, 1815–1883." Ph.D. dissertation, University of Texas, 1932.

Bowen, Nancy Head. "A Political Labyrinth: Texas in the Civil War—Questions in Continuity." Ph.D. dissertation, Rice University, 1974.

Budd, Harrell. "The Negro in Politics in Texas, 1867–1898." M.A. thesis, University of Texas, Austin, 1925.

Carrier, John Pressley. "A Political History of Texas During the Reconstruction, 1865–1874." Ph.D. dissertation, Vanderbilt University, 1971.

Crews, James Robert. "Reconstruction in Brownsville, Texas." M.A. thesis, Texas Tech University, 1969.

Crews, Litha. "The Know Nothing Party in Texas." M.A. thesis, University of Texas, 1925.

Dart, Justin Whitlock, Jr. "Edward Clark, Governor of Texas, March 16 to November 7, 1861." M.A. thesis, University of Houston, 1954.

Dobbs, Ricky Floyd. " 'A Slow Civil War': Resistance to the Davis Administration in Hill and Walker Counties, 1871." M.A. thesis, Baylor University, 1989.

Dorsett, Jesse. "Blacks in Reconstruction Texas, 1865–1877." Ph.D. dissertation, Texas Christian University, 1981.

Felgar, Robert P. "Texas in the War for Southern Independence, 1861–1865." Ph.D. dissertation, University of Texas, 1935.

Franzetti, Robert Joseph. "Elisha Marshall Pease and Reconstruction." M.A. thesis, Southwest Texas State University, 1970.

Friend, Llerena Beaufort. "The Life of Thomas Jefferson Chambers." M.A. thesis, University of Texas at Austin, 1928.

Gandy, William Harley. "A History of Montgomery County, Texas." M.A. thesis, University of Houston, 1952.

Giesenschlag, William Henry, Jr. "The Texas Gubernatorial Elections of 1857 and 1859." M.A. thesis, Texas A&M University, 1970.

Gray, Ronald N. "Edmund J. Davis: Radical Republican and Reconstruction Governor of Texas." Ph.D. dissertation, Texas Tech University, 1976.

Hall, Ada Marie. "The Texas Germans in State and National Politics, 1850–1865." M.A. thesis, University of Texas at Austin, 1938.

Heintzen, Frank W. "Fredericksburg, Texas, During the Civil War and Reconstruction." M.A. thesis, St. Mary's University of San Antonio, 1944.

Keener, Charles Virgil. "Racial Turmoil in Texas, 1865–1874." M.S. thesis, North Texas State University, 1971.

Kremm, Thomas Wesley. "Race Relations in Texas, 1865 to 1870." M.A. thesis, University of Houston, 1970.

LaPlante, Christopher. "Reconstruction in Dallas County, 1865–1873." M.A. thesis, University of Texas at Arlington, 1974.

Ledbetter, Billy D. "Confederate Texas: A Political Study, 1861–1865." M.S. thesis, North Texas State University, 1969.

McGraw, John Conger. "The Texas Constitution of 1866." Ph.D. dissertation, Texas Technological College, 1959.

Meiners, Fredericka Ann. "The Texas Governorship, 1861–1865: Biography of an Office." Ph.D. dissertation, Rice University, 1974.

Miller, Benjamin Hillon. "Elisha Marshall Pease: A Biography." M.A. thesis, University of Texas, Austin, 1927.

Moretta, John A. "Pendleton Murrah, Confederate Texans and States' Rights in the Lone Star State, 1863–65." Paper presented to the Houston Area Southern Historians Seminar meeting at Rice University, April 14, 1993.

————. "William Pitt Ballinger: Public Servant, Private Pragmatist." Ph.D. dissertation, Rice University, 1985.

Newsome, Zoie Odom. "Antislavery Sentiment in Texas, 1821–1861." M.A. thesis, Texas Technological College, 1968.

Nieman, Donald G. "Black Political Power and Justice: The Case of Washington County, Texas, 1865–1890." A paper presented at the annual meeting of the Texas State Historical Association, Austin, March 4, 1994.

Owens, Nora Estelle. "Presidential Reconstruction in Texas: A Case Study." Ph.D. dissertation, Auburn University, 1983.

Peters, Robert Kingsley. "Texas: Annexation to Secession." Ph.D. dissertation, University of Texas at Austin, 1977.

Ryan, Frances Dora. "The Election Laws of Texas, 1827–1875." M.A. thesis, University of Texas, Austin, 1922.

Sandlin, Betty Jeffus. "The Texas Reconstruction Constitutional Convention of 1868–1869." Ph.D. dissertation, Texas Tech University, 1970.

Scott, Paul R. "The Democrats and Their Opposition: A Statistical Analysis of Texas Elections, 1852–1861." Typescript in Texas A&M University Archives, College Station, Tex.

Shook, Robert W. "Federal Occupation and Administration of Texas, 1865–1870." Ph.D dissertation, North Texas State University, 1970.

Sinclair, Oran Lonnie. "Crossroads of Conviction: A Study of the Texas Political Mind, 1856–1861." Ph.D. dissertation, Rice University, 1975.

Smith, David Ryan. "Reconstruction and Republicanism in Grayson, Fannin, and Lamar Counties, Texas, 1865–1873." M.A. thesis, University of Texas at Austin, 1979.

Smith, Thomas Tyree. "Fort Inge: Sharps, Spurs, and Sabers on the Texas Frontier, 1849–1869." MS in possession of Thomas Tyree Smith, College Station, Tex.

Timmons, Joe T. "Texas on the Road to Secession." 2 vols. Ph.D. dissertation, University of Chicago, 1973.

Wallace, James Oldam. "San Antonio During the Civil War." M.A. thesis, St. Mary's University, 1940.

Weisel, Edward Berry. "City, County, State: Intergovernmental Relations in Texas, 1835–1860." Ph.D. dissertation, Rice University, 1975.

INDEX

Ab initio doctrine, 132, 146, 179, 180, 182

Abolitionists, 8, 17, 27, 29, 40, 43, 53, 58, 79, 80

African Americans. *See* Blacks

African slave trade, 8, 27, 31, 37, 102, 230

Age variables, in secession referendum, 49, 50–51, 52

Agricultural variables, in secession referendum, 46–49, 50–53

Alabama, 108

Allen, Richard, 227

American Party. *See* Know-Nothing Party

Amnesty oath, 129–30, 235

Anderson County: and secession referendum, 77, 80; and 1861 gubernatorial election, 98; white voter registration in, 167; black voting in, 176, 195; and 1868 constitutional convention referendum, 176; and 1869 gubernatorial election, 195, 210, 211; intimidation of black voters in, 210; election fraud in, 211

Angelina County: and 1861 gubernatorial election, 97, 99, 110; and 1866 constitutional referendum, 156n30; white voter registration in, 167; black voting in, 194; and 1869 gubernatorial election, 194, 199

Anti-secessionism. *See* Unionists

Arizona, 115

Armstrong, George, 221

Armstrong, Micajah L., 221

Arnold, Abraham K., 67

Atascosa County: and secession referendum, 61, 64; and 1861 gubernatorial election, 95, 96, 98; white voter registration in, 169; black voting in, 196; and 1869 gubernatorial election, 196, 199

Attaway, A. M., 180

Austin County: and secession referendum, 64, 72; and 1861 gubernatorial election, 95, 99; white voter registration in, 168; black voting in, 196; and 1869 gubernatorial election, 196

Austin *Weekly State Gazette*, 146

Baker, Cullen M., 222

Ballinger, William P., 16–18

Bandera County: and secession referendum, 61; and 1861 gubernatorial election, 96, 98; white voter registration in, 169; and 1869 gubernatorial election, 207, 208, 210

Baptists: and secession referendum, 48, 50, 52, 57; and slaveholding, 55; and 1860 presidential election, 57; and 1866 gubernatorial election, 152

Barkley, Benjamin F., 220

Bastrop County: and secession referendum, 61, 65, 70; and 1861 gubernatorial election, 95, 95n15, 96, 98; white voter registration in, 169; violence in, 175; black voting in, 195; and 1869 gubernatorial election, 195

Baylor, John R. "Jack," 115

Bee, Hamilton P., 107

Bee County, 169

Bell, James H.: in 1858 judicial election, 16–18; in 1864 judicial election, 119–23, 234; in Reconstruction government, 123; supporters of, and 1866 gubernatorial election, 151; on postwar political situation, 153–54; as moderate Republican, 182; as Hamilton supporter, 226

Bell, John, 39–40, 43, 45, 60, 70, 86, 88, 231

Bell County: white voter registration in,

The Shattering of Texas Unionism

Politics in the Lone Star State During the Civil War Era

DALE BAUM

In a rare departure from the narrow periodization that marks past studies of Texas politics during the Civil War era, this sweeping work tracks the leadership and electoral basis of politics in the Lone Star State from secession all the way through Reconstruction. Employing a combination of traditional historical sources and cutting-edge quantitative analyses of county voting returns, Dale Baum painstakingly explores the double collapse of Texas unionism—first as a bulwark against secession in the winter of 1860–1861 and then in the late 1860s as a foundation upon which to build a truly biracial society.

By carefully tracing the shifting alliances of voters from one election to the next, Baum charts the dramatic assemblage and subsequent breakup of Sam Houston's coalition on the eve of the war, evaluates the social and economic bases of voting in the secession referendum, and appraises the extent to which intimidation of anti-secessionists shaped the state's decision to leave the Union. He also examines the ensuing voting behavior of Confederate Texans and shows precisely how antebellum alignments and issues carried over into the war years. Finally, he describes the impact on the state's electoral politics brought about by the policies of President Andrew Johnson and by broad programs of revolutionary change under Congressional Reconstruction.

Baum presents the most sophisticated examination yet of white voter disfranchisement and ap-